To Peter on the
of your 60th bi
with affection,
Susan.

Conspiracy and the Spanish Civil War

Written by one of the most celebrated historians of the Spanish Civil War, Herbert R. Southworth, this book presents a fascinating account of the origins of the war and the nature and importance of conspiracy for the extreme right. It offers a highly detailed reconstruction of how a plot was concocted to justify the military uprising of July 1936 in Spain, and how the 'facts' of the plot were consolidated and disseminated by right-wing propagandists throughout Europe. Furthermore, the book explores how the myth of the Communist 'secret documents' was perpetuated well into the 1970s.

The latter part of the book, *The Brainwashing of Francisco Franco*, deals with the most influential reader of the documents, General Franco himself. Including an account of Franco's associations with the Entente Internationale contre la Troisième International, it represents a major contribution to the analysis of Franco's 'thought', and provides fascinating evidence of the depths and origins of his obscurantism.

Based on exhaustive research, and written with lucidity and mordant humour, this book acts as both an outstanding introduction to the vast literature of the war, and a monumental contribution to that literature.

Herbert R. Southworth was a leading historian of the Spanish Civil War. During a long and varied career, he worked at the Library of Congress, was a publicist for the Spanish Republic during the Civil War, and served with the U.S. Office of War Information in North Africa during the Second World War. In 1946, he founded Radio Tangier, which he managed until 1960. He built a huge collection of books on the Spanish Civil War and taught at the Universities of California and Vincennes, Paris. He wrote widely on twentieth-century Spain, including *El mito de la cruzada de Franco* (1963) and *Guernica! Guernica!: A Study of Journalism, Diplomacy, Propaganda and History* (1977).

Routledge/Cañada Blanch Studies on
Contemporary Spain
Series editors Paul Preston and Sebastian Balfour
*Cañada Blanch Centre for Contemporary Spanish Studies,
London*

1. Spain 1914–1918
   Between War and Revolution
   Francisco J. Romero Salvadó

2. Spaniards in the Holocaust
   Mauthausen, Horror on the Danube
   David Wingeate Pike

3. Conspiracy and the Spanish Civil War
   The Brainwashing of Francisco Franco
   Herbert R. Southworth

Also published in association with the Cañada Blanch Centre:

Spain and the Great Powers
Edited by Sebastian Balfour and Paul Preston

Conspiracy and the Spanish Civil War

The brainwashing of
Francisco Franco

Herbert R. Southworth

London and New York

First published 2002 by Routledge
11 New Fetter Lane, London EC4P 4EE

Simultaneously published in the USA and Canada
by Routledge
29 West 35th Street, New York, NY 10001

Routledge is an imprint of the Taylor & Francis Group

Typeset in Garamond by Taylor & Francis Books Ltd
Printed and bound in Great Britain by Biddles Ltd,
Guildford and King's Lynn

British Library Cataloguing in Publication Data
A catalogue record for this book is available from the British Library

Library of Congress Cataloging in Publication Data
Southworth, Herbert Rutledge.
Conspiracy and the Spanish Civil War: the brainwashing of Francisco
Franco / Herbert R. Southworth.
p. cm.
Includes bibliographical references.
1. Spain–History–Civil War, 1936–1939–Propaganda. 2. Fascist
propaganda–Spain–History–20th century. 3. Spain–History–Errors,
inventions, etc. 4. Spain–History–Civil War, 1936–1939–
Historiography. 5. Franco, Francisco, 1892–1975–Views on
Communism. 6. Communism–History–20th century.
7. International Anticommunist Entente. I. Title.

DP269.8.P7 S68 2001
946.081–dc21   2001041994

ISBN 0–415–22781–X

To Pierre Vilar and the memory of his wife
Gabrielle for their many kindnesses to me.

Contents

Prologue

Herbert Southworth became a major figure in the historiography of the Spanish Civil War as a result of the publication in Paris in 1963 of his book, *El mito de la cruzada de Franco*. It was issued by Ediciones Ruedo Ibérico, the great publishing house of the Spanish anti-Franco exile run by an eccentric and massively well-read anarchist, José Martínez Guerricabeitia. Smuggled into Spain and sold clandestinely, Ruedo Ibérico's books had enormous impact particularly after the publication of a Spanish translation of Hugh Thomas's classic work on the Spanish Civil War. From the first moments of the conspiracy that became the military coup of 18 July 1936, the rebels were falsifying their own history and that of their enemies. Hugh Thomas's book recounted the history of the war in a readable and objective style – in itself a devastating blow for the partisans of what they called Franco's crusade – and was therefore devoured hungrily by anyone who could get hold of a copy. Southworth did not narrate the war but rather dismantled, line by line, the structures of lies that the Franco regime had erected to justify its existence. The consequence of the arrival in Spain of both books was an attempt by the then Minister of Information, the dynamic Manuel Fraga Iribarne, to counteract their intellectual and moral impact.

There was created in the Ministry of Information a special department under the name Sección de Estudios sobre la Guerra de España. A young functionary of the Ministry, Ricardo de la Cierva y de Hoces, was to direct it. His job was, broadly speaking, to bring up to date the official historiography of the regime in order to repel the attacks coming from Paris. The principal weapon in the armoury of this new unit of intellectual warfare was provided by the purchase of the magnificent library on the Spanish Civil War built up over many years by the Italian journalist, Cesare Gullino. Southworth quickly became the department's main enemy. In comparison with Hugh Thomas, who was already well known after the world-wide success of his book on the Spanish War, Herbert Southworth was virtually unknown. However, there was another crucial difference between the two men. Thomas had written his great book on the conflict but the Spanish Civil War was not going to be the central objective of his life. He was already working on his monumental history of Cuba. Southworth, in contrast, dedicated his life to the study of the Spanish Civil War. Moreover, against la Cierva, who had the staff and resources of a ministry at his disposal, Southworth had his own arsenal – one of the world's greatest collections of books on the war.

As well as being an anti-Francoist author, Southworth was one of the investors who made possible the Ruedo Ibérico publishing house. That Ricardo de la Cierva y de Hoces saw Southworth as an opponent to be feared was soon revealed. They met in Madrid in 1965. Southworth told me later that la Cierva recounted to him how the police had orders to seize copies of *El mito de la cruzada* found when searching bookshops and the homes of political suspects. La Cierva proudly proclaimed that he recommended and even gave to his friends confiscated copies of the book. However, in Franco's Spain, what was said in private was often far removed from what was said in public. Ricardo de la Cierva wrote

> H.R. Southworth is, without argument, the great expert on the bibliography of our war, as seen from the Republican side ... His library on our war is the world's most important private collection: more than seven thousand titles. I am almost certain that he has read all seven thousand. And he keeps, in a tremendous photographic memory, all the important facts and all the relevant cross-references between these books.
>
> *Cien libros básicos sobre la guerra de España*
> (Madrid: Publicaciones Españolas, 1966, p. 40)

This praise was immediately followed by some ferocious, but superficial, attacks on the alleged deficiencies of Southworth's methodology.

Who was this Herbert Southworth, the legendary book-collector who for many years to come would be the legendary intellectual scourge of General Franco's dictatorship? His books would be quarried by the most serious specialists on the Spanish Civil War and his study of the bombing of Guernica would be one of the three or four most important of the many thousands of volumes written on the conflict. Even so, few people knew who he was because, lacking a position in a university, he lacked an easy label. Nevertheless, he had had an extraordinary existence. His writings as a whole contributed to the decision of the Francoist Ministry of Information to set up an entire department just to counter the demolition of regime propaganda. His extraordinary passage from poverty in the American West to crusading left-wing journalist during the Spanish Civil War had elements of a Steinbeck novel. His later transformation into a successful radio-station magnate and then into a scholar of world-wide reputation was reminiscent of one of Theodore Dreiser's self-made heroes.

He was born in Canton, a tiny Oklahoma town, on 6 February 1908. When the town bank, owned by his father failed in 1917, the family moved briefly to Tulsa in eastern Oklahoma. They stayed longer in Abilene, Texas, where his father prospected for oil. Herbert's principal memory of that time was reading his father's collection of the Harvard Classics. The theft of one of the volumes when he was twelve affected him so deeply that it was perhaps the beginning of his own obsessional book-collecting. He educated himself among the stacks of the Carnegie Public Library in Abilene. There, after months of reading *The Nation* and *The New Republic*, he decided to abandon Protestantism and the conservative Republicanism of the Bible belt. He became a socialist and an avid lifetime reader of what he joyfully called 'the muckraker's school of journalism'. It was to be the basis of his astonishing transformation into a formidable scholar in Europe.

He went to secondary school in Abilene until the age of 15. He worked at various jobs in the construction industry in Texas, then in a copper mine in Morenci, Arizona. There he learned Spanish working with Mexican miners. The collapse of the price of copper after the Wall Street crash left him unemployed. He then decided to work his way through Arizona University and when his savings ran out, he went to the Texas Technological College in Lubbock – better known as the birth-place of Buddy Holly. There he lived in acute poverty, paying for his studies by working in the college library. He majored in History with a minor in Spanish. The work in the library had deepened his love for books. With the encouragement of the college librarian, he left, in 1934, with only one thought in mind – to seek work in the world's most important book collection, the Library of Congress in Washington D.C. When he finally got a post in the Document Department, it was at a salary less than half of that he had received in the copper mines. Yet, although it barely allowed him to eat, he was happy just to be able to pass his days among the bookshelves.

When the Spanish Civil War broke out, he began to review books on the conflict for the *Washington Post*. Already emotionally affected by the struggle between fascism and anti-fascism, he always said thereafter that the events in Spain gave direction to his life. His articles brought him to the notice of the Republic's Ambassador, Fernando de los Ríos, who asked him to work for the Spanish Information Bureau. He left his ill-paid but secure government post in the library and moved to New York. There he worked with passion, writing regular press articles and pamphlets, including *Franco's Mein Kampf*, his anonymous demolition of José Pemartín's attempt to provide a formal doctrine for Francoism, *Qué es "lo nuevo"*. During this time, he took a Master's degree at Columbia University and formed an enduring friendship with his colleague Jay Allen, the distinguished war correspondent. While in New York, he also met and married a beautiful young Puerto Rican woman, Camelia Colón, although it was not to be a happy marriage. Herbert was devastated by the defeat of the Republic, although, after the war ended, he and Jay continued to work for the exiled premier Juan Negrín. They helped many prominent Spanish exiles who passed through New York, including Ramón Sender and Constancia de la Mora. Herbert also wrote a book about the Spanish fascist party, the Falange, which was rejected by publishers on the grounds that it was too scholarly.

Shortly after Pearl Harbour, Herbert was recruited by the US Office of War Information. In 1943, he was sent to Algeria to work for the Office of Psychological Warfare. Because of his knowledge of the Spanish situation, he was posted to Rabat in Morocco to direct Spanish-language broadcasts to Franco's Spain. At the end of the war, he decided not to use his demobilization air passage home but stay in Rabat, partly to await the fall of Franco but largely because he had fallen in love with a strikingly handsome and powerfully intelligent French lawyer, Suzanne Maury. When both were free to do so, they married in 1948. Knowing that there were no controls on broadcasting from Tangier, Suzanne advised him to buy a quantity of US Army surplus radio equipment with which he founded Radio Tangier. During that time, he travelled regularly to Spain in search of material for what would become the largest ever collection of books and pamphlets on the Spanish Civil War (which now resides at the University of California at La Jolla, San Diego).

The radio station was nationalized by the Moroccan government at midnight on 31 December 1960. Herbert and Suzanne went to live in Paris. He lost money in an effort to launch the potato crisp in France. That, the problems of finding an apartment big enough to house his library which was deposited in a garage, together with an incident in which he was beaten up by policemen during a left-wing demonstration, inclined him to leave the capital. The problem of his by now enormous library saw him move south where property was cheaper. In 1962, he and Suzanne bought the run-down Château de Puy in Villedieu sur Indre. Some years later, they moved to the faded magnificence of the secluded Château de Roche, in Concrémiers near Le Blanc. In the centre of the huge run-down house was a relatively modernized core, the equivalent of a four-bedroom house, where they lived. On the third floor and in the other wings lived the books and the bats.

Once established there, he began to write the series of books that obliged the Franco regime to change its falsified version of its own past. The most celebrated was the first, *The Myth of Franco's Crusade*, the devastating exposé of right-wing propaganda about the Spanish Civil War. Published in both Spanish and French by Ruedo Ibérico, it was decisive in persuading Manuel Fraga to set up the department solely dedicated to the modernization of regime historiography. Its director, Ricardo de la Cierva, in a losing battle with Southworth, went on to write eighty books in defence of the Franco regime. In 1965, Southworth wrote a second book, *Antifalange*, also published by Ruedo Ibérico, a massively erudite commentary on the process whereby Franco converted the Falange into the single party of his regime. It had significantly less commercial impact than *El mito*, because it was a minutely detailed line-by-line commentary on a book by a Falangist writer, Maximiano García Venero, *Falange en la guerra de España: la Unificación y Hedilla* (Paris: Ruedo Ibérico, 1967). García Venero was the ghost-writer for the wartime Falangist leader, Manuel Hedilla, who had opposed Franco's take-over of the single party in April 1937. Condemned to years of impris-

onment, internal exile and penury, the book was Hedilla's attempt to revin-
dicate his role in the war. Southworth's accompanying volume revealed such
knowledge of the interstices of the Falange that it provoked considerable
surprise and admiration among many senior Falangists. As a result of his
work on the project, Southworth had engaged in a flourishing correspondence with major Falangists. This continued until his death and was notable
for the tone of respect with which many of them treated him.

In 1975, Herbert Southworth's masterpiece appeared in Paris as *La
destruction de Guernica. Journalisme, diplomatie, propagande et histoire* (Paris:
Ruedo Ibérico, 1975), to be followed shortly afterwards by a Spanish translation. The English original appeared as *Guernica! Guernica! A Study of
Journalism, Diplomacy, Propaganda and History* (Berkeley, California,
California University Press, 1977). Based on a staggering array of sources, it
is an astonishing reconstruction of the effort by Franco's propagandists and
admirers to wipe out the atrocity at Guernica – and it thus had a very
considerable impact in the Basque country. The book did not reconstruct the
bombing itself but actually begins with the arrival in Guernica from Bilbao
of *The Times* correspondent, George L. Steer, together with three other
foreign journalists. From that moment, it is a work of the most fascinating
and meticulous research, which reconstructs the web of lies and half-truths
which falsified what really happened at Guernica. The most exaggerated
Francoist version, which blamed the destruction of the town on sabotaging
miners from Asturias, was the invention of Luis Bolín, the head of Franco's
foreign press office. To evaluate the work of Bolín and the subsequent
manipulation of international opinion about the event, Southworth carefully
reconstructed the conditions under which foreign correspondents were
obliged to work in the Nationalist zone. He showed how Bolín frequently
threatened to have shot any correspondent whose despatches did not follow
the Francoist propaganda line. After a detailed demolition of the line
pedalled by Bolín, Southworth went on to dismantle the inconsistencies in
the writings of Bolín's English allies, Douglas Jerrold, Arnold Lunn and
Robert Sencourt.

It might normally be expected that a detailed account of the historiography of a subject would be the arid labour of the narrow specialist.
However, Southworth, managed, with a unique mastery, to turn his study of
the complex construction of a huge lie into a highly readable book. Among
the most interesting and important pages of his book consist of an analysis
of the relationship between Francoist writing on Guernica and the growth of
the Basque problem in the 1970s. Southworth demonstrated that there was
an effort being carried out to lower the tension between Madrid and Euzkadi
by means of the elaboration of a new version of what happened in Guernica.
For this, it was crucial for neo-Francoist historiography to accept that
Guernica had been bombed and not destroyed by Red saboteurs. Having
conceded that the atrocity was largely the work of the Luftwaffe, in total
contradiction of the regime's previous orthodoxy, it became important for

the official historians to free the Nationalist high command from all blame. This task required a high degree of sophistry since the Germans were in Spain in the first place at the request of Francisco Franco. Nevertheless, the neo-Francoists set out to distinguish between what they portrayed as independent German initiative and the innocence of Franco and the commander in the north, General Emilio Mola. Therefore, Southworth analysed the massive literature on the subject to advance a clear hypothesis: Guernica was bombed by the Condor Legion at the request of the Francoist high command in order to destroy Basque morale and undermine the defence of Bilbao.

This conclusion was not apparently remarkable and scarcely went beyond the first chronicle sent to *The Times* by George Steer, and was no more than was regarded as axiomatic by the majority of Basques since 1937. However, the great French historian, Pierre Vilar, in his prologue to the book, pointed out the importance of what Southworth had achieved in returning to the event itself and removing layer after layer of untruth laid on by censorship, by diplomats serving vested interests and determined propagandists of Franco. In Vilar's view, what gave Southworth's work an importance far beyond the confines of the historiography of the Spanish Civil War was his determined quest for the truth, and his exposure of the way in which journalists, censors, propagandists and diplomats distorted history. In a terrain in which truth has always been the first casualty, the 'passionate objectivity' of Southworth rose up like a beacon and made it an object lesson in methodology. Southworth's research was based on an astonishing array of sources in seven languages amassed in many countries. On the advice of Pierre Vilar, the manuscript was presented in 1975 – successfully – as a doctoral thesis at the Sorbonne. He had already lectured in universities in Britain and France but this was the beginning of a belated academic recognition of Southworth's work in his own country. In the mid-1970s, he became Regents Professor at the University of California.

Herbert was never fully welcome in the US academic community because of his inveterate subversiveness and his mischievous humour. He made no secret of his contempt for Washington's policies in Latin America, which evoked for him the betrayal of the Spanish Republic. Everyday, as an avid observer of what he considered to be the hypocrisy of political theatre, he devoured a stack of French and American newspapers. Along with his political passion, he had a wonderful sense of the absurd and an irresistibly infectious laugh. He was particularly keen on multi-lingual puns, never ceasing to be tickled by the delivery to any restaurant table in Spain of a bottle of fizzy water with its label 'sin gas'. I remember on one occasion at a conference in Germany, the assembled participants were led by the director of the host foundation to see a sumptuous carpet, which we were proudly told, had once belonged to Adolph Hitler. Herbert dropped to his knees and began shuffling around, peering closely at the pile. Herr Direktor asked with concern what was the matter and was completely nonplussed when Herbert replied in his slow Texan drawl, 'I'm looking for the teeth marks!'

His demolition of the fake scholarship of others was often extremely amusing, most notably in his chapter entitled 'Spanica Zwischen Todnu Gabriet', in which he traced minutely how Francoist author after Francoist author cited a book which they had never read (Peter Merin's *Spanien zwischen Tod und Geburt* (*Spain between Life and Death*), but merely mis-copied its title. He once asked me to ensure that his gravestone carried the epitaph 'HIS WRITINGS WERE NOT HOLY WRIT / BUT NEITHER WERE THEY WHOLLY SHIT'. Despite his austere inquisitorial style, he was a rotund and jolly trencherman.

After the death of Franco, Herbert was regularly invited to give lectures at Spanish universities where he was a major cult figure. His influence was seen in the work of a new generation of British and Spanish scholars. Southworth's remorselessly forensic writings imposed new standards of seriousness on writing about the war. A pugnacious polemicist, he regularly took part in literary arguments, most notably with Burnett Bolloten and Hugh Thomas. Regarding his great Francoist opponent, Ricardo de La Cierva, he had already published a devastating demolition of his sloppy scholarship, 'Los bibliófobos: Ricardo de La Cierva y sus colaboradores', in *Cuadernos de Ruedo Ibérico*, 28–29 (December 1970 and March 1971). However, he ceased writing for a time. In 1970, he saw that his outgoings on books dramatically exceeded income and he decided that he must sell the collection. It was sold to the University of California at San Diego as 'The Southworth Collection' and remains the world's single most important library on the Spanish Civil War. With income from savings dwindling, he and Suzanne also had to sell the Château de Roche in 1978.

I had assumed that, as they had both entered their seventies, they would move to a modern house. Instead, they bought a medieval priory in the village of St Benoît du Sault, an intriguing but inconvenient house in which every room was on a different level and whose long and narrow stone spiral staircase led eventually to another bat-infested study. Inevitably, Herbert began to rebuild his collection and had started to write again. He enjoyed the friendship of Pierre Vilar, of numerous Spanish scholars and of the venerable Dutch anarchist thinker, Arthur Lehning. They lived happily in St Benoît until Suzanne's health broke down in 1994. Herbert nursed her devotedly until her death on 24 August 1996. He never recovered fully from that blow and, after a stroke, his health deteriorated. Although bed-ridden, with the devoted help of an English neighbour, Susan Mason, he continued to research. Only three days before his death on 30 October 1999 in the hospital at Le Blanc, Indre, he delivered a more fitting epitaph than that quoted above, in the form of the manuscript of the present volume – *Conspiracy and the Spanish Civil War: The Brainwashing of Francisco Franco*.

Professor Paul Preston
Series Editor

Acknowledgements

I undertook to write this, motivated by the encouragement of Professor Paul Preston. I have been able to complete the book only with the invaluable assistance of Sue Mason and Paul Preston. I here express my debt to each of them.

Part I

Conspiracy and the Spanish Civil War

I

I have always given to two specific, quite singular, chapters of the Spanish Civil War historiography a more inquisitive approach than to other categories of seemingly more fundamental significance – than, for example, to the military or diplomatic history of the struggle. These two specific parts are constituted by the journalism and propaganda of the Spanish conflict. They are to some extent interrelated, at least, overlapping. It is not hard to see why these two subjects are of considerable and continuing interest. The Spanish Civil War involved directly but a small part of the globe, but it drew toward Spain the attention of the whole world; thus the press that covered the Spanish War was more diversified in its actors and in its interpretations than the press that reported on the Second World War; thus the field open to propagandists during the Civil War was large and varied, but in the Second World War, where most of the independent countries of the world were themselves participants, the areas at the disposition of the conflicting propagandas were quite limited.

I was myself actively engaged in the propaganda war of the Spanish conflict, on the Republican side, with, I must now admit, meagre results. When, much later in life, I was able to dedicate a large part of my time to writing about the war in Spain, I devoted a very special attention to the problems of Spanish Civil War propaganda during (and after) the war itself. This activity may well have been caused in part by a sentiment of indebtedness to the Second Spanish Republic for having given me a cause to defend with passionate conviction and, perhaps, a deep desire to win, albeit belatedly, the propaganda war; but I must also confess that the nausea provoked in my being by the nature of the Catholic propaganda in favour of Franco during and after the war was one of the motives that kept the seat of my pants on the seat of the chair, in front of the typewriter.

Of all the arguments advanced by pro-Franco propagandists, during and after the war, the most entangled and the most absurd was that based on certain 'secret documents' that were alleged to prove that the Spanish Communist Party, in collusion with Spanish Socialists and even anarchists, as well as foreign Communists and Socialists and Comintern leaders, was plotting, on the eve of the military revolt in July 1936, to seize control – through an armed uprising – of the Spanish government, then already in the hands of the Popular Front.

I had never given more than a cursory reading to the various accounts of these 'secret documents' before the day in 1962 when I sat down to study them seriously as part of the preparation for what was to become *El mito de la cruzada de Franco*.[1] In delving into the complicated – and finally to me exciting – story of the 'secret documents', I found that the number and nature of their guarantors and sponsors were (or could seem too many persons to be) so important and serious that my own instinctive sentiments of being confronted by a poorly concocted imposture were not sufficient to disprove them, and I determined to do my utmost to reveal their – and of this I was convinced – spurious character. Proof was necessary for I could hardly ignore the opinions of Cardinal Gomá, Salvador de Madariaga, Jacques Bardoux, Hugh Thomas, Douglas Jerrold and others who seemed to give serious consideration to the 'secret documents'.

II

Ever since the Russian Revolution of 1917, it has been a profitable enterprise for conservative political movements in Western Europe to publish 'proofs' of a 'secret Communist plot' in order to win an election, or to justify a Rightist take-over of a government. One of the earliest of such schemes concerned the 'Zinoviev Letter', which helped to defeat the British Labour Party in the 1924 elections.[2] The most famous Communist Plot was that of the Reichstag Fire 'exposed' by the Nazis in 1933 in order to complete their conquest of the German State.[3] That only three years later another 'Communist Plot' supported by 'secret documents' should surface, in Spain this time, is hardly surprising.

The 'proofs' of the 'Communist Plot' in Spain consisted of four 'secret documents'. Document I was generally called '*Informe confidencial no. 3*'. It contained orders and watchwords for an uprising of the Spanish Left against the Popular Front, scheduled to take place between 10 May and 29 June 1936. Document II was usually entitled '*Informe confidencial no. 22/11*' and furnished the names of the members of the proposed revolutionary government and of the military and provincial authorities who were to form the 'National Soviet'. There was also an estimation of the size of the forces engaged in the operation, curiously labelled by its supposedly revolutionary authors the 'subversive movement'. The dates for establishing the also strangely labelled 'National Soviet' were, as in Document I, from 10 May to 29 June 1936. These two 'documents' were at times combined, and it is quite possible that originally they formed a single 'document' with II preceding I. (I have chosen to number the 'documents' in the order generally found in the published propagandas.) Document III was headed '*Informe reservado*'. It reported on a meeting said to have taken place in Valencia on 16 May 1936, attended by a delegate from the Third Internationale, by French trade union representatives, by a number of Spaniards (some just come from France) and by two Russian emissaries. Plans were made at this meeting for a revolutionary movement which would break out around the middle of June. Document IV contained general instructions for the 'neutralization of an army and its officers': It did not, in its first printed versions, refer specifically to Spain.

These 'documents' were used in pro-Franco propaganda, after the outbreak of the military rebellion, to justify the revolt of the generals; they were presented as proofs that Franco and the other military leaders had risen in revolt merely to forestall a Communist take-over of the Spanish government.[4] The country, aside from Spain, in which Documents I, II and III were the most widely diffused was England, and England was seemingly the base from which the initial distribution outside Spain was made. Documents I, II and III were given considerable circulation in France, and also appeared in the United States, Germany, Italy and Sweden. In contrast, Document IV first showed up in France, then in England and Italy and rarely appeared elsewhere, except in Spain.

Documents I and II were the most generally employed. This can be explained by the fact that they were the most Spanish of the four 'documents', being limited strictly to Spanish affairs. Document III was also frequently published, but since it dealt not only with Spain, but also with French and Soviet collaborations in Spanish revolutionary matters, the purposes behind its diffusion at times surpassed the limits of the Spanish frontier. Document IV was limited in its appearances outside Spain, perhaps because, as already noted, it did not clearly refer to a Communist conspiracy in Spain during the pre-war months, except in an Italian text and in one Spanish version.

The fact that exactly the same photographic reproductions of certain of the 'documents' were published in more than one country, that the same translations of some 'documents' are found in more than one publication in the same country, or in more than one country, that the same errors in figures and in spelling proper names appear in different copies allow us at times to trace the circulation of the 'documents' from one source to another.

III

The first known appearance of any of these 'documents' in the propaganda war following the outbreak of the Spanish conflict was in England. This was a highly restricted disclosure, and was kept from public knowledge until 1967; this manifestation of the 'documents' played no role in the public propaganda battles, either during the Civil War or later. Frederick Ramón

Bertodano y Wilson, Marquis del Moral,[5] who possessed both British and Spanish nationalities – he was born in Australia and had served England in three wars – sent photocopies of Documents I, II and III, with English translations, in a confidential communication to an official of the Foreign Office, with a covering letter, dated 30 August 1936. The letter read in part as follows:

> I have secured, after much difficulty, certain secret reports and orders of the Socialist-Communist Headquarters in Spain for the rising projected between 3 May and 29 June but postponed. The document is valuable for the list of Ministers of the 'National Soviet', liaison officers and other details of their colleagues of the French Socialist Party. I enclose a photocopy and I shall be glad if you will communicate it to the Foreign Office with my compliments. The man who sent it has risked his life in doing so. Unfortunately, I only received it three days ago...[6]

The Foreign Office discreetly let it be known to del Moral that it did not consider the 'documents' to be 'genuine'.[7] No specific reason was given for this judgement, but a glance at the 'photographic' copies forwarded by del Moral was sufficient to show that the pages were unconvincing as documentary proof of anything at all. They were constituted by three typewritten sheets, one for each 'document', and possessed no letterheads, dates, or signatures. There was nothing on the three pages to prove that they had not been typewritten an hour before being posted to the man at the Foreign Office. There is a strange error in the English text of Document III. In the paragraph numbered 8 of the Spanish text, there is a reference to a *Biblioteca Internacional*. In the English translation, the word 'Biblioteca' is rendered as 'Bookshop', instead of 'library'.

IV

The first public references that I have seen published outside of Spain dealing with the 'documents' are dated October 1936: one in England and the other in France. The English reference is found in the 'Historical Note' which served as a preface to the publication entitled *A Preliminary Official Report on the Atrocities Committed in Southern Spain in July and August 1936, by the Communist Forces of the Madrid Government, together with a Brief Historical Note on the Course of Recent Events in Spain*, first printed in London in October 1936. The title page bore these details: 'Issued by authority of the Committee of Investigation Appointed by the National Government at Burgos'.[8]

In the 'Historical Note' can be read:

All this time [Spring of 1936] there had been repeated and well-founded rumours that the Communists planned to seize power and declare a Spanish Soviet State ... The Communist risings were originally timed for some date between the 3rd of May and June 29th, but were subsequently postponed until 29th or 30th June. This gave the Right an opportunity which they were swift to seize.[9]

Further on in the 'Historical Note' it is stated:

If further evidence of the complicity of the Madrid Government were necessary, the appointment of Señor Largo Caballero as Prime Minister provides it, as he was openly designated as the President of the National Soviet of Spain... An interesting sidelight on the Communist plan was the provision made for a pretended 'Fascist' attack on the headquarters of C.N.T. as soon as the movement was begun ... It is thus established by documentary evidence that this great national movement was begun only just in time to forestall the Communist Revolution organized months before to establish a Soviet in Spain at the end of July.[10]

The 'Historical Note' is unsigned but there are indications that it was written by del Moral himself. At any rate, it was written by the man who received the English aviation journalist Nigel Tangye at Spanish Nationalist headquarters in London in December 1936, just before the journalist, carrying Nazi diplomatic recommendations, left for Rebel Spain to write favourably on the campaign of the Franco forces. Tangye described his host as:

a man with the finest features I have ever seen ... he was tall and slim, and his face revealed the breeding and culture that somehow one expects from the Spanish aristocracy. His hair, worn rather long, was white and in his eyes was a look of inestimable sadness.[11]

In talking of Tangye's projected trip to Spain, he advised the war correspondent: 'But before you go, read the book on the Spanish atrocities. In it I have written a brief history of the events that led up to the revolution.'[12]

Tangye's description could fit del Moral, as is attested by a letter from Sir Arthur Bryant, dated 23 July 1969. Sir Arthur was the writer of the preface to a follow-up volume, *The Second and Third Reports on the Communist Atrocities*, but he did not recall in 1969 who had prefaced the first volume.[13] The publisher of these *Reports*, and of a great deal of other Spanish rebel propaganda in England, was the London house of Eyre and Spottiswoode. The director of Eyre and Spottiswoode was Douglas Jerrold, a militant English Catholic, who played a prominent role in the story of the 'documents'. Unfortunately for the historian, the archives of Eyre and Spottiswoode were destroyed during a bombing of the Second World War, and there apparently remains no documentary trace of the authorship of the 'Historical Note'.[14]

If the author of the 'Historical Note' was del Moral, it was written by a man who knew that his 'documents' had been judged 'not genuine' by the Foreign Office, but this unpublicized judgement would not have been enough to stop a decided man like del Moral from his campaign in favour of Franco. Del Moral was probably the person most active behind the scenes in England on behalf of the Spanish Nationalists during the Civil War, just as his close friend Jerrold was one of their outstanding advocates in the public view.[15]

It must be underlined here that the first published appearance of a reference to the 'documents' outside Spain before or after the outbreak of the Civil War was in an effort to justify the military uprising.

V

The second public mention outside Spain in October 1936 to any of the 'documents' appeared in the feverishly pro-Franco Parisian weekly *Gringoire* on 9 October 1936: a French translation of Documents I and II, presented as a single 'document', the original of which had been reportedly found in Majorca among the papers abandoned by the Republican Comandante Bayo, who was defeated in his efforts to recapture the island in August 1936. The presentation read:

> The truth is that the national insurrectional movement was begun to prevent an enterprise of Sovietization of which the assassination of Calvo Sotelo was only the prelude. We have in hand a document which proves this fact in a preemptory manner. It was taken from the communists in the course of the action of the 28th Spanish infantry regiment at Palma de Majorca. It is the plan for a Soviet *coup d'état* which the Spanish patriots caused to fail.

The conclusion was: 'The execution of this plan was delayed several times, which permitted the Nationalists to organize to intervene in order to conquer and to save Spain.'[16]

This 'document' was, in so far as one can judge without the Spanish original which has apparently never been published, essentially the text of Documents I and II used by del Moral. There were slight differences in the spelling of certain names, and in the numbering of the 'watchwords'. The most significant change was that in the *Gringoire* paper, the earliest date for the eve of the uprising is given as 1 May, whereas del Moral's 'document' specified 10 May. Such differences can be explained as due to faulty typing, but in the case of instructions for an insurrection they could have led to catastrophe. And anyway, why different texts and so many copies? The reader of *Gringoire* – if he were of a sceptical turn of mind – might well have asked himself what these instructions for an uprising in Madrid in May and June were doing in Bayo's baggage in Majorca in August. Apparently, such questions were never asked by the editors of the paper. In this case also the purpose of the publication was to exonerate those accountable for the military revolt from any responsibility for the outbreak of the Civil War.

Another 1936 reference to the 'documents' can be discerned in one of the first books published in England on the Spanish Civil War, *Spanish Journey*, written by Eleanora Tennant. The author left Spain on 30 October 1936[17] and, since the publication date is given as 1936, it represents a record of some sort for rapid printing. Unsurprisingly, it was published by Jerrold's old firm, Eyre and Spottiswoode. Tennant gave no source for her information, nor did she give verbatim quotations, but she was certainly inspired by the 'documents' in general, especially by Document III, when she wrote

> The Nationalists only struck just in time as a Communist rising on a grand scale had been planned to take place a few days later. The complete plans for the Communist revolution which were prepared in May 1936, under the guidance of Ventura (a delegate of the Third International), have fallen into the hands of General Franco, so there is no secret about them.[18]

Still another early reference to the 'Secret Communist Plot Documents' outside Spain can be found in a booklet written by Federico de Echevarría, first published in all probability late in 1936 in Paris, then in London and New York. The French edition contains a preface dated 'November 1936' and the same date is found at the end of the text. The New York edition, however, had the date 'December 1936' at the end of the text. The French and American editions gave the following information, which evidently came from Document I:

> The instructions found in the possession of the Reds and published during the civil war prove that a great *coup d'état* was being prepared in order to set up the dictatorship of the proletariat in Spain. Originally it should have taken place in May, then it was postponed until June, and there were further postponements, the reasons for which are not yet known. Finally, it seems to have been fixed for July 30th. It was forestalled by the National Revolution.[19]

Echevarría did not indicate any source for these details.

Again, both of these authors, Tennant and Echevarría, used information contained in the 'documents' in order to absolve Franco and the military from any responsibility in starting the Spanish Civil War.

VI

The Popular Front electoral victory in Spain on 16 February 1936 presented Western Europe with a political and moral problem. It was the first time that a political coalition, including Socialists and Communists, had won a victory at the polls in this part of the world. Up to this moment, the expression 'revolutionary forces' in Spain referred by definition to forces of the Left. But now, the Left was in power and the Right in opposition. The first reaction of the conservative political and military elements in Spain was to begin doing what they had always up to then considered to be the base and vile prerogatives of the lower classes: they began plotting to overthrow a democratically elected government. (Of course, some of them tried to argue that the elections of 16 February 1936 were fraudulent, and the government illegitimate, but such arguments were unconvincing, and carried little weight in Spain before 18 July 1936, and did not become unconditional articles of faith of the Spanish Right until after that date.)

But however much the Spanish military and political conspirators might have instinctively believed that any government with the Socialists and Communists in it was by nature illegitimate, once they had launched their revolt and it had not immediately succeeded, they felt the need to explain and justify – especially in the Western political democracies – their 'revolutionary' behaviour. They refused the label of 'revolutionaries'. They were merely trying to *prevent* a revolution, a Communist revolution, that is. This is the sense of the argument advanced by del Moral to the Foreign Office, by the anonymous author of the 'Historical Note', by the editors of *Gringoire*, by Eleanora Tennant and by Echevarría.

In spite of their reactionary ideologies and their conservative dogmas, the Spanish rebels did not want to assume the role of 'revolutionaries' in the Western World, of agents for overthrowing a democratically elected government. They were, they argued in their propaganda, especially in the propaganda of the 'Secret Communist Plot Documents', but seeking to counter a real revolution, that is a social revolution of the Left. Thus, in the examples thus far shown of the pro-Franco propaganda in Paris, London and New York during the first months of the Civil War, the spokesmen of the Spanish Rebels appeal to the politically democratic sentiments of their public, denying the ultra-Rightist and undemocratic spirit of their revolt, and seek to shelter their uprising behind the protection of such sophistries as the 'Secret Documents of the Communist Plot'.

VII

It was in 1937 that the propaganda campaign outside Spain, based on the 'Secret Documents of the Communist Plot', began in earnest. On 14 January of that year, *L'Écho de Paris*, probably the French newspaper most influential on behalf of Franco, published Document IV. The publication of Document IV was prefaced by a long introductory essay over three columns, and the 'document' itself began on page 1 and continued on page 2. The headline read: 'HOW THE FRENCH COMMUNIST PARTY, FROM APRIL 1936, PLANNED REVOLUTION IN SPAIN'. The title over the 'document' itself stated: 'INSTRUCTIONS GIVEN TO THE RED MILITIAS FOR "NEUTRALIZING" THE ARMY'. The preface, signed by André Pironneau, read in part as follows:

The instructions addressed to the leaders of the Spanish Red militias, anarchists, communists, socialists, in order to 'neutralize' the army once these militias launched their attack, date from the end of April 1936.

They are not issued by some central Spanish organization but rather by 'technical services set up in Paris' sent to Spain at that time.

These technical services are those of the French Communist Party, closely collaborating with the Comintern and its representatives in France.

We can imagine the considerable interest aroused when we know the procedures advocated by the Communist Party since the elimination methods set out in the instructions to the leaders of the Spanish Red militias are the very same ones that would be used in France, if the case arose.

The 'document' itself consisted of thirty numbered paragraphs, with no direct references to the Spanish situation except the mention of 'the uniform of the civil or assault guard' in paragraph 15. Pironneau gave no proof whatsoever to support his gratuitous affirmations concerning the origin of the 'document' or its relations with the French Communist Party or with any 'Red militia' forces in Spain or elsewhere, nor did he indicate how the 'document' came into his hands, remarking only that 'The document we publish here has fallen into the hands of the [French] government.'[20]

VIII

On 15 February 1937, Jacques Bardoux, maternal grandfather of former French President Valéry Giscard d'Estaing, *Membre de l'Institut, Homme d'affaires* and prolific pamphleteer of Ultra-Rightist views, brought the *Gringoire* version of Document I and the *Écho de Paris* text of Document IV to the knowledge of an influential segment of French conservative opinion by publishing a long article in the *Revue de Paris* entitled *La guerre civile internationale. Moscou, Madrid, Paris*[21] and then, in a forty-seven-page pamphlet, *Le chaos espagnol: éviterons nous la contagion?*, Bardoux vouched for the authenticity of his copy of Document I, which he used, along with another 'document' dealing exclusively with France, in order to illustrate a parallel between the 'two operations France and Spain'.[22] The purpose of Bardoux's parallel was to demonstrate that at the VIIth Congress of the Third Internationale, held in Moscow in July–August 1935, plans were laid for a Spanish Revolution, then in progress.

> In March and April 1936, when the Frente Popular is in power, three or four months before General Franco has drawn his sword – the Russian government and its Communist Internationale are furnishing instructions, cadres, arms and munitions, to the revolutionary troops, who are to install, by force, at a fixed date, on the ruins of the Republic, a Soviet regime.[23]

Bardoux also guaranteed the authenticity of Document IV, writing, 'This document ... at first edited in French, with the collaboration of Russian technicians, then translated into Spanish and sent to Madrid, is authentic. I know that it is.'[24]

Documents I, II and III were cited during the first months of 1937 in England and the United States. Douglas Jerrold, a close English friend of del Moral and a well-known Catholic editor and publicist, in April 1937, wrote an article on the war in Spain in the London conservative monthly *The Nineteenth Century and After*;[25] this article was then published in the pro-Fascist New York monthly, *The American Review*.[26] Jerrold referred to Documents I, II and III, and he quoted extensively from I and III. He thus seems to have been, in April 1937, the first person to have written publicly about the three documents – I, II and III together – but he did not publish their texts in full. Writing of the detailed plans for a 'Communist uprising in Spain' in the summer of 1936, he declared:

> In May of last year the detailed plans were laid for a Communist rising in Spain in June or July 1936. These plans have been for some months in the possession of the Salamanca [Franco] government and the documents containing them are known to many journalists in England. They provide a careful timetable for the outbreak of the revolution and the organization of revolutionary cadres and give the personnel of the revolutionary government, with Largo Caballero at its head.[27]

Jerrold's quotations from the 'documents' differ slightly from the texts submitted by del Moral to the Foreign Office, but at the same time, they seem to be in all probability translations of the same Spanish original. The most significant difference is that the meeting said to have been held in Valencia on 16 May 1936 (Document III) was, in Jerrold's text, held on 15 May.

IX

Shortly after Jerrold quoted from the 'documents' in England, the Anti-Comintern in Berlin was revealing photocopies of Documents I, II and III, in an anthology of alleged Republican atrocities in Spain entitled *Das Rotbuch über Spanien*.[28] No source was given for the 'documents'. Parts of Document II were translated with these prefatory remarks: 'The secret plan for the uprising ... contained a precise synopsis of the total Bolshevik forces, it regulated the realization of the united action and gave as the goal of the combined action a Spanish Soviet Republic.'[29] The *Rotbuch* reproductions marked the first time that the three 'documents' were published in full together, and also represented the first time that photographs of Documents I, II and III were publicly exhibited.

It was probably this reproduction of Document I that Josef Göbbels cited in his 1937 Nuremberg Party Day speech, and which he described as 'an official document issued by the Moscow Comintern which I have before me'. Göbbels shouted that 'it has become clear from these facts that the Comintern came near to realizing its plans and was forestalled at the last moment by the strong personality of one man [Franco]'.[30]

The most significant fact to be gleaned from a study of the *Rotbuch* publication of Documents I, II and III is the indisputable proof that the *Rotbuch* copies are exact duplicates of those sent to the Foreign Office by del Moral. Each 'document' is on a single sheet, without letterhead or signature; each word is placed on the page in exactly the same position in both copies. Each misspelling is the same. The most expert typist in the world could not have realized a similar feat of manual reproduction. But, as indicated earlier, a short addition by hand had been made to the del Moral 'documents'. It therefore seems impossible that the Anti-Comintern Document I should be a photographic copy of the del Moral Document I, but the inverse is not out of the question. It is highly possible that del Moral had in August 1936 a photographic copy of the 'documents' later used by the Anti-Comintern; it is also possible that del Moral and the Anti-Comintern each received his photographic copies from a third source.

X

Also early in 1937, Cecil Gerahty, 'Special Correspondent' of the London conservative newspaper the *Daily Mail*, recorded in his book, *The Road to Madrid*, a translation made, he said, by himself, of Documents I and II, 'found in the Communist headquarters in La Línea, near Gibraltar', written on five sheets of paper.[31] The fact that such papers could exist near Gibraltar, outpost of the Empire, probably sent shivers up the spines of the *Daily Mail* readers. The 'documents' constituted, Gerahty wrote, a clear statement of the plot which the Syndicalists and anarchists were on the point of putting into execution when Franco forestalled them by a few days or perhaps even by a few hours ... These orders must have been effectively distributed throughout the country ... This Sovietic dictatorship is actually the present so-called Government ... Caballero's Soviet dictatorship in Valencia.[32]

In Gerahty's discovery, the paragraphs of Documents I and II were somewhat mixed up; in fact, in Gerahty's 'document' the material I have called Document II (using del Moral's numbering system) preceded Document I, and even included parts of the latter.

Gerahty had another proof of a Communist conspiracy, 'an exact translation of a leaflet I saw, found in a flower-pot in Triana'. As reprinted by Gerahty, it began: 'Fellow workmen. The 25th is the day arranged for our vengeance. All workmen are pledged to avenge our comrades of the María Luisa Park.' Gerahty explained that 'A few years ago some escaping prisoners were shot in María Luisa Park' and continued in detail:

> The month referred to is July, the date being exactly one week after the revolution actually began ... This is one of the many indications that Franco's move was only just in time to prevent a general massacre of the 'persons of order.'[33]

This anecdote is, of course, proof of but one thing: someone told Gerahty that he had found a paper in a flower-pot in the Triana sector of Seville. It can also, secondarily, show that Gerahty was eager to find a justification for Franco's revolt. It did not occur to him that Franco prevented a general massacre of the 'persons of order' through a general massacre of the Seville working class in Triana by Franco's troops, in great part Moroccan mercenaries.

XI

Another English supporter of Franco, the converted Catholic Arnold Lunn, a prolific pamphleteer for the Nationalist cause,[34] gave great significance to Gerahty's discovery, writing:

> The document contains detailed plans for a Communist revolution, and lists of those who are to constitute the National Soviet, a list headed by the President, Largo Caballero. The rising did not take place on the first date suggested in this document, but although postponed, the plan was not abandoned.[35]

In another reference to the 'Communist Plot', Lunn stated: 'Franco rose only just in time to forestall a *coup d'état* designed to inaugurate a Red dictatorship. The evidence for this is given in my book, *Spanish Rehearsal*.'[36]

Lunn's proof that the plan was not abandoned was found in Gerahty's other discovery, the leaflet left by an unknown agent in a flower-pot in Triana, on which was written the date of 25 July as 'the day arranged for our vengeance'. Lunn observed: 'This date was exactly one week after the war broke out. Franco was only just in time.'[37]

In 1939, Lunn elaborated on this 'discovery':

> An English journalist, Cecil Gerahty, discovered by chance in Triana ... a circular which announced July 25th as 'the day arranged for our vengeance'. This date was exactly one week after the war broke out. Franco cut the margin of safety very fine.[38]

If Franco's uprising were based on the paper in the flower-pot, it was cutting margins very fine indeed. Here it is worth noting that, although Jerrold had written in April 1937 that Documents I, II and III were familiar to 'many journalists' in England, and although it is evident from Lunn's texts that when he wrote *Spanish Rehearsal,* he had already read Jerrold's April 1937 article,[39] Lunn in his book referred only to Documents I and II and to these as found in the version of Cecil Gerahty, and took no heed of Jerrold's 'documents'.

XII

Later in 1937, Jerrold published references to Documents I, II and III, with quotations from Documents I and III, in his autobiography *Georgian Adventure*, a book in which he affirmed that the 'Communist rising ... was fixed for the end of June, or the beginning of July'. He also wrote:

> The plans for the Communist *coup*, which have now been in the hands of the Salamanca Government for some months, provide a careful time-table for the outbreak of the revolution and the organization of revolutionary cadres, and give the personnel of the Revolutionary Government to be set up, with Largo Caballero at its head.[40]

After quoting paragraph numbered (9) from Document III, Jerrold observed that 'the murder of Calvo Sotelo is thus proved to have been planned in advance as a definite stage in a revolutionary plot against the elected Government of Spain by the friends of Caballero'. This is Jerrold's second reference in less than two pages to a link between the murder of Calvo Sotelo and the plans found in the 'documents'.[41] He does not provide an iota of proof for the existence of this link.

If Jerrold had a sense of humour, and I sense no traces of it in his political writings, he would have found the situation amusing in which he was charging others with participation in a vast, though inexistent, conspiracy at a time when he was himself, by his own admission, one of the first foreign participants in the only real secret plan that did bring about the Spanish Civil War.[42]

XIII

Jacques Bardoux continued his research concerning the great conspiracy during 1937 and on 1 October published in the prestigious (in conservative circles and the libraries of French chateaux) *Revue des Deux Mondes*, an article entitled 'Le Complot Russo-Communiste'. In this article Bardoux gave a French translation of Documents I, II, III and IV.[43] In a brochure entitled *Staline contre l'Europe: Les preuves du complot communiste*, which appeared at about the same time, containing the same text with slight alterations, he gave the four 'documents' in both French and Spanish.[44] Bardoux in his presentation sought to demonstrate his objectivity:

> In the eyes of the court of public opinion, personal testimonies, however numerous, concordant and impartial they may be, will never have the same conclusive force as written evidence. But it is possible to find written proof that the communist *coup d'état* against the Frente Popular was to have taken place before 18 July 1936. Is it equally possible to demonstrate by documents that a liaison existed between Paris and Madrid, on the one hand, Moscow on the other, for the purpose of undertaking a simultaneous operation of force against the weakling governments of the Popular Front around the middle of June 1936? I believe so. Here are three pieces of evidence, of which I saw photocopies in London and whose authenticity I have verified. I am authorized to publish them.[45]

As an introduction to Documents I and II, considered by Bardoux to form a single document under the heading 'Instructions for the communist *coup d'état* and for the constitution of a Sovietic government', he wrote:

> This document arrived in London, through English hands. It was copied in June 1936 in the Madrid office of the *Unión General de Trabajadores*, socialist section of working class unity created by the III International.[46] It was communicated in August 1936 to several foreign governments, notably to the Holy See. Three other copies, which contain slight differences and whose texts are in my dossier, have been found in the archives of communist centres: at Lora del Río, a small

town in the province of Seville, in a village in the province of Badajoz, and at La Línea, near Gibraltar.[47]

In his second article and brochure, Bardoux presented Document III, with this introduction:

> This document – of which I have seen the photocopy – reached London in August 1936, through English hands. It had been copied in Madrid, in the offices of the *Unión General de Trabajadores* ...[48]

Bardoux's introduction to Document IV was more specific this time:

> The date for this Communist breviary is known: April 1936. The place where it was drafted is also known: Paris. The authors of the manual are known: the technical services of the French section, aided by Russian experts sent from Moscow. Drafted first in French, the instructions were then translated into Spanish and dispatched to Madrid.[49]

In his second article and pamphlet on the 'documents', Bardoux dropped all references to the *Gringoire* (Palma de Mallorca) 'document' which had however formed the basis for his first references to the 'documents'. Even the French version of Document I, in Bardoux's second article, is a completely different translation from that which he had used a few months earlier. Bardoux's chief contribution to our story lies in the fact that *Staline contre l'Europe* constitutes the only publication where the texts, seemingly more or less complete, of the four 'documents' were reproduced during the Civil War.

Just as Documents I, II and III, at least in their appearances after the outbreak of the Spanish War, can be traced back to London, so our knowledge of Document IV seems to have had a strictly Paris origin. This condition is easily explained: a Popular Front governed in Paris as it did in Madrid. Document IV was used by Bardoux to establish a revolutionary link between Paris, Madrid and Moscow.

One person who was to accept without question the 'documents' of Bardoux was the Comte de Saint-Aulaire, Ambassador of France, who wrote in 1938:

> Those who accuse Franco forget also that by the month of July 1936 all the preparations were made, by order of Moscow, to install the terror, the Soviet regime, in all Spain. On this subject, I refer to the revelations of M. Jacques Bardoux. The instructions of Madrid having been sent to every locality, several copies were handed to Franco ... Far from precipitating the catastrophe, Franco put limits to it by preventing it ...[50]

XIV

In 1937, Bardoux's first pamphlet was translated into English and published in London.[51] This translation, and Bardoux's later article in the *Revue des Deux Mondes*, inspired the English Catholic monarchist Robert Sencourt, who, in his 1938 book *Spain's Ordeal*, gave his own guarantee to Documents I, II, III and IV, citing as his sources Bardoux in *Chaos in Spain*; the *Revue des Deux Mondes*; *L'Écho de Paris;* and the *Letter of the Spanish Bishops*.[52] This latter document, which I shall analyse further on, was accepted without question by Sencourt. He wrote, 'These militiamen of the revolution were instructed regularly and were strongly armed. They were so thoroughly organized that in July 160,000 shock troops were already trained, with a further reserve of a hundred thousand.'[53] This outlandish affirmation was only too evidently lifted from Document II, but Sencourt, never a man to make a charge without a footnote of some sort, gave as his authority not the 'document' itself but the *Letter of the Spanish Bishops, 1 July 1937*. Sencourt did not realize that Cardinal Gomá was not a more reliable historical source than was Sencourt himself.[54]

Sencourt, following his guide Bardoux, treated Documents I and II as a single 'document'. He claimed, however, to have located five copies of this 'document', considering the 'document' transmitted to the Holy See (according to Bardoux) as another original; it was, in fact, merely a duplicate of one of the two 'documents' copied in Madrid in June 1936 (according to Bardoux). The other document copied in Madrid (Document III) was apparently not among those which, according to Bardoux, were communicated to 'several foreign governments, notably to the Holy See'.[55] Sencourt wrote, parroting Bardoux:

> All these three documents I, II and III are elaborations of the plans made in July 1935 by the Seventh World Congress of the Third International at Moscow: the plot to overrun the free countries under the mask of the Popular Front, and always under the guidance of a sovietic agent.[56]

(In all this imbroglio, it is amusing and at the same time educational to observe the manner in which several completely independent factors, absolutely worthless as proofs of authenticity, such as the existence of a 'document' in photocopy form, or the existence of a 'document' in the shape of a communication to 'several foreign governments, notably to the Holy See' are used by Bardoux and Sencourt to authenticate the 'documents'. It is also appropriate to underline at this time the fact that Sencourt, like Bardoux and others, was proceeding as though all 'copies' of his three (four) 'documents' contained the same texts, whereas, as a matter of fact, he had never seen the Badajoz version (nor has to my knowledge anybody else); the Lora del Río copy (as we shall see farther on, had two differing versions, and we do not know today the Spanish text of the La Línea original translated by Gerahty.)

XV

It was only in 1938 that complete English texts for Documents I, II and III were published in England and the three were printed together in a brochure entitled *Exposure of the Secret Plans to Establish a Soviet in Spain.*[57] This somewhat tardy appearance of the 'documents' in England is all the more surprising when we recall that Bardoux in *Staline contre l'Europe* (1937) wrote that he had obtained his copies of Documents I, II and III in England. It is also strange that the three 'documents' had been brought to public notice in Berlin a year earlier than in London. This 1938 English printing of Documents I, II and III was due to the initiative of a group called the Friends of National Spain, whose moving spirits were Jerrold, del Moral, Sir Henry Page Croft, Sir Charles Petrie and others.[58] (Since we know that del Moral had employed the 'documents' in August 1936, as had Jerrold in his April 1937 article, where he had written that 'the 'documents' ... are familiar to many journalists in this country', we can surmise that this comparatively unimportant publication under partisan auspices was adopted as a last resort, after the group had failed to have the 'documents' adopted officially by the British government or guaranteed by an independent press.)

The ostensible cause for the publication of the three 'documents' at this time was declared to be: 'the particulars given in *The Times* of 3 May 1938 on the ' "Comintern" organization in Spain', these 'particulars' being, according to the introductory paragraph 'confirmed by a study of the documents found in Spain immediately after the rebellion of 18th July 1936'. The article in *The Times* was a dispatch datelined 'Riga' and it sustained two theses difficult to uphold in the light of present-day scholarship: first, that the Soviet Union, far from sincerely promoting the Popular Fronts against Fascism and Nazism, was in reality preparing for 'civil war in "bourgeois countries" ' and, second, that 'the Comintern engineered the outbreak of civil war in Spain'.[59]

The 'particulars' concerning Spain in the Riga dispatch were in fact few, and did not justify their use to introduce this pamphlet on the 'documents'. The brochure did state that five 'copies of the plan have been found in different parts of Spain', and went on to affirm that the 'five documents' were 'almost identical, but in the interests of accuracy, slight variations in the names of individuals, etc., though of no importance, are shown in the text in italics'.[60]

The text of *Exposure* is highly confused concerning the contents of each copy of the 'Secret Plan', and the statement that the 'five documents' ... were published in full, side by side with French translations in the autumn of 1937 by Jacques Bardoux in *Staline contre l'Europe* was inexact.[61] In this booklet, as has been shown, Bardoux used but four so-called 'copies'. *Exposure* located three 'copies' in the same places as those indicated by Bardoux, but differed with him on the two others; *Exposure* included the *Gringoire* (Palma de Mallorca) copy – banned from Bardoux's second article, and situated Bardoux's primary source for the 'documents' as being 'the chief Communist Headquarters in Spain', although the French pamphleteer had given his source as the Socialist Trade Union, the UGT. In this manner, *Exposure* could indicate that four of the 'copies', all except that of *Gringoire*, had been found in an unidentified 'Communist Headquarters'.

The extracts from the 'documents' given by Jerrold in his article 'Spain: Impressions and Reflections' and later in *Georgian Adventure* are identical with the texts of Documents I and III in *Exposure*, which is hardly surprising in view of Jerrold's connection with the group responsible for the brochure. *Exposure* also published a photocopy of the Lora del Río 'document' in three pages;[62] this is in fact a combination of Document I, followed by Document II, in the same order as in Bardoux's article, but both appear under an overall title, 'Instructions and Countersigns', and the generally accepted title for Document I ('Confidential Report No. 3') is left out, while the same title for Document II ('Confidential Report No. 22') is retained. The text for these two 'documents' is essentially the same as the Spanish texts in Bardoux's second brochure. There would seem to have been at one time a common text, but whoever copied the Lora del Río 'document' on three pages (or a still earlier copyist) changed a word here and there, spelled a name differently, or even changed the order of three or four paragraphs. It is also of interest to observe that although Bardoux emphasized the importance of Document IV in his brochure, it is completely ignored by *Exposure*. In reality, the brochure of The Friends of National Spain was in all likelihood, and despite the gracious acknowledgement to Bardoux, based more on the 'English source' of Bardoux than on Bardoux's work. Finally, there was this pompous sentence: 'These documents, found in Spanish territory, are published with the permission and full authority of the Nationalist Government at Burgos.'[63]

Cecil Gerahty also returned to the charge in 1938, dealing with the 'documents' in *Spanish Arena*, the book he wrote in collaboration with William Foss. This tandem threw out the mixed-up copy of Documents I and II which Gerahty had discovered in 1937, the 'La Línea document', and in its place based their accusations of the 'Communist Plot' on Document I, as given in the English translation of Bardoux's first pamphlet, and on Document IV, translated in an abridged version from *L'Écho de Paris*.[64]

XVI

In his second 1937 pamphlet, *Staline contre l'Europe*, Jacques Bardoux signalled the existence in England of valuable documentation concerning the 'communist coup d'état for the establishing of a sovietic government'. This was, beyond any doubt, the material later used by an English businessman and sometime journalist, with interests and experience in Spain, Arthur F. Loveday. Such was Loveday's zeal to militate in the crusade against communism that just before the beginning of the war in Spain he became a convert to Catholicism, as had the ultra-racist Fascist sympathizer poet, Roy Campbell.[65] In Appendix II of his 1939 book *World War in Spain*, Loveday published English translations of the texts of Documents I, II and III.[66] This appendix was entitled 'Secret Documents detailing the plan for the establishment of a Soviet in Spain, the discovery of which was one of the immediate causes of the counter-revolution and the civil war'. The following pages bore the heading 'Secret Communist Documents'. In this appendix he also reproduced a photographic copy of the Lora del Río document. In its fundamental contents, aspects and details, Loveday's Appendix II seems to be a reprint of the 1938 *Exposure*. Loveday does not credit *Exposure* here, but he mentions it in his bibliography. Loveday's English translation is the same as that given in *Exposure*. However, Loveday's Lora del Río 'document' is not an identical copy of the one in *Exposure*. We therefore have two Lora del Río 'documents'. There is another detail difficult to explain. If Loveday, to give an air of authenticity to his exposition, wanted to reproduce a 'document', why did he not reproduce one of the 'documents' he claimed to have had in his hands in June 1936? Did he hesitate to reproduce a paper already labelled not 'genuine' by the Foreign Office? Did he know of the *Rotbuch* and prefer not to reproduce the copy already used by the Nazis? Or why did he not simply use the *Exposure* copy?

Loveday wrote in defence of his 'documents':

> ... there can be no further doubt that in May–June 1936, a proletarian rising against the already extreme Left government (Popular Front) of Spain and the establishment of Soviets under the dictatorship of Largo Caballero were fully prepared ... The sparks that set light to the conflagration and fixed the date of the rising of the Army officers were two: the discovery of the secret document containing the complete details for the proletarian communist rising with the establishment of a Soviet Spain, and the murder of the leader of the opposition in the Cortes, Señor Calvo Sotelo ... As regards the secret document detailing the instructions and outlining the procedure for the proletarian rising timed to start on some date in June or July 1936, its authenticity was doubted by some people, and the apologists of the Spanish Government attempted to discredit it, saying it was invented subsequently as an excuse for the Civil War. But there need no longer be any doubt about it in the minds of students of history ... The internal evidence of the document's authenticity is so great as to be overwhelming, for, not only were many of the plans and policies laid down in it actually fulfilled, but some of the very people indicated by name for various positions,

actually and subsequently filled them ... The document is so important, as conclusive evidence of the origins of the Civil War, that it is published as an appendix.[67]

Farther on in this same book, Loveday again refers to the 'document', by which word in the singular he would seem to mean both Documents I and II:

What would by itself be conclusive evidence of Communist-Soviet influence and intervention in Spain was provided in June 1936, by the discovery in Spain of the document to which reference has already been made ..., containing a complete and detailed scheme for the establishment of a Soviet in Spain ... its internal evidence is a striking proof of its genuineness. It was one of the sparks that started the Civil War: ... the historian cannot any longer reject it.[68]

Loveday's testimony is significant in that he, alone of all those who were writing about Documents I, II and III at that time, claimed to have seen them before the outbreak of the Civil War and could therefore testify that they had not simply been dreamed up after 18 July 1936. Alas, however, Loveday's explanations are among the more unbelievable of a propaganda campaign rife with fatuities. Loveday gave two contradictory accounts. The first one is found on pp. 55–56: 'It [Documents I–II] was stolen from the anarchist headquarters and a copy brought to England by the writer of this history in June, 1936, a month before the civil war broke out.' Then, on p. 176, he wrote: 'the documents consist of two confidential reports and a secret report, which came from the files of the Communist headquarters in Spain, and were brought to England in June 1936, by the author of this book'. Loveday was an extremely confused historian. In his first account, he stated that he had himself brought to England Documents I and II, stolen from the 'anarchist headquarters' (in Madrid? in Barcelona?) around the middle of June 1936. Then on another page of the same book, he avers that he brought to England, at the same time, copies of Documents I, II and III, taken from the 'files of the Communist headquarters in Spain'. Again, no city is indicated for this remarkable thievery, and how had the fruits of both adventures fallen into the hands of Loveday?

Loveday certified to the existence of five copies of the 'documents', four in the same localities previously identified by Bardoux and *Exposure*: Palma, Majorca; Lora del Río; a town near Badajoz; and La Línea. And the primary, quoted versions of Loveday? Are they not the same as those used by Bardoux as his text? Are they not the very 'documents' of which Bardoux had seen photocopies in London with his own eyes? Are they not the basis for the translations used in *Exposure*? All were declared to have been copied in, or stolen from, left-wing offices in Spain, just before the outbreak of the war – in three different offices, as a matter of fact.

Loveday had brought his copies out from Spain himself, or so he said in 1939, and Bardoux's copies had reached England *par voie anglaise*. On the other hand, Jerrold's 'documents' 'have now been for some months in the hands of the Salamanca Government', and the author of *Exposure* assured his readers: 'These documents, found in Spanish territory, are published with the permission and full authority of the Nationalist Government.' But then Bardoux and Loveday, whose 'documents' antedated the outbreak of the Civil War, also felt the need to assure their readers that they were authorized to use them. Bardoux: 'I am authorized to publish them.' By whom? Loveday was more explicit: 'All these documents were published with the permission and full authority of the nationalist government.'[69] Why should a Frenchman and an Englishman need permission from the Salamanca government to publish 'documents' that had left Spain before the war? or even after? It was doubtless to give the 'documents' a seal of approval, a semblance of authenticity.

Arnold Lunn guaranteed the authenticity of the 'Documents' printed in the *Exposure of the Secret Plan to Establish a 'Soviet' in Spain* in another book which he published in 1939, saying

> The Nationalist Government have recently issued a summary of documents discovered in Spain shortly after the outbreak of the civil war. These documents strikingly confirm the details given in *The Times* of May 3rd 1938, of the Comintern organization in Spain.[70]

XVII

England, Germany and France were not the only countries in which the 'documents' were employed for pro-Franco propaganda. As we have already seen, Jerrold published extracts from Documents I and II in *The American Review* in 1937. In 1939, Merwin K. Hart, an American with a background strikingly similar to that of Bardoux and of Loveday – all were right-wing businessmen with a gift for political pamphleteering – published *America, Look at Spain!*, a book with a highly argumentative pro-Franco content. This volume contained, as Appendix I, a 'document' entitled 'Instructions of the Communist International for Taking Over Spain', and presented to be the 'version found at Lora del Río'.[71] But the text was not the reproduction of the 'Lora del Río' copy, neither that of *Exposure* nor that of Loveday. It was the English text used in *Exposure*, and later in Loveday's book. Even the spelling is that of English usage and not American. This complicity is underlined by the fact that Hart placed in simple parentheses certain phrases which were in parentheses but also italicized in *Exposure* for the purpose of illustrating variations from one copy of a 'document' to another; all of these variant phrases are found in Hart's book, but incorrectly incorporated as integral parts into the 'document' itself. This rendered the parenthesized elements incomprehensible to the reader. Hart ignored, for unexplained reasons, Document III. He seemed to be, like Bardoux, fascinated by the idea of a 'photocopy', as if it gave credibility to a fraud. 'I have,' he wrote, 'in my possession a photostatic copy of the final instructions of the Communist International for the taking over of Spain.' And he added, 'I believe these documents are genuine.'[72]

XVIII

Pro-Franco propaganda in Germany and Italy enjoyed a role involving little exertion or discomfort; there was no rejoinder possible, pro-Spanish Republican arguments being prohibited there. As we have already seen, Documents I, II and III were sponsored by the Anti-Comintern for the German public. The chief vehicle used for the 'documents' in Italy was *La disintegrazione dello stato*, the first of the four volumes of *La guerra civile in Spagna*, written by 'Generale Francesco Belforte'.[73] 'Belforte's' use of Document IV is of special interest, being one of the longest texts known. He first mentioned it in a long quotation from Bardoux's first article and pamphlet, which referred to *L'Écho de Paris*, 14 January 1937.[74] Farther on in his book, 'Belforte' cited extensively from Document IV, which, as Bardoux had done, he declared to be of French origin, and first prepared in April 1936. But 'Belforte's' text for Document IV differs considerably from that of Bardoux. As indicated earlier, although Bardoux claimed that his Spanish text had been 'seized from beyond the Pyrenees', there is in his version but a passing reference to 'Guardia Civil y Asato [sic]' to link the 'document' with Spanish events. But 'Belforte's' Document IV begins with a first paragraph filled with mentions of Spanish Rightish political formations (FE [Falange Española], AP [Acción Popular], T [Tradicionalistas], and in a final paragraph called 'Avvertenze', the words 'Getafe' and 'Oviedo' clearly referred to Spain.[75]

Documents I, II and III – offered by 'Belforte' in the order of Documents III, then II and I, without any clear delimitation between the texts – were presented with these words:

> The Bolshevik revolution in Spain was decided by the Comintern on 27th February 1936 and almost immediately afterwards the news was received that, due to the terror which prevailed during the electoral campaign, to the violence incited during the elections and to the treachery of the Freemason Portela Valladares, the Popular Front, following orders from Moscow, had seized power.[76]

The first paragraph of Document III is given in resumé. The numbered paragraphs from 1 to 9 are direct quotations and paragraph 10 is left out.[77] Document II is printed in its entirety, except for the initial sentence, and paragraph 7 is omitted completely.[78] The last paragraph of Document I is not reprinted.[79] The headings of the three 'documents' are dropped and only the sub-heading of Document I, 'Instructions and countersigns' is reproduced.[80] Belforte does not specify the origin of his 'documents', but the Spanish references in Document IV would suggest that it – and perhaps the others – came from Nationalist Spain. Italian readers also learned about the 'documents' from the Milan edition of the Foss and Gerahty book.

Documents I, II and III were used in pro-Franco propaganda in Sweden, in a book by Ernest Bredberg, *Rebellen Franco och den lagliga regeringen*. He reproduced a copy of Document I, an exact duplicate of the page from the *Rotbuch*. Bredberg did not explain where the 'document' came from, but since the Anti-Comintern volume is in his bibliography and the copies are identical, we can conclude that the Nazi publication was his inspiration.[81]

One of the last appearances of the 'documents' before the outbreak of the Second World War was in *Histoire de la guerre d'Espagne*, written by two of France's best-known Fascist sympathizers, Robert Brasillach and Maurice Bardèche. These authors found Documents I, II, III and IV as given in Bardoux's second pamphlet convincing proof of how 'the Marxist groups communicate to their cadres the instructions to follow at the moment of the seizure of power'.[82]

Another short reference to the Bardoux 'documents' was published in Lyon in 1939 by Léon Ponçet in a pamphlet entitled *Lumière sur l'Espagne*, with a preface by General de Castelnau, leader of the extreme Catholic Right in France, President of the Fédération Nationale Catholique, described by René Rémond as 'a glorious soldier whose prestige is much valued, but he is a man of the Right, because of his family traditions and his royalist convictions' (*La Droite en France, de 1815 à nos jours*, Paris, Aubier, 1954, p. 194). Ponçet considered Bardoux's second treatment of the 'papers' 'well documented' and, he continued:

> what the most impressive is, without a doubt, the written proof that the communist coup d'état in Spain was to have been launched before 18th July 1936, thus before the military uprising. There are three papers and M. Bardoux saw photographs of them in London and thus he has been able to verify their authority.[83]

In this detailed examination of how the 'documents' were used for pro-Franco propaganda outside Spain during the Civil War, I have drawn attention to three centres of distribution: London, Paris and Berlin. In London, the Marqués del Moral, Douglas Jerrold and Arthur F. Loveday were the principal actors; in Paris, the man responsible was Jacques Bardoux; and in Berlin, the main source was the Anti-Comintern. A curious fact, for which I have until now not found a satisfactory explanation, is that London, Paris and Berlin were using copies of exactly the same material.

Who among them started the chain? Or was there another agency of which I have found no trace?

XIX

The 'Secret Documents of the Communist Plot' played a sporadic role in Nationalist Spain during the Civil War and if we judge their importance by the published references, we must conclude that they were more appreciated by ecclesiastics and their literary camp-followers than by military commentators or ordinary journalists.

The single most influential utilization of the 'documents', during the war or later, was that by Cardinal Isidro Gomá, Primate of Spain, who on 1 July 1937 authorized the publication of the *Carta Colectiva del Episcopado Español*, an appeal to the Catholic Bishops of the entire world. This document constituted an extraordinarily tendentious interpretation of the issues at stake in the Spanish War. Aside from its wide publication in Nationalist Spain, the *Carta Colectiva* received enormous publicity in all the countries where the Catholic Church had any importance.[84] We can affirm that at this period the 'documents' reached the zenith of their glory. Although the *Collective Letter* did not refer to the 'documents' as such, information that had originated in Documents II and III was cited therein at length.

Cardinal Gomá was apparently a firm believer in the revolutionary conspiracy of the Spanish Left. He wrote in the *Collective Letter*:

> the movement [Franco's] did not come about without those who originated it having previously informed the public authorities so that legal means could be used to oppose the imminent Marxist revolution. This effort had no effect and the conflict broke out...[85]

The Cardinal also wrote:

> there is documentary proof that in the detailed plan for the Marxist revolution that was being prepared, and which would have broken out all over the country if civilian-military movement had not prevented it, there were orders for the elimination of the Catholic clergy and of well-known right-wingers and for all industry to be 'Sovietized' and communism to be established.[86]

Cardinal Gomá was quoting from Document III when he informed the Catholic faithful all over the world of the 'Communist Plot'. His prefatory words were:

> On 27th February 1936, following the Popular Front triumph, the Russian Comintern gave orders for the Spanish revolution to begin and

financed it with vast sums of money. On the following 1st May, hundreds of young people publicly demanded in Madrid 'bombs, gunpowder and dynamite for the coming revolution'.[87]

He then quoted from Document III:

On the 16th of the same month [May], USSR representatives, with Spanish delegates from the III International met at the 'Casa del Pueblo' in Valencia. Their 9th resolution was: 'To put one of the Madrid areas, No. 25, formed by police agents on active duty, in charge of eliminating political and military figures who would play a prominent role in the counter-revolution.[88]

Cardinal Gomá was referring to information contained in Document II when he wrote: 'Meanwhile, from Madrid to the most isolated villages, the revolutionary militias were given military training and were heavily armed, to the point that, when war broke out, they had 150,000 assault soldiers and 100,000 resistance fighters.'[89]

Gomá commented upon these untrue and unproved assertions with the smug conclusion: 'These are the facts.' When the reader reflects on the unarmed, untrained condition of the Spanish workers on 18 July 1936, without defence against the military rebels, the Cardinal's demonstrably false declarations remain among the most unjust falsehoods of the many uttered by the supporters of Franco.

Men of the accepted moral and intellectual stature of Cardinal Gomá do not have to give sources for their declarations (above all, not to the credulous faithful), even when, or especially when, they are as patently exaggerated as in the paragraph quoted above.[90]

XX

There is a slight possibility that the Cardinal (or one of his collaborators) borrowed these absurdly exaggerated figures concerning the forces at the disposal of the Republicans at the beginning of the war from a small book published during the first months of 1937 by F. Ferrari Billoch, a Catholic expert on Masonic, Jewish and Communist plots,[91] who quoted from Documents I and II.[92] This version differs in considerable measure from others known. Ferrari Billoch's 'informe número 1' is del Moral's Document I, but that 'document' was officially called 'Informe Confidencial no. 3' and Ferrari Billoch's 'document' is only about half as long as was del Moral's. Ferrari Billoch's last paragraph is of special interest. It reads: 'The orders are to execute immediately all counter-revolutionary prisoners. The Republicans of the Popular Front will be invited to support the movement and, if they refuse, they will be expelled from Spain.'[93] These two sentences are much more rational and politically plausible than those found in the same place in the 'documents' of del Moral, the *Rotbuch*, Bardoux, Loveday, etc. In the del Moral 'document', the words 'all the counterrevolutionary prisoners' are given as 'all the antirevolutionaries'. The words 'the Republicans of the Popular Front' of Ferrari Billoch are written in del Moral's 'document' as 'the revolutionaries of the Popular Front …'. In the historical context of Document I, it is much more reasonable to write of executing 'the counter-revolutionary prisoners' under arrest, than of executing 'all the antirevolutionaries', just as it is far more understandable to offer collaboration and, in case of refusal, expulsion to the 'Republicans of the Popular Front' than to offer the same to the 'revolutionaries of the Popular Front'.

Del Moral called his second 'document' 'Informe confidencial no. 22', but Ferrari Billoch entitled his 'document' containing a similar content 'Informe Confidencial número II'. It began: 'The dates of 11th May and 29th June are confirmed for unifying the movement according to the results of the elections for President of the Republic.'[94] Del Moral's copy reads somewhat differently: 'The dates of 11th May to 29th June are confirmed for launching the subversive movement according to the results of the elections for President of the Republic, as stated in the previous report.' One 'document' proposes the 'unification', the other the 'initiation' of the movement. Could it be that one typist heard a word pronounced in one way, and another typist heard the same word pronounced differently? Del Moral gave two dates, comprising a seven-week period, 'for the initiation of the subversive movement …'. Such indefinite planning seems to me to be a curiosity in revolutionary conspiracies. But Ferrari Billoch was equally obscure, in writing that the dates of 11 May and 29 June are fixed for the 'unification of the movement'. The only acceptable reading would be a cross between the two texts, that is, for example, 'the dates of May 11 to June 29 are confirmed for the unification of the movement …', that is seven weeks in which to unify the conspiratorial movement.

XXI

In comparing the 'documents' of Ferrari Billoch with those of del Moral, one can find, as almost always in comparing any two copies of the 'Secret Documents of the Communist Plot', differences in the spelling of proper names. One can also wonder at which moment someone decided to add the adjective *subversive* to the word *movement*, an addition that made the del Moral 'document' far less convincing to the critical reader. Persons who sponsor 'subversive movements' do not usually label them as such. At any rate, Ferrari Billoch published the same figures as those used by Cardinal Gomá for the Assault (offence) and Resistance (defence) forces, but he did not cite from Document III, and it was from this 'document' that came the only quotation from the 'documents' in *The Collective Letter of the Spanish Bishops*. Ferrari Billoch commented thus on his 'documents':

> The Marxist revolution was being prepared in this way, in great detail, a revolution which would turn Spain into a Soviet province and subject it to the tyranny and cruelty of the men of the Comintern.
>
> The fact that these instructions came from Moscow has also been verified – can we not now see how they are brazenly helping the Spanish Reds? And they are not even helping them through the official Communist Party, but rather by the secret organization of cells and committees that blindly obey the secret orders from the Comintern.[95]

XXII

A likely source for Cardinal Gomá's citation from Document III is a booklet of 147 pages, published in Burgos in 1937 – probably during the first months of that year – entitled *España vendida a Rusia* and written by the RP Teodoro Toni SJ, like Ferrari Billoch, a specialist in Jewish, Masonic and Communist conspiracies.[96] Father Toni published Documents I and II, reversing del Moral's order and presenting them as a single 'confidential report'. In the presentation of his 'documents' – Documents II and then I – Father Toni wrote: 'Certainly, the Communist Party armed its officials and prepared for the uprising. There is a secret report giving the details of this. The text is as follows.'[97] Father Toni also published Document III in its entirety, but the first paragraph is given as a summary in Toni's prose and not as part of the quoted 'document'.[98] Toni's 'documents' could easily have been the product of a negligent typist copying and occasionally 'correcting' del Moral's 'documents'.

The 'documents' of del Moral and of Father Toni possessed in all probability a common source, but there are puzzling dissimilarities between the two copies. For example, in Document II, Toni's version, the '*Commander*' of '*the liaisons*' is named as 'Ventura, of the U.R.S.S. and of the Second International', which is obviously inexact, whereas del Moral identifies the supposed representative of the Soviet Union as 'of the III International', which would have been more convincing.

There are, of course, the usual number of names spelled differently in each 'document'. In the 'Mando General de las Milicias' in Document II, del Moral named as the delegate for Levante, one 'Sapia', whereas Toni gave his name as 'Rápida'. Among del Moral's 'zona[s] de Asalto' we find 'Alicante'. This province is missing from Father Toni's list. In the version of Document I supplied by Teodoro Toni SJ, under the heading 'The general instructions' (which are in the singular in del Moral's text), we find listed under '2–3 in 5' the phrase 'General capture of the revolutionaries', but in the del Moral 'document' the phrase reads 'General capture of the counter-revolutionaries'.

Del Moral's text is obviously the correct one on this detail, and the failure of Father Toni to perceive the contradiction shows the negligence of his work.

There are equally curious discrepancies between the two copies of Document III. Aside from the numerous proper names spelled differently in each copy – 'Garbins' (Toni) and 'Garpius' (del Moral); 'Loupine' or 'Lupovino' (Toni) and 'Supovine' (del Moral); 'Combin' (Toni) and 'Comlin' (del Moral) – there is in the paragraph numbered 8 a reference to a 'Biblioteca Internacional'; in the del Moral text these words are followed by 'Chamartin de la Rosa', but in Father Toni's version the words become 'San Martín de la Rosa'. And in paragraph number 1, Toni mentioned 'premises called the Office of International Studies' which in del Moral's copy became simply 'called International Studies'. And so on.

Father Toni's booklet constitutes, in so far as I have been able to discover, the only publication in wartime Spain in which Documents I, II and III are all reproduced (with omissions, additions, changes, etc.) and the only one in which Document III appeared. It is regrettable that we do not know where Father Toni found his 'documents'. However, Father Toni did give a source for Document IV, to which he made a passing reference, mentioning *L'Écho de Paris* and André Pironneau. This article, he pointed out, 'publishes the instructions that the Red militias were already receiving from the end of April 1936. They wanted to *neutralize* the army first of all so that they could then win more easily.'[99]

XXIII

Father Toni also made a revealing statement concerning Documents I and II, as follows:

> The newspaper *Claridad*, published this same information, with a few very small differences, at the end of May 1936, calling it *fantastic*. The Popular Front knew that the Right already had these plans and wished to publish them themselves in order to nullify their effect, so they attributed them to their opponents' inventive fantasies.
>
> They clearly were not fantasy. The facts have shown it all to be true, at least fundamentally. What it meant is that they also had their spies, just as we did on our side ...[100]

A similar reference linking *Claridad* and Documents I and II appeared in another book published in the Rebel Zone during the Civil War. This book appeared in Valladolid, probably in 1937; the authors were G. Orizana and José Manuel Martín Liébana, and the book was entitled *El movimiento nacional: Momento, espíritu, jornadas de adhesión, el 18 de julio en toda la nueva España*.[101] These journalists had as the basis for their allusions to the two 'documents' a newspaper article which had appeared in *El Diario Palentino* on 7 August 1937. According to Orizana and Martín Liébana, the article was widely reproduced throughout the Rebel Zone.[102] One such reproduction can be seen in *El Diario de Navarra* of 8 August 1937.

The Palencia newspaper wrote that a Nationalist General Ferrer had convoked journalists to the office of the civil governor of the province (perhaps on 6 August) and had there showed them 'very detailed information concerning the details of repressive plans, movements and projects contained in secret documents found during searches carried out a few days ago at the homes of extremists in our town'.

El Diario Palentino reproduced large extracts of 'documento confidencial número 3', which was in reality Document I followed by Document II, 'so that one can see how far the extremist left movement was to spread throughout Spain.' An editorial comment in the Palencia newspaper read as follows:

> The Civil Government has provided us with an interesting document showing what type of fate would have befallen us under the yoke of Moscow and the revolutionary coup being prepared by the 'Reds'. But, as the saying goes, 'he who strikes first, lives to strike again'. And, it seems that, on this occasion, we have beaten them hands down.

This interpretation was the clear objective of the military communication and of the newspaper articles. It was also the purpose of Orizana and Martín Liébana: to justify the uprising. In their book one can read:

> It appears undoubtable that the Marxists had a plan. A newspaper in Palencia published it and many others copied it from there. *Claridad* tried to discredit the information by ridiculing it, but no-one could be convinced by this journalistic trick.

One of the authors here prudently added, 'I do not give any credit to the document or take any credit away from it, I simply reproduce it here for anyone who wishes to read it.'[103] The parts of the 'documents' reproduced in the Valladolid book are about 90 per cent faithful to the text used by del Moral.[104]

XXIV

Another Spanish Jesuit, Father Constantino Bayle, a prolific pro-Franco propagandist during the Civil War, also reproduced parts of Documents I and II in 1937.[105] His first page of Document I is an exact copy of the reproduction that Loveday was to publish in 1939, as the Lora del Río copy. But Father Bayle gave to his photocopy merely the title, 'Evidence of the planned Red revolution'. Bayle gave the same title to his extract of

Document II, which bore the heading 'COPY OF THE CIRCULAR SENT TO THE UGT ORGANIZATIONS'. This copy of Document II differs considerably in detail from others known. The political affiliation of the members of the 'National Soviet' is not indicated and again there are variations in the spelling of proper names.

XXV

Both Franco and Mola, early in the war, declared to have had a foreknowledge of the 'Communist Plot'. The German Consul in Tetuán cabled to his government on 24 July 1936 that Franco had told him: 'The Nationalist uprising was necessary in order to anticipate a Soviet dictatorship, which was already prepared.'[106] And Mola on one occasion early in August 1936 informed a journalist that a Communist revolt that would have destroyed Spain 'was being prepared for 29th July',[107] but the date given in Documents I and II was '29 June' and not '29 July'. Then in 1938, José María Iribarren, Mola's first biographer and his war-time private secretary, wrote that the General in June 1936 was aware of the detail given in Document II: 'The revolutionary militias had 150,000 assault troops and 100,000 resistance fighters.' This phrase was followed by: 'The revolutionaries were so confident that they fixed 1st August as the date of the revolution.'[108] This was forty-eight hours after 29 July. The figures quoted by Iribarren could have come from the fifth paragraph of Document II, but they are also found in *The Open Letter of the Spanish Bishops*, which dates from 1 July 1937. Anyway, it is hardly likely that either Mola in the spring of 1936 or his secretary, José María Iribarren in 1938 really gave the slightest credence to such evidently false figures. But there are other references in Iribarren's book to a Communist rising and it comes clearly from Document II:

> In the meantime, the communists, seeing their hour approaching, were getting ready. There was a note on Mola's desk calendar in his office on the back of the page for 19th April ... The note was a copy of a 'confidencia' he had received around that time. It referred to a coup d'état being prepared by the communist leaders (Maurín, Mitje, Martí, Fernández and others) for 11th May.[109]

It is a historical fact that the first step towards such a revolt was never attempted; Iribarren does not tell his readers why, nor does he produce any proof that the conspiracy did exist. But he does write after his tale of the conspiracy that: 'That "confidencia" made Mola hasten preparations.' Thus the 'confidence' of 19 April served the same purpose as the 'Secret Communist Plot Documents'. It served to justify the preparation for the real conspiracy, the military rebellion, which Iribarren was recounting in his book. On this same theme, he wrote farther on:

> In July everything was ready. When the communists, who had initially fixed the date for their coup as 1st August, found out that the army was trying to steal a march on them, they decided to set it for the 21st July; I heard Mola talk about the 26th. This meant that the 'Uprising' was arranged for the 12th, it was postponed because of the Pamplona 'fiestas' and was fixed for the 15th. But he had to defer it until the 20th to ensure support from certain quarters.[110]

Such baseless accounts are of interest only in that they demonstrate the widely felt need to link the justification of the military revolt with a Communist conspiracy.

Iribarren's 1938 book was the second one that he had published on the life of Mola during the Civil War. His first book, published in 1937, was far less voluble about 'Communist plots' as the justification for Mola's plotting. In 1937 Iribarren had written that in March 1936 Franco and Mola had met in Madrid and agreed that both of them would support an uprising, under three conditions. None of these mentioned a 'Communist Plot'.[111] Iribarren also wrote that Franco had told a Portuguese journalist early in August 1936 that the military revolt was originally set for August, but that events were precipitated by three factors; these were: (1) 'the fear that some supporters would cease their support as time went on', (2) 'the corrupting activities perpetrated by communist cells (the results had already been seen in the ships' crews) were increasingly alarming', and (3) 'because we had heard that with the complicity of the Casares Government and the President of the Republic, a communist revolution was being prepared'.[112] This conspiracy involving Casares Quiroga and Manuel Azaña was less credible than the one advanced in the 'documents'.

Iribarren continued:

> Indeed, once the railway strike was announced from the middle of July on, the leaders and more prominent members of the Right jailed, a death sentence passed on the others, and the orders and instructions for the Red rebellion distributed, it was a matter of days before it broke out.
>
> According to some, the date for this Soviet coup d'état was set for 10th August. More accurately, it seems that the date was set for 29th July.[113]

XXVI

Sometime during the war, probably in 1937, Jerrold's article in *The Nineteenth Century and After* was translated into Spanish and published in Salamanca by the DEPP.[114] The Spanish translation of excerpts of Document I used here does not correspond to any other known version,[115] so we may suppose that in spite of the fact that in England in 1937 Jerrold claimed to have been quoting from copies of 'plans [which] must have been for some months in the possession of the Salamanca Government', his translators could not find the original in Salamanca and merely translated Jerrold's translation back into Spanish. Thus, Jerrold's error of fixing the Valencia meeting for 15 May rather than a day later was perpetuated in Spain itself.[116] On the other hand, the word 'biblioteca' used in paragraph numbered 8 of del Moral's Document II, which was wrongly translated as 'bookshop' in del Moral's English copy of Document III, but which was correctly translated into the English word 'library' by Jerrold, was, in Jerrold's Spanish edition, turned into 'librería', the Spanish word for 'book-shop', that is the word mistakenly used by del Moral in his English version sent to the Foreign Office. In other Spanish-language versions – Toni (1937, that is, in all probability, before the publication of Jerrold's article in Spain); and Arrarás (1940, that is a year or two before Jerrold's Spanish publication) – the word used is 'biblioteca' and not 'librería'.

XXVII

The 'Estado Español' of the Spanish rebels, on 21 December 1938, in the person of the Minister of the Interior (Gobernación) Ramón Serrano Suñer, created a *Comisión sobre ilegitimidad de los Poderes Públicos Actuantes en 18 de julio de 1936*, and in the course of its investigations, the Commission, in a publication authorized on 15 February 1939, gave its approval to part of the contents of Document III. The Commission was formed by twenty-two personalities of the judicial, legal, university and political elements who had adhered to the Franco cause.

Among the members of the Commission were ten ex-ministers of Rightist governments and thirteen former deputies of the Right (sometimes the same person). Among the better known names were the President of the Commission, Don Ildefonso Bellón Gómez, magistrado del Tribunal Supremo; Don Antonio Goicoechea y Coscuyuela, President of the Real Academia de Bellas Artes; Don Eduardo Aunós Pérez, former minister of General Primo de Rivera (and minister-to-be of General Franco); and Don Rafael Garcerán Sánchez, a former law clerk of José Antonio Primo de Rivera, who had found ephemeral notoriety during the Civil War.[117]

These eminent figureheads countersigned the following assertion:

2. The following 16th May [1936], authorized representatives from the USSR met with equally authorized representatives from the III International in Valencia at the 'Casa del Pueblo' and adopted the following resolution: 'To entrust one of the Madrid areas, No. 25, with eliminating political and military figures who would play a prominent role in the counter-revolution.'

This information and the quotation evidently came from Document III, but the exact wording does not correspond to any of the other known texts of Document III in Castillian. The source given for the above-cited paragraph 2, as well as for three other paragraphs stated that: 'From the content of the different documents in the appendix of this *Dictamen*, but especially from the report presented to the Non-Intervention Committee by the Portuguese Government, it appears clear ...'.[118]

But there is nothing attributed to the Portuguese government in the published *Apéndice I* of the *Dictamen*, and in the 'Response of the Portuguese Government to the accusations formulated by the Soviet Government', printed in the volume *Portugal ante la guerra civil. Documentos y notas*, there is nothing taken from Document III.[119] At the same time, all the other details enumerated on paragraphs 1–4 on pp. 67–68 of the *Dictamen* are to be found in the Portuguese statement of 22 October 1936, which is presumably that cited by the *Dictamen*. The fact that no date was given for the Portuguese document in the *Dictamen* serves to exemplify the shoddiness of this piece of propagandistic argumentation.

XXVIII

Then, in 1939, the official Nationalist publishing house Editora Nacional produced a Spanish edition of *Exposure* in Bilbao.[120] The contents of this brochure, *Exposición del plan secreto para establecer un 'Soviet' en España*, were not organized in exactly the same manner as the English original. The Spanish booklet consisted of the introduction to *Exposure*, plus the photographic reproduction of Documents I and II (Lora del Río copy), and a printed copy of Document III in Spanish; in all probability, a translation from the English of *Exposure* rather than the utilization of the Spanish original of del Moral. I say 'in all probability', for here as in the translation of Jerrold's article the English word 'library' is converted into '*librería*' or 'bookshop', instead of the original Spanish word '*biblioteca*'. An interesting detail is that the Spanish translations of excerpts from Documents I and III in Jerrold's article, and the reproduction of Document I in *Exposición* and the translation of Document III from *Exposure* all have different Spanish texts. Yet, all these 'documents' were supposed to have had the same origin from original copies in Spain. An equally perplexing situation concerns the reproduction of Documents I and II, labelled in *Exposure* the Lora del Río copy.

This is reproduced in *Exposición*, but certain words underlined in ink or pencil in *Exposure* are free of such markings in *Exposición*, forcing us to the conclusion that the photocopies in the latter publication were taken earlier than the ones used in the English brochure. Also, the copy reproduced in *Exposición* is not identified as the Lora del Río copy; in fact, so sloppy is the editing that no presentation whatsoever is made of the photocopy. At any rate, two copies of a 'document' containing about two-thirds of Document I were reproduced in Nationalist Spain during the war: one by Father Bayle, and one in *Exposición*, and there are some differences in their wording. (Strange evidence in a 'document'.)

Among the wartime publications of Rebel Spain, I have found but one reference to Document IV, and that is a translation of the article in *L'Écho de Paris* of 14 January 1937, published in a booklet entitled *El por qué del movimiento nacional español*, edited by SPES, an acronym for Servicio Prensa Española Sur-Americana.[121] This brochure was constituted by 104 pages of text, plus forty-seven unnumbered pages. These unnumbered pages are in reality a reproduction of the Rebel propaganda pamphlet *España Roja*. The principal collaborators of the SPES were, in this order: Professor Vicente Gay, Juan Pujol and Victor de la Serna. All of these were at one time or another recipients of Nazi funds and it is highly probable that SPES was itself subventioned by the Nazis.[122] Insofar as I have been able to discover, this translation of Document IV was not used in other presentations of the 'document'.

XXIX

Once the Second World War had begun in September 1939 – although it did not immediately deserve this global title – Western Europe and the two American continents found less and less time to discuss such past history as the Spanish Civil War. But one book significantly dealing with the 'documents', *Spain* by Salvador de Madariaga, appeared in London in 1942.[123] Madariaga was the best-known Spanish intellectual in the English-speaking world. He had passed a great part of his public life outside Spain – at the League of Nations, in France, in England and in the United States: a distinguished Chair at Oxford, representing Spain at the League of Nations, an ambassadorship at Washington, then at Paris, as well as his publications in English and French and in his native tongue, all had contributed to the renown of his name. But the world outside Spain paid little attention to the fact that he had also held the post of Minister of Public Education, then of Justice, in one of the reactionary Centre-Right governments of Alejandro Lerroux in March and April 1934, or that he was extremely hostile to the Spanish Left. This led Madariaga into making unreasonable analyses of the 'documents', which were unworthy of his reputation as a historian.

Madariaga's source was Loveday's first book, which he had evidently read with unscholarly carelessness. The Spanish diplomat summed up his thoughts about the 'documents' in this manner:

> If the documents reproduced [by Loveday] in translation (and one of them in photographic reproduction) are forgeries, they are very thorough, and it is easy to understand that Mr Loveday should have taken them for genuine. If they're true, they would prove the existence of a plot for a revolutionary rising timed for May or June 1936. I incline to think they are genuine, for I know that one of the prominent men involved in the conspiracy said in a European capital towards December 1935 'If we win the general election, we shall be in office in the spring ... and if we don't, also.' It was moreover given as certain in Moscow at the beginning of 1936 that there would be a proletarian Republic in Spain that summer. Since the conspirators won the election, this would explain why the rising did not take place. All that, without being mathematically proved, seems tolerably certain.

To protect himself, Madariaga added:

> But it is extravagant to put these papers to the use Mr Loveday does and to have them preceded with a title which says: 'Secret documents detailing the plan for the establishment of a Soviet in Spain, the discovery of which was one of the immediate causes of the counter-revolution and the Civil War.' It is enough to glance at the documents to see amongst the names of the leaders of the alleged rising some of the staunchest anti-communist revolutionaries of Spain.[124]

Madariaga's opinions were authoritative in English-speaking countries concerning Spanish affairs, and his ill-founded judgement on the 'documents' was to have a heavy responsibility in perpetuating their influence. I shall discuss Madariaga's analysis of the 'documents' in detail further on.

XXX

In Spain itself, contrary to what was happening outside the country, the ending of the Civil War and the beginning of the War in Europe intensified rather than slowed down historical writings on the Spanish Civil War. The victors sought to justify their rebellion and the extremes of its violence (which did not stop at the official ending of the fighting) by references to the 'Secret Documents of the Communist Plot'.

Felipe Bertrán Güell, in 1939, used both Documents III and IV. His book, one of the first to try to cover in detail the numerous Rightist conspiracies that prospered in Spain almost from the day the Republic was proclaimed, entitled *Momentos interesantes de la historia de España en este siglo*.

La España de 1936. Preparación y desarrollo del alzamiento nacional,[125] began its version of Document IV with a paragraph concerning Spanish Rightish political organizations, greatly resembling the opening paragraph of 'Belforte's' text. However Bertrán Güell's complete text was about two pages shorter than that of 'Belforte' – although including some of the first paragraphs which 'Belforte' had given only in resumé – and did not include Belforte's final paragraph with Spanish geographical indications.

Bertrán Güell's introduction to his 'document' merits attention. It read:

> Meanwhile, Russia gave her final instructions for building on the chaos of the Hispanic branch of her dictatorship of terror and blood. The document containing them was simultaneously taken to Madrid in the month of July by Soviet technicians who entered Spain through Port-Bou, Barcelona and Cádiz.[126]

Bertrán Güell also quoted from Document III, without indicating the 'document' as his source. The lines he cited were a shortened version of what Cardinal Gomá had written, but all the words used were to be found in the Cardinal's text, and may well have come from *Carta Colectiva*. His original introduction to the quotation was 'On 16th February, in the "Casa del Pueblo" in Valencia, representatives of the III International had already adopted, among others, the following resolution ...'.[127] Gomá had given the date usually found in the text of Document III, that is 16 May not 16 February – a date that might well have come to the mind of Bertrán Güell because it was the date of the Popular Front elections of 1936.

XXXI

F. Ferrari Billoch also published a text of Document IV in a 1939 book: *La masonería al desnudo. II parte: Entre Masones y Marxistas ... (Confesiones de un Rosa-Cruz)*. This book was presented as a 'third edition' on the title page, but the text is preceded by a 'Prologue to the second edition', and the contents are presented as being the book that Ferrari Billoch had prepared for publication just before the military revolt and which did not have time to be printed before the uprising. 'I luckily saved all the printing proofs from the Asiatic hurricane that demolished my home in Madrid.'[128] This book printed in Santander[129] on 31 August 1939 may be the first publication, but the second printing. At any rate, the contents, including the text of Document IV, were presumably written before the war.[130]

(In his own prologue, Ferrari Billoch stated that José Calvo Sotelo had written a prologue for the proposed 1939 publication, but that it had been lost. 'The sheets, illuminated by his sharp intelligence, remained unpublished, its contents perhaps mounted between the matrixes of the typesetter.'[131] Calvo Sotelo was lucky, for the sponsoring of such trash as that of Ferrari Billoch would have added nothing to his intellectual reputation. Another of Ferrari Billoch's books, *La Masonería al desnudo. Las logias desenmascaradas*, had appeared early in February 1939, just before the elections, with a prologue by Antonio Goicoechea y Cosculluela,[132] so we may conclude that the approbation of such unenlightened, obscurantist documentation was widespread among the Rightist intellectuals who backed the military revolt.)

The Document IV of Ferrari Billoch resembled that of Bertrán Güell; the texts are at times word for word the same. However, Ferrari Billoch's version is longer, or more 'complete'. On the other hand, the Spanish version of Bardoux varies greatly from that of Ferrari Billoch (Bertrán Güell), in wording if not in meaning. Belforte's text could conceivably have been a translation of the 'document' reproduced by Ferrari Billoch, but the Italian text has only in summary two pages of the first part of Ferrari Billoch's 'document', which is thus the most complete reproduction of Document IV that I have found. Here is Ferrari Billoch's chronology of the arrival of the 'document' in Spain:

> As is known, those present at the funeral of a Guardia Civil lieutenant on 16th April 1936 were treacherously attacked by groups of Marxist militias. In view of the failure of the attack which had been arranged with the coup in mind and intended to fill the revolutionary proletarian masses with enthusiasm, Paris was requested to send Soviet technicians to Madrid. These latter simultaneously entered Spain through two border crossings: Port-Bou to Irún and the ports of Barcelona and Cádiz. It was thus easy for some of them to reach Madrid.[133]

This chronology, placing the arrival of the 'document' in Spain in April 1936, is essentially that of Perroneau and Bardoux, and is far from the date of July put forward by Bertrán Güell.

Ferrari Billoch also reproduced Documents II and I, in that order, as a single 'document', with no general heading.[134] This is not the text Ferrari Billoch had given in 1937, but is word for word the version published by Father Toni in 1937. He did not explain the origin of his 'document' but prefaced it with these intriguing words:

> This other report – a new, clear demonstration that the Communist Party is taking the organization of its movement very seriously – has been secretly going the rounds in Sovietizing revolutionary circles. However, *Claridad* has just published it and has qualified it as a 'fascist fantasy.'
>
> A lot of us – all of us know – that the report reveals genuine plans drawn up by the Rebels, plans not yet implemented, despite the ruses of the Spanish Lenin's newspaper. But they realized that the report was already in the hands of hostile elements and they wished to discredit it.

As a result, it may have been amended: in any case, it is still of great interest.[135]

It seems to me that the book of Ferrari Billoch was quite probably written before the war and perhaps intended for publication at that time. This is the third reference found in a pro-Franco text concerning a commentary on Documents I and II in Largo Caballero's newspaper *Claridad*.[136] If we accept that Documents I, II and IV were prepared for publication in a book sponsored by the extreme Right in Spain before the Civil War, then knowledge of them in Spain at that time is confirmed, and the pre-war existence of Documents I and II (but not necessarily Document III) as proclaimed by del Moral, Loveday and others is corroborated.

XXXII

More important to the general public than the volume of Ferrari Billoch, as a commentary on the 'secret documents', were two works actively promoted by the Franco regime, both of which appeared in Madrid in 1940. Each was written by a journalist, converted by the circumstances into a historian, and each author was known to be, at least for the moment, a great favourite of Franco. One book was under the general literary direction of Joaquín Arrarás, Franco's first biographer; the other was by Manuel Aznar, later Franco's ambassador to the United Nations. Arrarás wrote the 'official' interpretation of Spanish history from 1909–1939, *Historia de la cruzada española*, published from 1939–1943 in eight volumes and 4,434 pages, on glossy paper, with thousands of photographs and coloured illustrations. Arrarás defended every point of Franco's Civil War propaganda, including the authenticity of the four 'documents'. In Volume II, after paragraphs of 'economic chaos', 'rashes of strikes' and 'excesses everywhere', Arrarás described the 'Red plan for revolution in Spain' with these prefatory words:

> But there is already a plan to implement the heart and soul of the propaganda. The revolution is set out in some documents which are being circulated among Marxist organizations. Explanations are given in these documents of how to carry out the attack, the forces needed to do so, the locations of reserves and arsenals and, certain of victory, the leaders who will direct the future march of the victorious revolution.[137]

Arrarás then reproduced his versions of Document II, followed by Document I; the first under the heading 'Confidential Report No. 2' and the second under the title 'Confidential Report No. 3'. I have not found these headings on other copies of these two 'documents'. However, the texts of Arrarás's Documents I and II correspond in most respects to other known copies, and they differ here and there only in details. For example, the grammatical fault in the lead-off paragraph of Document II, 'the dates are confirmed ...', is exactly as in del Moral's copy, but the grammar is correctly given in Father Toni's version. Del Moral's 'Soviet Nacional' contains fifteen 'Comisarios' plus the President and the representative from the Third International. Arrarás lowered the number of his Commissars to thirteen, but this was four more than Toni had allowed. In Toni's 'Soviet', there were no jobs for Galán, Alvarez, Angulo Baráibar, Vega, José Díaz or Javier Bueno. Arrarás, on the other hand, while giving posts to Baráibar, Vega, José Díaz and Javier Bueno, eliminated Galán, Alvarez Angulo and Jiménez de Asúa. Interestingly enough, the first nine names in each list are exactly the same, and one may speculate that the typists' attention in each case began wandering at exactly the same point, and while names were dropped out, the beginning of the list always followed the same order in each 'document'. One highly interesting anomaly among these three sets of Document I and II is that whereas del Moral presented as the final member of his 'Soviet Nacional' one 'Ventura, delegate of the III International', both Toni and Arrarás transformed this personage into 'Ventura Delgado, of the III Internacional'.

Arrarás also reproduced the greater part of Document III.[138] Exactly as had Father Toni, Arrarás began with a resumé of the first quite long paragraph of Document II as found in del Moral's copy. The ten 'agreed upon points' in the texts of Father Toni and Arrarás are almost word for word as in the copy that del Moral had forwarded to the Foreign Office. Two obvious misspellings in del Moral's copy – 'centricistas' (in the centre politically) and 'sesignado' (resigned) – were correctly written as was the geographical place name 'Aranda del Duero', which del Moral had given as 'Aran de Duero'. In 'Point' 9, where del Moral had situated the meeting for 10 June at the 'Biblioteca Internacional Chamartín de la Rosa, calle Pablo Iglesias II', Toni had located it as the 'Biblioteca Internacional de San Martín de la Rosa, calle Pablo Iglesias II' and Arrarás had written 'Biblioteca Internacional de Chamartín de la Rosa' without any street indication. Perhaps it was not the typist's eye which wandered, but that of the person who was *dictating* to the typist. Anyway, all these unexplained variations permit the researcher to wonder which copy was in reality the original and to ask himself how many *different* variants of the 'documents' were in circulation. At any rate, accuracy in the 'instructions' was important.

Volume II of Arrarás's many-paged history seems to have been the only book published in Spain to contain the texts of the four 'documents'. It thus joins the distinguished company of the French pamphleteer, Jacques Bardoux, whose booklet, *Staline contre l'Europe* is the only other work that, to my knowledge, gave warranty to the four 'documents'. Arrarás presented Document IV as a production of the 'laboratories of the Comintern'.[139]

XXXIII

One of the less comprehensible activities of the *Franquista* historians is their use or lack of use of the instruments placed at their disposition. Why did the police functionary, who wrote highly successful anti-Communist books under the pseudonym 'Mauricio Karl'[140] before, during and after the war, never refer to the 'Secret Documents of the Communist Plot'? He certainly knew of them, and if he did not use them in his propaganda, we can ask ourselves why. Another case in point concerns Manuel Aznar, who had made himself a reputation with his journalism during the Civil War and who doubtless had all official Spanish doors opened to him for the writing of the *Historia militar de la guerra civil de España*, published in Madrid in 1940, and which must be considered the official history of the war from the viewpoint of the regime at that time.[141] Aznar's book, although published in the same year as the first volume of Arrarás's *political* history of the war, made no direct references at all to any documentary status for the details found in Documents I, II and III. However, he did insist that a Communist revolution (to be led by Largo Caballero?) was being prepared in Spain in the spring and summer of 1936. He was certainly influenced by Document III when he wrote:

> The leaders of universal Communism had already decreed that, on a specific date in May 1936, the methodical campaign of criminal agitation being fought over the bleeding body of Spain would culminate in an assault on the political Power and in the establishment of a regime of Soviets set up on the familiar trilogy of the revolutionary soldiers, workers and peasants.

But the time dictated by Moscow was too short:

> The date in May agreed upon in Moscow would not come to anything since the preparations made for the decisive battle did not seem sufficient. The Communists decided to transfer the great operation planned to the 29th July of the same year, or perhaps to the 1st August.

These details about the delay in launching the 'Communist revolt' permitted Aznar to explain how Franco was able to anticipate the conspirators of the Left. A few lines farther on, Aznar made what appears to be clear, although indirect, references to Documents I, II and III, and at the same time offered an explanation for the great number of copies of the 'documents' found throughout Spain:

> The international revolution was so convinced of victory that, in spite of their well-known fondness for secrecy, the principal Marxist agents and leaders no longer kept their objectives secret. Not only did the

Government and the police know about this official and secret Comintern documentation itself, with all its instructions, orders and counter-orders, addressed to the revolutionary Centres in Spain, but quite a large number of copies were circulated which any Spaniard who wished to know about it could easily read.[142]

But although Aznar made no direct contribution to the story of Documents I, II and III, he did introduce a new element to the propaganda concerning the 'Communist Plot'. Despite Franco's political exile in the Canaries, Aznar wrote, he was well aware of the dastardly plots of the Spanish Left, and 'had detailed and exact reports on the resolutions the Comintern had adopted to make the revolution in Spain possible and triumphant'. Franco 'knew the dates that the Marxist revolution had set to attack us', and this knowledge was the primary cause of his missive dated 23 June 1936 to the Minister of War, Casares Quiroga.[143] This somewhat long letter expressed, Franco wrote, his fears lest the changes brought about in the military commands by the Popular Front should provoke unrest in the armed forces. At the same time, Franco reassured the Minister that there was no doubt about the loyalty of the officer corps. Franco, who knew of the preparation for the revolt, was lying to his Minister. The 'letter' has been the subject of varying interpretations.

This is the only reference of which I know that links the 'Communist Plot' to Franco's letter. Although Aznar chose not to name Documents I, II and III, he gave an inordinate amount of attention to Document IV, as I shall show a few pages farther on.[144]

XXXIV

One other work, published in Spain in 1940, mentioned the details found in the 'documents'. This volume, written by Lieutenant Colonel of Cavalry Alfonso Gutiérrez de la Higuera and Luis Molins Correa, was entitled *Historia de la revolución española. Tercera guerra de independencia*. Here, as in many other works of its sort, the legal government of the Republic was presented as 'groups of invaders' which 'rapidly and violently seized all the national redoubts, using the impunity given by the use of power', whereas the military conspirators were described as 'another group' which 'wrapping themselves in patriotic secrecy, were preparing to strike for once and for all; to break out against the rabble who were trampling on Spanish soil'.

These two historians invoked details from Document I:

We know the reasons why the general uprising was set for June 1936, but was deferred until the month of August, by virtue of instructions received from the Comintern in Moscow, and we still have the original. These instructions advocate a general strike and decree that individuals on the blacklist will be executed. The plan of rebellion in Bolshevist Madrid: a pretence of an attack on the unions and in protest, the immediate declaration of a general strike ...[145]

Gutiérrez de la Higuera and Molins Correa gave no source for this information.

XXXV

In 1945, the Servicio Histórico Militar, a section of the Estado General del Ejército, published the first and only volume of a work entitled *Historia de la guerra de liberación, Antecedentes de la guerra*.[146] This work used material from the four 'documents'. Details from Documents I and II – the source given was Arrarás – were preceded with these words:

> As far as Spain was concerned, there was already a complete plan of revolutionary action which was set out in great detail in the secret reports numbers 1 and 2 of the Marxist 'general staff'. The members of the future *National Soviet* to be headed by Largo Caballero, were named in these secret reports.[147]

Document III, however, was not referred to, but the information therein was resumed in a short paragraph as a historical fact. As frequently happened in such references to Document III, special attention was drawn to paragraph 9, in which, according to the Servicio Histórico Militar,

> Among other additional resolutions, it was also decided to eliminate political and military figures who would play a prominent role in the counter-revolution. The Madrid communist area number 25, made up of active government police agents, was given this mission.[148]

A footnote, profiting from hindsight, affirmed: 'Note that the assassination of Calvo Sotelo had already been planned much beforehand even in the smallest detail.'[149]

Document IV was more extensively quoted.[150] These extracts are quite similar to the texts of Beltrán Güell, Ferrari Billoch and Aznar, but here and there are words and phrases not found elsewhere. The citations from Document IV were prefaced by remarks to indicate that there were two parallel conspiracies: the military and the Right, the trade unions and the Left.

> The military uprising being prepared could not be excessively delayed if the extreme left's subversive objectives were to be overtaken, since, at that time, they were also busy making their own preparations. On 21st

[April 1936], the Madrid Socialist Group proposes a total reform of the party's programme in a really revolutionary sense ... At the same time, the Comintern draws up a complete plan in order to reduce the Army's resistance, which was the only real obstacle in the path of the revolutionaries.[151]

XXXVI

At this point, I want to review the various texts, more or less complete, of Document IV found here and there – and under the circumstances nobody does really know what constitutes a 'complete text' of such a 'document'. We now have under consideration the following: (1) *L'Écho de Paris* (1937, French) – Bardoux (1937, French and Spanish); (2) 'Belforte' (1938, Italian); (3) Bertrán Güell (1939, Spanish): (4) Ferrari Billoch (1939, Spanish); (5) and (6) Aznar, Arrarás (1940, Spanish). I do not want to consider here the texts constituted by but a few paragraphs, for evident reasons. Each of the longer versions of Document IV with which I deal here gave an account of the origin of the 'document'. Bardoux, 'Belforte', and Ferrari Billoch attributed their 'document' to Paris and Soviet counsellors. Bertrán Güell, Aznar and Arrarás had their 'document' from the Soviet Union, Moscow or the Comintern. All roads led to the Soviet Union, frequently passing through Paris.

Each text has significant differences from the others. The paragraphing is changed in each copy. The paragraphs in the *L'Écho de Paris* – Bardoux copies (1937) are numbered, from 1 to 30. In all the other copies, the paragraphs are distinguished by letters, except in that of Arrarás, which is neither numbered nor lettered. The Ferrari Billoch copy, the most complete in its text, is lettered from A to LL, plus the *'Advertencia'* (warning), that is fourteen sections, some sections having more than one paragraph if compared with Bardoux's copy. Ferrari Billoch's copy is similar to that of Bardoux in meaning as is that of Arrarás, but not in wording or form, and Bardoux's copy – which he said came from Spain – lacks the first and final paragraphs of Ferrari Billoch's copy, that is the very paragraphs which refer to Spain. These paragraphs are also lacking in the text of Arrarás, as are Ferrari Billoch's paragraphs F and G, and parts of H, all of I, part of J, all of K and L, part of LL and the *'Avvertenza'*.

The references to Spain are more numerous in the 'Belforte' and Ferrari Billoch texts than in the other four. The first paragraph of 'Belforte', of Bertrán Güell, of Ferrari Billoch and of Aznar are all similar in construction, with precise indications of Spanish Rightish political groups; but in no two are the lists of these political groups composed of the same names; there are omissions and additions. The final *'Avvertenza'* of 'Belforte', with its references to Spanish geographical locations, is not reproduced by Aznar, and in fact appears in Spanish only in Ferrari Billoch's copy. Aznar's text lacks not only this final 'Avvertenza' but also the three paragraphs which precede it in both 'Belforte's' text and Ferrari Billoch's. The fact that the Spanish references found in some copies of Document IV appear, save for a word or so, at the beginning and at the end of these 'documents', suggests the probability that this 'document' was prepared in France or elsewhere as a basic 'document' of universal utility. The Spanish references were then tacked on to the master copy.

The historiography of Document IV varied from one commentator to another, but each version followed the same basic outline: the 'document' was drawn up either in Moscow, Paris or Madrid by Soviet agents. Pironneau, in prefacing his French text of Document IV, had given the end of April 1936 as the date of its composition, by French Communists, 'in close collaboration with the Comintern and its delegates in France'. The 'document' was forwarded to Spain by 'technical services in Paris'. Bardoux, who offered the first published Spanish text alongside the French of Pironneau, confirmed the date of April 1936; the place of drafting: Paris, and the authors: 'the technical services of the French section, aided by Russian experts sent from Moscow'. According to Bardoux, a Spanish translation was then forwarded to Spain but the Spanish text he published had been found 'on the other side of the Pyrenees'.

The next version we have of Document IV is that of 'Belforte', who related that on 16 April 1936, Soviet technical elements were requested from Paris by Madrid; these were to enter Spain either by Irún and Port Bou, or by Barcelona and Cádiz. The 'soviet technical elements' did not bring Document IV with them, but rather proposed 'the following methods which were adopted without discussion and immediately passed on to the members of the vanguard'. 'Belforte's' text contained both a beginning and an ending with precise Spanish references. The historiography of 'Belforte's' 'document' is in direct contradiction with those of Pironneau and Bardoux, both as to the persons who drew up the 'document', the place where it was written, and as to the final text. Bardoux's Spanish text was a direct translation of his French text. If, as he claimed, the 'document' had come from Spain, why did it lack the beginning and ending with clear Spanish references?

The next known text of Document IV is that of Beltrán Güell, who informed his readers that it had come from Russia, that it had been sent 'simultaneously' to Madrid, in July 1936 by 'Soviet technicians' who entered Spain by four routes: Irún, Port Bou, Barcelona and Cádiz. This 'document', as shown above, was incomplete, compared with that of 'Belforte'. A similar account of the origin of Document IV was given by Ferrari Billoch, who wrote that after the 'failure' of the attempt of 16 April to arouse the Spanish masses, Madrid requested from Paris the dispatch of Soviet technicians to Spain. 'These latter simultaneously entered Spain through two border crossings: Port Bou to Irún and the ports of Barcelona and Cádiz. It was thus easy for some of them to reach Madrid.' '[A]fter some meetings', the Soviet technicians proposed what eventually became Document IV, and it was accepted without discussion. In spite of differences, the accounts concerning the origins of Document IV, as given by 'Belforte', Beltrán Güell and Ferrari Billoch, have much in common.

Arrarás and Aznar published their accounts of the sources for Document IV in the same year, 1940. They more or less agreed on the origin of the 'document': Moscow. Here is Arrarás's story:

> This often announced proletarian dictatorship can only be achieved through the use of violence. This has been postulated a thousand times by Largo Caballero and his followers. And by a methodical, organized and scientific violence, following the techniques of the Comintern laboratories, which is where the plan for the attack on and the breaking down of the Army's resistance, the most difficult and dangerous obstacle for the revolution, has been prepared. [See n. 154.]

There remains the version of Manuel Aznar. He began his story by giving his warranty to the general idea of a 'Communist Plot' and its confirmation by a widespread diffusion of 'documents'. Aznar twice described the origins of Document IV.

> There is a very interesting document dating from this time ... It is, shall we say, the GENERAL ORDER OF OPERATIONS issued by Moscow only a few days before the general offensive was to begin. This document was distributed to all communist cells in Spain on 6th June 1936.[152]

Four pages farther on, he wrote:

> These instructions arrived in Madrid, as I said above, during the month of June 1936. I myself was able to read them because, shortly afterwards, they were placed in the secret files of our military leaders. Another version, even more specific, was distributed to all the active international revolutionary cells halfway through the month of July. The new document placed great emphasis on not allowing the officers from the various garrisons to join their regiments on receiving orders to return to their barracks.[153]

I have found no other versions of Document IV.

XXXVII

After the end of the Second World War, historical interest in the Spanish Civil War began anew outside the Peninsula, at times taking on the aspect of a prolongation of the war-time polemic between Rebels and Republicans. In 1940, a Spanish Socialist exile in England, A. Ramos Oliveira, published what is probably even today the best reasoned analysis of the 'documents' ever written:

> The famous Communist plot, organized in Moscow, against which the Spanish generals and aristocrats rose a few hours before it was due to explode, was a fantastic subterfuge, an alarm without serious foundation; although the invention of this bogey gave positive aid to Hitler, Mussolini and Franco in places where any cock-and-bull story about Russia or the Spanish Republic fell on fruitful ground. On the other hand, those who believed in good faith in the existence of a sinister plot against Spain, conceived and organized in Moscow, failed to perceive that, faced with the Hitler menace, it was in the interests of the USSR to foster a *rapprochement* with France and England – interests which would not be furthered by Moscow fomenting civil war in Europe or in any isolated country ... And nothing could have been more foreign to Soviet interests than the hostility which would have been aroused in the capitalist democracies by an attempt to create a new Communist plot, like those who were the easy victims of this propaganda implicitly accused Moscow and the Third International of negligence, which in itself would destroy another of the arguments which were used to terrify devout ladies and owners of property; for it is not clear how the agents of Moscow and the politicians of the Kremlin, who, according to the extreme Right, are so subtle and dangerous, could have organized a conspiracy for the month of July 1936, which would cause civil war to break out and deliver the government into the hands of the Spanish Communists, and yet forget the absolute necessity for supplying them with arms. War, civil or otherwise, is waged with arms; and those who maintain that Russia provoked the Spanish war, imply that Russia and the men of the Third International are imbeciles. The fraudulent story of the Communist plot in Spain – a story about as authentic as the Protocols of the Elders of Zion – has all the characteristics of the mare's nests invented for political reasons to justify the tactics of the opposition. The game is as old as the history of political and religious struggles. It was a fabrication – but one which damaged the Spanish Republic, because vast sectors of world opinion, not all of them capitalist, lent ear to it.[154]

XXXVIII

This judicious evaluation of the Communist plot stories has unfortunately received little attention. In fact, in 1949, three years after Ramos Oliveira's analysis had appeared, Loveday reaffirmed his fervent belief in the relevancy and authenticity of Documents I, II and III, grossly contradicting himself in the process. One who rallied to Loveday's position at this time was R.M. Hodgson, KCMG, KBE, who had represented the British government at Salamanca during the latter part of the Civil War. His 'foreword' to Loveday's 1949 edition contains some of the most ill-informed statements about the Spanish Civil War publicly expressed at this time by an Englishman with diplomatic responsibilities during the Civil War.[155]

In one place Loveday asserted, concerning, it would appear, Documents I and II,

Just as there can be no further doubt that in May–June 1936, a proletarian rising against the already extreme Left government (Popular Front) of Spain and the establishment of Soviets under the dictatorship of Largo Caballero were fully prepared ... The immediate sparks that set light to the conflagration and fixed the date of the rising of army officers were the murder of the leader of the opposition in the Cortes, Señor Calvo Sotelo ... and the discovery of the secret document containing details for the proletarian communist rising with the establishment of a Soviet Spain ...

As regards the secret document detailing the instructions and outlining the procedure for the proletarian rising timed to start on some date in June or July 1936, its authenticity was doubted by some people, and the apologists of the Republican government attempted to discredit it, saying it was invented subsequently as an excuse for the civil war. But there need no longer be any doubt about it in the minds of students of history. It was stolen from the anarchist headquarters: a copy was received in England by the writer of this history in June 1936, a month before the civil war broke out and handed to the British Foreign Office, who curiously enough rejected it. Subsequently, during the course of the war, copies of it were found at Communist–Socialist headquarters in Majorca, Seville and Badajoz, after their capture by General Franco's army and its authenticity was proved and generally accepted (see Madariaga's 'Spain').

The internal evidence of the document's authenticity is so great as to be overwhelming, for, not only were many of the plans and policies laid down in it actually fulfilled, but some of the very people indicated by name for various positions, actually and subsequently filled them (cf. Largo Caballero, Belarmino Tomás, Margarita Nelken, etc., etc., etc.).

The document ... is so important, as conclusive evidence of the Communist causes of the civil war ...[156]

A few pages farther on, Loveday referred to Document II:

What would by itself be conclusive evidence of prepared Comintern–Soviet influence and intervention in Spain was provided in June, 1936

by the discovery in Spain of the document … containing a complete and
detailed scheme for the establishment of a Soviet in Spain … its internal
evidence is a striking proof of its genuineness … attempts at first were
made to declare it a forgery. A copy of the document was first discovered
in Spain and received in England in June 1936, by the author and given
to the British Foreign Office, which foolishly rejected it; various other
copies were subsequently discovered in other communist centres in
Spain … its authenticity had then to be generally accepted.[157]

Then, as in his first book, Loveday reproduced the three 'documents' in an
appendix with this preamble: 'The documents consist of two confidential
reports and a secret report, which were obtained surreptitiously from the
files of the communist headquarters in Spain and were received in England
in June 1936 by the author of this book.' He then wrote that 'no less than
four other copies of the two confidential reports [were] subsequently found
in different parts of Spain', adding to the three he had already mentioned,
the La Línea 'document'. Again, he said that 'All these documents were
published with the permission and full authority of the Nationalist
government.'[158] Despite the copyright ownership which Loveday
attributed to the Nationalist government, the full panoply of the five
'copies' was never exploited in Spain, save in the translation of the English
booklet *Exposure.*

There appear in these quotations from Loveday several features which I
want to underline. First, he noted that the three 'documents' had been
'rejected' by the Foreign Office. This was, I believe, the first public reference to this rejection, and can be taken for proof that Loveday's 'documents'
were those which del Moral presented to the Foreign Office and which
were considered not 'genuine'. Another interesting detail is that Loveday,
who in 1939 had given two contradictory explanations of how he had
obtained the 'documents', now changed his story to give two other
differing accounts, making four contradictory versions in all. In 1939, he
averred that he had brought the papers to England himself; now he stated
that he had *received* them in England. In 1939, he once gave an anarchist
source for the 'documents', then a Communist source. He repeated this
confusion in 1949.

If, as seems certain, the Loveday 'documents' and the del Moral 'documents' are the same, it is a bit strange to observe that whereas Loveday's date
for reception of the papers was around the middle of June, they were given
to del Moral only on 27 August, and sent to the Foreign Office only on 30
August, that is seventy-five days later.[159] Another item of interest is the
evident conviction of Loveday that the fact that other copies of Documents I
and II had been found in different places as Majorca, Seville (province),
Badajoz (province) and the town of La Línea was a proof of their authenticity.
Was not such a dispersion of 'secret' documents a reason to doubt their
authenticity?

It is also to be noted that Loveday is quite ambiguous in his reference to the 'documents'. At times he speaks of 'the document' and apparently means Documents I and II; at other times he obviously covers all three 'documents' when he refers to 'the document'. As in his first book, the 'document' was found on one page at the 'anarchist headquarters'[160] and on another page, at the 'Communist headquarters' in Spain.[161] Exactly what did he mean by the 'anarchist headquarters'? By the 'communist headquarters'? In which Spanish city were these headquarters located? What did he mean by the 'communist-socialist headquarters' in Majorca, Seville and Badajoz, where three 'other copies' of the 'secret documents' were found?[162] Loveday himself was not quite certain, for on another page of his book he located the Seville 'document' at the 'communist headquarters in Lora del Río', and the Badajoz 'document' at the 'communist headquarters in a village near Badajoz', and the Majorca 'document' not at the 'communist-socialist head-quarters' but among the papers of Commander Bayo'.[163] And on this page Loveday added the La Línea 'document' to the list, as in his first book, saying that it too was found at the 'communist headquarters'. It seems obvious that 'anarchist', 'socialist' and 'communist' are interchangeable and equally denigrating words for him. Two other observations: Loveday prided himself on Madariaga's seal of approval and Loveday did not reproduce here the Lora del Río document as he had done in his 1939 book.

XXXIX

In 1951, an enthusiastic supporter of the Franco cause, Richard Pattee, who had at one time been a high functionary in the US State Department, gave his uncritical approbation to the Loveday 'documents':

> The existence of a communist plot for the summer of 1936 has been amply demonstrated with documentary proof ... Loveday ... has done us the service to reproduce in English translation the full documentary evidence on this point. They are secret, confidential documents outlining the plans for the establishment of a Soviet regime in Spain. The details are illuminating in the precision with which they provide for every contingency.[164]

Another true believer in all the propaganda of the Franco rebellion was S.F.A. Coles, an English journalist, who also lectured at the NATO Defence College at Paris. In 1955 Coles unhesitatingly sponsored the 'documents'.[165]

XL

Taking the opposite side of the controversy in 1956, an American university professor, David T. Cattell, a specialist on the Soviet Union and the Spanish Civil War, gave a lucid political analysis of the four 'documents'. Cattell sought to view the 'documents' in the context of the political situation in Spain itself, and of Spain in the developing European crisis. He noted the contradictions involved in Gerahty's description of Documents I and II as being anarcho-syndicalist in origin, and continued, challenging that very part of Document II, which, through Cardinal Gomá's patronage, had been accepted by the Catholic hierarchy all over the world:

> That the document was of communist origin, is equally improbable. The document names 150,000 shock troops as the basis of the revolt, yet the communist party did not total anywhere near that number at this time. Furthermore, if such a plot was planned it would have depended on the previous arming of the working class, yet when the military uprising occurred there was a great scarcity of arms among the workers. It was only the distribution of arms by the government on July 19 that allowed the workers to form into militias.[166]

After observing several weak points in Loveday's presentation, Cattell made this conclusion concerning Documents I and II:

> The one possibility is that there was a plan on the part of the whole revolutionary Left to revolt and establish a Popular Front Government. But why was a revolt necessary when the Popular Front, through its majority in the Cortes, already controlled the government? The revolutionaries certainly could have gained the support of the Left Republicans under Azaña who all along had been in favour of the formation of a Popular Front government. No force, therefore, was necessary to carry out the aims of this alleged plan. Finally, the only deduction which can be made concerning this document is that it was prefabricated by the Nationalists for propaganda purposes.[167]

Concerning Documents III and IV, Cattell reached this conclusion: 'Since no proof whatsoever has been brought forth to support the origin of the documents, they can be disregarded as evidence in the case.'[168]

Cattell, however went further and offered a rebuttal of the whole conception of a Communist plot in the overall European picture of the time, aside from the weakness of the 'documentary' evidence presented:

> Up to this point, the specific evidence investigated would not lead to a conclusion that there had been a communist plot to seize power. A

consideration of the general Russian policy at this time equally reveals the impossibility of such a plot.[169]

XLI

Another exponent of the ideology of Franco's defenders, Claude Martin, published a life of Franco in France in 1959. He wrote that during the spring of 1936, 'Communist Party circulars addressed to their cells came into the possession of the Military Information Service which left no doubts as to the Comintern's wish to attempt a coup', [170] intended to eliminate the political, military and financial leaders of the Right. This could be a reference to Documents I, II and III. Martin also referred to Document IV as given by Aznar ('The instructions of June 6') and concluded: 'The Army leaders had no doubt: the communist revolution would break out on 29th July or 1st August ... We therefore had to be ready to take the initiative and make it fail.' [171]

XLII

In 1960 two significant judgements on the 'documents' were published by Englishmen. One was by Hugh Thomas, a one-time Labour candidate for the House of Commons and later ennobled by Margaret Thatcher; the other was an English United Press war correspondent on the Republican side, Burnett Bolloten, who later became a citizen of the United States.

Thomas's initial positions about Documents I, II and III, were expressed in his 1961 general history of the Spanish Civil War (probably the best-known narrative account of the conflict). In his later, and much superior, editions, he was to change his mind. However, the publication of his second edition in 1965 did not, understandably, have the same impact as the first. The enormous commercial success of the first edition effectively ensured that the majority of readers would have read what he first wrote about the documents rather than his later corrections.

In Thomas's 1961 edition, the only authority on the 'documents' cited is Loveday's 1939 book, and it appears in a footnote. Thomas did not explicitly mention Loveday's 1949 book at all in connection with the 'documents' despite its presence in his bibliography. Still, the flagrant contradictions in Loveday's 1939 account of the manner in which the 'documents' came into his possession should have been enough to put doubts into his mind.

It seems to me possible that Thomas's opinions on the 'documents' were influenced by Loveday (1939) as analysed by Madariaga (1942). However, Thomas did not mention Madariaga in relation to the 'documents'. Thomas referred to Madariaga's 1942 book a number of times in his text – usually in footnotes – and in his bibliography. It is reasonable to suppose that Thomas was aware of the study of the Anglo-Spanish professor-diplomat touching on the problems posed by Documents I, II and III. Certainly, their conclusions were similar. Madariaga wrote, 'If the documents reproduced … are forgeries, they are very thorough, and it is easy to understand that Mr Loveday should have taken them for genuine … I incline to think they are genuine.' Thomas, in similar vein, concluded 'I have come to the conclusion that the three documents … are not forgeries … The fact that these documents were probably genuine …'.[172]

If, as seems to be the case, Thomas did not take a look at the revised editions of Madariaga's 1942 book – for example, the New York edition of 1958, in which all references to the 'documents' are left out, with no explanation of this omission – it is regrettable. It seems probable that Madariaga did see Loveday's 1949 edition, with its two new explanations of how Documents I, II and III came into the possession of the one-time English businessman in Barcelona, and that even for Madariaga, harsh critic of the Spanish Republic, four different versions of the same event were too much.[173]

Thomas's commentary on the three 'documents' is found in a fairly long footnote, based on these lines of text:

> All sorts of plots and plans to achieve this were now prepared. Despite the fact that the establishment of a Communist *régime* in Spain would have been contrary to the general lines of Stalin's moderate foreign policy at that time, the Communist Party of Spain, intoxicated by their capture of the Socialist Youth, continued to feed Largo with flattery and to egg him on to more and more extreme statements.[174]

This citation had followed extracts from inflammatory speeches, one by Margarita Nelken, the other by Largo Caballero (dated 24 May). Thomas gave no further particulars concerning 'all sorts of plots and plans', save in his footnote on the 'documents'. Thomas's opinions, by the sheer number sold, were, after those of Madariaga, probably the most influential in the English-speaking countries and elsewhere, in the interpretation of the 'documents'. As we have seen, the propaganda of the 'documents' after the outbreak of the Civil War was largely orchestrated from London. There is a direct line from del Moral to Jerrold to Loveday (or Loveday to del Moral) and with subsidiary lines to Bardoux in Paris, to 'Belforte', to Hart, etc., and then to Madariaga and on to Thomas.

Here is Thomas's conclusion:

> I have come to the conclusion that the three documents alleged to have been found in four separate places after the start of the Civil War, and

making plans for a Socialist-Communist *coup d'état* by means of a simu-
lated rising of the Right are not forgeries.[175]

Thomas's reasoning was that since the 'first reference' he had found to 'those
documents' (Loveday) was in *Diario de Navarra* of 7 August 1936, they
could not have been fabricated between 18 July and 7 August, for this latter
date is 'rather early for clever propaganda forgeries'.[176] In fact, the *Diario de
Navarra*, which mentioned not three 'documents' but only Documents I and
II, was dated 8 August, which could have weakened Thomas's cause by
twenty-four hours, but since the *Diario de Navarra* openly acknowledged its
own source to have been the Palencia newspaper cited earlier, dated 1
August, there was even less time to fabricate 'clever propaganda forgeries', a
mere two weeks. However, Thomas went on to write:

> The fact that these documents were probably genuine does not mean
> that the plans they envisaged were ever likely to be put into effect. They
> were dreams more than blueprints, or rather plans for hypothetical
> circumstances which might never arrive.[177]

Thomas then continued that the fact that the 'documents' were 'probably
genuine' did not mean that they 'justified the generals' uprising, since the
plans of these latter were already very advanced before their enemies had
begun to prepare their own'.[178] The net effect of this analysis was to declare
Documents I, II and III 'probably genuine' but without significance.

Hugh Thomas's consideration of the historical and political problems of
the 'documents' led him into several errors. First, he concluded, following
Madariaga, that the 'documents' 'were probably genuine', which was, as we
shall see, inexact; and second, he declared them to be if 'forgeries' then
'clever forgeries'. Third, Hugh Thomas, in deciding that the 'documents'
were 'genuine', concluded that they were Republican plans and not the
production of the military rebels; and fourth, he made no effort to analyse
the 'documents' in the context of the Spanish political scene, nor in that of
the Soviet Union and the European political situation.

A spin-off from Thomas's book brought a new guarantee to the 'documents', this time from Sir Charles Petrie, who reviewed Thomas's book in a
popular London weekly immediately after its publication. Petrie seized on
the occasion to affirm his faith in the proofs of the 'Secret Communist Plot'.
He wrote: '... it is clear that Franco's blow forestalled one by the
Communists. Documents which fell into the hands of the Nationalists
proved that the plans of the extreme Left were complete ...'! Petrie then
repeated 'facts' found in the three 'documents' and offered this judgement,
'Russian complicity was fully established.' He observed that the original
dates for the Leftist revolt had been changed and concluded that 'this change
of plans enabled the Nationalists to get their blows in first'.[179]

XLIII

Hugh Thomas was a talented young graduate of Cambridge, where he was President of the Union, published a novel or two, stood for the House of Commons for the Labour Party in an unwinnable constituency, and then produced for the twenty-fifth anniversary of the outbreak of the Spanish Civil War the first scholarly general history of the conflict. His book gained the encomiums of the English intellectual establishment (Cyril Connolly, Philip Toynbee, etc.); he won a world-wide reputation, became a professor in one of the newly founded English universities. Successfully launched from the Centre-Left, he gradually moved to the Right and seventeen years after having published his book on the Spanish War, he declared himself for the Tory Party.

Thomas had begun his career as a writer of fiction, of imaginative prose, and, in his historical work, at times, his narrative instincts sometimes seemed to gain the upper hand. In 1975, in my book *La destruction de Guernica*, and in later editions, I called attention to Thomas's method of structuring his historical narrative, which was much as a novelist might do, and which occasionally led to a greater elasticity than appeared justified by the facts themselves.[180] An example may be found in the way in which he incorporated in the same chapter two events of the war: the bombing and burning of Guernica by the Rebels and the siege of Santa María de la Cabeza by the Republicans.[181]

I considered this linkage, though theoretically indicated by the chronology, to be, in reality, unjustified. He placed in contraposition the Franco atrocity in Guernica and the alleged Republican 'savagery' in Santa María de la Cabeza: two examples of Iberian bloodthirstiness. Thomas objected to my comments in a book review published in *The Times Literary Supplement* and a discussion ensued.

Mr Thomas had written in 1961:

> The defenders were surrounded by 20,000 Republicans, who seemed likely to be as savage as Red Indians. Doubts and difficulties arose. The attacks began again. Aircraft and artillery led the way. The heroic Cortés was wounded on April 30, and on May 1 the International Brigade and the militia of Jaén broke into the sanctuary. For a while slaughter was general. The sanctuary was burned. Flames engulfed the Sierra.[182]

In my 1975 book on Guernica, first published in French, I had written:

> This basic anti-Republican prejudice on the part of Crozier can be seen in his account of the end of the siege of Santa María de la Cabeza, in Jaén province. According to Crozier, it ended with the 'overrunning of the improvised fortress by the Republicans, and the slaughter of the defenders' ... However, in reality, the vanquished were treated with a

generosity rare in the Spanish Civil War, and certainly nothing like it can be found in the accounts of Nationalist treatment of Republican prisoners. See *Epopeya de la guardia civil en el santuario de la Virgen de la Cabeza*. Also la Cierva, *Historia ilustrada*, II, p. 207. Crozier perhaps obtained his impression of a 'slaughter' from Hugh Thomas, who wrote concerning the surrender of the sanctuary, 'For a while slaughter was general' … In Thomas's book, this account followed that of Guernica, and the English historian doubtless credited the Republicans with this atrocity in order to keep things in balance.[183]

In his review in *The Times Literary Supplement*, Hugh Thomas wrote:

Mr Southworth is entitled to read my chapter like that if he wishes. In fact, my arrangement was logical since I had adopted a chronological approach to my account. That Nationalist redoubt did fall on May 1, five days after Guernica. [I presume Mr Thomas means 'five days after *the attack* on Guernica', for the town itself fell only on April 29.] On April 26 itself, the fighting there was, in the words of Captain Cortés, 'tough and murderous' (*tenaz y mortifero*). There is thus a perfectly good reason for considering the two events close together.[184]

Mr Thomas seemed to have disregarded the first lines in my note concerning Santa María de la Cabeza, and I replied as follows:

The chronology he [Hugh Thomas] observes is 'logical' and I can but agree. However, it is clear from my text that I was protesting, not against his chronologically 'logical' treatment of the two events in the same chapter, but against the serious errors of fact in his dramatic ('The defenders were surrounded by 20,000 Republicans, who seemed likely to be as savage as Red Indians') account of the siege of Santa María de la Cabeza. Mr Thomas wrote: 'The heroic Cortés was wounded on April 30, and on 1 May the International Brigade and the militia of Jaén broke into the sanctuary. For a while slaughter was general. The sanctuary was burned. Flames engulfed the Sierra.'

This dramatic account was demonstrably inaccurate. There was no 'International Brigade' at the final assault on the sanctuary. The attacking forces, 'who seemed likely to be as savage as Red Indians' were in number not even 20 per cent of those to whom Mr Thomas referred. The sanctuary was not burned. No flames 'engulfed the Sierra'. This early text of Mr Thomas was vividly written, it made for exciting reading, but it was not history based on facts.

More importantly, it is inexact that after the Republican forces 'broke into the sanctuary, for a while slaughter was general'. There was no 'slaughter', general or otherwise. This can be confirmed by both Republican and Nationalist accounts (*Trayectoría*, 1971, by Antonio Cordón, who commanded the Republican forces; the Civil Guard's own official history of the siege; and *Historia ilustrada de la guerra civil española*, by the neo-franquist historian Ricardo de la Cierva).

I suggested in my Guernica book that Mr Thomas had used his account of the siege of Santa María de la Cabeza in an effort to balance a Rebel atrocity (Guernica) against a (supposed) Republican atrocity (Santa María de la Cabeza). In my 1964 book, *Le mythe de la croisade de Franco*, I argued that Mr Thomas tended to seek to equalize the blame for atrocities between the two contending parties, 'de couper la poire en deux' (split the difference). I can give many examples, but I consider the accounts of Guernica and Santa María de la Cabeza, placed side by side, classic examples of the method.[185]
Mr Thomas's reply did not justify his original choice of words:

> Santa María de la Cabeza. The attack on this Nationalist redoubt was undertaken by the Army of the South. Their effectiveness ... surpassed 20,000 men, although the 16th Mixed Brigade which carried out the assault, was, of course, smaller. Everything points to the fighting being extremely violent. The Republican artillery fire was considerable. The defending commander died of wounds and I think about 100 out of the 400 defenders were killed.[186]

XLIV

In the 1977 revision of his *The Spanish Civil War*, Thomas made substantial corrections in his account of the siege. Laid aside was the comparison with 'savage indians', but Thomas maintained the encirclement by 'twenty thousand Republicans'.[187] Antonio Cordón, the superior officer of Martínez Cartón, wrote that during the occupation of the Cerro by the Civil Guards the number under arms was around 700[188] and that the number of the attacking forces was hardly superior to three times the defenders.[189] Thomas now eliminated from his scenario the aviation, for the good reason that the Republicans had none. He also left the 'brigada internacional' on the cutting-room floor, despite the colour it added to the story. And in the new version there was no 'slaughter', 'general' or otherwise. But Thomas could not cut out all the scenic effects and retained the lines: 'The sanctuary was burned. Flames engulfed the Sierra.'[190] Thomas did not mention the fact that none of the occupants of the sanctuary was mistreated or brutally punished after the surrender. I now want to include the epilogue to the affair, written by Antonio Cordón. After insisting on the generous treatment given the survivors, he wrote:

> But the same thing did not happen to those who, whether soldiers or not, had been in Andújar on our side when the Nationalists entered

town after the Nationalist victory in 1939. From what I know, Pérez Salas was shot, one of the doctors who treated Cortés, Dr. Velasco, was shot, Rey Pastor was shot along with many more. Others spent long periods in prison.[191]

Thomas's 1961 book quickly became accepted as a classic on the subject. Its substantial sales had the effect of institutionalizing the errors regarding the 'slaughter' at Santa María de la Cabeza, and such careless conclusions as those concerning the 'Secret Documents of the Communist Plot'. As for the influence of Thomas's debatable account of Santa María de la Cabeza, we can read in Brian Crozier's *Franco* of 'the overrunning of the improvised fortress by the Republicans and the slaughter of the defenders'.[192] Carlos Seco Serrano, a Barcelona university historian, in his *Historia de España. Epoca contemporánea*, writes of those 'who survived the slaughter that came after the final assault'.[193] Crozier gave no source for his account of the siege of the sanctuary, but he refers frequently to Thomas's book in his notes. Seco Serrano gave no source either, but in the first edition of his book (1962) he quoted from Thomas in the caption placed under a photograph of Santa María de la Cabeza. Also in that first edition, Seco Serrano published a bibliography on the Spanish Civil War that was practically in its entirety copied from Thomas's book. It is therefore reasonable to assume that on the question of Santa María de la Cabeza, the accounts of Crozier and Seco Serrano were following that by Hugh Thomas.

Earlier, in 1963, in *El mito de la cruzada de Franco*, I pointed out how Thomas did not take a firm stand on the numerous polemical issues where the Rebel and Republican interpretations differed. He sought to find a middle position. This was true not only of the 'Secret Documents of the Communist Plot' but also concerning the siege of the Alcázar, the Massacre of Badajoz, the Murder of Calvo Sotelo, and a number of other events, including the Siege of Santa María de la Cabeza. An exception was Mr Thomas's account of the atrocity of Guernica, where he clearly favoured the Republican version as, overwhelmingly and outspokenly, did the bulk of English public opinion.

In his 1975 *The Times Literary Supplement* review of *La destruction de Guernica*, Hugh Thomas made an effort to justify the campaign of misinformation carried on in England and the United States during the Civil War by Douglas Jerrold and Arnold Lunn in defence of the Franco cause. Thomas wrote that Jerrold and Lunn in 1937

> were indeed convinced that as Mr Southworth says (though using the words as a denunciation) the Civil War was a 'holy war, a Christian crusade to save the Catholic Church; as well as western civilization, from oriental threats, and from communism'. Hence, they would champion what their friends said and stick to it.[194]

It seems odd to find virtue in the sincerity of the political positions of Jerrold and Lunn concerning the Civil War, inasmuch as most of what they wrote about the war in Spain was incorrect and they could hardly have failed to know it.[195] I am still amazed that persons holding the beliefs of Jerrold and Lunn could think 'the Catholic Church, as well as western civilization' could be 'saved' by lying and by endowing the Spanish people with forty years of Francoism.

Thomas went on with an elaborate pun:

> These Christian gentlemen had, however, been fundamentally affected by the terrible atmosphere of a witch's sabbath which characterized Nationalist Spain in those days. To understand this atmosphere requires a more equable spirit than that of Mr Southworth who approaches his victims with all the generosity with which the Count of Monte Cristo approached his enemies. Was the origin of Danglar's treachery to be sought in the number of pregnant girls in the Rue du Chat Qui Pisse in Marseilles in the Napoleonic era? Such pedantry would have been swept aside by Edmond Dantes with contempt, just as Herbert Southworth, the Count of Anti-Cristo, tries to sweep aside sceptical historians of the next generation. With Dantes, as with Mr Southworth, you must take a side.[196]

Mr Thomas seemed to wish to persuade his readers that he, unlike myself, was above taking sides. In fact, by coming to the defence of Jerrold and Lunn, he was surely taking sides.[197] Jerrold had, after all, boasted of having tried to get machine-guns for José Antonio Primo de Rivera's Falangist *pistoleros*.[198]

XLV

Hugh Thomas's evaluations of Documents I to III are of interest because of the world-wide sales of his book, and of the influence of his book on later historians. Burnett Bolloten's comments on Documents I to IV are of import to this study because of the development and structure of Bolloten's 1961 book (and of its several subsequent revisions).[199] This book, which was begun in 1938–1939 and published for the first time in 1961, is in its essential purpose, an all-out attack on the Spanish Republic and its leaders, on all its leaders, but especially on Juan Negrín. All other books of this political bent, if they deal with the 'documents', accept them without question as being authentic. On the contrary, Bolloten's attack on the Republic dismisses the 'documents' with a few well-analysed sentences. His text of reference reads as follows:

Russia was not blind to the dangers of German intervention in Spain, but anxious not to give body and colour to attacks that pictured her as the open patron of world revolution, lest she antagonize the moderate parties in the Western democracies on whom she based her hopes of an anti-German front, she adhered in August 1936, to the international non-intervention agreement, which had been proposed by France in order to prevent an extension of the conflict and undertook together with the other countries participating in the accord not to send arms to Spain.[200]

Bolloten's treatment of the 'documents', like that of Thomas, was in the form of a long explanatory footnote, of which I quote the relevant parts: 'This concern for Western opinion does not concur with the charge presented by the rebels to justify the rising according to which the communists had conspired to establish a Soviet regime in Spain during the summer of 1936 ...' (Bolloten here gives two sources: Aznar's *Historia militar* [Document IV] and *Exposure* [Documents I to III]. He then argued:

for it is obvious that had they even attempted to establish such a regime they would have ruined the Comintern's hopes of a rapprochement with the Western powers. For this reason alone – to say nothing of the fact that they certainly did not have the necessary strength – the charge may be safely discounted.[201]

Bolloten's analysis of the European period when the 'documents' were supposed to have been written approaches those of Ramos Oliveira and Cattell, both of whom appear in his bibliography, but are not cited on this matter. But Ramos Oliveira was an ardent Republican, and Cattell was not antagonistic to the Republican viewpoint. I have discussed elsewhere the problem of Bolloten, but I wish here to explain briefly how this pro-Republican analysis of the 'documents' appeared in a book primarily hostile to the Republican cause. Bolloten began to write with a vision of the Civil War favourable to Juan Negrín, but his finished manuscript speaks well of no Republican leader. His judgement concerning the 'documents' comes from the period when he was writing a pro-Republican, pro-Negrín account of the Civil War, and when he was putting together his 1961 manuscript he could not bring himself to throw out the already written facts which he knew to be essentially correct. This interpretation of Bolloten's text is confirmed by the revisions of *The Grand Camouflage* in 1977, 1979 and 1980, in which Bolloten swung still further to the Right and to some extent reneged on his first remarks concerning the 'documents', but without ever firmly admitting to his readers, or perhaps even to himself, that he had made this turnaround.

Bolloten's analysis of the 'documents' has another distinction. It is the only published text refuting the 'documents' that appeared in Spain during the Caudillo's lifetime. In fact, *The Grand Camouflage* was published in Barcelona but a few weeks after its first appearance in London, under the high patronage of Manuel Fraga Iribarne, then director of the Falangist think-tank, the Instituto de Estudios políticos, and shortly thereafter, Minister of Information and Tourism. Bolloten found fault with the translation of his book, and had another one made, which came out in Barcelona in 1967. The lines referring to the 'documents' are essentially the same in each translation. Bolloten's book, with a number of pro-Republican interpretations of the period (mostly dealing with the immediately pre-war months), was an absurdity in Spanish Civil War historiography published in Spain, due to the influence of Fraga Iribarne, who saw the need for a drastic change in the antiquated Francoist propaganda concerning the conflict. Burnett Bolloten, with an explanation of the 'documents' much more Leftist than that of Hugh Thomas, was curiously enough able to achieve what Thomas could not do: get his book published in Franco Spain.

Bollotten had now, in 1987, arrived at the point of no return. He had been firmly adopted by the Spanish Right, with Ricardo de la Cierva taking the place of his patron, formerly held by Fraga Iribarne. This was emphasized in chapter 33 of la Cierva's 'Nueva y definitiva historia de la guerra civil' (*Epoca*, Madrid, 16 June 1986), where Bolloten is saluted by la Cierva as 'the first historian of the Republican zone' and praised for his 'masterly research' in *La revolución española* (1980).

XLVI

In 1962 and 1963 two other references to the 'documents', one in Germany and one in France, appeared. Helmuth Gunther Dahms, a right-wing German historian, specializing in the period before and during the Second World War, published in 1962 a study of the Spanish War extremely favourable to the Franco cause. He gave to his readers the details of Document II, with the 'National Soviet' treated not as a project, but as a reality, a creation of Largo Caballero, Jesús Hernández and Francisco Galán.[202] He gave no source for this information. Dahms also accepted at face value Aznar's account of Document IV, writing: 'The opposing camp [to the military conspirators] was also proceeding with its revolutionary plans and, on 6th June, the Communist Party gave "precise orders and instructions" to all its members for launching the combat.'[203]

A French writer, almost paranoic concerning the Popular Front of 1936, who used the pen-name of 'Georges-Roux', wrote a general history of the Spanish war in 1963. He exaggerated the number of deaths among the Spanish clergy,[204] wrote inexactly concerning the siege of the Alcázar and proclaimed his belief in Documents I, II and III; 'The authenticity of these three documents is arguable and they cannot be entirely believed. However, a left-wing historian, such as Hugh Thomas, holds that these texts are "probably genuine". They are, at the very least, credible.'[205] There are at least two errors in the previous quotation. The first is to call Hugh Thomas a 'historian of the left' and the second is to call the texts of Documents I, II and III 'credible'. 'Georges-Roux' expressed his conclusion concerning the three 'documents' as follows:

> Two rebellions, one Marxist, the other military, are being planned. They are symmetrical, two sides of the same coin, almost simultaneous. Which one will break out first? Two monsters are preparing to devour one another over the corpse of the Republic. Which one will eat the other?[206]

XLVII

For the period ranging from 1945 to 1963, I have found authors, writing in Franco Spain, who accepted the authenticity of one or more of the 'documents' in their historical writings. Of these, one was a university professor, one was a general in Franco's army, one a close collaborator of General Mola just before the war and later, another, a police expert on Masonic and Jewish matters, etc.

As I have already indicated above, José María Iribarren, a pre-war secretary to General Emilio Mola, wrote in 1938 that Mola was aware, before the outbreak of the war, of information found in Document II. Fourteen years later, another pre-war conspirator with Mola, B. Félix Maíz, claimed for Mola pre-war knowledge of the four 'documents'.[207]

Under the date of 14 April 1936, Maíz cited in *Alzamiento en España*, subtitled 'From a diary of the conspiracy', six paragraphs of Document IV,[208] but these extracts, whose contents resemble in their meaning and very closely in their wording parts of paragraphs B, D and H of Ferrari Billoch, are not at all similar in their wording to Bardoux, Beltrán Güell or Aznar. However, six lines of the extract from paragraph H are word for word in the text found in the book of the Servicio Histórico Militar. The text used by Maíz may well have been the text from which the Servicio Histórico Militar took its extracts, but since the Servicio reproduced extracts from paragraphs C, D, E, H and LL, and Maíz used extracts only from B, D, and H, we have but a few phrases for comparison. In the case of the quotations from paragraph D, they are word for word the same in *Servicio* and in Maíz. In the case of extracts from paragraph H, there are very minor differences.

Maíz introduced his references from Document IV in this manner: 'Revolutionary FURY is planning an offensive against the Government. What is Bela-Kum [sic] doing in Barcelona? ... Let us look at some of the National Revolutionary Committee's instructions ...'[209] Maíz gave no details about these 'instructions'.

From time to time, Maíz refers to his '*diario*', but it is never clearly indicated when entries from this diary and another composition begin. It is perhaps under the date of 5 May that Maíz first mentions details that also appear in Documents I and II. He wrote: 'The Communist Party, in one of its "Secret Reports", has drawn up a plan for the first hours of its Movement in Madrid.'[210] This is followed by a text which, at times, is quite different from the standard contents for Document I. It is much shorter and about half of the material is not found in other versions of Document I. However, ten lines are word for word the same in del Moral, Bardoux (Spanish), *Rotbuch*, Toni and Arrarás, except for some punctuation marks.[211]

Maíz seems to have been a maniac on the subject of espionage, which renders his text difficult to follow, for it contains more allusions and hints than facts. On one page, he wrote:

> Our spies within their camp have supplied us with very important data on the development of the communist revolutionary bloc. Some of this success, and I say so in honour of the truth, has been achieved by foreign agents. Not all the delegates and agents in Spain have been sent officially by the Komintern. Communists who are *not communists* have also been in the country. *They are actually anti-communists and foreigners.* 6-WIW-9 is a double agent, a Spy and a Counter-Spy ... This agent has already left Spain after having carried out his mission. He has the names of the Supreme Council of the 'SPANISH SOVIET!'

Then there follows a list of the members of the 'Soviet'. Like most of such lists from Document II, it differs in details from the others. On the same page we can read: 'Mola dictates: "Take note of these agreements. They are links in a new chain. Insist in Valencia upon the need to obtain precise information of the result of the meeting on the 16th." '[212]

Elsewhere, Maíz wrote, under the date of 17 June:

> Largo Caballero demands from his lieutenants that a speedy conclusion be brought to the task of structuring the militias that will bear the shock of the seizure of power. According to his calculations, up until 15th June there are in excess of 250,000 men making up the large formations of 'Assault and Resistance'.[213]

It is worthwhile noting that, since the death of Franco, not a single letter of this 'secret' information has been confirmed.

These figures for 'Assault and Resistance' are exactly those of Document II. Maíz was thus telling us that Mola had faith in the authenticity of Documents I, II, III and IV. Or was Maíz merely yielding to the conspiratorial fantasies which abound in his book?

XLVIII

Early in the 1950s, the Franco regime began publishing a series of propaganda pamphlets under the general title 'Temas Españoles'. These served from time to time as a vehicle for the 'Secret Communist Plot Documents'. In 1953, Enrique del Corral, in no. 29 of the series, published a biography of Calvo Sotelo. He wrote:

> Strikes are taking place uninterruptedly and in 'Secret Report No. 2' the details of how and when the communist revolution is to take place are clearly laid out. Largo Caballero is to preside over the National Soviet … The number of weapons available is stated …[214]

The details from Document II are followed by the textual reproduction of the 'point nine' of Document III, which del Corral interpreted as the 'basic symptom in Calvo Sotelo's life: his death, which was already rapidly approaching'. This same interpretation had been given, in a handwritten notation to the last line in the first paragraph of Document I, in the copy handed in to the Foreign Office. Corral, as was by now the habit in Franco Spain, did not feel the need to give the origin of his 'documents'.

Material taken from Documents I, II and III was evoked in 1954 in another pamphlet of the series 'Temas Españoles', written by Blasco Grandi and entitled *Togliatti y los suyos en España*. Grandi did not mention the 'documents' as such, nor did he give any source for the information which he used. In this brochure, the author considered the alleged Valencia meeting of 16 May to be an undisputed historical fact, and insisted that 'one of the most significant facts that became clear during the Valencia meeting' was the revolution jointly projected for the two countries: Spain and France. According to Grandi, all the projects contained in Documents I and II, including the formation of the 'Soviet Nacional' under the chairmanship of Largo Caballero, were the result of the Valencia meeting. The killing of Calvo Sotelo was interpreted, as in the handwritten marginal note in the del Moral copy of Document I, to have been the execution of the plans set forth in Document I.[215]

XLIX

Early in the 1950s, a publishing house funded by the Franco regime, Editora Nacional, began a series entitled 'Colección Libros de Actualidad Política', and no. 16 of this series, *Historia política de la zona roja*, written by a university professor Diego Sevilla Andrés, appeared in 1954. Sevilla Andrés did not mention specifically the 'documents' or the material contained therein, but he considered valid the arguments presented by the 'documents', that is the conspiracy of the Spanish Left, which the military uprising had forestalled. 'In short, the 18th July represented the finishing line of a race and the person who got there first was the one who would be able to control events.'[216]

Nine years later, the author of *Historia política de la zona roja* published a second, revised edition, this time as part of a series called 'Libros de Periodismo Rialp', a collection directed by the prominent intellectual of the Opus Dei movement, Antonio Fontán. Despite the name of the 'Collection', the book was more a pretence at history than at journalism. In this new edition of his book, among other changes, Sevilla Andrés added more than a page of text (two paragraphs) in which he introduced the subject of Documents I, II and III as proof of the 'Marxist' plot. It seems strange that Sevilla Andrés did not write about the 'documents' in his earlier version – for they had been widely commented on in Spain since 1936–1937, but the direct cause of these two new paragraphs was the translation of Hugh Thomas's book in France in 1961. Sevilla Andrés began his exposition in this way: 'The Marxist coup d'état was meticulously planned. Three documents clearly detailing the plans for the Marxist uprising were found in Lora del Río ... Those documents are not forgeries and Thomas himself accepts them.'

After citing Thomas's expression of confidence in the 'documents' of Loveday, Sevilla Andrés then quoted Thomas's words to the effect that their authenticity 'does not mean that the plans referred to in them were to be put into action'. The Spanish writer, however, perceived the contradictions in Thomas's middle-of-the road position: 'the long documents, the numerous copies and the distribution of the same was nothing more than a distraction employed by ... men of the Left'. And then: 'It must be supposed that Thomas does not believe that the leaders of the conspiracy against the disorder in Spain were ignorant of their adversary's movements especially since this latter was not very cautious.'

Sevilla Andrés considered that Franco's letter to Casares Quiroga of 23 June 1936 'and the various private and public appeals made by men on the Right to the government', were inspired by knowledge of the three 'documents'. Thus, argued the Spanish university professor, it was the knowledge of the 'Communist Plot' that turned the Spanish Right towards rebellion, despite its desire to remain within the framework of legality, 'collaborating with the Republic'.[217]

L

Eduardo Comín Colomer described by his friend and publisher "Mauricio Karl" as 'a writer, police inspector, professor at the school of Police and theoretical secretary of the Division of Social Investigation of the General Directorate of Security',[218] wrote concerning the 'documents' at least three times, in 1955, in 1959 and in 1967. We shall take up the first two of his efforts at this time. In 1954, Comín Colomer published in two volumes: *Historia secreta de la segunda república*. The primary targets of his research: Freemasons. He did not refer to any of the 'documents' but he did use material that came from Document II. Under the heading 'The Communist preparations', he wrote:

> There is no doubt that prominent persons of Soviet sympathies began plotting from the moment that the conspiracy known as the Popular Front was established. Right from the start of the Republic, prominent Soviet sympathisers began arriving at Warsaw railway station en route to Spain in order to lay the foundations, step by step, for the necessary conditions for the revolutionary explosion.
>
> But, logically, everything had to come to a head at the precise moment. 'Popular Frontism' was the catalyst for the atmosphere, and although it acquired great importance at the Comintern VII Congress when it was launched by George Dimitrov, the Secretary General, it is interesting to remember that Freemasonry had already been tirelessly working for a 'single front of the Left' for some considerable time previously, and the greatest political extremes are included in this classification.
>
> The Marxists, as is known, had painstakingly drawn up an insurrection plot which was to be led by a 'national Soviet'.[219]

There then followed a list of the chosen: fifteen *comisarios*, plus the President of the 'Soviet', Largo Caballero, and his *asesor* (consultant) Ventura, 'a delegate of the Comintern' whom Comín identified as Jesús Hernández; this identification was correctly done, according to Hernández himself.[220] These seventeen names are the same as those found in the del Moral 'document', with more or less the same posts.

The interest of this group, for Comín Colomer, lay not so much in their Socialist or Communist political affiliations, but in their links to Freemasonry. 'We can therefore see,' he wrote, 'that out of 17 members of the "National Soviet", no less than eight were active militant Freemasons and it was precisely these people who held the key posts …'.[221]

Four years later, in 1959, Comín Colomer cited long passages from Documents I, II and III in a revised edition of *Historia secreta de la segunda república*, under the general heading 'Soviet Plan'. As a prelude to the material taken from Document II, Comín wrote: 'Everything was so well prepared that there was already a National Revolutionary Committee, also called a "National Soviet" …'.[222] Before he reproduced in its entirety Document III, as previously published in *Exposición*, Comín declared that the English translation by the 'Amigos de la España Nacional en Inglaterra' 'provided certain information on the secret plan to establish Sovietism in our country, and this plan was exactly the same as the information found in various documents discovered immediately after 18th July 1936!'[223] After the reproduction of Document III, he summarized: 'As is clearly shown in the document, the revolution was a fact.'[224]

Comín Colomer did not give the full texts of Documents I and II, but he wrote fairly long summaries, which were considerably doctored as to names, and to the political or intellectual tendencies of the Leftists mentioned. Comín was especially alert to the supposed Masonic affiliations of the alleged members of the 'National Soviet' – eight of the seventeen members, he pointed out, were Freemasons. He took away from the anarcho-syndicalist Pestaña his portfolio of Posts, Telegraph and Telephones given him by *Exposición*, which had erroneously labelled Pestaña as being a 'socialist'. (He also incorrectly identified Ventura, delegate of the Comintern, as Victorio Codevila, 'who used the name of Luis Medina in the Red zone'.)[225]

The only source given by Comín Colomer for his extracts from the three 'documents' was the Spanish translation of the English pamphlet *Exposure*. Comín was reputed to have extensive files on all the political subversives of Spain and access to the Spanish police archives. Why did he not then quote from the original copies in Spanish of the three 'documents', from which the English editor claimed to have taken the information? Instead, he relied on a Spanish translation from the English translation of the supposedly original 'documents' in Spanish.

LI

Towards the end of the 1950s, Editorial AHR of Barcelona launched a series of twenty books under the general title, 'La Epopeya y sus Héroes'. One of these books, published in 1957, entitled *Guerra de liberación (La fuerza de la razón)*, was written by General José Díaz de Villegas. This work, exemplary for its political obscurantism, was, unfortunately for Spain, normal for the Spanish barracks. As was to be expected, Díaz de Villegas subscribed whole-heartedly to the propositions found in Documents I, II, III and IV.[226] Before giving details from Document IV, Díaz de Villegas wrote: 'From now on, events will definitively accelerate. The Comintern is sending to Spain a plan for the annihilation of the Army.'[227] Referring to Documents I and II, he affirms:

> There appears to be an unending chain of assaults, thefts, sacrilegious acts, robberies and general desecrations. We have reached the very eve of the revolution. The Marxist General Staff are distributing their 'Instructions' numbers 1 and 2. Largo Caballero will be appointed head of the National Soviet ...[228]

The Spanish general declared, concerning Document III: 'The communists are meeting with delegates of the Comintern in Valencia. The date for the Red revolution has been set for the middle of the month of June 1936.'[229]

Díaz de Villegas spoke again of Documents I and II, reasoning that the failure of the 1934 uprising in Asturias had been closely studied by the Communists and its defects corrected:

> in short, the October 1934 revolution had been crushed ... This is the lesson that had to be studied and which was indeed studied in Moscow by experts on 'armed insurrection' and 'coups d'état' and then the facts deduced from this cold analysis would be passed on to the executors in Spain.[230]

Giving his attention again to Document I, the military historian stated:

> The plan for the Red uprising in Madrid – and similar types of action had been studied in other cities, according to each case – for the revolution planned for 1st August was, essentially, different from the previous one [October 1934] and was much more detailed.[231]

After giving details from Document I, Díaz de Villegas wrote, indicating Document I, 'a secret "report", bearing number 22, later completed these instructions'.[232] He thus attempted to draw together the two papers.

One of the General's conclusions:

> This is why and how on that day, 18th July 1936, when the Nationalist Movement had scarcely begun, anticipating by a few days the uprising planned by the Reds, and with the noble rebellion in Madrid drowning in blood, I immediately realized that the communist Staff had planned everything in minute detail, from the attack on the barracks, particularly the Montaña barracks, the meticulous occupation of the capital, armed militia guards being placed in all official centres, streets, garages, squares and important buildings. This was not a case of improvisation, as was revealed in the act. The revolution had been planned and studied in great detail by the Marxists and had been led by foreign experts.[233]

Díaz de Villegas then gave in detail the substance of Document II, commenting on these details from time to time. In repeating the figures taken from Document II, concerning the 'revolutionary' forces of 'assault', 'resistance' and 'trade union militias', he affirmed that

> the Red forces were probably greatly superior ... That is, a complete army made up of nothing less than 450,000 men ... These are figures that could explain why the Uprising was crushed especially in the largest two Spanish cities: Madrid and Barcelona.[234]

Discussing the figures in Document II dealing with armament, Díaz de Villegas argued:

Furthermore, this time the militias were much better armed than at the
time of the attempted revolution of October 1934 ... It is apparent that
they had an impressive arsenal, in addition to which, even before the
Nationalist Movement began, the weapons stored at various depots were
given to the mob by the Red Government.[235]

Díaz de Villegas did not take the trouble to tell his readers the source of his
information, evidently taken from Documents I to IV. He was not addicted
to footnotes, but with the repeated references to the 'documents' in the
Spain of Franco, their credibility had become unchallenged. Earlier writers
in Spain who dealt with the 'documents' 'revealed' the secrets of the
'Documents'; by 1957, their contents had fallen into the public domain.

It is worthwhile, however, to stress that the military historian Díaz de
Villegas accepted as gospel truth the exaggerated military 'facts' contained
in the 'documents', especially in Document II, concerning the number of
troops ready for the Leftist 'revolt', and the armament stocked for such an
enterprise. It is difficult to imagine how a general officer of the Spanish
army could have printed such nonsense in 1957, or even twenty years earlier.
It is a well-documented fact that in Madrid when the military revolt broke
out, the Government of the Republic tergiversated, refusing to give arms to
the people, for at least twenty-four hours. In Barcelona, it was certainly not
the Communists who animated the spontaneous resistance to the military
rebels, the Communists were not that strong in Catalonia.

The references to the 'documents' found in the works published in Spain
from 1945 to 1963 contributed nothing to the history of their origins. Only
two of the six authors gave sources: Sevilla Andrés and Comín Colomer. The
first found his inspiration in Thomas's book, the second in *Exposición*. These
are English sources, based on Spanish 'documents'. Yet neither of the
Spanish writers sought a Spanish confirmation of the 'documents'. Such
research was not necessary for their public. The allusions of Maíz are so
fictionalized that one can easily imagine that the author's fantasies were
enlightened by the mentions of the 'documents' that he had previously read
here and there. There is little that is new in his elucubrations. The conclusion that we can draw from these writings is that the validity of the four
'documents' was by 1963 an integral part of the historiography of the
Spanish Civil War, seen from the Franco propaganda offices. We can also
accept the fact that the research facilities on the Spanish Civil War available
to pro-Franco writers in Spain, as well as their own research capacities, were
extremely limited.

LII

In 1962 and 1963 when I was working on *El mito de la cruzada de Franco*, I
was forced to undertake a serious study of the 'Secret Communist Plot

Documents'. This had never before been attempted. I had found a considerable number of opinions advanced about them, but nobody had really tried to discover their origins, to compare the various copies and texts, or to analyse them word by word. I began this work with the intimate conviction that they were completely fraudulent, and even today I cannot understand how anyone with the slightest knowledge of 1936 Spain and 1936 Europe could ever have imagined them to be genuine.

There were three approaches to a determination of the authenticity of the 'documents' from the materials that I had in hand in 1962; this time limitation, of course, excluded the del Moral 'documents', which did not become available until 1966, and some published writings of which I did not then know. These three means of attacking the problem were: (1) an examination of the physical appearance of the 'documents', as photocopied and as textually reproduced; (2) a review of their purported origins; and (3) a study of the relevance of their contents to their historical context. By 1963, several persons, through their knowledge of the political situation in 1936, in Spain and in the world, had made a correct interpretation of the 'documents', notably Ramos Oliveira and Cattell, who had labelled them falsifications; but their arguments were based on logic and not on visible, verifiable evidence. Such logical arguments did not impress those who espoused the thesis that the 'documents' were trustworthy and did not need to make an effort to provide proofs of their authenticity. Their own convictions about the validity of the 'documents' were founded on their faith in the general belief in a Communist plot, any Communist plot.

Let us take a look at the physical aspects of Documents I, II and III, the only ones of which I then possessed, or now possess, material presented as reproductions of the original copies. These were found in the Nazi *Rotbuch* and, much later, in the del Moral copies. They were textually the same as those of Bardoux. The two photocopies of the Lora del Río 'document' (Loveday 1939 and Bayle 1937) differed not only from each other, but also from that of the *Rotbuch*. Physically, all three bore the trademarks of the same manufacturer – a lazy, indifferent typist. The essential point is that there was absolutely nothing in the appearance of the *Rotbuch* copies to convince anyone of their documentary value. They were typewritten on white paper, without letterheads and without signatures; they were undated. Any typist with a machine equipped with Spanish accents could have produced the 'documents' in less than an hour's time. No businessman would have risked a penny on a communication of this nature, but in the case of the 'documents' we find three *hommes d'affaires*, each in his own way a staunch defender of the capitalist system: Bardoux in France, Loveday in England, and Hart in the United States, each asking his readers to have confidence in Documents I, II and III.

Madariaga, writing in English, expressed his belief that the three 'documents' of Loveday, if 'forgeries' were very 'thorough' forgeries.[236] The Compact Oxford English Dictionary gives this definition of 'forgery': 'The making of a thing in fraudulent imitation of something; also especially in the forging, counterfeiting, or falsifying of a document.' It is impossible to grant the label of 'forgery', thorough or otherwise, to a simple typewritten, unsigned, undated sheet of paper, without even a letterhead in lieu of signature. The physical description of the 'documents' was in itself sufficient to discredit them completely before an unprejudiced observer. They cannot even be called attempts at 'forgery'. The person or persons who wrote them could never have been convicted in a court of justice for having committed 'forgeries'. They are imagined compositions, but not 'imitations' of anything.

To place the 'Secret Documents of the Communist Plot' in perspective, the reader can look back to n. 2, concerning the 'Zinoviev Letter'. This false document had all the qualities of a true 'forgery'. It had what the 'Secret Documents of the Communist Plot' lacked: a letterhead, an official sender, a receiver and a signature. The 'Zinoviev Letter' exposes the amateurishness of its Spanish imitators and emphasizes the credulity of those who believed in the Spanish sheets of paper.

The various accounts of the origins of the 'documents' were not more convincing than was their physical aspect. The *Gringoire* document was said to have been found in Palma de Majorca in 1936 in the baggage abandoned by the Republican forces of Captain Bayo. Gerahty produced the La Línea document, but then curiously let it drop, preferring the *Gringoire* document, sponsored by Bardoux, who in the meantime had renounced the *Gringoire* document without any explanation, choosing in its stead the 'documents' he had found in London. The *Rotbuch* was silent as to the origins of its 'documents'. Arnold Lunn cited Gerahty as his authority, although his friend Jerrold had already quoted from Documents I, II and III, hinting that he had received them from Salamanca. The origins of the Lora del Río and the Badajoz 'documents' were still more vague than those of the La Línea and Palma de Majorca 'documents'. The source of the Loveday documents was even more unlikely, for two contradictory explanations were presented in 1939 and two others, basically different, in 1949. Madariaga accepted Loveday's two inconsistent accounts of 1939, but apparently four differing versions were too much even for him, inasmuch as he did not renew his approval of the three 'documents' after 1949.[237] But Madariaga's guarantee, given to Documents I, II and III in 1942, encouraged Loveday to republish them ten years after his first edition. The 'authenticity [of Document I] was proved and accepted generally (see Madariaga's "Spain")', Loveday wrote with satisfaction in 1949.

The proliferation of copies of the four documents was generally interpreted by their defenders to be a further verification of their authenticity, whereas it was, in reality, a cause for doubting their validity, as I shall show later on.

LIII

Finally, let us study the contents of the 'documents' in their historical context: the Spanish context and the European context. Here we find a series of opposing 'facts' that should have withdrawn the 'documents' from the serious consideration of everybody, including Josef Göbbels. We can dismiss the fantasies of Bardoux, Lunn, Jerrold, Loveday, Cardinal Gomá, Sencourt, Hart, Pattee and others who lived in a special world inhabited by Left-wing conspiratorial monsters, from whom they drew the inspiration for their propaganda. The acceptance of Documents I, II and III by Madariaga and then by Hugh Thomas is a more distressing spectacle.

The details of the contents of the three 'documents' cannot be accepted in the general framework of the Spanish internal political situation in the Spring of 1936, nor can they and the purposes attributed to them be admitted within the political boundaries of the European problems of the same period.

Let us now observe the details found in Documents I, II and III. To have confidence in Document I, we must believe that in the spring of 1936 there was a possibility for concerted action among the Spanish Socialists, the Spanish Communists and the CNT for a *coup d'état* intended to *overthrow* the Popular Front. The conspiracy was presented as a plot against the Left-Centre government of the Republic (described in all Francoist propaganda as a government of the extreme Left), and not at all as a plot against the Right. Document II demands that we accept a situation in which well-known partisans of the moderate Socialist Indalecio Prieto, such as Jiménez de Asúa and Belarmino Tomás, were involved in a revolutionary plan, in collusion with outstanding members of the Spanish Communist Party, to bring the Left-wing Socialist Largo Caballero to power. To acknowledge the genuineness of Document III, we must be persuaded that the French Communists were preparing to help to carry out a *coup révolutionnaire* in Spain around the middle of June 1936, in collaboration with the French Socialist leader, Léon Blum; that the Comintern leader Dimitrov, the French Communists Maurice Thorez and Marcel Cachin, the French Socialist Vincent Auriol, the Spanish Anarcho-Syndicalist José García Oliver (in company with the dissident anarcho-syndicalist Angel Pestaña) and Largo Caballero were all implicated in this Soviet–Franco–Spanish conspiracy. These positions are so extremely far-fetched that even Madariaga, after proclaiming his faith in the authenticity of the 'documents', felt obliged to point out the only too-evident flaw in the contents of the three 'documents'. ' It is enough to glance at the documents to see amongst the names of the leaders some of the staunchest anti-Communist revolutionaries of Spain.'[238]

Another unbelievable detail: we are informed in Document II that the Left political parties and trade unions had at their command thousands of armed men ready to stage a revolutionary struggle just before the outbreak of the Civil War, an assertion that the most fervent partisan of the military uprising would not dare to advance, since with Franco's death, his defenders lost their monopoly control of the Spanish press. The lack of arms among the working class was one of the reasons for Franco's immediate victory in provincial capitals where the Socialists, Communists and Anarchists were theoretically dominant, for example in Seville and Saragossa.

LIV

Now we can turn our gaze to the 'documents' and their credibility as viewed in the overall picture of the European political situation during the first half of the year 1936. We have already quoted the analyses of Ramos Oliveira and Cattell. I shall now cite, for the second time, an opinion concerning the four 'documents', based on a limited study of their sources (Aznar and *Exposure*), by the British-American historian Burnett Bolloten, expressed in 1961 – and later qualified as I shall show farther on:

> It is obvious that had they even attempted to establish such a regime they would have ruined the Comintern's hopes of a rapprochement with the Western powers. For this reason alone – to say nothing of the fact that they certainly did not have the necessary strength – the charge may be safely discounted.[239]

This is one of the paragraphs most fraught with interest among all the writings about the 'documents', because the author, in the book in which it appeared, and years later in three other versions of his first book, based his primary thesis on contradicting this paragraph, while at the same time he continued to repeat it.[240]

LV

Among those who analysed the 'documents' in consideration of their international implications was Salvador de Madariaga; in spite of (or because of?) his experience as Spanish Ambassador in two important Western capitals and as delegate to the League of Nations before the Second World War, he held a view of the world in the first six months of 1936 (and forever after) not unlike that of Bardoux, Jerrold, Loveday and others of their ilk. He wrote:

> I know that one of the prominent men involved in the conspiracy said in a European capital towards December 1935 'If we win the general elections, we shall be in office in the Spring, and if we don't, also.'[241]

This 'prominent' man is nowhere named, so we cannot question him. What is significant in the above paragraph is that Madariaga considered the 'conspiracy' to be a fact. This statement must be taken into account, in weighing the contradictions of Madariaga's paragraphs. Madariaga continued: 'It was moreover given as certain in Moscow at the beginning of 1936 that there would be a proletarian Republic in Spain that summer.'[242] I have found no substantiation elsewhere for this misplaced piece of information. The one-time diplomat and lifelong writer of historical works then argued: 'Since the conspirators won the election, this would explain why the rising did not take place. All that, being mathematically proved, seems tolerably certain.'[243]

In some sectors, Madariaga possessed a wide margin of tolerance, hence the intellectual negligence and the mathematical ignorance of this affirmation. Let us squarely regard the embarrassing lack of logic in Professor Madariaga's reasoning. His statement can rationally mean but one thing: for him, the 'conspiracy' was a pre-electoral event. But a simple reading of the Loveday 'documents' – Madariaga's sole source – is more than enough to show us that it was impossible for them to have been written before the elections of 16 February 1936. Document I refers to the 'final details of the Movement after the coming 3rd of May ...'. Let us concede that the references are for the year 1936, although the year is nowhere given with precision in any of the four 'documents'. (If the 'documents' did not refer to 1936, then they are even less credible as historical 'documents'.)

Document II mentions the forthcoming 'elections for the President of the Republic'. Alcalá-Zamora was dismissed from the presidency on 7 April; the election for commissioners to vote on his successor took place on 28 April; Azaña was elected to the presidency on 10 May. Document II could have been written between 7 April and 10 May. It could not have been written before that time.

Document III concerns a meeting which supposedly took place on 16 May. If the 'document' were 'genuine', as Madariaga contended, it could hardly have been written before that date. It also contains a reference to Casares Quiroga as Prime Minister, a post he assumed only on 13 May 1936. Incidentally, it seems far beyond the realms of probability – even if we accept the still more improbable hypothesis in which Spanish members of an unknown entity called 'la Central del Comité Revolucionario de España', who were said to have recently talked with French Communists and trade union members, met with Comintern delegates in Valencia to plan a revolutionary uprising in France and Spain – that only three days after Casares's nomination to the post of Prime Minister, and three days before the appearance of the government before the Cortes, an assassination of Casares and the details of his personal guard should have been a matter of serious discussion before a revolutionary meeting. Document III also mentions the struggle between Largo Caballero and the Prieto factions of the Socialist Party concerning the convocation of a National Congress of the PSOE; this inter-party fight took place between 9 March and 25 May, that is not before the elections of 16 February 1936.

But if Documents I, II and III were written after the 16 February elections, as is evident from the texts of the three 'documents', Madariaga's reasoning comes tumbling down and nothing at all is 'mathematically' or otherwise 'proved'. If, having won the elections, the alleged conspirators abandoned the 'plot', they would hardly have continued to manufacture 'documents' and leave them all around the country. If Madariaga had followed his initial argument to its logical conclusion, he would have written something like this: *the fact that the potential conspirators won the elections explains why the conspiracy never took place and the 'documents' in question are falsifications.* Madariaga's reasoning thus rests on nothing more solid than his unquenchable hatred of the Spanish Republic and the Spanish Left.

Having proclaimed to the world his inclination for the genuineness of the Loveday 'documents', and having written of the 'conspiracy' as an uncontested fact, Madariaga then pirouetted with this pious declaration:

> But it is extravagant to put these papers to the use Mr Loveday does and to have them preceded with a title which says: 'Secret documents detailing the plan for the establishment of a Soviet in Spain, the discovery of which was one of the immediate causes of the counter-revolution and the Civil War.'[244]

If, as Madariaga affirmed to his readers, the 'documents' were 'genuine' and the 'conspiracy' a fact, it is difficult to understand why Loveday should have been excoriated for having published them as being 'genuine' and as proofs of a 'conspiracy'. A man of lesser reputation than Madariaga could have been ridden out of the intellectual community on a rail, because of such unscholarly confusion. But this is not all: the whole story of Madariaga and the Spanish Civil War confirms these illogical synopses and faulty interpretations of events on the part of the conservative Anglophil. I have found in no subsequent editions of his book any acknowledgement by Madariaga of his unjustifiable 1968 error concerning Documents I, II and III.

LVI

Madariaga was one of those Spanish intellectuals who, greatly honoured by the new Republic of 1931, turned against that Republic in its hour of peril, as did, among others, Ortega y Gasset, Marañón, Pérez de Ayala and Unamuno. I do not mean here to indicate that the majority of Spanish intellectuals, writers and university professors did not support the Republican cause during the Civil War. The contrary is well known to have been the true situation. It was precisely those to whose ambitions the Republic had given impulse and support who denied the Republic at the critical moment.

Madariaga's Spanishness, in fact, consisted largely of his birth certificate and his passport. He was chiefly educated in France. In 1917, he published the first of his many books while living in London. At the end of the First World War, he began an off and on again career as an international civil servant. In 1928 he accepted a chair of Spanish literature at Oxford. In 1931 the Republic named him Ambassador to Washington and he resigned his chair in Oxford. According to his own statement, in 1936, when named to Washington, he had been living abroad since 1916. He was named Ambassador to Paris in 1932, while also serving as Spanish delegate to the League of Nations in Geneva. He had also been elected deputy to the Consituent Cortes in 1931, on the regionalist ORGA (Organización Regional Gallega Autonóma) ticket. He left the Paris embassy when named Minister of Public Instruction in the reactionary government of Alejandro Lerroux in 1934.[245] Gil Robles took the pains to underline the fact, in his 1968 memoirs, that the post had been offered to three others, who turned it down, before it was given to Madariaga.[246] Very shortly thereafter, the government fell and Madariaga returned to his writing, while continuing to represent Spain at Geneva, without, according to his own testimony, either nomination or salary.[247]

After the Popular Front victory in 1936, President Azaña appointed Madariaga to represent Spain at Geneva. His activities there provoked a polemic led by the Spanish Socialists and, early in July 1936, Madariaga resigned from his post. In view of his known political ideas, it could hardly have been expected that he should work for very long with a government of the Left. He had suffered a great disappointment late in 1931 when Azaña was forming his first government. Azaña offered him the Ministry of Hacienda, which he declined in expectation of an offer of the Ministry of Foreign Affairs. In 1974 he wrote some revealing lines on the subject: '... and I was left wondering why I was not appointed Minister of State [for Foreign Affairs], which was what all Europe expected'. But Azaña named Luis de Zulueta and not Madariaga. Why? Madariaga asked himself.

> Objectively, of course, I should have been the Minister. Of course, in everything that was essential and important in politics, I was the Minister and, of course, for years everyone in Europe thought that not only was I a Minister of State, but that rather I was *the* Minister of State for the Republic.[248]

Evidently, the Spanish Republic had not come up to Madariaga's expectations. When Civil War broke out, Madariaga left Spain and lived in England, where he used his influence and numerous friendships to denigrate the embattled Republic. Thomas Jones, long-time secretary of Lloyd George, kept a diary. On the date of 25 September 1936, Madariaga described Franco to Lloyd George as being 'capable, courageous and pure', while declaring the Republican leaders to be stupid, and he assured the

English statesman that Franco would be in Madrid in the following month, at which time, Madariaga prophesied, he would probably make concessions to the peasants.[249] In his diary entry for 3 November 1936, Jones wrote:

> Madariaga is more optimistic than anyone else about the possibility of Franco – however moderate he may be – granting a leftist programme to the peasants once he has taken Madrid and Madariaga said: 'There is a 50% chance that Franco will do this'.[250]

Madariaga's activities behind the scenes were commented on by the American Ambassador to Italy, William Philips, in a communication to his government on 23 April 1937:

> While García Conde [Franco's ambassador to Italy] hoped that Madariaga might be willing to go [to Washington], he said that neither Madariaga nor his particular group are willing to serve Franco at present, preferring to keep apart from the situation until victory for one side or the other seems more certain.[251]

While Madariaga was busy trying to keep in the middle of the road in his secret manoeuvres – at times frankly veering to the Right – he kept silent in public. I well remember an evening in the early winter of 1936 when Madariaga gave a lecture in Washington DC, at the Wardman Park Hotel. I have forgotten the title of his talk, but I know that when questioned about the war in Spain, he refused to comment on that problem, to the disappointment of his audience.[252]

LVII

Madariaga's true feelings about the Civil War appeared in his book *Spain*, edition of 1942, published at a time when it could have influenced the sentiments of the greatly bombed Britons into kinder feelings about Francisco Franco. Not only did Madariaga defend the fraudulent 'documents' as being 'genuine', he took up similar positions against the Republic whenever the opportunity presented itself. One of the more unscholarly episodes of Madariaga's defence of the Spanish Rebels concerned the massacre at Badajoz, which is recognized everywhere today and at the time as a high point in modern military savagery. Madariaga wrote, concerning atrocities during the Spanish Civil War, 'Impartial information proved after the event that both sides sinned equally.' In a footnote, he added:

> A typical case is that of Badajoz. Major McNeill-Moss in his *Siege of Alcázar* has examined the reports which were current at the time of the atrocities committed by the Rebels when they took the city in 1936. I

believe that he has proved that there was a good deal of fabrication of telegrams and reports on the event by Press individuals or agencies interested in blackening the record of the Rebel Army; but I believe also that what remains as undoubtedly true is bad enough.[253]

Madariaga, writing about the massacre of Badajoz, shows us how difficult it is, even for a man who has studied at the French *Polytechnique*, to drive his car down the exact middle of the road. McNeill Moss's book was a flagrant piece of Rebel propaganda, a fact which Madariaga failed to point out when he recommended its pages to his readers. The arguments of McNeill Moss concerning Badajoz are false from beginning to end. The only real 'fact' to be garnered through a study of McNeill Moss's book was one which he unwittingly 'proved': the directors of the Havas Agency and United Press chose to lie to Luis Bolín and the Rebel censorship rather than to defend their correspondents and lose their chance to make money by continuing to report on the Spanish Civil War. I can say without fear of contradiction that the 'proofs' of McNeill Moss which convinced Madariaga – and on which he made no further research whatsoever – were incomplete and their interpretation totally fallacious. However, as they were, they were good enough for Madariaga, who was ready to be convinced that the Republican accusations concerning the Badajoz atrocities were themselves false and exaggerated.[254]

Madariaga was a narrative historian, a writer of agreeable prose, little of it based on important research, and, more usually than not, founded merely on gossip picked up here and there. In a passage from Madariaga's paragraph on the 'Secret Documents of the Communist Plot' which I have already quoted, there is an eloquent sample of the Madariaga method, which I shall quote again:

> I know that one of the prominent men involved in the conspiracy said in a European capital towards December 1935: 'If we win the general election we shall be in office in the spring ... and if we don't, also.' It was moreover given as certain in Moscow at the beginning of 1936 that there would be a proletarian Republic in Spain that summer.[255]

No serious historian could pay attention to such blatherings. If such phrases were extracts from a journal, with precise names, places and dates, they could at least be treated with attention, but not in their present state. Another example:

> From a confidence made by Señor Gil Robles to a foreign ambassador and from another confidence made by Azaña to a common friend, I am in a position to assert that neither side expected a victory at the polls in February.[256]

In weighing the 'facts' on which he built his interpretation of the Civil War, he permitted his deeply felt life-long political and social prejudices to decide which facts were true and which were false. His judgement of these facts was thus from the beginning unbalanced.

LVIII

Madariaga took an ambiguous stand on the Spanish Civil War, where he had, however, a clear choice: Hitler, Mussolini and Franco on the one side, with Stalin, the European Left and the Spanish Republic on the other. He reacted vaguely to Fascism only when bombs began falling on London. In 1974, in his book *Españoles de mi tiempo*, he made it clear where his sympathies lay. He was opposed to the man who supported the war of the Republic against Franco, the Church and the Axis when Ambassador in London, Pablo de Azcárate; and favourable to the man who deserted from the Republican ranks, Julio López Oliván.[257] Azcárate, in 1976, reproduced translated extracts from an article by Madariaga entitled 'Spain's Ordeal', published in the *Observer* of London, 11 August 1936. Madariaga qualified Franco as 'having no political ambitions whatsoever, with a clear and noble sense of duty and exemplary patriotism'. Madariaga, in this same article, wrote lines which he did not care to reproduce in his later books, saying that a Rightist victory would be no more than an episode in the history of Spain,

> unless Franco, together with his most important followers, rises above the motley reactionary mass surrounding him and becomes the instrument of a disciplined revolution. If he becomes a dyke, he will be swept away by the current, but if he becomes a channel, he can still save Spain and possibly also Europe.[258]

Alas, Franco could not save Europe. Once again, Madariaga failed in his self-appointed role of prophet.

Pablo de Azcárate had served the League of Nations for fourteen years when, late in August 1936, he was asked to take the post of Ambassador in London. He abandoned his position in the League, which could even then have appeared as a life-long job – he was First Under-Secretary-General of the League – to undertake a work which many perceived to have a life term of weeks, if not days. Madariaga showed in his writings a hearty dislike for Azcárate.[259]

He wrote quite frankly that he considered that the high post in the League of Nations given to Azcárate should have gone to himself.[260] Azcárate returned Madariaga's feelings, but with more elegance. He evaluated Madariaga's ambiguous activities during the Civil War as follows: he wrote, swept along by his impulsive character, he was not content to adopt an attitude of being discretely and expectantly neutral, but rather hoped to be *au dessus de la melée* and ... to play the role of referee between the two contending parties. He did not realize that the feelings surrounding his personality in Spain were enormously different from those which would have been necessary, as far as political prestige, moral authority and general respect are concerned, not only in order to successfully come out of the enormously difficult task he proposed embarking upon so lightly but also to embark upon it under conditions which were the minimum necessary for him not to appear, in the eyes of Spaniards on both sides, to be imbued with that which most effectively and irremediably sterilizes initiative: the absurd.[261]

When Madariaga came out openly and noisily against the Franco regime in 1954 – eighteen years after the outbreak of the Civil War – it was at a moment when Franco had already abandoned the label of Fascist-Falangist for a more acceptable trade mark, at least in the opinion of his protector in Washington, such as 'organic democracy', etc. Spain was a more Fascist country during the Civil War than in 1954. Even as late as 1942, when Franco still had his options for a Fascist choice wide open, Madariaga wrote as follows concerning José Antonio Primo de Rivera:

He was a brave, intelligent and idealistic young man, utterly disqualified for dictatorship by an irrepressible sense of humour, but he held that Communism was inevitable and that therefore it was best to travel towards it by way of an authoritarian system such as fascism.[262]

Perhaps Madariaga also had an 'irrepressible sense of humour' or, at any rate, a highly original conception of the nature of Fascism.

In a book published in Spanish in New York in 1959 (*General, márchese usted*),[263] Madariaga printed a copy of a letter he had addressed to Franco in November 1954 and in which he had pounded on the table and admonished Franco to abandon his power. (This letter had no known effect on El Caudillo but had it been written during the Civil War, it would have rendered more credible Madariaga's newly sought reputation as an anti-Fascist.) This book was, apart from the 1954 letter, composed of talks against the Franco regime delivered over the French-controlled state radio from 1964 to 1967.

It is difficult to situate Madariaga in the Spanish political organigram, for the simple reason that his life was not really that of a Spaniard. He was conservative, nay reactionary, in matters social and political, but at the same time he was anti-clerical and indifferent to the monarchy. Had he passed his life in Spain, he would have been ostracized from conservative society as were the first Spaniards to divorce in 1932. His tardy conversion to opposition to Franco was counter-balanced by his innate anti-Marxism and anti-Sovietism. For a person of his international reputation, his political reasoning was astonishingly immature. His declared stands on the Russian Revolution, the Spanish Civil War, the struggle between Fascism and anti-Fascism were evasive and thoughtless. He wrote in 1955:

> It is also appropriate to consider ... the efforts being made by the Soviet Union to win the affection of the Spanish regime. I already prophesied this years ago. Opposition between the communist and falangist regimes has never seemed to me to be essential. Communism is politically fascist and fascism is economically communist.[264]

LIX

Already in 1950, the Congress for Cultural Freedom (CCF) had been founded in Paris; and later, various affiliates were set up in European capitals and in the United States (the American Committee for Cultural Freedom, ACCF). The CCF had many eminent European intellectuals on its directorate, and Madariaga was named a 'Presidente de Honor'. A penetrating analysis of the ACCF and the CCF was published in New York in 1967, by Christopher Lasch.[265] Lasch pointed out that the CCF, when formed, had among the most conspicuous of its delegates 'militant anti-Communists (some of them also ex-communists from the European continent and from the United States'.[266] Again, Lasch observed that the ACCF 'was based [on] a coalition of moderate liberals and reactionnaries (both groups including a large number of ex-communists) held together by their mutual obsession with the communist conspiracy'.[267] The revelation by the *New York Times* on 27 April 1966 that the CCF was being funded by the CIA through 'dummy' foundations brought about the disappearance of the CCF and the ACCF. Madariaga occasionally contributed to the monthly *Cuadernos*, published in Paris by the Spanish-language affiliate of the CCF, under the direction of Julián Gorkin, an ex-Communist and, during the Civil War, a leader of the verbally ultra revolutionary POUM (Partido Obero de Unificación Marxista).[268]

Madariaga, like all other intellectuals of the 1930s and 1940s, was forced to pronounce himself on Fascism and anti-Fascism. The examination papers he turned in from time to time, reluctantly, won him failing marks. While scathingly fault-finding anyone who defended the cause of the Spanish Republic, he detected in certain Falangist activities a 'heroism' that he never observed in the resistance of the Spanish working class to Falangist-Fascist violence. Despite his career in international affairs, Madariaga had little understanding of political science, and his attempts to explain Fascism were ludicrous. I have already quoted Madariaga's bizarre remarks concerning J.A. Primo de Rivera, published in 1942. In his chapter concerning Ramiro de Maeztu in *Españoles de mi tiempo*, written in 1947 when Madariaga had already lived through the First World War, the Russian Revolution, the Spanish Civil War, the Second World War and the Decolonization, he offered this simplistic and provincial definition of Fascism: 'I believe, in fact, that Maeztu should be considered as one of the creators and perhaps the founder of Fascist ideology.'[269] And again, 'I believe there can be no doubt as to Maeztu's importance as the definer and propagator of fascist ideology.'[270] Madariaga was referring to a little-known book by Maeztu, first published in English as *Authority, Liberty and Function in the Light of the War* (1916) and then in Spanish in 1919 as *La crisis del humanismo*.[271] Maeztu's more widely read book of the immediately pre-Civil War ascendant Fascist years, *Defensa de la Hispanidad*, while reactionary and ultra-clerical, did not fit the Fascist pattern. Maeztu's 'crusade' was not so much European as Spanish American, the Roman Catholic revenge for 1789.[272] The Spanish Fascist (Falangist) programme, foreseen in conjunction with the Axis Powers, and spelled out by Franco to Hitler, envisioned Spanish imperialism as expansion into Africa, a colossal, unrealistic stupidity, involving lands hardly worth fighting for, as a glance at the map today will show.[273]

Gorkin and the ex-Falangist Dionisio Ridruejo seem to have been Madariaga's closest collaborators in the bustling activity of the 1960s, the chief purpose of which was to ensure that the eventual departure of Franco would not result in a Leftist government in Spain. An important element in this activity was the Munich Congress of Europeanists in 1962. According to his own 'Calendar of the life and work of the author', Madariaga from 5 to 8 June 1962 'presided over the domestic and foreign joint Europeanist delegation at the Munich Congress of Europeanists'.[274]

In fact, both in the Munich meeting and its repercussions, and in the diverse operations of the Congress for Cultural Freedom, Madariaga was deeply involved with other right-wing activists whose chief interest was to facilitate the changeover from Franco to a Centre-Right government.

LX

In Ridruejo's posthumous book *Casi unas memorias*,[275] there are reproduced one telegram and two letters, dated 1962, 1963, bearing two signatures: Gil Robles – Ridruejo. The frontispiece of *Casi unas memorias* consists of a photograph of Gorkin, Madariaga and Ridruejo in Bruges in 1963. Madariaga, while venting his spleen against anyone who defended the Spanish Republic, found in Dionisio Ridruejo, 'an eloquent preacher of the empire',[276] a man who merited his 'friendship and admiration', words that can be found in the prologue which Madariaga wrote for *Casi unas memorias*.[277] Madariaga – and this is worth recording here – had refused a meeting with Dr Juan Negrín during the war, because he considered the Republican leader to be 'an unfortunate man in the hands of the Russians, and I wanted no contact whatsoever with him'.[278] Ridruejo, who had fought to establish Fascism in

Spain and had worn Hitler's uniform on the Russian front, fighting to make Hitler master of Europe, was in Madariaga's eyes a far more worthy person.

In his prologue to *Casi unas memorias*, Madariaga gave still another interpretation of Fascism: it was the natural offspring of the Russian Revolution. 'The first dictator of the century was Lenin. His descendants, called Mussolini, Hitler, Franco and *tutti quanti* were born later. It is therefore a matter of record that 20th century dictators emanate from socialism.'[279] This simplistic formula shows how little Madariaga had learned during his lifetime.

Madariaga offered a general amnesty to the Falangist-Fascists of Spain, and, indeed, of the world. These poor fellows were, he explained, persons who had arrived to maturity 'at a time of total political depression when the failures of the League of Nations and the Russian Revolution lie scattered among the Western democracies'. The crisis of 1929, in Madariaga's analysis, was not in any sense a 'failure' of the capitalist system, from which the world emerged at the price of the Second World War. 'These young fascists, Nazis, Falangists see themselves as *leftist revolutionaries...*' Madariaga then referred to 'anticapitalist' phrases found in fascist literature, such as 'socialistas' (socialists), 'nacional-socialistas' (national socialists), 'nacional-sindicalistas' (national syndicalists) and 'juntas de ofensiva nacional-sindicalista' (reunions of national syndicalists), without pointing out that most of those who gargled such expressions, if they survived, joyfully entered into the capitalist society, with additional points for past capitalist-Fascist services.[280]

Madariaga sought to explain why Ridruejo, the minstrel-agitator of the Phalanx, reacted as he did when he saw the Handwriting on the Wall. This elucidation lay in the realm of poetry.

> More than anything else, Ridruejo was, in his heart, a poet ... And Primo de Rivera served as the prototype or model for what Dionisio was to become. Despite his speeches and statements, José Antonio was a poet who saw Spain in a dream as beautiful and unreal and who impatiently wished to make it an immediate reality. Dionisio was a 'soldier' of the Falange who wished to elevate José Antonio in order to 'save' Spain. It would be and could have been many things; but *this* Falange of José Antonio always saw itself as idealistic and blameless.[281]

LXI

This sentimental slobbering over the lyrical basis of Falangist violence can be explained by the total lack on the part of Madariaga of any sound political viewpoint. This accounts for the nebulous prose with which Madariaga sought to relate Ridruejo's break with the Franco regime:

Can we be surprised that this being, forever young, and in his very soul practically a child, should feel ill at ease when the enthusiastic and heroic Falange began to ferment? Once the early days, the heroic era were over, it lost no time in changing its style from ceremonies with action to ceremonies without and from words to wordiness. Is there any more bitter suffering for the poet than to have to listen to verbiage? Someone, some day, will pinpoint the moment when the Movement became gestures and verbiage. This is the time when Ridruejo left the Movement in order to move about and left ideology in order to think. Others followed, in almost the same set of circumstances. The reason for their disagreement was the same for all of them: the contrast between what for all of them was total unselfishness and what for the Caudillo was total ambition.[282]

Madariaga's passionate defence of actions of the pre-war and wartime Phalanx cannot be overlooked. He had simply neglected to keep up to date on the various interpretations of Falangist history. Nine years earlier I had attempted an explanation of the rupture of certain Falangist intellectuals with the Franco regime – Ridruejo, Montero Díaz, Tovar Llorente and Laín Entralgo – which gave a more reasonable meaning to their actions than had Madariaga. I referred to the phrase 'crisis of disillusionment' used by Enrique de Sotomayor in his talk entitled *Frente de Juventudes*.[283] I wrote in 1967 as follows:

This 'crisis of disillusionment' could only have as its basis the discovery, made as much by Ridruejo as by other Falangist intellectuals who had duly assimilated the National-Syndicalist undertaking, that Spain would not take part and could not take part in the Second World War; that the Axis was condemned to losing the war and that without the victory of the Axis Powers, Spanish territorial expansion, the Spanish empire, was not possible. The moment of coming face to face with the truth varied from one person to another. But at one time or another, each one realized that his dreams were courting disaster and that the promises made by the Falange could *never* be kept.[284]

Madariaga's ramblings on the subject of Fascism and Falangism are not our principal interest here, but they do constitute an example of how his mind worked. He did not bother to study Fascism, nor to do research on the matter; he just offered the first analysis that came into his head, on the problem of the 'documents', on the massacre of Badajoz, and on Falangism and Fascism, as on the intellectual itinerary of Ridruejo and his colleagues.

LXII

The attitude of the Franco regime towards Madariaga was ambiguous. Although his writings apparently irritated Franco from time to time,[285] the regime utilized Madariaga's virulent attacks on the PSOE, Juan Negrín, Julio Alvarez del Vayo and other Republicans in its own propaganda. This was rendered possible and easy because of the contradictory positions frequently adopted by Madariaga. In 1959, Franco's propaganda services published a booklet entitled *¿Qué pasa en España? El problema del socialismo español*[286] made up of quotations and reproductions from Madariaga's writings, especially *Spain* and *España*. Another propaganda publication of the Franco government which took advantage of Madariaga's ambivalent declarations was entitled *Madariaga versus Madariaga*. It was composed of three brochures, the pages unnumbered, joined together by a paper wrapper bearing the title given above, without editor or date. The subtitle was: 'Extractos de: *Anarquía o jerarquía, Ideario para la constitución de la tercera república*, Madrid, M. Aguilar, Editor, 1955; *Spain, a Modern History*, London, Jonathan Cape [1961?]; *Democracy versus Liberty? The Faith of a Liberal Heretic*, London, Pall Mall Press Limited.'

LXIII

An allied operation was carried out by historians loyal to the Francoist positions. Madariaga was by far the most quoted of the exiled writers. He can be said to have been the anti-Republicans' favourite 'Republican' exile. Arthur F. Loveday cited Madariaga five times and called him 'perhaps the most distinguished politician, diplomat and historian among the exiles'.[287] Arnold Lunn considered *Spain* to be a 'brilliant book',[288] and described Madariaga as 'that eminent author'.[289] Diego Sevilla Andrés, Professor of Political Law in a Franco university, wrote: 'It appears that Madariaga views the Uprising as an attempt to save the Republic from Marxism.'[290] Rafael Calvo Serer, a distinguished member of *Opus Dei*, associated Madariaga with Pedro Sainz Rodríguez, writing that both 'fully confirm the Republic's responsibility for the outbreak of the civil war'.[291] He went on, 'Furthermore, for Madariaga, in his *Spain*, the rebellion by Largo Caballero's socialists deprived the Left of legal arguments against the rightist uprising in 1936.'[292] On another page, he wrote, 'Salvador de Madariaga, the best-known writer in exile, presents a historical and political ideology that, in many respects, is the same as that espoused by the Nationalist intellectuals; as shown by José Pemartín in a resounding study (*Arbor*, October 1953).'[293]

Sir Robert Hodgson, London's representative to the Nationalist government during the Civil War, and author of the Foreword to Loveday's second book, wrote concerning Madariaga, 'His book on Spain is a mine of information and I have frequently had recourse to it.'[294] Brian Crozier, a biographer (and admirer) of Franco, quoted Madariaga, 'the most impartial of all the observers', on the errors of the Spanish Republic,[295] but in an overall judgement, while accepting Madariaga's opinions in general, 'especially on failure of the Spanish Republic', considered his view on Franco 'obscured by a blind spot'.[296]

Another enemy of the Republic (a fact which he tried carefully to hide), Burnett Bolloten, used Madariaga with caution in the early texts of his work,[297] but in his 1979 English text and his 1980 Spanish version, he quoted Madariaga's *Españoles de mi tiempo* to denigrate Pablo de Azcárate in a particularly disgusting and unscholarly manner.[298] Bolloten, throughout his career, had always chosen a selective bibliography and, at this point, while citing Madariaga on Azcárate,[299] he did not have the historian's carefulness to quote Azcárate on Madariaga,[300] although Azcárate's book was listed in the bibliography and even used to attack Azcárate in Bolloten's text.[301] Madariaga was Bolloten's, as he was every other anti-Republican's, handy hatchetman.

LXIV

Finally, Madariaga's true place in the history of modern Spain was given him by Ricardo de la Cierva who, in his *Los documentos de la primavera trágica*, called him up four times as a witness for the Franco regime, and reprinted eleven pages of his diatribes against the Spanish Republic.[302] La Cierva continued with this attitude towards Madariaga in his 1973 highly illustrated *Francisco Franco: Un siglo de España*, in which he cited the 'distinguished philosopher of contemporary Spanish history'[303] more than thirty times, never to impair his reputation, even on the pages concerning the Munich reunion of 1962 of the moderate Right-Centre opposition to Franco. Madariaga was a highly quotable person, especially on the pages dealing with the October 1934 Asturias uprising[304] and on the divisions within the PSOE in the spring of 1936. Concerning the latter point, la Cierva quoted what he described as 'Madariaga's accurate opinion'.[305] La Cierva also wrote: 'Gil Robles himself, together with Calvo Sotelo and Madariaga, was the most reliable recorder of the anarchy [in Spain during the months preceding 18 July 1936].'[306]

Madariaga is further called upon in one of la Cierva's recent volumes dedicated to the exploits of his hero Francisco Franco.[307] Here he insists more than in the past on the influence of Madariaga's book *Anarquía o jerarquía* on the intellectual processes of Francisco Franco. The greatest homage paid to Madariaga by la Cierva was to attribute to him a part of the inspiration that made Franco, in the eyes of la Cierva, a statesman, a political philosopher. In referring to Franco's declarations of 22, 23, 24 and 25 July 1936, he found in them traces of the following: 'the feeling of unity given in the speech of José Antonio in la Comedia: the criticism of the democracy and the *organic* alternative according to the modernization of Madariaga: the nostalgia and cleansing experience of the Dictatorship'.[308] Concerning the date of 16 November 1938, when Franco decreed the date of 20 November to be a day of national mourning in sorrowful memory of J.A. Primo de Rivera, la Cierva wrote in a resumé of the reasons

> why Franco, who had followed Salvador de Madariaga's proposals on organic democracy with great interest and who had studied in depth and assimilated José Antonio's speech in la Comedia as his own, decided to use the organic formula and José Antonio's doctrine, overlaid with demagogic concessions – according to Franco – as the cement for his unitarian populism.[309]

Such phrases may be the verdict of history: the Spanish intellectual, Salvador de Madariaga, in collaboration with José Antonio Primo de Rivera, inspired the political programme formulated by Francisco Franco, according to the one-time official hagiographer of the Caudillo, Ricardo de la Cierva. In such a case, the man who had desperately wanted to be the Foreign Minister of Spain will have finished as the second-rate adviser of the third-rate Dictator of the Spanish side of the Iberian Peninsula.

I have taken advantage of my readers' trust – if they have followed me up to this point – because Madariaga merits attention. Although not a research historian, and despite having his own political agenda, his reputation for sage objectivity helped to keep alive for more than a generation the myth of the 'Secret Documents of the Communist Plot'. He probably influenced Hugh Thomas in his own discussion of the 'documents'. Indeed, if Madariaga had produced a serious study of the 'documents' in 1942, in all probability Thomas would not have adopted the interpretation of the 'documents' that he published in 1961 and which contributed in its turn to justifying a continued belief in their authenticity.

LXV

I wanted to *prove* the falseness of the 'documents' by something more material than a logical argument. The logical demonstration had been made by Ramos Oliveira and Cattell. It had no effect on those who 'believed' in the 'documents'. Since the 'documents' existed, there must have been an agency behind them, a past history not well defined in the numerous references that I had found.

After I thought I had practically exhausted my research on this problem, I looked again at the reference suggesting a link between *Claridad*, Largo Caballero's Madrid daily, and the 'documents' published in the book by Orizana and Martín Liébana: '*Claridad* sought to deride the documents [Documents I, II], by ridiculing them.'[310] Two other books, one by Father

Toni in 1937 and the other by Ferrari Billoch in 1939, had mentioned *Claridad* in connection with the 'documents', but I was not in 1963 aware of these references. Earlier in this work, I have given quotations from these three books.

The clear reference to *Claridad* in the book by Orizana and Martín Liébana was too tempting for me to consider my research complete without tracking down this clue, and since *Franquismo* was still in flower, I thought it more prudent to drive to Madrid from France, where my wife and I had been living for many years, than to carry out enquiries by correspondence. In the Hemeroteca Municipal of Madrid, in less than an hour's time, I had found the proof that I was looking for. In the 30 May 1936 number of *Claridad*, I found a reproduction of Documents I and II, with a denunciation of their fabrication and distribution:

> The document we publish here has been taken from an idiot, a fascist leader, by an excellent comrade. In this case, the people involved are of less importance. What is important is the damage caused by stupid items such as this being wisely distributed, maintaining an atmosphere of criminal unease and provoking pusillanimous or ingenuous people into imagining that labour orgnizations are sects of people truly possessed by the devil ... who dream only of annihilating half of humanity ... That this damage has been done is indisputable. As final proof, we publish below some instructions which have been widely but quietly circulated, which prove how this provocation has made an impression on certain simple minds. It is one more piece in the plan of agitation and terror that the fascists are developing with the aim of creating a favourable climate for their sinister plans.[311]

In my 1963 book *El mito de la cruzada de Franco* (and in an enlarged, revised version in French, a year later),[312] I exposed Documents I and II for the cheap counterfeits they were. In the same sense, I could dismiss Document III and Document IV, which were sponsored by the same counterfeiters. This exposure had curious and varying results. But, first of all, I want to return to Madariaga and Thomas, who bore considerable responsibility for the perpetuation of the belief in the 'documents'. Neither Madariaga nor Hugh Thomas seem to have made any effort to discover the facts about the 'documents'. Madariaga was an easy to read narrative writer of historical events, but never a research historian. His account of the Loveday 'documents' was based on anecdotes, not on research. In all truth, I had the great advantage, when I was writing, of possessing most of the written accounts in which the contradictory evidence of the 'documents' abounded – above all, the *Rotbuch* – for it is in the visual presentation of the three 'documents' in the Anti-Comintern book that the viewer is struck by the fraudulent aspect of the 'documents'. This undocumentary appearance of the 'documents' is far more forceful there than in the reprinted translated pages of

Bardoux, *Exposure*, Loveday, etc. It is significant that the pages turned down by the Foreign Office in 1936 were clones of the *Rotbuch* 'documents'. The partial nature of the sheet of the so-called Lora del Río 'document' does not provoke the same reaction in the investigator as does the page found in the *Rotbuch*.

If Hugh Thomas had had sufficient curiosity about the 'documents', he could have unearthed the essential fact about the 'documents' from the Orizana and Liébana book which was listed in his bibliography. The weak suggestions of Madariaga and Thomas concerning the 'documents' were indications of, let us say, intellectual sloppiness.

LXVI

In the organization of this book, I had intended to use the publication of my 1963 book *El mito* as the watershed for all discussions concerning the 'documents'. After the publication of *El mito*, it was impossible for any rational being to assert that Documents I and II were proofs of any 'plot' whatsoever, or that they were 'secret' or 'Communist' or even 'documents'. And if Documents I and II were counterfeits, it was extremely difficult to maintain that III and IV were genuine. Therefore any comment on the 'documents' published later should have to take into consideration the arguments of my book. There are two books – one by an Englishman, K.W. Watkins, *Britain Divided*, published also in 1963, the other by Gabriel Jackson, *The Spanish Republic and the Civil War, 1931–1939*, published in 1965, but written earlier – which escape from my original schema. By a curious coincidence, probably caused by the attrition of time that grinds away at all historical mythology, the books of Watkins and Jackson, like *El mito*, all three written and published at about the same time, and each of the three independently of the others, argued that Documents I, II and III were falsifications.

If I go into detail to display the ratiocinations of Watkins and Jackson in some detail, it is to illustrate how historians, possessing more or less the same materials with which to judge the 'documents' as those that Madariaga and Hugh Thomas had at their command, nevertheless arrived at opinions totally opposed.

Watkins's examination of the Loveday 'documents' is one of the most thorough ever made based entirely on observations and political deductions on the 'documents' themselves, and it is regrettable that he allowed this exposition to be marred by his inexplicable tolerance for the text of Madariaga concerning the 'documents'. But let us concentrate on his highly interesting dissection of the 'Red' plot. First of all, he dwelt on the international situation, and quoted the Comintern leader Dimitrov as having been 'moved to complain' in 1935 'that among members of the Communist International only too often "a desire made itself felt at times to substitute for the concrete analysis of reality and living experience some sort of new scheme, some sort of new, over-simplified lifeless formula, to represent as actually existing what we desire, but does not yet exist" '.[313]

The English writer drew this conclusion:

> At this stage, it can be said that, whilst the Spanish Communist Party was a revolutionary party which aimed eventually to establish the dictatorship of the proletariat, the above analysis indicates that it was not planning an armed insurrection in Spain in 1936: this, for the simple reason that the very preconditions which it regarded as essential for success did not, as yet, exist.[314]

Watkins then directed his attention to the 'alleged documentary proof of this plot ... the straightforward task of assessing the authenticity' of the Loveday documents.[315] He addressed himself to three questions: 'How did Mr Loveday obtain them and present them to the British public? How and where were they originally discovered? What conclusions can be drawn from their own internal evidence?'[316]

In answer to the first question, Watkins studied the two Loveday books, with their four contradictory versions of how he had obtained the 'documents', and declared:

> It should surely not be asking too much of a writer who claims to be making an authoritative study of an important historical event that he himself should be clear as to whether he brought certain documents to Britain or merely received them here.[317]

Watkins then applied himself to the problem of the four different discoveries of the 'documents', aside from those of Loveday, and decided:

> It might be thought that the discovery of a single document would result in a flimsy case and that this 'scatter' of documents would greatly strengthen it. Such a view would merely betray a complete ignorance of communist theory and practice. It is precisely this 'scatter' which casts the gravest doubts on the 'discovery'.[318]

And:

> If groups of Anarchists had distributed such documents or left them lying about it might be understandable. But that the Central Committee of the Communist Party, contrary to international Communist practices, should have allowed the documents to get into the hands of local leaders in a village or small provincial town ... is absolutely unthinkable ... A professional revolutionary party, possessing the strength and power which Loveday and others have attributed to the

Spanish Communist Party, would not have done so. In fact, those who produced these documents overreached themselves.[319]

As for the contents of the 'documents', Watkins, after noting Madariaga's two reservations that the Popular Front, having won the February elections, the Communists could work through the Cortes, with the attaching prestige of legality and right, and the presence of so many well-known anti-Communists in the list of Ministers, offered other reasons for not accepting the 'documents'. Watkins stressed the fact that the Spanish workers had no armament when the war broke out – thus contradicting the 'documents' and the fact that the alleged number of 'Assault Fighters' and 'Resistance Fighters' far surpassed the number of Communist Party members, even accepting the party's official figures.[320]

Watkins also quoted Cattell's 'interesting line of argument concerning the USSR's policy at that time', an argument that Thomas had not heeded, although Cattell's *Communism and the Spanish Civil War* was listed in his bibliography.[321]

The well-organized arguments of Watkins concerning the Loveday 'documents' have a convincing quality that merits our respect, but they bear the minor flaw of his blindness toward the position of Madariaga. The fact that Madariaga accepted Loveday's first book with its two contradictory versions of how he acquired the 'documents' is dismissed as of no consequence, although it does underline Madariaga's uncritical approach to the problem.

Watkins nowhere poses the question of why the experienced diplomat and authority on foreign affairs Madariaga did not see the weak spots in Loveday's presentation of his 'documents', weak spots that were visible to Watkins himself. Watkins quoted Madariaga's paragraph on the 'documents' at length, without insisting on the fact that Madariaga did write: 'I incline to think they [the documents] are genuine' and that he did treat the 'conspiracy' as a reality. Madariaga was perhaps beyond criticism in a doctoral dissertation in Great Britain.

Watkins was unjust to deride Loveday, a businessman turned newspaper correspondent-propagandist, for his lack of 'academic standards', because it was Madariaga, the proud dweller in academe, who, in his treatment of the Loveday 'documents', betrayed 'academic standards' and not the former President of the British Chamber of Commerce in Barcelona. Madariaga was extremely severe with non-Spaniards who made mistakes on details of Spanish history, as shown in his mention of Professor Arnold Toynbee's 1937 *Survey* for the Royal Institute of International Affairs, where he warned readers that Toynbee's

theories on the Spanish background, as set forth in Part I of the *Survey* for 1937, are highly debatable and lead this distinguished scholar to conclusions of a most hazardous character which no well-informed Spanish authority would substantiate. Unfortunately, these theories are not without a certain influence on a number of aspects in the narrative of the Civil War, so that this work, otherwise so excellent, has to be handled with caution.[322]

If Professor Toynbee made mistakes in the 1937 *Survey*, as Madariaga alleged, they are unlikely to be of the gravity of the numerous errors of fact concerning the Spanish Civil War committed time and time again by the Spaniard, of nationality if hardly of spirit, Salvador de Madariaga.

LXVII

Gabriel Jackson challenged the authenticity of the 'documents' as forcefully as had Watkins, but his arguments were based more on Spanish political realities than were those of Watkins, whose book was oriented to the impact of the war in Spain on British politics. The copies of the 'documents' that Jackson was refuting were not very precisely identified, but from his text, it is evident that he was referring to Documents I, II and III.[323] 'There are many improbable things in these documents', wrote Jackson. First of all, the attitude of the Third International in 1936 did not conform to the picture given in the 'documents'.

> The Communist International in 1936 was oriented entirely toward the establishment of an anti-fascist front of all bourgeois and proletarian forces opposed to fascism. In Spain, the Communists openly criticized the Caballero Socialists. The Soviet-plan documents ask one to believe that Communists wished to overthrow the French and Spanish Popular Front governments, and that a planning committee including several Russians would prepare a commissar list with a Caballerist majority.[324]

Then the American historian found many unacceptable political contradictions amongst the conspirators named in the documents. Among them, Jackson pointed out,

> As commissar of Justice, they named Luis Jiménez de Asúa. Then along with Thorez, José Díaz, Gregori Dimitrov, Caballero and others, Vincent Auriol was to be one of the guiding spirits. The anarchists David Antón, García Oliver and Angel Pestaña were also named.[325]

This was an 'incredible combination of names' for

> Jiménez de Asúa was a constant supporter of Prieto and of legal, parliamentary government. He was a principal author of the Constitution of 1931. However, as the defending lawyer for the peasants of Castilblanco and for various Socialist leaders after Asturias, he earned the kind of

blind hatred which would lead the Right to imagine him as a 'commissar of justice'. Vincent Auriol was a parliamentary French Socialist, but he had come to Spain on behalf of the International League for the Rights of Man to ask Alcalá-Zamora and Lerroux to amnesty the Socialist leaders condemned to death in February 1935. This action would easily qualify him to be placed among the Soviet leaders by a rightist propagandist. As for the anarchists named, David Antón was one of the extremist CNT leaders who made cooperation with the UGT most difficult. Pestaña, on the other hand, had been converted to reformist ideals and was equally at odds with both the CNT majority and with the Caballero Socialists. The Right, however, would very easily be able to picture these men working together under Largo Caballero to build a Soviet Spain.[326]

Continuing this analysis founded on the 1936 reality of the disagreements among the Spanish organizations of the Left, Jackson asserted that 'neither does the plan for a Soviet concur with the known events of June 1936' for the following reasons:

> The UGT and CNT leaders were completely absorbed in their mutual rivalries arising from the construction strike. The Caballerist leaders in late June were pleading with the CNT to accept mediation so as *not to* destroy the authority of the Casares government. Largo Caballero was in England and France during late June and early July. Finally, no evidence is ever offered for the statement that the plan was postponed until August 1. But such a statement is not necessary to account for the utter lack of 'Soviet' activity between May 11 and June 29 and to justify the military rising of July 18 as a preventive measure.[327]

Jackson, in his review of the 'documents', is imprecise as to which 'document' he is concerned with, but since he refers to Thomas's book and Thomas's stated source is Loveday, we can presume that Jackson is dealing with Documents I, II and III. At one stage of his argumentation, the American historian uses a form of proof by the negative: Maximiano García Venero, in his three-volume *Historia de las internacionales en España* (described by Jackson as 'the best documented study made in Spain of the revolutionary Left'), did not mention the 'documents' and this fact is considered by Jackson to be a proof of their doubtful authenticity.[328] Jackson contrasted this non-publication with Hugh Thomas's discovery of a reproduction of the 'documents' – in reality, only I and II – in the *Diario de Navarra* of 7(8) August 1936, and Thomas's 'conclusion that the *Diario* documents were not forgeries'.[329] Next, Jackson stated that 'These documents received wide international publicity when published in the London *Times* on 3rd May 1938 and the following year in Bilbao.'[330] My own research had turned up no reproduction of the 'documents' in *The Times* of 3 May 1938 or on any other date, and I am inclined to think that Jackson's references to *The Times* resulted from a misreading of the first paragraph of the brochure *Exposure*, printed in London, in fact very shortly after the 3 May 1938, and of which a translation appeared a year later in Bilbao.

These strictures are, however, in no wise intended to deprive the well-reasoned conclusions of Jackson and Watkins (along with earlier ones of Cattell and Ramos Oliveira) from their deserved award for being praise-worthy deductions leading to the truth concerning the 'Secret Documents of the Communist Plot'. None of the arguments advanced by any of the four historians mentioned above was, to my knowledge, ever to receive an echo in the *Franquista* historiography of the Spanish Civil War.

I must underline the fact that Jackson wrote: 'Practically all the Nationalist officers to whom I spoke accepted as fact that this accusation [of the 'Secret Documents of the Communist Plot'] was true ...'[331] and gave as his own opinion that 'the documents were drawn up by badly informed rightist elements'.[332] Part of the remaining problem was then to find out who were these 'badly informed rightist elements'.

LXVIII

Since Documents I and II were reproduced and denounced in a Madrid daily on 30 May 1936, they could hardly have been after that date 'secret documents' for anybody. It was therefore absolutely impossible for an honest man to argue that Franco and the other generals rose in rebellion in July 1936 to foil a dastardly plan so 'secret' that everyone in Spain could have read about it in a Madrid newspaper forty-five days earlier. And, as a matter of fact, not one of the defenders of the Franco cause, after the publication of *El mito*, came forward to reproduce any of the four 'documents'. The methods used by the Franco camp were most oblique. If, as happened once or twice, the 'documents' were mentioned as historical papers of value, this gesture was accompanied by a failure even to mention the evidence concerning them brought up in *El mito*. The 'documents' were not defended in a factual confrontation, but allowed to disappear in a cloud of oblivion, while the rebuttal moved to another, undocumented, plane. But at first I had the naivetée to imagine that absolute proof of the falseness of the 'documents' would undermine the faith even of those who desperately desired to believe in the 'Communist Plot', if only because they could not confront the reality of the illegality and illegitimacy of their 'Cruzada Nacional'.

El mito de la cruzada de Franco was, of course, under interdiction of public sale in Spain until the death of Franco. Nevertheless, the demolition of the propaganda based on the 'Secret Communist Plot Documents' became more or less bruited about, and the temptation of replying to *El mito* became irre-sistible among the true believers. The first sign of this new developing polemic – the first that I have found – was in a publication by that ardent defender of the four 'documents' in 1940, Joaquín Arrarás, who twenty-five years later backslid in his *Historia de la segunda república española (texto abreviado)*. After pointing out various references to reproductions of the 'documents' (more or less quoting them exactly as he had found them in *El mito*), and insisting on the following details: 'Salvador de Madariaga in *España*, and the North American (!) Hugh Thomas, in *The Spanish Civil War*, accept the authenticity of the documents proving the Marxist conspiracy to establish a proletarian dictatorship.'[333]

Arrarás wrote as follows:

> Among those who deny the authenticity of this evidence, the most vehement and excessive is the Englishman (!) Herbert Rutledge Southworth, in his pamphlet entitled *El Mito* ... Southworth maliciously states that the documents were used against the Popular Front as capital proof to justify the 'generals' uprising against Spanish democracy'. No such thing exists. The documents, whether apocryphal or genuine, will always be insignificant with regard to the pile of arguments or testimony offered by the revolution unleashed on 16th February 1936 ... Those documents neither add or subtract anything important from Spanish political reality at that time.
>
> The Marxists' plans are categorically recorded in the speeches of Largo Caballero, González Peña, La Nelken and others in the pages of *Claridad*, *El Socialista*, *Mundo Obrero* and in dozens of pamphlets and revolutionary weeklies which signify as much as all the clandestine documents. A proletarian dictatorship, as is constantly being announced by the Marxists, cannot be established without a violent struggle and this latter cannot be unleashed without pre-military organization, based on the Red militias that abound all over Spain ...[334]

Arrarás did not tell his captive Spanish audience of the publication of Documents I and II on 30 May 1936, which would have enabled his readers to judge for themselves of their validity; instead he mounted a counter-campaign to show that the 'documents' now had no importance. They could be true or false, the 'Red Menace' and the 'Secret Plot' were a reality that could not be denied. This is the same upside-down reasoning that has kept alive for decades another false document – notably in the Rebel Zone during the Civil War and in Franco Spain during the lifetime of the dictator: the Protocols of the Elders of Zion.[335] The 'documents' were false, but the 'plot' was real. In Spain in 1936, there was one conspiracy, that of the military. There was no other.

As a matter of fact, the exposure of the falseness of the 'Secret Communist Plot Documents' offered a confirmation of the considerable preparations of the military plot. The false 'documents' constituted an integral part of the conspiracy of the Spanish generals. It was early in 1937 that the competing factions among the Insurgents began to unveil details of their contribution to the right-wing conspiracy, each party – the military, the Carlists, the Alfonsists, the Falangists, etc. – seeking to gain credit for the victory which was growing larger and nearer on the horizon. It is quite possible that, as the claims and counter-claims on the patent rights to the 'Movimiento Nacional' were made public, the need was felt to insist on the early left-wing plot which did not exist.

(It must also be noted that in 1965 Hugh Thomas, in a first revision of his *Spanish Civil War*, made amends for the first, equivocal evaluation of the Loveday documents, writing in his altered text, 'In fact, it seems certain that these [documents] were forgeries, made before the rising and possibly deceiving those who later propagated them.'[336] As I have already pointed out, the Loveday 'documents' did not, in a legal or technical sense, merit even the appellation 'forgeries'. And since Thomas was himself among 'those who later propagated them', it was but natural that he should show an indulgence for the former believers. In his first edition, Thomas was less than adept in judging 'forgeries'. Moreover, his 1961 text, along with that of Madariaga, contributed to the perpetuation of the 'authenticity' of the Loveday papers even beyond the year 1963. In one case, as we shall see, Thomas's 1961 testimony was used by Luis Bolín in 1967, despite Thomas's 1965 correction. On the credit side, Thomas in 1965 repeated his conviction of 1961 that 'the establishment of a communist regime in Spain would have been contrary to the general lines of Stalin's moderate foreign policy ...'.)[337]

LXIX

Luis Bolín was an Anglo-Spanish journalist greatly influenced by the thinking of ultra-conservative English Catholics, such as Douglas Jerrold, Sir Arthur Bryant, Arnold Lunn and so forth. An ardent monarchist, he defended to the last the tenets of faith of the Franco Crusade, even when it was downright silly to do so. Bolín was probably the man who provoked through maladresse the controversy over the destruction of Guernica.[338] Thirty years after the Condor Legion bombed Guernica, in 1967, he published his memoirs, *Spain: The Vital Years*, first in English, a language with which he was quite at ease, and later that year in Spanish.[339] Comparing the two texts, it seems likely that the Spanish is not a direct translation of the English (nor the English of the Spanish) but each reflects a free rewriting of the other. Bolín believed in the 'Secret Communist Plot Documents' and in the 'plot' itself. He gave five pages to a discussion of the 'documents' in 'Apendice II' of his Spanish edition[340] ('Appendix I in English),[341] entitled 'Realidad del Comunismo en la Crisis Española', after having earlier affirmed in his text, 'a communist rebellion had been set for the end of July or beginning of August'.[342] Farther on in his book, he elaborated on this 'communist movement' in part as follows:

Specific circles have doubted the existence of this plan [Document IV], but it is certain that the leaders of the aforementioned party [Communist], issued categoric and detailed *orders and instructions* on 6th June 1936 for a communist rebellion which the Nationalist Uprising was able to frustrate ... During the summer of 1936, the passivity or complicity of the Popular Front Government increased the likelihood of success for a conspiracy of this type [postponed until mid-August, it was forestalled by the Nationalist revolt]. The corresponding plans came to light near Seville and in other places, in August 1936 and I was one of the first people to see them. [No-one on our side knew of these plans until they came to light near Seville, in August of 1936 where I myself saw them a few weeks after the start of our rebellion.] In 1940, they were reproduced in their entirety by Manuel Aznar in his brilliant *Historia militar de la guerra de España*...[343]

The sentences bracketed above contain phrases found in the English edition of Bolín's book that are absent from the Spanish. The reader may find these changes of interest. Also, incidentally, Aznar's 'brilliant *Historia*' is merely 'informative' in English. The lines quoted in Spanish in the preceding paragraph are followed in the English edition by two pages of details concerning the contents of Document IV.[344] In Spanish, Bolín contented himself with this comment on the 'orders and instructions' given in Document IV: 'It is sufficient to say that they were drastic, detailed, radical and implacable: if they had been put into effect, they would have been extremely bloody.'[345]

Fortunately for Spain, Francisco Franco was ready and waiting to prevent this imaginary bloodbath, preferring his own.

Bolín, a one-time head of the Spanish Insurgents's military censorship in Seville, was one of the last of the true believers in the propaganda of the Franco crusade – there were also Professor Jeffrey Hart of Dartmouth College, who, in 1973, came to the defence of Bolín's pronouncements on Guernica,[346] and the journalist Brian Crozier, who has been claiming for years that Guernica was never bombed by the Germans[347] – and the last one known to persist in affirming his faith in the 'documents'. He prolonged the confusion that reigned among pro-Franco historians concerning Document IV. Bolín, as shown in the long quotation above, claimed that the first knowledge of Document IV among the Spanish Nationalists was in August 1936, when a copy was found near Seville 'and in other places', and that he, Bolín, was among the first to lay eyes on it. Here he contradicts the author of the 'brilliant *Historia*', who wrote that he had himself in June 1936 seen the 'instructions' which 'very quickly came to enrich our military leaders' secret archives'.[348] It is important to note that neither during the war, nor since, have copies of 'orders and instructions' been shown to historians. These contradictions were underlined by Bolín's claim that it was the plans he had himself seen in August 1936 which were 'reproduced in full' by Aznar, who claimed that they were the 'document' he himself had read in

June. Bolín had been a mediocre newspaperman, according to one professional English source,[349] but in his remarks concerning Document IV he offered his readers a real 'scoop', thirty years after the event. No other pro-Rebel authority on Document IV had ever revealed its discovery in August 1936, not only in Seville, but also 'in other places'. Not Pironneau, nor Bardoux, nor 'Belforte', nor Arrarás, nor Ferrari Billoch had been so precise.

Bolín also quoted a few sentences from the inevitable vademecum of all pro-Franco historians of the Civil War, *Spain* by Salvador de Madariaga, in which the Spanish Socialists were blamed for the violence in Spain during the spring of 1936 and the Fascists exculpated.[350] Bolín used the 1961 edition of Madariaga (see above) in which the Anglo-Spaniard had quietly without explanation removed the 1942 paragraph dealing with the Loveday 'documents'. Presumably, Bolín was unaware of Madariaga's earlier work and its expressed belief in the authenticity of Documents I to III.

Bolín, the Rebel specialist in propaganda, then cited the first ten lines of n. 1 on p. 108 of Hugh Thomas's 1961 edition of *The Spanish Civil War*. This citation was, alas, but half of what Thomas had written. Bolín dishonestly repeated what Thomas had said when his foot was on the right side of the fence, and failed to prove what he had said when his foot was on the left side of the railing. Bolín needed someone with a good reputation to champion the 'documents' and Thomas was his man. Bolín was doubly dishonest, for the ambiguous words of Thomas in 1961 had been repudiated in 1965, two years before the appearance of Bolín's book.

Having used both Madariaga and Thomas, the two historians of the Spanish Civil War appearing to be on the middle of the road, Bolín turned to another enigmatic figure of Spanish Civil War historiography, Burnett Bolloten. As I have already noted, Bolloten opposed the authenticity of the 'documents' with an analysis of Soviet foreign policy in 1936. But, first of all, Bolín recommended Bolloten's work, which 'must be read by those who enjoy studying this exciting period of Spanish history' and which he considered 'in the main, well documented'.[351] The 'well documented part', from Bolín's viewpoint did not include Bolloten's judgement of Documents I to IV. This aspect of the debate was one that most of the partisans of the validity of the 'documents' and the existence of the 'plot' chose to ignore. Bolín confessed that the arguments of Bolloten 'seemed logical' but then wrote that they 'fail for two reasons'.[352]

The first reason was that the 'the Nationalists did not have to invent anything in order to justify their Uprising; it was the Republic that provoked them with the necessary justification by their disastrous actions over a five-year period'.[353] This commentary is obviously based on the incomplete quotation from Thomas's book, in which the English historian hesitated to accept the 'documents' as having been written after 18 July 1936, and considered them to be of Leftist origin if concocted before that date. The lines cited above from Bolín's Spanish text are quite different from the previously published English, in which Bolín wrote: 'the events of the preceding years amply justified the military revolt; no attempt was made to justify it by publishing plans for a communist conspiracy'.[354] But, as anyone who has had the patience to follow this textual examination up to here can testify, almost from the first month of the Civil War – for example, del Moral in London – efforts were made by Spanish Nationalist agents or sympathizers precisely to justify the attack against the Spanish Republic by revealing 'plans for a Communist conspiracy'. One must be naive indeed to think that Bolín was unaware of such endeavours, inasmuch as many of them were carried out by his close English friends.

It can be noted here that Bolín in 1967 was remarkably ignorant concerning the bibliography on the subject on which he was pontificating. In 1967 – as was evident to a reader of any of the following: *El mito* (1963), Arrarás's *Historia de la segunda república (texto abreviado)* (1965) or Thomas's 1965 revision – the position of those who were challenging the genuineness of the 'documents' was not that they were written after the outbreak of the war to justify the 'Alzamiento', but that they were written before the war to prepare certain sectors of the Spanish Right for the coming 'Alzamiento'.

> In the spring of 1936 there were probably hundreds of copies of documents I and II which were passed from person to person in Spain and which terrified the already terrified members of the Spanish Right. This tension in the air was considered necessary in order to obtain the support of the bourgoisie for the Generals' uprising.[355]

None of these works is in Bolín's bibliography, which, as a matter of fact, refers to no book published after 1964, three years before his own publication. Nor had he assimilated the standard pro-Franco texts on the 'documents' written before 1963.

Bolín continued his observations on Bolloten's discussion of the 'documents':

> When the plans for a communist revolution came to light near Seville, I was the head of the Military Press Office in that city and was in constant contact with foreign journalists. No-one made me divulge those plans which is what would have happened if they had been drafted for propaganda purposes.[356]

Document IV was, in all probability, written along with Documents I and II and doubtless also Document III, as part of the propaganda campaign preparatory for the military uprising. Whether or not Bolín found the 'plans' in Seville in August 1936 is beside the point. As we know, copies of Documents I and II and also III were scattered all around Spain. And when we study Bolín's career as a Press Officer, detested by the majority of the foreign press corps, it becomes clear that the war correspondents, except for the German, Portuguese and Italians, would not have believed his story of the 'documents'[357] had he shown them around. Another detail: Bolín, in discussing the 'documents', uses the word 'drafted', which carries with it the connotation of skilful preparation. Now, one can believe in the 'documents' or disbelieve in them, but no one can claim that they were 'drafted'. They were either prepared, as Jackson wrote, 'By badly informed rightist elements', or by careless scribes for stupid readers. It is hard to believe that Bolín, deeply implicated in the monarchist section of the military conspiracy, knew nothing of the 'documents' before the war. However, throughout his paragraphs on the 'documents', he takes the position, following the 'facts' found in Thomas's truncated citation, that they were fabricated after 18 July 1936.

Bolín continued his analysis of Bolloten's comments, presenting his 'second reason', with sentences in which his English text did not always concord with his Spanish text. In English, he wrote:

> Equally unwarranted is the assumption that Communists in Spain would have hesitated to act in a manner contrary to the Comintern's policy. Spanish Communists, in July 1936, had yet to be taught discipline and submission to their masters; they did not attach much importance to the Comintern.[358]

This was greatly shortened into Castilian: 'the hypothesis that the Spanish communists were incapable of acting independently of the Comintern lacks credibility'.[359] He went on in Castilian:

> Neither did the lack of forces with which to establish themselves overly concern them; they counted on the force of others, less intelligent than themselves but docile with regard to their plans, and the suggestion that in July 1936 someone on our side is drafting conspiracy plans, complete in every detail and imbued with a genuine Communist character, supposes a great lack of understanding of the way in which the Movement against the Republic was planned – scant detail with regard to the plan, total absence of Machiavellian design and complete disregard of public opinion abroad and of anything apart from the individual consciences of those involved in the rebellion.[360]

But, Bolín was arguing with his own phantasms, for few people except himself in 1967 were believing that the 'documents' had been elaborated in July 1936 or were feeling called upon to deny that he and his collaborators had 'faked' a Communist conspiracy in July 1936. As the principal architect of the counter-charges, I was proclaiming, with proofs in hand, that the 'documents', at least Documents I and II, had been prepared before 30 May 1936. Bolín's refusal to accept the debate on this unchallengeable terrain was strange indeed, for, according to Loveday, Documents I, II and III had been fabricated before the war, and Loveday was the accepted authority for the 'documents' in England. Bolín was most certainly aware of del Moral's efforts to foist his 'documents', which later became known as Loveday's 'documents', onto the Foreign Office. How then could Bolín affirm that ' no attempt was made to justify it [the military revolt] by publishing plans for a Communist conspiracy' when every other pro-Insurgent propagandist, beginning with del Moral, was basing his propaganda argument on the 'Secret Documents of the Communist Plot'?

LXX

Another recidivist in dealing with the 'documents' was Eduardo Comín Colomer, who, in 1967, revised his arguments of 1955 and 1959. (Like many of the pro-Franco pamphleteers of the time, he felt the need to counter the evidence produced in *El mito*, but he did not want to name the book in his own text.) In 1955 and 1959 he had given his enthusiastic endorsement to Documents I, II and III. By 1967, he preferred to forget his commitments of the past, and began his analysis of the 'documents' by referring to the 'experience of October 1934' as a reference for the revolutionary intentions of the Spanish left. Speaking of the end of May 1936, he wrote:

> It was certain that Spain was rushing not towards chaos or anarchy, as everyone has said in an attempt to explain the disorder simply, but rather Spain was rushing towards Bolshevisation. And perhaps, as a result, a sharp blow had to be given to bring the reality of the tragic situation into focus.[361]

The 1967 references of Comín Colomer to the 'documents' began not, as in his previous books, with *Exposure*, but with citations from *Claridad* of 30 May 1936, which the Spanish reader might well have thought to be the fruit of Comín's own industrious research. This time, he wrote about only Documents I and II, completely forgetting Document III. After quoting the explanatory lead-off paragraph in Largo Caballero's newspaper, he observed:

> The strange thing is that these so-called reports were said to be genuine, but in the sense that they were Marxism's own revolutionary plans. They were doubtlessly drawn up by someone who knew about Marxist methods, on the basis of the October 1934 instructions ... We therefore insist that they were reports drawn up by someone who knew about insurrectionary operations in urban areas.[362]

Comín Colomer flaunted his experience as an official of the political police to warrant confidence in Documents I and II. The latter, which he labelled as 'Secret Report Number 20', possessed 'a good many details that justify this description'. Instead of offering a rationalization for the contradictions and improbabilities found in the composition of the list of conspirators, he assured his readers that 'In the first part, they point out the possibility of a National Soviet with the names of fairly well-known political figures as members of the most extreme wing of Marxism.'[363]

The savant of Spanish Leftist political secrets then made the following revelation:

> The gross error was in stating 'Ventura' to be from the USSR and a delegate of the Third International, when this name was the pseudonym used by Jesús Hernández Tomás. We clarified this in the first part of this History, when dealing with the Spanish delegates who took part in the VII congress of the Comintern.[364]

But Comín, in his 1959 book, had 'clarified' the matter of Ventura's identity otherwise: 'Let us clarify the obscurity of this figure's [Ventura] identity. He was simply Victorio Codivila who used the name of Luis Medina in the Red zone.'[365] Evidently, one cannot always trust the confidential files of the police.

Comín Colomer then resumed his new interpretation of Documents I and II as follows: 'in brief, none of this went beyond reports, although it has been gradually accepted as a revolutionary plan prepared by Marxists'. 'But, it must be understood that,' he went on,

> the fact that such documents were no more than reports based on plans for October 1934 does not mean that the Spanish Bolsheviks had no revolutionary plan. They did have one and it was quite complete. As far as Madrid was concerned, they had changed some of the basic points planned for that earlier day of insurrection and, because of the availability of more human resources, they were able to have objectives that were impossible on the previous occasion. Furthermore, the operational plan had to be different. This time, Marxism would not spill out onto the streets to begin the fighting, but rather, since the Marxists were certain that fascism would rise up against them, the role of the militias, as initial shock troops, would be equivalent to a counter-offensive.[366]

That is, Comín considered the Spanish Left to have been provocateurs of the Right, aware of the military plot and merely waiting for the uprising in order to annihilate its participants. To support his argument, Comín reproduced extracts from an article which, he wrote, had been published in the Madrid daily *Ahora* of 1 August 1936 and which showed the Director de Seguridad (Director of Security), Alonso Mallol, in full possession of all the details of the movements of the rebels in Madrid, on the night of 18–19 July 1936, giving the necessary orders to dominate the revolt with the aid of the Casa del Pueblo. This article, which seems highly propagandistic and intended to credit the Republican government on the night in question with more aid to the working class than it really gave, is the only proof presented by Comín in support of his thesis. He wrote:

> So, the fact that the Casa del Pueblo, as the central headquarters of the 'urbanized' militias, had its men ready and armed, irrefutably showed that there was indeed a revolutionary plan, a counter-offensive planned in great detail which would face the uprising imposed on the Spanish Right by Popular Frontism during the development of its tactics of provocation. It is also certain that this plan would have been changed into a plan of offensive if those people officially placed beyond the margins of the law by the government's belligerent attitude had not been able to react.[367]

The proof of the 'Communist plot' advanced by Comín Colomer in 1967 was even weaker than that which he had previously proposed, based on the 'documents'. But his efforts to renew his charges of a Communist conspiracy provide evidence of his deeply felt need to justify the military uprising as being merely a desperate reaction to prevent a Communist take-over of Spain.

LXXI

Another waffling point of view on the 'documents' was advanced, also in 1967, by Brian Crozier, an Australian living in London, in his highly favourable life of Franco *Franco. A Biographical History*. Crozier based his remarks on Documents I, II and III as given in Loveday's two books:

> A fierce controversy has raged over the authenticity of these documents. I do not propose to enter into it, because I consider the documents unimportant, even if genuine, and in any case of little relevance to what happened in Spain in July 1936.[368]

Why did Crozier consider the 'documents' unimportant?

> The Nationalists began conspiring at the beginning of March, long before the existence of a precise communist plot was suspected. In a more general sense, of course, they did fear a communist revolution, or at any rate revolutionary anarchy, and that fear was one of their reasons for conspiring. The rapid deterioration of law and order after the advent of the Popular Front strengthened their view that military action had to be taken.
>
> All this would have happened even if no documents had ever been discovered. But in any case, the accepted Nationalist version of the facts is now that the documents were found by Nationalist forces in various

places *after the July uprising had started*. It is therefore no longer argued that the uprising was timed to forestall a communist coup (foreign supporters of the Nationalists were, in any case, freer with this argument than the Nationalists themselves). As Joaquín Arrarás comments: 'The documents, apocryphal or authentic, were always insignificant'.[369]

As Crozier unconsciously recognized in this narrative, 'the Nationalists' were ready to conspire from the moment that the Spanish Right, despite its overblown optimism, realized that it had lost the elections of 16 February. The 'conviction that military action was necessary' was spontaneous ('at the beginning of March') and needed no 'rapid deterioration of law and order', a process to which the forces of the Right were delighted to give their aid and encouragement.

The ambiguity of Crozier's arguments appears in the second of the paragraphs quoted just above. He is quite right in saying that the military revolt would have taken place, 'even if such documents had not appeared'. But every little bit helps. On the other hand, Crozier does not really say anything when he writes that 'the accepted Nationalist version of the facts is that these documents were found by Nationalist troops in different places after the July uprising began'. (It should be pointed out that in his original English Crozier wrote that 'the accepted Nationalist version of the facts is now that the documents were found ...'.[370] The important word 'now' was dropped by the translator, who sought to give some meaning to the phrase.) Neither myself nor any other disbeliever in the authenticity of the 'documents' ever took the trouble to doubt that copies of the 'documents' were found here and there after the outbreak of the Civil War. What I was writing in *El mito* was that the 'documents' found 'in different places after the July uprising began' were falsifications of alleged 'documents'. The controversy never centred around the problem of whether or not some 'documents' were found; it centred around the problem of the true nature of the 'documents' found. Crozier was wrong to include the word 'now' in his phrase; his 'accepted version' was not that of 'now' (1967), but that which first appeared late in 1936 and had continued even after I had published *El mito*. An example: Luis Bolín's 1967 book.

Perhaps it was the evident confusion of Crozier himself about the 'documents' that caused his translator (who had already dropped the word 'now' from Crozier's work) to reverse completely the meaning of the following phrase from Crozier's English text: '(foreign supporters of the Nationalists were, in any case, freer with this argument than the Nationalists themselves)'.[371] I do not know who used the argument most. All used it when it was thought necessary, beginning with Franco himself in August 1936. Without knowing any precise method of weighing the contents of each publication, I am inclined – after making this study – to believe that the 'documents' were used during the Civil War more outside

Spain than in the country itself, but that after the end of the Civil War, the situation was slightly reversed.

Crozier's rebuttal to the denunciation of the 'documents' is of the highest interest, for he, consciously or not, goes to one of the root causes of the Spanish Civil War: the historical, political and social ignorance of the Spanish Right, above all, of the Spanish military and the Spanish clergy. Crozier refuses to enter in the debate concerning the authenticity of the 'documents', but at the same time he assures us that Franco and many of his colleagues believed firmly in material such as that contained in the 'documents'. Crozier writes, referring apparently to the month of May 1936:

> By now, Franco, in common with a number of Nationalist leaders, was convinced that the Soviet Union had prepared precise plans for a communist uprising, and Franco Salgado quotes him as saying that despite all the difficulties that lay ahead, a military uprising was the only way left to forestall a communist takeover.[372]

And Crozier goes on to explain Franco's behaviour in this manner:

> The point that interests us here is that Franco himself was among the leading figures on the Nationalist side who believed that precise communist plans existed for the liquidation of all Army officers and men, of whatever rank, known to be anti-communist, in the event of a 'conflagration'. A copy of the communist orders to this effect, dated 6th June, is said to have fallen into the hands of the Army's intelligence service and to have reached Franco in the Canaries. He took them seriously enough to double the guard at his headquarters and order additional security measures.[373]

Crozier's authorities given here are Claude Martín and Luis de Galinsoga – General Franco Salgado. The reference to 6 June comes from Aznar via Martín, that is from Document IV.

Crozier explained the conduct of Franco and his fellow conspirators by their sincere belief in an imminent Communist seizure of power in Spain. At the same time, he wrote, in justification of the belief, as follows: 'Let us, however, be quite clear what we are talking about. In a general sense, there *was* an international communist policy for Spain. Its main lines were laid down in Moscow and its details overseen in Spain by Comintern agents. This much is beyond dispute ...'[374] But the simple fact that there was a Soviet *policy* for Spain does not, in ordinary political language, mean that there was *ipso facto* a conspiracy to overthrow the government of the Popular Front. In fact, every serious student of the European diplomatic situation in 1936 now writing inclines to the idea that the Soviet Union wanted a bourgeois-Left government in Spain, with which to collaborate on a general European front against Hitler. (Crozier, in a footnote, did refer to the arguments of Watkins and Jackson concerning the 'documents', but he did not accept these arguments, despite his references to them as 'an ingenious and thoughtful refutation of their authenticity'.)[375] What Crozier did prove, if we accept his analysis of Franco's interpretation of the political situation in Spain in the spring of 1936, is that an officer corps badly informed on politics, history and social policies can be disastrous for any country, as, indeed, it was for Spain.

On the matter of Franco's sources of political information, Crozier is helpful and loquacious. He writes that Franco revealed to him that he was for many years a fervent reader of a Geneva publication entitled *Bulletin de la Entente Internationale Anticommuniste* (also called *Bulletin de la Entente Internationale contre la III Internationale*). Crozier explains that this was the source through which Franco 'in 1928 first began a systematic study of communism and followed communist tactics in Spain throughout the life of the Second Republic'.[376] A mind formed by such literature would quite naturally have believed in the authenticity of the 'Secret Documents of the Communist Plot'. Finally, what we can learn from Crozier is that Franco helped launch the Civil War because he was ignorant of the realities of the world in which he lived. (See Part II.)

LXXII

Of the three Spanish commentators on the 'documents' in the years immediately following the publication of *El mito* in 1963, each had his peculiar importance. Arrarás was the historian with the heaviest load of 'secret documents' on his back. He had endorsed all four in 1940. Bolín was also a long-time soldier in the Franco propaganda army, but his importance for our story lies in his English heritage. He influenced and reflected the extreme Right of the English Catholics, perhaps more than he did the Spanish Right. The third man, Ricardo de la Cierva, was a high functionary in the Ministry of Information and Tourism under Fraga Iribarne when he began a well-financed effort to bring the pro-Franco propaganda on the Civil War out of its obscurantist origins into a streamlined, modern expression.[377] He failed, but the task was beyond the limits of human endeavour. His place in the history of the propaganda of the Franco regime is assured and it is of interest to contrast his techniques with those of Arrarás and Bolín.

The method of la Cierva, later an ephemeral Minister of Culture after the death of Franco, was more subtle than his elders in the work he began in 1965 to reform the bases of the Francoist justification of the military revolt of 1936. He generously gave with his left hand and then sought to take back with his right hand. He first mentioned the 'documents' in 1967 in his 738-page volume *Los documentos de la primavera trágica*; the four 'documents' concerning the 'Secret Communist Plot' were omitted, because, he wrote, after the analysis found in *El mito*, 'there is not the slightest doubt that these documents are, at the very least, debatable. The photocopy provided by Southworth seems to us to be decisive. And I do not believe it is appropriate to provide debatable documents.'[378]

Having admitted the evident falseness of Documents I and II (and with them III and IV), la Cierva argued in this fashion:

> It seems to me that to attempt to reduce the causes of the subversion and the Uprising to a dispute over papers is to take historical analysis to absurd, bureaucratic grounds. But, whoever, after evaluating the documents produced in this book, denies the clear existence of immediate aggressive aims on the part of Spanish communism during the tragic Spring could not be accused exclusively of historiographic duplicity. He will have to learn to read again.[379]

But the reduction 'of the causes of the subversion and the Uprising to a dispute over papers' was the work of the propagandists of the Spanish Rebels and not of the defenders of the Republic. The undeniable fact is that, whatever may have been the excesses of vocabulary by the partisans of Largo Caballero and the spokesmen of the Spanish Communists, the besieged intellectual defenders of the Spanish Right have never produced a single document or action that would confirm the authenticity of their charges of a Leftist attack on the government of the Popular Front. There is no doubt that some of the 'documents' in la Cierva's book can be interpreted as verbal incitations to violence, and there is no doubt that these words were never followed by plans or actions by the Spanish Left to revolt against the Spanish government. In fact, why should they have done so?

It was the Spanish Right that plotted and revolted against the legal government of the Spanish Republic. The 'Secret Documents of the Communist Plot' are an important part of the written evidence concerning the military plot. La Cierva considered them not worth printing in his volume, preferring 'irrefutable testimony'. Among the 'irrefutable' documents available to him were those which, written during the months preceding the Civil War, began appearing in the Nationalist zone late in 1936 and which constituted indisputable proofs of the authentic conspiracy to overthrow the government of the Spanish Republic. It is significant that la Cierva did not publish these papers.

Another item of possibly considerable interest in la Cierva's book was the following: 'We possess an original series of the famous documents, in the Salamanca Archive which was obtained in Madrid in November 1936 at a house on the Calle de Princesa.'[380] A comparison of the 'documents' found by la Cierva in Salamanca with those used by the *Rotbuch* and del Moral, or even other scraps known in photocopy, could be of help in unravelling the puzzle of their real origin. Unfortunately for my own research, the authorities at Salamanca are today unable to lay their hands on the la Cierva copies.[381] It is equally regrettable that la Cierva gave no further details, for example, defining exactly which 'documents' he had found, their physical condition, etc.

Two years later, in 1969, la Cierva approached again the theme of the 'documents' in his *Historia de la Guerra Civil Española. Tomo primero. Perspectivas y antecedentes. 1898–1936.* After having reviewed at some length the exposure of the 'documents' as realized in *El mito*, and admitted that 'the publication of the first two documents in the issue of *Claridad* for 30 May 1936 completely invalidates them as 'secret proof', he took his stand:

> We will not tire the reader out with further details about a matter that we have always believed to be completely trivial; we do not wish to divert him from the true historical problem with regard to the reality of communism in the Spain of 1936.

He disdained the 'documents' but he reclaimed the 'plot'.[382]

La Cierva then revealed one of the essential factors in the labyrinthine ways of the 'documents'. He stated that he believed 'to have found the person who today claims to be the author of all these documents, and he is probably the author of the first two and perhaps of the third'. Who was this person? It was 'the writer, Tomás Borrás, who wrote them in his house in Madrid and distributed them by Falangist and military means after having reproduced them with the assistance of a typist who was working precisely in the Ministry of War'.[383]

La Cierva summed up the problem of the 'documents' as follows:

> The documents, therefore, were born false, as a piece of Falangist agit-prop and were used very effectively by Spaniards and foreigners during the Civil War. For the Nationalists and their supporters, these documents were genuinely believed to be articles of faith, and in this capacity, they even influenced very genuine documents, such as the most famous document of the entire Civil War, the Bishops' Collective Letter. Prior to the Civil War, those in power paid little attention to these documents of which they were doubtlessly aware; none of the important, right-wing newspapers reproduced them. Their later influence was due not to their scientific authenticity – which did not exist – but rather to the weakness felt in the 1930s for 'secret papers' – justly pointed out by Southworth – and because many Spaniards and Europeans believed that their fear and their ideas about communism were reflected in these 'documents'.[384]

La Cierva then turned back in his tracks and wrote: 'To deny the authenticity of the documents now – and we are the first to do so – does not mean to deny the deep and very real roots of that fear and danger.'[385] La Cierva adopted, in speaking of the 'documents', the position of all the advocates of the defence of the military rebellion: the 'documents' were false, as he made more clear than did his colleagues; but the Communist menace was nonetheless there and the uprising was justified.

In attributing to Borrás the authorship of the 'documents', la Cierva did him no flattery. As has been shown throughout this study, the 'documents' were concocted by someone unlearned about the political situation in Spain, or too lazy intellectually to care about what he was doing. Borrás should have known more about the Spanish political scene in the spring of 1936 than did the author of the 'documents'. On the other hand, the 'documents' may have been written by someone so contemptuous of his eventual readers that he took no pains to produce a convincing paper. (Whoever the author might have been, he was right to do the careless job that he did, for it was accepted by so many eminent ecclesiastics, historians and journalists, and also by men of the business world.) But who were the readers sought by Borrás, or by whoever did draw up the 'documents'?

Curiously, la Cierva, whose comments I have reproduced with no significant omissions, tells us how the 'documents' were utilized *after* the outbreak of the war, but he says very little about their political existence before 18 July 1936. But it was for his pre-war reading public that Borrás was writing; certainly he never imagined the hectic career of the 'documents' after 18 July 1936. La Cierva insists that, before the war, 'none of the important, right-wing newspapers reproduced [the documents]', and that 'those in power paid little attention to these documents', of which, he added, they doubtless knew.[386] La Cierva, whose career as a propagandist was probably the most important held by anyone in Spain during the end of the Franco years, is trying to make us believe that, had, for example, *ABC* or *El Debate* thought the 'documents' important, one or the other, or both, would have revealed their secrets. But la Cierva certainly knew that the significance of the 'documents' lay completely in their 'secret' nature. Had any newspaper of the Right published them, they would have been exposed, the improbability or the impossibility of their supposed 'facts' uncovered. The power of the 'documents' lay in their surreptitious use, passed from hand to hand, furtively, never in the light of day. La Cierva insists on their 'Falangist agit-prop' origin. I am more inclined to see in all this the hand of the military conspirators, or the hands of both.

Nevertheless, la Cierva does give us the essential clue about the 'documents' in naming Borrás (and his accomplice) as the persons 'who distributed them by Falangist and military means ...'.[387] Exactly what does he mean by 'distributed'? Here, we can take a backward glance into the record of the 'documents' after the fighting had started. We are told that copies were found, during the first months of the war, in different places in Spain: near Seville, near Badajoz, in Majorca, in La Línea, and so on. Now, if the 'documents' were really sent to these provincial outposts by the supposed Leftist conspirators, these amateurish plotters were criminally careless, inasmuch as there was no valid reason whatsoever for this general distribution. (The reader can reflect on the fact that no copies of the *real* documents written by the *real* military conspirators were ever found by the Republican authorities during the war.)[388]

La Cierva gives us the explanation for this dispersal of 'secret documents' around Spain. Borrás and his helpers shipped out to the provinces bundles of copies of the 'documents', especially I, and II, perhaps III, and it was inevitable that copies be 'discovered' here and there during the war. La Cierva also furnishes us with an explanation for the many differences in the wording of the copies found in one place and in another. We can imagine a scene where the typist is seated before a typewriter, writing, while someone else dictates. Both of these persons know that absolute fidelity to the dictated text is not essential. The foreign names do not need correct spellings; it is enough that they sound like foreign names, and for many of them, that they seem Russian or Central European. Even the placing of the sentences in the paragraphs and of the paragraphs in the whole text is of slight importance. Thus we have found copies of the 'documents' with diverse ways of spelling surnames, even Spanish surnames, with lines dropped out, with paragraphs inverted, etc. The 'documents' were not held to be deathless prose by the person who reproduced them, nor were they considered to be real 'instructions' to anybody.

The various copies of the 'documents' which were found scattered around the Peninsula by the Spanish Rebels, and which were interpreted as proof of the ramifications of the 'secret Communist plot', were in reality a proof of the ignorance and the amateurishness of the propaganda factory which was at the origin of the whole story of the 'documents'.

LXXIII

Also, in 1969, there appeared in Spain a justification of the military revolt conceived on bases slightly different from those of Arrarás, Bolín or la Cierva, and on a complete acceptance of the 'documents' as falsifications. This proposal came from José María Gil Robles, who before the Civil War was the leader of the political forces of the Vatican in Spain (and of the Guelphs in Spain in the first half of the twentieth century), ideologically allied with the 'clerical fascists' of Dollfuss and others of such ilk. Gil Robles considered that the danger to Spain in the spring of 1936 came not from the Spanish Communists, but from the Spanish people; 'The real danger lay not in a movement of communist tendency but in the climate of anarchy which permeated the air on all sides.'[389]

The real danger to the Republic, of course, came not from the Spanish people, or the Spanish Communists, but more directly from the Spanish military and their right-wing political allies, such as Gil Robles. Nevertheless, Gil Robles's analysis of the 'documents' made in 1968 seems to me to have been, along with that of Bolloten, the most level-headed and well-reasoned published in Spain during the reign of Francisco Franco. The Catholic leader wrote:

> Never have I believed in the possibility of a communist rebellion at that time [the first part of 1936] and much less in the direct participation of the Komintern. Without wishing to go into the problem of clarifying the authenticity of the documentary testimony – analysed in depth, especially by Southworth – it does not appear likely that the Soviet Government favoured taking action in Spain at that time. From 1931, the Spanish Republic and the Soviet Union had not even exchanged ambassadors, although they were on the point of doing so before the 1933 elections. Faced with the threat of Hitler, Stalin was in favour of a rapprochement with England and France. The Franco-Russian Treaty and the resolutions of the VII Congress of the Third International testify that the European revolution was subordinated to the policy of containing German imperialism. And nothing could awaken greater hostility in the European democracies than the attempt to install a communist state in Spain.[390]

Gil Robles while refuting the 'documents' and the charges of the 'Communist Plot' nevertheless upheld the righteousness of the military uprising. He could hardly have done less, inasmuch as he was cognizant of the conspiracy against the legitimate government of the Republic and did nothing to avert it. He was an accomplice, and it served him little. A popular revolt was the constant nightmare of the leaders of the Spanish Right, aware of their unjust rule, but it would be difficult to plead that the 'climate of anarchy' which the Catholic chieftain thought to see all around him in the spring of 1936 would have been worse than the Civil War and the forty years of Francoism.

LXXIV

The atmosphere *fin de régime* that prevailed in Spain with the ageing and then with the death of El Caudillo seemed to draw together the die-hards of Francoism by means of a defiant plea in justification of the military insurrection, frequently accompanied by an invocation of the 'documents'. One such, published in 1975, but doubtless written before the death of Franco, was the poorly organized exposition on the 'documents' proffered by the novelist-historian José María García Escudero in the third tome of his four-volume *Historia política de las dos Españas* (1975). This author gave a highly muddled account of the uses made of the 'documents', revealing among other details the bibliographical weakness of historians of the Civil War in Spain at the time.[391] García Escudero's treatment of the problem of the 'documents' turned around the publication in *Claridad* of Documents I and II on 30 May

1936, as shown in *El mito*, and the subsequent change of heart by Hugh Thomas in his 1965 Penguin edition, and the acceptance, with reservations as already related, by R. de la Cierva of the *Claridad* argument.[392] This latter position was viewed somewhat as high treason by García Escudero, who sought to dismiss the *Claridad* argument with a question and answer. The question: 'Does its publication [in *Claridad*, 30 May 1936] constitute decisive proof of its falseness?' García Escudero's reply: 'I would not go so far; if we suppose that the documents were genuine and that there were reasons to suppose that they had fallen into enemy hands, the intelligent procedure would have been to publish them as forgeries.'[393]

Thus, after recalling la Cierva's nomination of Borrás as author of the first two 'documents', García Escudero added, 'Another matter is that there was no need to forge anything in order to convince those who were already greatly convinced and they had only to step out into the street to convince themselves still more.'[394] In defence of his position, this arch-founder of the uprising invoked the

> impressive list of orders and instructions for the revolution quoted by Maíz in his book, in such numbers and in such a way that it seems difficult to deny their authenticity, although it would be more difficult to guarantee their seriousness.[395]

And, finally, García Escudero called to his aid the conclusion of la Cierva already cited, that 'to attempt to reduce the causes of the subversion and the Uprising to a dispute over papers is to take historical analysis to absurd bureaucratic grounds',[396] and applauded the decision of the Ministry of Information functionary to discard from his anthology *Los documentos de la primavera trágica* the four 'documents' and to include the 'authentic documents', 'the circulars, instructions and reports of the Spanish Communist Party Central Committee, its members' speeches and its statements to the press'.[397] The ultra pro-Franco historian added:

> Historians who at the moment are suffering from such a strange attack of documentalism are deliberately turning their backs on the real atmosphere of those incredible months. The extremist uprising could be seen in every glance, on every corner. It was an authentic community-wide certainty. No document was required ...[398]

In his search for a substitute to take the place of the discredited 'documents', he drew the picture 'of the two trains setting off on a hopeless race to be the first to arrive'. In this case, 'the documents were fundamental', for they 'showed that the rebels did nothing more than get an advance on what their adversaries had already prepared for a set date'.[399]

On the other hand, 'if there was no such preparation, if one of the trains was stopped, then the responsibility would rest entirely with the other [the military rebels]'. García Escudero did not want to admit too much, and instead drew another picture:

> I am not saying that this has not been shown, but that a different comparison is certainly preferable: two travellers in the Argentine pampas are looking out towards the horizon and perceive the threatening approach of the floods they are expecting and suddenly realize that, little by little, the ground they are standing on has become waterlogged and the water reaches their knees and is still rising and they are forced to react without losing any time. Although there is no danger of a frontal attack. Although there is no specific plan for revolution.[400]

Above, García Escudero was quoted as referring to the lack of any need to 'forge anything in order to convince those who were already greatly convinced', and he is himself all too evidently one of those for whom, 'documents' or no 'documents', the justification of the military revolt of July 1936 is the ideological keystone. All the written proofs contrary to this justification could not budge his beliefs an inch.

LXXV

In 1976, the year after the death of Franco, two more books dealing in part with the 'documents' appeared in Spain. Both were written from the viewpoint of the armed forces on the Rebel side. They may well have been, and in all probability were, written before the death of El Caudillo. One was a fairly complete revision by B. Félix Maíz of his 1952 book *Alzamiento en España*, now titled *Mola, aquél hombre*; the other book was by José María Gárate Córdoba, who fought in the Civil War as a *Requeté* and later became an army colonel and a military historian.

Although Maíz's books are at times cited as source material, I would class them as being among the most poorly organized of those concerning the Spanish Civil War. In books where chronology is of paramount importance, chronological confusion reigns. Also, in reading Maíz's books, we must remember that before he published his first book, which appeared in 1952, the texts of the four 'documents' had already been published in Spain, singly or in diverse groupings, time and again, and all four of them had even been gathered in one single volume, the second tome of Arrarás's *Historia de la cruzada española* in 1940, that is twelve years before Maíz's first book. If the 'documents' played the role in Mola's activities that Maíz claims, then Mola was far less informed than generally supposed.

In *Alzamiento en España*, Maíz reproduced information which came from Document I and attributed it to a messenger just arrived from Paris, one 6-WIW-9, 'split personality. Spy and counterspy'.[401] This courier-spy, in Maíz's first book, reached Pamplona, Mola's headquarters, early in May, quite probably before 6 May.[402] But in this same book, other information found in Document I was said to have been furnished to Mola only on 9 May.[403] Such contradictions should place Maíz's 'documents' in the doubtful category in anyone's mind. Then, in *Mola, aquél hombre*, other material of the same nature is revealed in paragraphs apparently concerning events of 1 July, and the man known as 6-WIW-9 is not at all involved at that time,[404] although he does appear frequently elsewhere in the book, identified as an agent of Admiral Canaris of the Abwehr.[405] Also, on 1 July, there are meditations by Maíz such as:

> The danger of the final days in June passed. Who gave the order to suspend the 'Red coup'? ... Or ... would we have to wait until 1st August to go arm in arm with the French Popular Front? There was paralysis in revolutionary circles. Action, information and espionage groups came to a complete standstill.[406]

This extract from a cheap mystery novel can only mean – if we are to believe Maíz – that on 1 July Mola had feared a 'Red' revolution on 29 June, as indicated in his Document I.

In his 1952 book, Maíz, under the heading of his notes for 5 May, date of the elections of Cuenca, reproduced material from Document II, the list of the 'members of the Supreme Council of the "SPANISH SOVIET"', and he says that 6-WIW-9 left Spain with the roll of names at that time.[407] But in his second book, Maíz revealed the names of the members of the 'Spanish Soviet' only under the diary date of 1 July.[408] There is thus a difference of sixty days between one book and the other in recording the names of the members of the 'Consejo Supremo del "SOVIET ESPAÑOL"'. Nor is Agent 6-WIW-9 directly implicated in the 'documents' at this time in Maíz's second book. It is, in fact, only during the final pages of *Mola, aquél hombre* that 6-WIW-9 comes on the stage, in his new description as an agent of Canaris, collaborator of Juan de la Cierva, and of a German First World War aviation ace, expelled from the Nazi movement, turned arms merchant, Veltjens.[409] However, in his new book, Maíz has changed the sobriquet of Canaris's agent from 6-WIW-9 to 6-WIM-9.[410] And WIM is credited with having delivered, 'among his outstanding services to the Nationalist conspiracy', the names on the 'Spanish Soviet' and information contained in Document III, at an imprecise date.[411] This all forms part of the murkiness of Maíz's story.

Maíz's recital about the 'documents' is the object of a commentary by Angel Viñas, who, in his authoritative study *La alemania nazi y el 18 de julio*, while confirming Mola's relations with la Cierva and Veltjens, placed in doubt the milder extravagances of Maíz's imagination:

> So, we must assume that agent WIM did not have much luck on his mission since among the supposed services he gave to the conspiracy

were, nothing less than providing information regarding 'the meeting of the revolutionary council in Valencia on 16th May, with a complete copy of the resolutions adopted and with a list of the delegates present both at the meeting in Valencia and at the later one in Madrid on 12th June ... the list proposed to the Comintern with the names of the future Spanish Soviet ...' However, it is well-known that these documents are simply, subtle pieces of propaganda, used by the Nationalists during the war and after the war. They have absolutely no value at all.

It comes as a surprise, therefore, that Maíz chooses to revive this story and attribute the origin of the documents to no less than an agent of Canaris who did not even give them to his colleagues or to the German embassy, but did give them to the conspirators.[412]

I have already noted above a reference to information contained in Document III found in *Mola, aquél hombre*. In Maíz's first book there were several small items referring to the 'documents', but they were contradictory among themselves and then were later contradicted by Maíz himself in 1976. One, under the date of 5 May, reported that 6-WIW-9 had brought a communication which read in part as follows: 'The members of the Revolutionary Committee are given orders to meet in Valencia on 16th May.'[413] Then, under the date of 13 June – it is a frustrating experience to try to follow Maíz's dates – there was a citation from Article 9 of Document III, followed by this sentence: 'We have heard that Dimitrov, Auriol and Thorez will meet Largo Caballero and other members of the National Committee in Madrid.'[414] But it is evident that if Mola had Document III in his hands at that time (and he did, according to Maíz, have at least a good copy of the citation from Article 9), he should have known that the meeting in Madrid was allegedly scheduled for June 10.

But this account was contradicted later by Maíz himself when he wrote in 1976:

> As a result of confidencias received in the Unión Militar Español during the first ten days of the month of May, attention was given to a highly probable date quoted for a meeting of the Communist Revolutionary Council in Valencia with foreign members of the international party. It seems that the meeting was held in Valencia.
>
> And so it was. On the 16th, with a plenum of those mentioned, the following resolutions were adopted:[415]

There followed the first nine points of Document III, but not the preliminary paragraph nor the tenth point, or (j). On this detail, Maíz explained:

> One final paragraph, j), closed the council's meeting, but a tear on the copy paper which was sent to the General from Madrid renders it illeg-

ible. Some single words can be seen, such as: 'Coordination ... liaisons ... dependent organizations ...'[416]

Whereas the first nine of the points agreed upon in Valencia according to the text in Maíz's book are with slight changes, the same as in other copies of Document III, I have found in no other copy of point 10 (j) the words 'coordination' or 'dependent organizations' or their equivalents.

Maíz offered, in 1976, a curious confirmation of the meeting scheduled for Madrid on 10 June: according to Document III, it did not take place on that date, he wrote, but 48 hours later, that is on 12 June. He also addressed himself to the question: why did the projected Red uprising not take place on 29 June? His answer:

> The men were not ready. That was the main reason why the 30th [sic] June coup failed. The revolution could not rub shoulders with men who did not dare to go out into the streets with guns in their hands and death everywhere ... The internal crisis of all that intrigue delayed their action, giving more time for a Nationalist reaction to be set up to face their plans.[417]

This reasoning, based on bad faith and a faulty analysis of a non-existent situation, cannot withstand the facts of history. The Spanish working class did not shrink from the fight, and if, in some localities, they failed to seize a rifle during the first day or two of the struggle, it was because the governmental leaders, reluctant to arm the workers, refused to them the armament that the military chiefs, in places where they won immediate control, eagerly handed out to Falangists and *Requetés*.

But Maíz was not incapable of learning, at least in an instance or two, as is shown by the fact that, although in his first book he placed Bela Kum [sic] in Barcelona under the heading 14 April, in his second book at the same date, he changed Bela Kum into Erno Geroë, 'agent of Bela Kun'.[418] In Maíz's first book, at times an anti-Semitic and anti-Masonic tract, he published as an Appendix, 'textual copies of some of the provisions of the *Protocols of the Elders of Sion*'.[419] These pages are omitted from his new edition, perhaps through prudence counselled by the changing times. Nevertheless, it is instructive to find Maíz in 1952, with Francoism triumphant, proclaiming his faith in two of the most notorious political falsifications of the century.

For Maíz, his belief in the 'documents' and his confidence in the argument that the military revolt preceded the 'planned Communist uprising' but by a hairsbreadth were the two parts of a whole. Expressions confirming this joint credence, found in his two books, have already been cited. There are others, for example, this quotation from *Mola, aquél hombre*, probably concerning 2 July: 'A short distance separated the date for the joint action by the French and Spanish Popular Fronts. The Director [Mola] had proof of such a possibility. First of August?'[420]

Still another example from Maíz's 1976 book. Shortly after 14 June (Yagüe's return to Morocco), he wrote:

> Will the rumours about a Red coup be confirmed for the end of this month? Someone suggests that if this were a fact then the Nationalist uprising would not take place. 'It is possible that the date could be changed, but it is certain', said Captain Lastra last night, 'that in the North, twenty companies with twenty captains will revolt, and below, the Army of the Protectorate will join them ...'[421]

LXXVI

Another figure involved in the uprising from the first day and who defended the credibility of the 'documents' in 1976 was José María Gárate Córdoba, author of numerous works on the Civil War, and more precisely for our study, the book *La guerra de las dos Españas (Breviario histórico de la guerra del '36)*. Gárate Córdoba accepted the authenticity of the 'documents' but he did not identify them with precision, and it is not at all certain that he was referring to more than Documents I and II. Essentially, he precognized the general idea that there existed documentary proof of a 'Communist Plot', and he did not bother to go into details of this 'proof'. He wrote in his text, seeking to demonstrate that there was a contest to see who could rise up first against the Republican government – the military plotters or the Communist conspirators:

> The dates for the uprising were changed too many times, and the chronological order in which the garrisons were to rise up remains a mystery ... According to what we have been assured, the communists initially set their coup for 1st August, but when they found out that the Army was trying to get ahead of them, they decided to set it for the 21st; the secretary heard Mola say that it was for the 26th and, as a result, the Uprising was set for halfway through the month.[422]

The footnote attached to this last sentence contained Gárate Córdoba's thoughts concerning the 'documents'.

> The orders for the 'Red Revolution' of the 1st of August stirred up controversy to the point that they could be considered apocryphal. García Escudero, based on La Cierva, states that they were forgeries and that Tomás Borrás confessed to being the author, but he is writing a book on the subject and the author can now say that the radio announcer and variety artist, Pepe Medina, one day in the Spring of

1936, announced that in the Ministry of War a typist was copying some strange instructions dictated by a group in which there were two Russians. Borrás got him to make another copy for himself. He made a further printing of the three or four pages he had, at night at the Huerto press, calle Nuncio 7, which he then widely distributed. The newspaper, *Claridad*, on seeing that the orders had been discovered, tried to publicly discredit them as being a 'fascist' forgery, attempting to lay the blame on Marxism. This alibi was useful and the above has generally been believed. But the perfection of the plan reveal the General Staff's expertise in calculation, logistics, and coordination. In his book, Borrás intends to demonstrate once and for all their authenticity.[423]

Gárate Córdoba's note on the 'documents' constituted a far more formal defence of the 'documents' than did the numerous but vague references to extracts from the 'documents' found in Maíz's book. Maíz seemed completely oblivious of the polemical atmosphere that had always surrounded the different versions of the 'documents', and in fact he never referred to them as entire compositions, but quoted from time to time excerpts that in fact corresponded to items in the 'documents', but which were treated as separate scraps of information forwarded to the former Jefe de la Seguridad by a 'confidente' (informer). Gárate Córdoba, although never going into detail concerning the 'documents', did profess his confidence in the authenticity of the 'documents' of which Tomás Borrás claimed to be the author according to la Cierva (Documents I, II and perhaps III), and of which Borrás claimed to be simply the distributor in wholesale quantities according to Gárate Córdoba ('three or four pages').

Thus, Gárate adopted a position concerning the 'documents' that contradicted that of la Cierva, while at the same time he was proclaiming his admiration for the historical work of la Cierva, describing his *Bibliografía general sobre la guerra de España (1936–1939)* as 'his imposing bibliographical study'.[424] La Cierva's book is in reality an outstanding monument of the sort of unscholarly and trashy work that distinguished the intellectual product of the Franco era, save for several rare examples that appeared in the final years of the regime. Gárate's explanation for the exposure of the 'documents' in *Claridad* is merely that which was put forward by Father Toni in 1938 and it is no more convincing in 1976 than it was when first pronounced.

LXXVII

The two versions of what Borrás did in the spring of 1936 are contradictory. The more believable is that supported by la Cierva, in which Borrás wrote the 'documents' and then distributed them throughout Spain. Gárate's account is more complicated, more melodramatic. There we have two of the standard characters for the espionage story, the 'pair of Russians', who apparently were working in the Ministry of War in the full light of day. The Minister of War after 13 May was Casáres Quiroga, hardly considered to have been a person with a bloody knife between his teeth. Borrás's first story of having as his helper a stenographer from the War Ministry is far more credible. Then Borrás, according to Gárate, had copies 'printed' which he 'widely distributed' throughout Spain. But all of the copies ever shown in photocopy have been written on typewriters and never in printed form. Surely, if printed copies had been distributed 'widely' one copy would have surfaced in the more than sixty years since 1936. Moreover, if the 'documents' were to be presented as 'secret', it would seem unlikely that they would have been handed around in printed form. But then the physical task of writing a thousand sheets, even including copies, would have been a long and tiring job. On the other hand, the fact that there are so many differences within the texts, in the spelling of the proper names and the geographical places, in the disposition of sentences and paragraphs, would definitely rule out the theory of a single printed edition.

To whom were these printed copies of Tomás Borrás's work 'distributed'? Did Borrás keep a copy of the original of the 'strange instructions'? Or of the printed instructions? Again, if Borrás had wanted to alert Spanish public opinion to the coming danger, it would seem that his normal reaction would have been to arrange for publication of the 'documents' under headlines in *ABC* or *El Debate*. Instead, he kept them seemingly secret, which was the most effective manner in which to use a falsification. And if, as Gárate insists, the 'perfection of the plan reveals the expertise of the General Staff in calculation, logistics, coordination', the authors could have been military plotters more logically than Communist conspirators.

The argument for discarding the hypothesis of Borrás as author of the 'documents' lies in the stupidity of the Spanish and European political references found in Documents II and III, and even in Document I. Was Borrás so ill-informed about Spanish politics? How could a Spanish journalist with any knowledge of the Spanish political scene in the spring of 1936 have composed these absurdities? Because he thought his eventual readership was too naive or too ignorant to detect the contradictions and the improbabilities? But if so many supposedly knowledgeable persons such as Cardinal Gomá, Jacques Bardoux, Douglas Jerrold, Arnold Lunn, the Comte de Saint-Aulaire, Robert Sencourt, Arthur F. Loveday, Robert Brasillach, Maurice Bardèche, Richard Pattee, Jesús María Iribarren, Félix B. Maíz, José Díaz de Villegas, Manuel Aznar, Eduardo Comín Colomer, Professor Luis García Arias, Professor Salvador de Madariaga, Professor Hugh Thomas, Luis Bolín and Colonel Gárate Córdoba expressed belief in their authenticity, it is hardly surprising that Borrás's provincial clients, or even those in Madrid and Barcelona should have paid them equal attention.

LXXVIII

In 1980, the novelist-historian, Luis Romero, who jumped about intellectually much in the manner of la Cierva and Crozier, referred to the 'documents' ambiguously in his book *Cara y cruz de la República, 1931–1936* as follows:

> The international conspiracy which was preparing for a proletarian rebellion for August and which was offered as justification for the military uprising, has been fully disproved; the documents were falsifications and can be attributed to propaganda and provocative hoaxes. It can be stated that no such fixed-term revolutionary plans existed, and that the documents which were later produced were quite inadequate, even as falsifications.[425]

Romero went on to pronounce this verdict:

> That political and trade union forces, with power and influence and revolutionary ability, as had been shown in Asturias, should intend to overthrow the bourgeois government and establish a proletarian dictatorship is something that is likewise proven, to the point that a refusal to admit it would be equivalent to denying the evidence.[426]

Romero then quoted from a speech by the Communist Antonio Mitje delivered around the middle of May 1936. That this 'evidence' is elusive can be deduced from the words of Romero that follow: 'What must be found out and what is difficult to clarify is the proportion of verbalism and effective projects in the boasts made in public about the revolutionary plans.'[427] Romero therefore had no 'evidence' that justified his previous affirmation, and we can easily 'deny the evidence'. Moreover, he himself continued in this fashion: 'If a more or less generalized revolutionary coup had taken place, an even stronger edition than that of October 1934, unforeseeable situations would have been reached, unforeseeable at that time and now difficult even to imagine.'[428]

The feeble argument of Romero, who tries to justify the Franco rebellion by appealing to the theoretical possibility that Spanish 'revolutionaries' might have been seeking to overthrow the Popular Front government, is an exemplary manifestation of the problem facing the *Franquistas* when they write about the 'Secret Documents of the Communist Plot'.

Romero tried another ploy when he mentioned Maíz's *Mola, aquél hombre*. Maíz, he wrote, in continuing to express belief in the reality of the international Left conspiracy, was merely showing how widespread among a large number of civilians and military personnel was the sentiment that all they were doing in conspiring and rebelling was to 'anticipate' an insurrection from the Left.[429] Thus, the political intoxication based on ignorance and obscurantism could justify the action of the 1936 military rebels.

LXXIX

In 1984, a historian, Luis Suárez Fernández mentioned the 'documents'. After referring to Crozier, Franco-Salgado, the Entente Internacional Anticomunista, *Mundo Obrero* and speeches by Largo Caballero, Suárez Fernández gave this opinion:

> We do not intend here to enter into the controversy of whether the documents furnished by Loveday in 1939 about the communist plan of rebellion for that summer are genuine or not. In a case of doubt, such as this, the historian must remain silent.[430]

Suárez Fernández then recommended García Escudero's analysis of the 'documents'.

LXXX

I refuse the sophistry of Arrarás, la Cierva, Crozier, Romero, Suárez Fernández and such. A true historian in the place of la Cierva would have included the 'documents' among the significant historical papers of the spring of 1936 – among the most significant. The fact that the 'documents' were faked from the beginning does not eliminate them from the scrutiny of the historian. When a counterfeiter presents false merchandise at the bank, and trickery is discovered, the affair does not end with a joyous shout of 'Well played!' Documents I, II, III and IV did not have the value that their manufacturers and distributors assigned to them. They were counterfeit for this reason, but this false quality does not keep them from existing. They are historical documents. They played a role in the preparations for the assault against the legally elected government of the Spanish Republic and, later, in the international propaganda campaigns of the Nationalists, during and after the Civil War.

The mere fact that the 'documents' cannot today be used against the Spanish Left of 1936 does not constitute a valid reason for excluding them from the history books – once they are placed where they belong, labelled and identified. Now that we know the general history of the 'documents', they become documents in fact, and are no longer the pseudo-documents that they always were when being fraudulently manipulated by the Nationalists and their supporters. They are no longer propagandistic evidence in the hands of the Spanish Right against the Spanish Left of 1936. They are historical evidence in the accusations of the Spanish Left against the Spanish Right of 1936. It is not difficult to understand why la Cierva, Crozier and others prefer to forget about them, as they prefer today to forget about many other things. I have been, over the years, accumulating these details precisely because I believe they should not be forgotten: the 'Secret Documents of the Communist Plot' remain one of the key exhibits in the exposition entitled: Conspiracy Against the Republic.

LXXXI

One explanation for the attempts by Franco apologists to throw the 'documents' into the trash can of history is quite probably their realization that the 'documents' vividly illustrate, among other things, the intellectual mediocrity of Franco's partisans. Even Romero felt the need to acknowledge that the 'documents' were 'quite imperfect even as falsifications'. That a paranoical anti-Communist malady had pervaded the extreme Right of Western Europe and, to some extent, North America before the outbreak of, and during, the Second World War is evident to readers of this book. Does it not also underline the cultural decline of that Right and of such ageing institutions as the Roman Catholic Church?

Most of the manipulators of the 'documents' undoubtedly believed in their genuineness. But what, then, are we to conclude concerning the knowledge possessed and the intelligence exercised by these persons? The effectiveness of the 'documents' seems to have been most profound in Western Europe and North America. Merwin K. Hart was a nonentity on the American scene. The American Catholic Church – hardly renowned for its cultural accomplishments – although it was the prime mover of pro-Franco propaganda in the United States, did not apparently try to sell the 'documents' to its clients. The man responsible for first publicizing the 'documents' in the United States, Seward Collins, had in all probability continuing relations with some international network of pro-Fascist propaganda, as had Merwin K. Hart. Richard Pattee was at one time, as I have pointed out, a high functionary of the United States Department of State.

The public for the 'documents' was apparently much larger in Europe. England provided the largest cast of protagonists for sponsoring the falsifications. Jerrold was the editor of a respected right-wing monthly, *National Review*, and the leading figure in the publishing house Eyre and Spottiswoode. Robert Sencourt possessed a firm reputation in English conservative and monarchist historical circles. Loveday, the most persistent advocate of the 'documents', was a conservative businessman, perhaps without great intellectual pretensions, but he did serve as correspondent for *The Times* in Chile from 1914 to 1920 and as correspondent for the *Morning Post* from 1927 to 1933, and was the author of several published works.[431] Lunn was a prolific writer on popular Catholic issues and a skiing enthusiast.

Jacques Bardoux, the French flag-bearer for the propaganda campaign on the 'documents', was a well-considered personality on the French Right, *Membre de l'Institut*, a frequent contributor to such pillars of conservative thought as the *Revue des Deux Mondes* and the *Revue de Paris*. The Comte de Saint-Aulaire, *Ambassadeur de France*, had served the Quai d'Orsay in Madrid and other capitals for many years. A historical work by 'Georges-Roux' was honoured by the Academie Française. Robert Brasillach, who was executed by the French government for collaboration after the Second World War, is still considered one of the intellectual luminaries of the extreme Right in France.

Cardinal Gomá was, for all the obscurantism of his thought and writings, Primate of Spain. Fathers Constantino Bayle and Teodoro Toni were well known pamphleteers of the Society of Jesus in Spain. Arrarás, Iribarren, Aznar, Comín Colomer, Ferrari Billoch, Bolín, Maíz and their likes were honoured writers and journalists who played up to a public based generally on the church or the army.

I see no reason to believe that all of these persons – the Primate, the ambassador, the businessman, the *Membre de l'Institut*, the prominent editor, the State Department functionary, the hack writer – that all of them did not sincerely believe in the authenticity of the 'documents'.

LXXXII

If I have demanded, kind readers, so much of your time and patience in relating the avatars of the 'Secret Documents of the Communist Plot' it was because I know of no other method for giving you the full volume of the story. I had the choice of writing it in detail in more than a hundred pages or of condensing it in a long paragraph. I have evidently chosen the first solution.

The propaganda campaigns based on the 'Secret Documents of the Communist Plot' were curious, perhaps unique, particularly in the history of the propaganda of our times: they had two, even three manifestations. It is now my considered opinion, after studying the evidence shown in this volume, that the 'documents' were conceived in the spring of 1936 by persons close to the military conspirators. The authors were beyond any doubt aware of the military plot, and saw in the 'documents' an arm of psychological warfare. The 'documents' were distributed clandestinely inside Spain during the months preceding the uprising, to influence the military caste – I suspect, especially among the junior officers – and the timorous bourgeoisie, and to prepare the general atmosphere in Spain for an acceptance of the necessity for the rebellion. Since it is likely that bundles of copies dispatched to provincial capitals were, in turn, copied again locally, one can imagine in the thousands the actual number of copies typewritten and distributed.

This was the first life of the 'documents', one usually confined to the limits of Spain. Documents I and II seem to have been those most frequently used, with Document III lagging behind quite a bit. This may have been a mere matter of distribution. Document IV could have been intended for a more restricted, professional category of readers, not necessarily Spanish.

Despite the considerable number of quotations, extracts and reproductions given for the four 'documents', I have undoubtedly failed to unearth a certain number – perhaps in South America and in the North American Catholic press – but I flatter myself that I have discovered enough material to give to the readers a general idea of the development of the usages of the 'documents'.

LXXXIII

The second career of the 'documents' was purely accidental. It began with the failure of the *pronunciamento* and the prolongation of what had become the Civil War. We do not really know how the 'documents' were presented to their furtive readers in Spain before the outbreak of the Civil War, but it is not difficult to imagine the confidential phrases employed. Now, after 18 July 1936, the prefatory arguments were produced in the full light of day, and they were utilized in London, Paris and New York (also in Berlin and Rome) more frequently than in the Spanish provinces. It is true that the del Moral 'documents' were for thirty years a diplomatic secret, but they soon fell into the public domain via Jerrold, Bardoux, the Friends of National Spain, Loveday, etc., once the diplomatic ploy had failed. The objective behind the distribution of the 'documents', once the war had lasted a few months, was to show that Franco, a true democrat, had risen in rebellion only when it was the sole recourse remaining for Spain to be saved for Western Civilization and Christianity against the Asiatic Hordes. This second life of the 'documents' lasted more or less until 1963, when the pre-war publication of Documents I and II in the Madrid press was revealed.

LXXXIV

The third appearance of the 'documents' developed after 1963, when last-ditch defenders of the Franco cause accepted the falsity of the 'documents' simply as a hook on which to hang their arguments in favour of the 'Communist Plot', documented or not. Or even, still insisting on the validity of the 'documents', they mentioned the charges against them in order to proclaim their historical 'facts', to show that the 'documents' were authentic whatever proofs existed to the contrary. The sleight of hand was rendered possible by the refusal to take into consideration the 1936–1939 position of the Soviet Union in favour of a French–English–Soviet Union pact against the Hitler regime, that is by a refusal to study the international reality of the period in which the Spanish Civil War took place. This refusal was aided by the lack of neutral or non-Fascist interpretations of the

European, international history of the period available for readers in Spain during the Franco era. So, despite the detailed analysis of the 'documents' that I have demonstrated in the preceding pages, I am afraid that for so long as the Spanish Right and the Spanish armed forces will feel the need to justify the *Alzamiento*, there will come forward credulous minds to express their belief in the 'Secret Documents of the Communist Plot'. Logic and reason will little avail against them.

LXXXV

Concerning the dates for the composition of the 'documents', if we discard the idea that they were written by a Spanish Eric Ambler or John Le Carré of the epoch – let us remember that there is absolutely nothing in the photographic reproductions of Documents I, II and III to show that they were not really extracts from an espionage novel – and adopt the obvious position that they were composed for internal propaganda in Spain, we can, as already suggested, fix quite approximate dates for Documents I to III. Document I was written before 3 May 1936; Document II, between 7 April and 10 May. Since Documents I and II were published in Madrid on 30 May 1936, they were certainly written before that date. From its contents, we must conclude that Document III was produced between 16 May and 10 June. It is difficult to pinpoint the dates for Document IV. According to several Spanish Rebel sources, it was known in Spain before the outbreak of the Civil War, even in April 1936.

Did Borrás write the 'documents', or more possibly did he write I and II, and perhaps III? I do not really know. There are numerous errors of nomination among the Spanish and other political persons mentioned. Not all of these can be attributed to the mistakes of a typist. We certainly do not possess in the del Moral–*Rotbuch* photocopies an original of Documents I, II or III. There are unforgivable errors in these three 'documents', in the spelling of Spanish words and Spanish names. It is difficult to accept the fact that the original copy was so stupidly composed. But there are other errors in these 'documents'; there are mistakes in political affiliations, rendering Document II unbelievable and Document III downright silly. The faults in spelling can be put to the charge of the typist, but not the whole composition of the 'Soviet Nacional' in Document II, nor the names of the international conspirators in Document III. These contradictions have at times led me to suspect a non-Spanish origin (although a Spaniard might easily have been responsible for the untrustworthy lists of the Spanish plotters), but I have been unable to find even a slight suggestion of such a source, either in the publications of the Entente Internationale contre la III Internationale,[432] of Geneva, or of the Anti-Comintern[433] of Berlin. For lack of alternative candidates, let us assume that the author of at least Documents I and II, and perhaps III, was Borrás.

Whether Borrás or another author conceived the 'documents', I am strongly inclined to believe that Documents I, II and III were drawn up by the same person or by the same team of persons. It also seems to me to be highly possible that Document IV had another source, perhaps more military and less political. All four 'documents' at their inception were intended to serve but one purpose: to brainwash slow-thinking elements of the Spanish Right in the psychological preparations for the military putsch. Later the field of operations for the 'documents' was extended to all of Western Europe and to the Americas, from 1936 to 1963. Since then, the employment of the 'documents' has apparently been limited to Spain itself.

LXXXVI

It is of primordial interest to observe that the problem of the 'documents' (of their origins and legitimacy), which began in the Peninsula, then had a long and poisonous growth outside Spain, has now returned to its native ground. It seems to me evident that propaganda 'facts' thrive for only so long as their usefulness continues to serve a cause that is vital, or thought to be such. The propaganda campaigns of the First World War, for example, notably that sponsored by British information services, which placed in accusation the conduct of the German Army in Belgium, hardly outlived the war itself.

The propaganda battles that centred around the 'Secret Documents of the Communist Plot' were among those of the present century that have had the most vitality, the most enduring lives, the most frequent reappearances. Why were these pieces of paper published, discussed, defended and attacked with so much ardour for so long a time (and even today they serve as a point of reference in polemical books on the Civil War), when they so obviously present absolutely no credibility? The explanation is that the thesis involved was considered necessary for the Franco cause. This thesis was: the Communist menace to Spain justified the Franco uprising. There were three methods of trying to prove that the menace existed: (1) by the 'Secret Documents of the Communist Plot'; (2) by a serious study of the political situation in Spain in 1936; and (3) by a rigorous political analysis of the European and international situations.

The best proof was obviously the 'Secret Documents of the Communist Plot', if these were indisputably documentary evidence. The 'documents' were far from complying with this simple definition but they were able to serve in the special clandestine operations involving the 'documents' during the weeks preceding the Civil War. If we can judge by the quality of the 'documents', nobody engaged in the conspiracy was capable of turning in a serious study paper on either the second or third method: on either Spanish internal political problems or on the European and International political scenes in the spring of 1936. Had such persons existed and had they done their work well, they would have produced reports of little use for the arguments of the conspirators. The 'documents' were all that the conspirators had, but they could have been composed with more competence.

Once the *pronunciamiento* had gone into the stage of Civil War, the propaganda area involved spread beyond the limits of Spain. These propagandists, usually volunteers, who now came to the defence of the Rebel cause in England, France and elsewhere (but also in Spain) found copies of the 'documents'. These were trashy proofs of nothing, but the new advocates of the Franco rebellion, usually moved by Catholic-inspired anti-Communism, were even less well equipped to recognize the intrinsic worthlessness of the 'documents' than theoretically were Borrás and his fellow workers. Anyway, the foreign champions of the Franco cause had only the 'Secret Communist Plot Documents', Documents I, II, III and IV, to work with.

Still, their acceptance of this flimsy material can be considered to show that they realized that the secondary evidence extracted from speeches by Communist leaders and Largo Caballero was not so convincing as a 'document' on paper, however weak its contents might be.

As for the arguments based on analyses of the Soviet position toward the European situation in 1936, and the Soviet search for a united front against Hitler, these elements were never, to my knowledge, brought up by any spokesman of the Spanish Right, except in that quoted above by Gil Robles in 1966 (who was then a spokesman for whom?), and he confirmed what Ramos Oliveira and Cattell had already written. It was inconceivable that the Soviet Union could favour a Communist uprising in Spain in 1936. (In 1967, Bolín had come up with the most original comment on such an event: the Spanish Communists were indifferent to the wishes of the Soviet Union.)

LXXXVII

Why was the need for the justification of the uprising viewed as so basic and necessary by the champions of the rebellion? We must not forget that Spain had been contaminated by the ideas of the French Revolution, despite the defeat of Napoleon by the combined forces of England and the reactionary elements of Spain, with the Catholic Church in the avant-garde. The overthrow of the legally elected government of the Popular Front by dissident generals and colonels was difficult to defend, in Spain and in Western Europe or in the Americas. But the 'documents' reversed the diagram: it was the Leftist forces of Spain, Largo Caballero (the 'Spanish Lenin') first of all who had planned to revolt against the Popular Front, and the Spanish military had merely reacted to forestall the 'Communist' revolt. That this argument would not withstand five minutes of intelligent scrutiny is beside the point; the Spanish Right wanted to believe in the argument and no one took the time to study its contradictions.

LXXXVIII

Why have the arguments incorporated into the 'documents' been able to survive through their various metamorphoses of place and time for so many years? Why do they still have a certain propaganda value? It is because the war in which they made their initial appearance has not ended. The basic theses of the 'documents' are still expounded during the intermittent skirmishes.

The Spanish Civil War was essentially class warfare. The propaganda used by the Right during the war, of which the arguments founded on the 'documents' were a key element, may continue to appear now and then whenever the class struggle becomes acute. The Spanish Right will not for decades desist from its efforts to justify the armed rebellion of 1936. The present armistice of 'national reconciliation' is just that – an armistice. This situation is evident in the Rightist propaganda of today, denigrating the wartime Republic and its leaders, and justifying the military revolt and forty years of Francoism. There is also the propaganda of epidemic proportions in praise of repentant Falangists and others of that sort, such as Ridruejo, Tovar, Areilza and so forth.[434] While eulogies are showered upon erstwhile defenders of the 'new order' of Adolf Hitler, those who fought against Fascism are unremembered and their names are considered obscenities. The name of Juan Negrín is never spoken.[435]

Not everybody had a bad time while Franco was in power. After all, the Civil War gave to the Spanish Right forty years in which to plunder the Peninsula.

LXXXIX

Pierre Vilar has written perceptively: 'Any analysis of the Spanish war that is not an analysis of the class struggle on a worldwide scale will have no significance.'[436] This statement is applicable to the problem presented by the 'Secret Documents of the Communist Plot'. In their first, pre-Civil War phase, they were an element of the Class War inside Spain itself. During the Civil War and for years afterwards, by their utilization as propaganda in many foreign countries, they became, as Pierre Vilar wrote, engaged in 'the class struggle on a worldwide scale'. Then, with the death of Franco and the gradual return to democracy in Spain, the problems of the Spanish Civil War withdrew into Peninsular borders, where the 'Secret Documents of the Communist Plot' continue from time to time, to reflect the class struggle in Spain.

The existence of the 'Secret Documents of the Communist Plot', and in fact the whole episode of the Spanish Civil War, can be attributed to the gut conviction of the Right in Western Europe and elsewhere that the political parties of the Socialist–Communist–Marxist variety have no right to win an election and take power. They are permitted to participate in elections (sometimes) but are not supposed to win. No political personality of our epoch epitomized more clearly or more brutally this manner of viewing democratic electoral processes south of the Rio Grande than did President Ronald Reagan.

It can hardly surprise my readers that, more than sixty years after the false document of the 'Zinoviev Letter', Ronald Reagan should also present a false 'document' to world opinion. I cite the following from an article published in *El País*, Madrid's foremost daily, dated 17 November 1985 and signed by the newspaper's Washington correspondent, Francisco G. Basterra:

> Since becoming President, Reagan has been repeating a false quotation from Lenin in which, allegedly, the father of the Soviet revolution states: 'We will take over Eastern Europe. We will organize the masses in Asia. We will move into Latin America and will not need to take over the United States. It will fall into our hands like ripe fruit.' One of Gorbachov's main advisors had to angrily appear on American television to announce that Lenin had never said these words.
>
> The White House, surprised because after searching among Lenin's books and speeches in the Library of Congress, was unable to find the quotation and had to admit a few weeks ago that it was apocryphal material. It was never used by Lenin and the President borrowed it from the *Blue Book* of the John Birch Society, an extreme right-wing organization.

I have no reason to doubt the good faith of President Reagan. I am certain that he believed in the authenticity of his quotation. I am also persuaded that, while yielding to the evidence that the quotation in itself was false, he was also convinced of the reality of his own 'Communist Plot', as were the numerous personalities who sponsored the 'Secret Documents of the Communist Plot'.

The 'Communist Plot' is a far too useful weapon in the war between the classes to be easily abandoned.

Part II

The brainwashing of Francisco Franco

I

In referring to Brian Crozier's life of Franco and to his remarks concerning the 'Secret Documents of the Communist Plot', in the first part of this book, I mentioned also the work and publications of the Geneva-based Entente Internationale Anticommuniste (EIA). Crozier attributed to this organization a dominant influence on the vision held by Franco – and other high-ranking officers of Spain's military forces – of the political, social and economic problems of their time. I have since then found sufficient other references to the EIA and to Franco's relations with it to convince me of the validity of Crozier's opinion on this point.

I now recognize that the propaganda of the EIA (bulletins, meetings, etc.) was quite different from that of the 'Secret Documents of the Communist Plot'. The 'Secret Documents' originated as a form of *disinformation*, propaganda intended by the authors to mislead those who received the information. This form of propaganda was exactly in the mould of the 'Protocols of the Elders of Zion'. The authors knew that the documents presented to the public were false. However, in the case of the publications of the EIA, the authors believed in the exactness and integrity of what they published and said. Dominated by their religious, social, political and, finally, racial prejudices, they were as much victims as were those who read, heard and believed the outpourings of the Entente.

In the light of present-day Spanish Civil War historiography, the work of the Entente was far more effective in Spain itself than was that of the 'Secret Documents'. Unknown to the Spanish public at large, the EIA's arguments and positions were efficacious because they were targeted, insofar as their Spanish readership was concerned, on a small élite group of high military officers. The publications of the EIA were not discussed by the press or in public debate, cases in which better educated, better informed minds could easily have exposed the shallowness of the Entente's facts and arguments.

Even before agents of the Spanish military began brainwashing naive Spanish Rightists with multi-copied versions of the 'Secret Documents' in the months just before the outbreak of the Civil War, highly placed officers of the Spanish armed services were themselves being brainwashed by the EIA with propaganda of a totally different Communist plot.

II

I am now returning to that part of Crozier's book in which he wrote of what Franco said to him about the Entente. Crozier, after one of his conversations with Franco, concluded that the General's introduction to the Geneva publication was one of the most significant events of his life during 1928, an event equal in importance to the birth of his daughter Carmencita. But whereas the birth of his daughter brought joy to Franco, the information from Geneva carried by the bulletins of the EIA brought only 'knowledge and a spur to action – the knowledge of an enemy, and the ambition to defeat him'.[1]

Crozier's text is of the greatest interest, for it was based on what Franco told him. It was published during the Caudillo's lifetime; it has never been repudiated. On the contrary, it has been confirmed again and again. Concerning Franco and the EIA, Crozier wrote:

> For it was in 1928 that Franco, whose experiences of 1917 had already alerted him to the danger of Bolshevism, first began a systematic study of communism. He started subscribing to a Swiss anti-communist publication, the *Bulletin de la EIA* – the journal of the *Entente Internationale Anticommuniste*, of Geneva, whose President was the late National Councillor Aubert.
>
> It was Franco himself who mentioned the bulletin to me, saying that he had been a subscriber for many years and, through it, had had access to much material about the Comintern which few people bothered to study. That way, he followed communist tactics in Spain throughout the life of the Second Republic.[2]

Crozier informs us of the considerable weight that this reading had on Franco's manner of viewing the political scene in Spain:

> He was aware, for instance, that the Spanish Communists were under orders to foment strikes and violence, in order to provoke repressive measures by the authorities. This, he said, enabled the Socialist deputies to make speeches in the Cortes calling for the banning of the *Guardia Civil* and for further cuts in the Army.[3]

Franco was an active subscription agent for the *Boletín*, according to Crozier:

Until the Civil War began, Franco never missed an issue of the bulletin, and he was careful to notify the publishers of his changes of address when he transferred to the Balearics and to the Canaries. Moreover, he persuaded certain other officers to subscribe to it. As a result, he claims, the events of 1936 did not come as a surprise to them, and they were ready to deal with the Communists.[4]

III

Franco was, it would seem, in the years before 1967, the date of publication of Crozier's biography, quite preoccupied with recollections of his relationship with the Entente. In that same year, another biography of Franco appeared, written by George Hills, who was, like Crozier, a journalist. Hills also mentioned Franco's connection with a Geneva propaganda organization, but he did not give its name. Hills' book on Franco, like Crozier's, was a highly sympathetic treatment of El Caudillo, and of the latter's view of the world and communism.[5]

Hills wrote, concerning Franco's point of view in 1928: 'Henceforth, he saw it as his responsibility that he should prepare young men for the battle he already begun to see ahead. And ... now as a General began to take an ever greater interest in politics, economics and social problems.'[6] Franco stated to Hills:

It was while I was director of the Zaragoza Military Academy that I began to receive regularly a Review of Comintern Affairs from Geneva. Later I discovered that Primo de Rivera had taken out several subscriptions and thought I might be interested in it. I was. It gave me an insight into international communism – into its ends, its strategy and its tactics. I could see communism at work in Spain, undermining the country's morale, as in France.[7]

Franco told Hills that the Communist propaganda then circulating in the Spanish army was ineffective because it was a translation of material originally written for use in France. Franco viewed the problem of Communism always with regard to France, as did the Swiss-based Entente.

His worry was what might be going on under the surface, particularly among officers and N.C.O.s, not the leaflets and pamphlets confiscated from time to time in barracks ... Franco was already becoming aware that there were other groups of individuals to whom a later age would give the names of crypto-Communist and fellow-travellers. It was the flank attack and not the frontal feint that he considered dangerous.[8]

Hills presents to his reader a Franco with his nose always buried in a serious book. Speaking of his strike-breaking activities in Oviedo in 1917, Franco told him:

> I came to ask myself what it was that drove people, ordinary decent people, to strike action and acts of violence, and I saw for myself the appalling conditions under which employers were making people work – but as I deepened my enquiries I began to see that no easy solutions were possible. So I began to read books on social questions, on political theories and economics, to search out some solution. Those put forward by socialists and anarchists could lead only to chaos and to an even worse state of affairs than the ills they sought to remedy.[9]

It should have been quite easy for Franco to realize that the scenes he was describing, in which 'ordinary decent people' were brought to 'strike action and acts of violence' were simply scenes of class warfare. It must be underlined that Franco viewed a strike by working men to protest against what Franco himself called 'the appalling conditions under which employers were making people work' as inadmissible conduct, as he showed in 1917.

Hills himself added this to the above quotation, 'Franco thereafter became well-known for his reading of books into the early hours of the morning.'[10] Writing about Franco during the first years of the Republic, Hills described him as 'a general who was known to spend his free time, when not riding, fishing or shooting, in the reading of history and book after book on politics and economics, and to have done so for many years'.[11] In support of this affirmation, Hills gave a footnote, which in no way clarifies in any detail Franco's bookish interests, but does confirm his addiction to reading the bulletins of the EIA: 'He took out a personal subscription to the bulletins on Soviet affairs from Geneva, when, with the advent of the Republic, the subscription would no longer be borne by the Government (conversation with author).'[12]

Either Franco was mixed up in his dates, or Hills misunderstood him. The Republic continued to pay for Franco's subscription to the EIA bulletins for three years and it was only on 16 May 1934 that Franco personally subscribed to the EIA publications, in a letter written in faulty French. If the letter had been an official one, it seems probable that Franco would have used the services of a functionary who knew French better than did the General, but this letter was doubtless private and secret, although the letterhead was that of 'General Francisco Franco'. The letter reads as follows:

Palma de Mallorca (Spain) 16 May 1934
Secretary of the Entente International against the III Internationale

Sir:

I have learned of the great work which you are carrying out for the defense of all nations against communism, and I should like to receive, each month, your highly interesting bulletins of information, so well documented and so efficacious. I wish to cooperate, in our country, with your greatest enterprise and to be informed about such questions. I shall be grateful if you will let me know the conditions under which I may receive each month your bulletins.

Please accept, Sir, my admiration for your great enterprise and my gratitude.

I am very truly yours,

(signed) Francisco Franco

Address: General Francisco Franco, Military Commander of the Baleares[13]

Hills did not quite understand the nature of the EIA *Bulletin*. It was not so much a 'Bulletin about Soviet affairs' of a serious character, as might seem to be the case in view of the text which preceded the note, but could rather be described as a publication which, while specializing in references to, and articles on, the Soviet Union, was also the outspoken defender of all regimes and political organizations with reactionary, ultra-Rightist programmes, in Europe and the Americas and in the European colonies. It was this opposition to social change which appealed to Franco and his fellow officers, and it is precisely this fact which is important for us today.

IV

Hills nowhere gives his readers the titles of the books which Franco was so busily engaged in reading in his free moments. Crozier is hardly more explicit, writing that at this same period Franco 'now set about conscientiously improving his education and widening his technical and theoretical grasp of military science'. He adds:

He devoured books that seemed likely to contribute to the educative needs of a higher officer in a country where there is no tradition of divorce between the armed forces and politics. History and sociology, politics and science, seasoned the inevitable diet of military works and periodicals.[14]

We can glean from Crozier one subject of Franco's reading and one title: the future Caudillo was 'fascinated by works on Napoleon' – a detail offered to Crozier by Joaquín Arrarás – and another item which confirms the first, found by Crozier in the biography of Franco by S.F.A. Coles, to the effect that during the Civil War, 'Franco sent a special emissary into Republican territory to secure a copy of Machiavelli's *The Prince*, annotated by Napoleon.'[15]

The vague and imprecise references to Franco's reading by Crozier and Hills leave us, nevertheless, with one clear fact: Franco was an assiduous reader of the bulletins of the EIA.

Nowhere did Hills mention the title of the publications that Franco had received from Geneva, dealing with 'Soviet affairs'. This title was in French. Hills possessed a complete mastery of the Spanish language; his mother was Spanish-speaking and he was born in Mexico. Crozier, however, while born in Australia, grew up in France and spoke French fluently. These details probably explain why Crozier gave to his readers the name of the Entente, and Hills merely implied the existence of an unnamed entity. To resume the circumstances of their engagement with Franco's biography, one can say: Crozier sympathized fundamentally with Franco because of the visceral anti-Marxism common to both men; Hills, on the other hand, was attracted by Franco's strong Catholic convictions, which he ardently shared.[16]

But what I want to emphasize now is that both biographers, Crozier and Hills, considered the *Bulletin de la Entente Internationale Anticommuniste* to have had a determining influence on the political direction of Franco's thinking.

V

If my sources are complete, it was then to two non-Spanish journalist-historians – Crozier, a Britisher born in Australia, and Hills, an Englishman born in Mexico – that Franco first revealed his relations with the EIA. Since Franco's death, other details concerning Franco and the EIA have been published by Professor Luis Suárez Fernández, a highly conservative Spanish historian, who has published eight volumes bearing the title *Francisco Franco y su tiempo*. If Franco had revealed his rapport with the Entente to anyone previously to his talks with Hills and Crozier, the fact was unknown to Suárez Fernández, whose work is based on material found in the Fundación Nacional Francisco Franco. Suárez Fernández remarked in a footnote that 'in private conversations with his biographers, Crozier ... and Hills ... the Caudillo referred to this publication [*Bulletin de l'Entente Internationale Anticommuniste*] as being important'.[17]

Suárez Fernández, as I shall show farther on, made numerous other references to the EIA. The first volume of his work contains eleven chapters; chapter 10 is headed 'L'Entente Internationale Anticommuniste'.[18] Of the twenty-six pages in the chapter, hardly one concerns the EIA,[19] but the title of the chapter demonstrates the importance given by Suárez Fernández to the EIA in Franco's life.

Suárez Fernández himself is too befuddled concerning the chronology of Franco's connections with the Entente to serve us usefully as a guide, but he does possess information that can be beneficial if correctly interpreted and controlled. For example, he situated Franco's first contacts with the EIA, as had Crozier and Hills, 'Between 1928 and 1931', emphasizing a few lines farther on this phrase: 'Let us remember the fact. From 1929 Francisco Franco had shown himself to be a determined enemy of communism ...'.[20] During these three years, wrote Suárez Fernández, 'some of the key ideas which are later repeatedly developed in his speeches as leader are shaped, based on his reading and experience'. And Suárez Fernández immediately linked this sentence with the Entente:

> Franco began to receive a *Bulletin de l'Entente Internationale Anticommuniste*; the first subscription reached him officially, paid for by the Government, but he later continued the subscription and paid for it himself ... He was unswerving in his opinions: communism, in theory and in practice, is the threat hanging over Western Christian civilization, which it aims to destroy; to fight against it, therefore, is an unavoidable duty for all governments sharing the ideals of humanism which are more or less close to the roots of Christianity.[21]

But, before assuring us, on pp. 197 and 198, that the determining year for Franco's great political decision was 1929, Suárez Fernández had already, in his 'General Introduction', told us that the year of Franco's resolution was 1934, when Franco was

> sent as Governor [sic] to the Balearic Islands ... he could reveal his exceptional gifts in one particular field, that of logistics and fortification, which he deemed to be of the utmost necessity because clouds were beginning to gather over the Mediterranean. It was at this time [1934] that he established contact with international sources of information and news distribution on the subversive processes being encouraged by the Soviet Union. Franco was always a convinced anti-communist.[22]

Franco may have been and, given his upbringing and military education, probably was 'a convinced anti-communist', but he did not begin to realize this fact until he had begun reading the bulletin of the Entente.

Suárez Fernández again, more than 250 pages into his text, confirmed the date of 1934 as being that of Franco's political conversion, in these words:

It was at this time – May 1934, or perhaps before – that Franco acquired a political commitment. An *Entente Internationale Anticommuniste* had been established in Geneva, gathering together those people who were convinced of the need to prepare for the battle against the communist revolution. The Entente's services provided reports, secret in part, the contents received through confidential channels. Franco signed up on 21st June 1934, stating that he wished correspondence to be in French, and received reports and material until the war. There is no doubt that these reports determined his attitude in 1934 and 1936; he felt certain he knew that the Comintern was preparing an attack on Spain.[23]

In all probability, it was the answer from Geneva to Franco's letter of 16 May 1934 which contained the formula of adherence to the principles of the Entente, the formula which Franco in turn addressed to the EIA in Geneva on 21 June 1934. I have found no indication that Franco was ever a member of the International Council of the EIA, an advisory body of the Entente which held annual meetings 'which many representatives attended, from all the European nations, the United States, Latin American republics, Japan and Australia. These meetings were usually held in Geneva, but also took place in Paris, The Hague, London and Brussels.'[24] However, the other military hero of the Entente, Marshal Mannerheim, the ultra right-wing Finnish military leader, was declared in 1940 to have been 'a member of the International Office of the EIA for several years'.[25]

VI

I have already remarked on the fact that Hills, while insisting on the serious role that the bulletins of the EIA played in the political development of Franco, did not retain from his talks with El Caudillo the name of the Entente. This lapse on the part of Hills, or perhaps on the part of Franco, resulted in a misunderstanding of the chronology of the Entente's influential entry into Franco's life by the historian Juan Pablo Fusi. On this matter, Fusi quotes Hills and Suárez Fernández, but downplays Crozier, the most lucid witness, at this point.

In one place, in his book *Franco*, Fusi wrote:

Franco, who on 21st June 1934, had become a member of the Entente Internationale Anticommuniste, saw the Asturias insurrection as an attempted communist revolution and as far as he was concerned the only important matter was that the left and the Catalanists were acting in violation of the law.[26]

Here, Fusi allows his reader to place Franco's adherence to the ideas of the Entente on 21 June 1934, but five pages earlier he had written:

> The Director of the Military Academy [Franco] was already an anti-communist and a conservative; in Zaragoza, he subscribed to a bulletin dealing with matters about the Comintern which was published in Geneva, and he was convinced that communism was already at work in Spain ...[27]

As I have already shown, Franco's initiation into the ideological rites of the Entente began in 1928 and continued until the outbreak of the War in Spain, that is Franco was a constant reader of the EIA bulletins for longer than seven years. The 'bulletin' to which Franco had subscribed when in Zaragoza, according to Fusi's chronology – in reality, Franco did not himself subscribe but accepted a subscription offered by Primo de Rivera, paid with government funds – was the same 'bulletin' to which Franco himself subscribed in 1934 when, as Fusi writes, he 'became a member of the Entente Internationale Anticommuniste'. This was a continuing relationship from 1928 to July(?) 1936.

VII

We have for our inspection still another recent commentary on Franco and the EIA, that of Ricardo de la Cierva:

> Shortly before leaving Madrid, [General] Primo de Rivera gave him, as he did to other influential officers in the young Army, a subscription to the *Bullein {de} l'Entente Internationale contre la Troisieme Internationale*, an anti-communist bulletin published in Geneva, the editor being the future federal [sic] parliamentarian, Aubert.[28]

(It seems to me to be evident that la Cierva meant to write that Franco, 'shortly before leaving Madrid' to go to the Military Academy at Zaragoza, received a subscription *to* the *Bulletin from* General Primo de Rivera. This error, in English, is called a 'dangling participle' or a 'confused participle'.)

While on the subject of la Cierva, I want to draw the reader's attention to the fact that whereas Crozier, Hills and Suárez Fernández gave high marks to Franco for having the intelligence to have discovered, disseminated and known how to interpret the EIA Bulletins, la Cierva is more reticent as to the accuracy of the information given in the publications sent from Geneva, writing in continuation of the phrases quoted above:

Emilio Mola, another recipient of a subscription [a present from Primo de Rivera] noted in particular that some of its assessments were exaggerated and he personally gathered a realistic body of knowledge about communism in Europe and Spain which was unsurpassed by any other Spaniard of his time in the public arena.[29]

Do these qualifying phrases mean that la Cierva has changed his chapel of worship from that of Franco to that of Mola? Such a supposition might be bolstered by one of the last sentences in what la Cierva calls 'The contents of this new version', as follows: 'Neither the Franco family nor the Franco Foundation have assisted with documented information, in spite of express requests on the part of the author, who operates completely independently.'[30]

VIII

I have now presented four testimonials to the facts that, beginning in 1927–1928, Franco was an avid reader of the publications of the Genevan enterprise of misinformation called the EIA, and that he firmly believed in what he read in these publications.

It was hardly surprising that Franco was strongly attracted by the pseudo-scholarship of the EIA publications. Their contents were doubtless what he had been seeking for many months. Franco's intellectual under-development was normal for a Spanish officer of that time. He was a specialist in military science, totally lacking in the general culture which a leader of the people should have – but does not always have – in this century and in Western Europe. His political and social views were those of the military academy, frankly reactionary; his religious commitment was one of unquestioning fidelity to Roman Catholic obscurantism, not unlike the rigid Calvinism of Théodore Aubert, the outstanding personality in the founding and development of the Entente, or the medieval religiosity of Georges Lodygensky, the chief White Russian supporter of the EIA, whose political motivations appear to have been in great part based on his dedication to the Russian Orthodox Church.

IX

By cross-checking and comparing facts gleaned from Crozier, and others from Hills, la Cierva and Suárez Fernández, we can state with assurance the following: in 1928, General Primo de Rivera, using public funds, had propaganda from the Geneva-based *Entente Internationale contre la III Internationale* sent to a number of young, promising and already superior officers, among them Franco and Mola. The government-paid subscriptions to the publication seem to have been cancelled early in 1934; Franco then renewed his subscription with his own money. These two dates, 1928 and 1934, are confused, as are other matters, in the mind of Suárez Fernández, but in reality the link between Franco and the Entente was a continuous affair from 1928 to the outbreak of the Civil War, as Crozier makes abundantly clear. It seems also that the reading of the EIA publications was widespread among a certain category of Spanish officer, friends and later co-conspirators of Franco. It also seems probable that after the end of the Civil War, Franco began anew to receive the EIA *Bulletin*; it is certain that he was in communication with the Entente, but the extent of these relations remains for the moment obscure. There would not seem to have been any political reason why mail from Geneva would not pass through France and reach Madrid during the Second World War.

X

There are, evidently, other sources for information concerning Franco, Spain and the Entente. First of all are the EIA publications and the EIA archives.

Franco lost his collection of EIA publications during the Civil War, according to both Crozier and Suárez Fernández. I found it difficult to locate such publications, as I shall explain a bit farther along. The archives of the EIA were also said to have disappeared or to have been destroyed. Crozier and Suárez Fernández gave conflicting testimony as to what had actually happened to them. Crozier wrote:

> General Franco's collection of files of the Bulletins *de la EIA* was lost, together with other possessions, when his Madrid house and its contents were sequestered by the Republican authorities after the 1936 military rising began. The *Entente Internationale Anticommuniste* itself, which had maintained close relations with the Anti-Komintern, destroyed its own files, for reasons of Swiss neutrality, on the outbreak of world war in 1939. Some of the details I give, which supplement Franco's own recollections, were obtained on my behalf by the Spanish Ambassador in Berne, Don Juan de Lojendio, Marques de Vellisca.[31]

Suárez Fernández gave two accounts of the disappearance of the EIA archives, completely contradictory. On one page, he wrote, in a footnote, 'The Entente's archives, in Switzerland, were destroyed in order to erase any suspicion of association with the Anti-Komintern.'[32] This version agrees more or less with that of Crozier. But then, seventy-five pages later, Suárez Fernández, in another footnote, following the mention in his text of the papers furnished to Franco by the 'Entente's services which provided reports, secret in part of the contents received through confidential channels', wrote that Franco, together with his many books and papers, also lost these reports during the war, including the report on the 1935 Comintern meeting and the Dimitrov report which declared that communism would soon take over once the Popular Front had won the elections. In 1962, Victor de la Serna, attaché to the embassy in Berne, was given the job of getting in touch with Doctor Engels, who was trying to revive the Entente, in order to get hold of that Report. But the Entente, which had broken up and scattered its archives in order not be confused with the Nazis, could no longer find it.[33]

This information is attributed by Suárez Fernández to 'The Office of Victor de la Serna in December 1962'.[34]

These two accounts of the disappearance of the EIA archives, one given to Crozier at an unspecified date, the other to a Spanish diplomat in 1962, cannot both be exact. If the archives were destroyed, they were not simply dispersed, but lost forever; on the other hand, were they scattered here and there, hidden perhaps, they might some day come to light. I found it impossible to believe that Aubert, founder of the Entente and an unshakeable believer in the anti-Communist cause, would, of his own free will, have permitted the complete destruction of his life's work.

When I began research on this subject, I was primarily interested in Crozier's book because of what he had written, or rather had not written about the 'Secret Documents of the Communist Plot'. I had reviewed the two biographies, one by Hills and one by Crozier, when they first came out[35] and it was while rereading them later that my attention was drawn to the Entente. I began wondering if the Entente had published something about the documents. Moreover, I reasoned that even if the archives of the EIA had been burned to ashes, there should be a collection of the published EIA material in the great libraries of Western Europe and North America. Thus, while concentrating on the 'Secret Documents', I also sought, from time to time, with little success, material on the Entente.

It was only when I found Suárez Fernández's comments on the Entente and his evaluation of its influence on the political education of Franco that I began to see the Entente, not as a subsidiary to the problem of the 'Secret Documents of the Communist Plot', but as a corollary, distinct but equal – perhaps superior – in importance to all the other Rightist endeavours to destabilize the Spanish Republic, in Spain and elsewhere.

XI

After many fruitless enquiries in Europe and North America, I finally discovered two depositories in which there was a considerable amount of EIA material. One of these was the Hoover Institution on War, Revolution and Peace at Stanford, California, the principal think-tank of the American right; the other was the Bibliothèque Publique et Universitaire of Geneva. In the first of these libraries, I found not only many copies of the EIA *Bulletin* but also, in the archives, an unpublished typescript by Georges Lodygensky, written in French, entitled *Face au Communisme: Le mouvement anticommuniste internationale de 1923–1950*, 2 volumes, 118, 96 pp.[36] I have been able, through the kindness of the Hoover Library staff, to obtain, in recent years, a number of pages each year of the Lodygensky Manuscript. This is, to my knowledge, the most detailed account of the history of the Entente available as of this day.

The Bibliothèque Publique et Universitaire of Geneva possesses a great number of EIA *Bulletins*, reports and booklets, all in French, but the collections are incomplete. The Schweizerische Landesbibliothek in Berne has a fairly complete set of an EIA publication dating from 1939 through 1949. (The Entente materials in Geneva and Berne complement each other, in the sense that the German-language material in Berne was largely given over to internal Swiss matters dealing with Communism, whereas the French language publications in Geneva were usually concerned with international affairs.)

However, after many months of intermittent research on the problem of the 'dispersed' or 'destroyed' EIA archives, I found, on a page of Lodygensky's typescript, a handwritten 'NB' saying that the archives of the EIA had been deposited in the Bibliothèque Publique et Universitaire of Geneva. I wrote to this institution, with which I had already been corresponding, signalling this discovery and asking for a confirmation. I did not receive an answer. Nevertheless, by chance and persistence, which, in such problems of research, go hand in hand, I was able to obtain unquestionable proof that the archives of the Entente were deposited in the Bibliothèque Publique et Universitaire of Geneva by Théodore Aubert, before his death, with an absolute interdiction to reveal their existence before 1975.[37] At the expiry of this period, the son of Théodore Aubert, Edouard, who had but little interest in the work of the EIA, prolonged the period of secrecy until 1991. Edouard died in 1985. His son Jean-Pierre, apparently more concerned with the history of the Entente than was his father, later decided to open the archives to research.

The curious feature of this situation is not that the Archives had been closed to research for a certain number of years. This happens frequently. The oddity of this state of affairs is the secrecy decreed around even the acknowledgement of the existence of the Archives of the Entente, let alone the revelation of their hiding place. However, it is not difficult to find the reason for the mystification surrounding the EIA Archives. The information forwarded to Brian Crozier from Swiss sources, and that received by Franco, also from Swiss sources, were intentionally misleading. The EIA Archives were too precious in the eyes of Théodore Aubert for them to be destroyed 'when the Second World War began, because of Swiss neutrality', as Crozier uncritically wrote, or for them to be dispersed in order that the Entente not be 'confused with the Nazis', as Victor de la Serna reported to his Caudillo.

The post-war climate in Switzerland, which had been before the Second World War the seat of the League of Nations, and had not been favoured as the home of the successor of the League, the United Nations, was hardly auspicious for the continuation of the Entente, as I shall show in detail a bit farther on. The EIA, however, did continue until 1950. The atmosphere of the Cold War, although not hostile to anti-Sovietism, was ill-disposed to forgive the open collaboration of Aubert and his friends with German Nazism and Italian Fascism. Had anyone among the Spanish diplomatic and consular representatives in the Helvetic Confederation been of scholarly bent, he could, without too much trouble, have consulted the incomplete collections of the EIA *Bulletins* in the official libraries in Berne and Geneva, and found out that far from dispersing its archives when the Second World War broke out, the EIA continued its collaboration with the Fascist movements of Europe until the eve of the Nazi defeat. It was not too difficult to know where the sympathies of Aubert, Lodygensky and their financial backers in the Entente lay, before, during and even after the Second World War.

XII

What I have written in the following pages concerning the Entente comes almost exclusively from two sources: (1) pages from the Lodygensky memoir, and (2) EIA publications, notably the periodical entitled *Bulletin d'Information Publique* and three resumés of EIA activities, *Neuf ans de lutte contre le bolchevisme* (Geneva, 1993), *Dix-sept ans de lutte contre le bolchevisme* (Geneva, 1940) and *Théodore Aubert et son oeuvre* (Geneva, 1932), by Dimitri Novik.

I have encountered difficulties in obtaining copies of the EIA publications for the early years. The Hoover Institution has nothing before 20 June 1933. The British Library has twenty-six items, mostly single pages, dating from February to September 1925, plus four pamphlets published between 1924 and 1929. The Library of Congress has a few copies of EIA *Bulletins* for 1939, and four copies of the publication entitled *Documentation*, one for 1935 and three for 1939. These are kept in a 'sample file'. The New York Public Library seems to have a bit more for 1939 and 1940. Even the holdings of the Bibliothèque Publique et Universitaire, the most extensive I have found concerning the EIA, are far from complete, despite the status of this institution as the legal deposit library for the Geneva Canton. I do not know the reason for the fragmentary state of this material in the great libraries I have consulted, but I strongly suspect that it is the result of two factors: the distribution strategy of the Entente, and the complete indifference of the scholarly world to the work of the EIA, which did not seek out its readers

among the habitués of public and university libraries, but targeted its publications among influential persons and groups thought to share its
conservative ideology.[38]

XIII

The Entente Internationale contre la Troisième Internationale – the name
was changed around 1938 to the Entente Internationale Anticommuniste
(EIA) was founded in Geneva late in 1924 by a member of the Geneva bar
named Théodore Aubert, with the close collaboration of a White Russian
refugee, well-connected with the Comité International de la Croix Rouge
(CICR), the medical doctor Georges Lodygensky.

Aubert was born on 8 September 1878 at Geneva. His family came from
the French Dauphiné towards the end of the seventeenth century, fleeing
Catholic persecution of the Huguenots, and settled in Geneva. 'They were
received into the bourgeoisie in 1702.' Théodore Aubert studied law at the
University of Geneva and was admitted to the bar in 1901; he later became
a member of the Bar Council and a delegate to the Grand Council of the
Swiss Bar.[39]

During the First World War, Aubert was mobilized as an infantry officer
and served in 1917–1918 as a special delegate of the Swiss Federal Council
to visit prisoners of war and civilian internees in France, Switzerland having
assumed the representation of the diplomatic interests of the Central Powers
when the United States entered the war. In December 1918, Aubert was in
Berlin as a delegate of the CICR. Here he had the task of looking after the
interests of Allied war prisoners, especially the Russians. He was thus
present at the outbreak in Germany of the social conflicts that followed the
German defeat. In May 1919 he was again in France as a delegate of the
CICR and during the following months he visited 'concentration camps
situated in the liberated areas of France'. Aubert then took part in the
Conference of the International Law Association, again as a delegate of the
CICR.[40]

Georges Lodygensky had been before the Revolution of 1917 the official
delegate of the Tsarist regime to the Comité International de la Croix Rouge
(CICR) and continued this work in Geneva after the end of the First World
War. This was possible because Switzerland had refused to recognize the
Soviet Union after the Russian Revolution, and, in fact, did not recognize
the Soviet Union until after the end of the Second World War. Throughout
the history of the Entente, one encounters frequent liaisons and helpful
contacts between personalities of the CICR and the leading spirits of the
EIA.

XIV

A tenuous relationship between Switzerland and the Soviet Union had begun in 1918, the year in which a Soviet delegation – the Berzine Delegation – visited Switzerland for the first time and was expelled *manu militari*. An article in the *Encyclopaedia Britannica* (1926) shows how far a generalized fear of the Soviet Union prevailed in the Confederation. The author of the article, Carl Burckhardt, identified as an 'official of the Swiss Federation', explained the expulsion of the Soviet delegation as follows:

> the Soviet delegation acted mainly as an organ of propaganda and espionage, and the revolutionary tendencies of the general strike in that year were undoubtedly aggravated by its influence. The difficulties of the military in countering these tendencies, together with the suffering caused by a widespread epidemic of influenza, roused public feelings and the delegation was requested to leave the country.[41]

This quotation might seem to indicate that Swiss public opinion somehow linked the influenza epidemic with the Soviet mission, an example of the irrationality frequently found in such situations.

XV

Two important events in Swiss history preceded the founding of the Entente: the first was closely allied with a European phenomenon of the time, inspired by the social unrest resulting from the world war and the Russian Revolution. It began in 1918 and was called in each country, the Civic Union, (*Union Civique*). The second event came later in 1923. This was the murder of the Soviet representative in Rome, Vorovsky, in Swiss territory. Théodore Aubert was active in founding the Swiss *Union Civique*, and he achieved wide notoriety in successfully defending the accomplice of the assassin of Vorovsky.

The Civic Unions were right-wing paramilitary groups formed to combat workers' organizations in many European countries. The Swiss Civic Union had been formed after the general strike of 1918, by Aubert and some of his friends. Colonel de Diesbach, who commanded the detachment of dragoons that escorted the Soviet mission to the frontier, was later a member of the Permanent Bureau of the Entente.[42]

Dmitri Novik, Aubert's hagiographer of 1933, while relating the story of the Swiss general strike of 1918 and the forced departure of the Soviet mission, struck the proper note for the Entente's gallery of authors dealing with social unrest. He wrote, 'This is insufficient to root out evil. The strike will continue.' The strike, employed by the Swiss workers, was viewed as evil incarnate. Novik continued:

Troops were mobilised while, at the same time, civilian groups were established in several Swiss towns to maintain order and ensure the functioning of public services. Aubert was the chief initiator of this movement. After the strike was suppressed, for several years he was in charge of managing the Civic Unions in French-speaking Switzerland. It was thus that he was called on to study from very close at hand the various subversive movements and, in particular, Bolshevism. Aubert was also in contact with the leaders of Civic Unions in France, Germany, Belgium and Holland, thus widening his international relationships, for which he had prepared the ground during the course of his various missions. These relationships would later be of use to him.[43]

Novik, while presenting Aubert as a resolute enemy of the right of the workers to strike, tried also to show him to be 'a sincere friend of the working class' and added that 'he is beginning to be recognized as such in working class environments'. Novik explained that Aubert was in favour of class collaboration. 'It is useless to insist that Aubert is strongly in favour of the most robust social reforms based on intelligent cooperation between employers and workers.'[44]

XVI

On 10 May 1923, Vyatzlaw Vorowsky, the Soviet representative in Rome, who had come to Lausanne to act on behalf of his country at an international conference which, among other matters, concerned the Dardanelles, was shot to death with a revolver by Maurice Conradi, who held both Russian and Swiss citizenship. He had as an accomplice, a White Russian émigré, Arcadius Polounine. A press report of the time read,

> At 21.00 hours, on 10th May 1923, the Soviet agent Vorowsky was shot in the Cecil Hotel restaurant by a 'Swiss Russian', Maurice Conradi, a former voluntary officer in the 'White' Russian army. Conradi also wounded two other Soviet agents acting as Vorowsky's bodyguards: Ahrens and Divilkowsky. He then laid down his weapon and asked for the police to be called, adding 'I have done something good for the whole world.'[45]

The assassination of Vorovsky involved both the White Russian movement and the Tsarist section of the CICR. When Lodygensky returned to Geneva from Russia after the Revolution, in April 1920, he continued to occupy the two rooms comprising the offices of the Russian Red Cross, while at the same time, engaging occasionally in the practice of medicine, especially with clients among the Russian refugee colony. Dr Lodygensky himself used one of the two rooms; the other one contained the archives of the Russian Red

Cross. It was there that Arkady Pavolvitch Polounine worked with two female secretaries. Polounine had been sent to Geneva to work as first secretary under Lodygensky by the White Russian general, Peter Nicolaievitch Wrangel.[46]

The assassin Conradi, or 'executioner', as Lodygensky preferred to name him, had met Polounine during the Russian Civil War, when both were with the White Russian Armies. Later, on 25 March 1923, Conradi came to the Russian Red Cross in Geneva to see Polounine, according to the former's pre-trial testimony, confirmed by Aubert's address to the jury in November 1923.[47] However, Lodygensky, writing many years later, stated that Conradi had come to see him seeking medical advice.[48] Both of these reasons for Conradi's visit to the Russian Red Cross offices may well have been exact.

In the course of the conversation between the two former comrades in arms, 'they also renew their conviction that Bolshevism should be destroyed'.[49] 'Together, Conradi and Polounine decided to do what they could, within their limited resources, to achieve this end. Then, to render the act useful, it was a matter of deciding whom should be executed. Polounine mentioned Vorowsky.'[50] After this conversation, Conradi travelled to Berlin for reasons unknown; on his return, Polounine gave him a sum of money.[51] A short time later, Conradi, who was in Lausanne awaiting the arrival of Vorowsky, sent an urgent letter to Polounine requesting a hundred Swiss francs. Polounine not only sent the money, but joined with it a note which, unluckily for Polounine, Conradi lost at the scene of the crime.[52]

XVII

Lodygensky was quite naturally standing at his traditional post at the Russian Orthodox Church in Geneva on the Sunday morning, 13 May, after the assassination. Polounine appeared; the two men looked at each other, apparently to signify a meeting after the service. Polounine then disappeared.[53]

Lodygensky was called to the telephone during luncheon. A police agent requested him to come to the Russian Red Cross offices immediately. There he found a number of policemen in civilian dress, and Polounine, who was under arrest. A policeman demanded to look into the files belonging to Polounine, and Lodygensky showed him the relevant cabinets. Lodygensky continued, 'the police were going through the files. Although I appeared totally calm, I did not feel any the less worried. But, fortunately, the police search was only superficial and they failed to examine other Red Cross papers.' The policemen left and, as Lodygensky wrote,

> Ill at ease, I picked up Polounine's file, leafed through it meticulously and discovered a letter from Conradi. This document left no doubt as to

the fact that the former comrades in the White army had already established close contact from the first time Conradi came to Geneva. It goes
without saying that I immediately destroyed such a compromising
document.[54]'

Lodygensky feared to be arrested in his turn, but, nevertheless, sought to use
his time to find a lawyer to defend Polounine.

Lodygensky and Aubert were on a more than friendly basis. The White
Russian delegate to the CICR had met Aubert almost immediately after the
former's return to Geneva from war-torn Russia, and had related to the
lawyer his first-hand impressions of the Revolution. They saw each other
frequently thereafter, and when Polounine arrived in Switzerland,
Lodygensky presented the White Russian officer to Aubert. 'The latter
immediately appreciated the true worth of my assistant's vast intelligence
and extraordinary learning.'[55]

XVIII

This background explains the reasons why Aubert at once offered his
services to defend Conradi's accomplice, Polounine. Aubert was assured of
support from the White Russian émigrés, of the Tsarist embassy still functioning in Paris, and of the Tsarist Red Cross in Geneva and in Paris.
Lodygensky noted, 'The archbishop of our parish, the Venerable Orloff, told
whoever wished to listen that he would pray without respite for justice and
truth to triumph in the Lausanne trial.'[56]

Aubert became so deeply involved in the defence of Polounine that he
abandoned completely the other work in his law office, leaving it entirely in
the hands of his associate. (The defence of Conradi had been confided to a
lawyer of the Lausanne Bar, Sydney Schoepfer.)[57] Aubert made no attempt to
plead the innocence of Polounine, correctly persuaded that the letter signed
by his client and found at the scene of the killing could easily be considered
as proof of complicity.[58] Instead, Aubert spent his time drawing up 'an
irrefutable bill of indictment against anti-religious and inhuman communism'.[59] To this end, testimony was solicited from members of the White
Russian colonies in Western Europe, from persons associated with the
Tsarist Red Cross and from members of the Russian aristocracy then in
exile.[60] A number of Russian writers living in France and Switzerland were
also recruited.[61]

XIX

The consolidated trials of Conradi and Polounine were held in Lausanne, in
the great hall of the Casino de Montbénon, in order to have enough room to

hold the large number of journalists, Swiss and foreign, expected to come to cover the trials[62] which lasted eleven days, from 5 to 19 November 1923. Aubert spoke for a total of nine hours, on two days, 11 and 15 November.[63]

According to EIA sources, Aubert's address to the Lausanne jury was widely translated,[64] but we shall deal with only two printings, the French original which was entitled *L'Affaire Conradi*, with a subtitle *Le procès du Bolchevisme*,[65] and an English-language version which bore the poorly inspired title *Bolshevism's Terrible Record: An Indictment*.[66] The French transcript had, according to Lodygensky, this unusual origin: several days before the end of the trial, Aubert received the visit of a stenographer who had been engaged by the 'partie civile communiste' (Communist plaintiff) to record the transcript of the trial, intending to use it as propaganda, but the 'partie civile', realizing that the cause was lost, refused to pay the stenographer, who then offered his work to Aubert at a low price.[67] This scenario is possible, and it is certain that during those months preceding the trial Lodygensky was in extremely close contact with Aubert. However, it is clear from the Lodygensky typescript that Aubert was reading a prepared text to the jury and that he had, at the end of his nine-hour plea to the jury, a fairly accurate text concerning what he had said in the courtroom.[68]

It is significant that the first transcript of Aubert's courtroom plea was entitled *L'Affaire Conradi* and not 'L'Affaire Polounine'. This underlines the evident fact that the trial of Conradi, the actual assassin, was far more important than that of his accomplice Polounine. A surprising amount of evidence against Polounine had accumulated during the preliminary investigation by the examining magistrate, as Aubert admitted in his speech.[69] However, it was unlikely that the jury could have condemned Polounine, unless it had previously condemned Conradi; whereas, one could imagine the contrary: Conradi condemned and Polounine set free. Thus, Aubert's arguments, of necessity, frequently encompassed the defence of both men. I have not seen Schopfer's defence of Conradi, but it was probably more legalistic than was Aubert's, which was 99 per cent political.

XX

The central argument of Aubert's address before the Criminal Court of Lausanne in justification of the killing of Vorowsky was that Conradi (and Polounine) had been seized by an 'irresistible force' which drove them to the murderous act. According to the law in force in the Canton of Vaud, of which Lausanne was the capital, anyone possessed by such an 'irresistible force' to commit a crime could not be held responsible for his or her behaviour.

Aubert proposed to the jury several incidents from Polounine's life to illustrate the 'irresistible force' which propelled the White Russian officer to become an accomplice to murder. Among the events to which Aubert assigned responsibility for Polounine's homicidal mania was the decomposition of the Russian Imperial Army:

> At that time, Polounine does not belong to the White army. He does not belong to the Korniloff detachments, but he suffers deeply. He suffers because a short time after the revolution was unleashed, the decomposition of the army becomes terribly apparent; this decomposition had begun under Kerensky and was initiated by Bolshevik agents who were working – I can here solemnly declare – with German gold and on Germany's behalf.
>
> What is therefore the reaction of an officer such as Polounine to such circumstances? He sees the army he loves falling apart, he sees his country, for which he is ready to lay down his life, about to be considered a criminal country! Do you not understand that at that moment an irresistible force took hold of him, this same irresistible force that leads us on to the battle field, that makes us die for our country and for our honour?[70]

Another circumstance of the Russian Revolution, and a very important one, which, according to Aubert, weighed heavily in the determination of Polounine's conduct, was the Treaty of Brest-Litovsk, by which Russia signed a separate treaty of peace with Germany:

> What memories did Polounine bring with him to Geneva? The memory of his country's dishonour, because of the betrayal of Lenin, because of the betrayal of Brest-Litovsk, the memory of that horrendous cruelty, of that misery, of that terror, of those nurses he had saved who had been so atrociously tortured. And his own family had not been spared. I will go on no further. Once again, here, Polounine appears as he is, in the purity of his motives, as a patriot. He has acted only on behalf of his motherland and sacrificed himself for his motherland. He left this latter while she was being crucified. She is still on the cross.
>
> Like the Princess Kourakine, whose evidence you have heard, Polounine, of peasant origin, was thinking of Russia, 'this great dishonoured martyr, dismembered and bathed in blood'. Thus, always present was the irresistible force, the irresistible force of the desire for justice, the irresistible force of passionate love for his country; this country Russia.[71]

During the first hour of his plea, Aubert challenged the State's Attorney, insisting on attenuating circumstances based on the 'irresistible force':

> You, the State Attorney, have said that Polounine did not warrant any mitigating circumstances since, in his case, there was neither provocation nor irresistible force. Let me say, however, that there was a force,

and an irresistible force in the portrayal of Bolshevism such as we listened to last week, and so irresistible that you yourself, Sir, have yielded to it ... so, you have experienced the effects of this irresistible force which Polounine obeyed ...; but on Polounine, a Russian citizen who has seen blood spilt and who has lived through these horrors, this irresistible force exerted an influence a thousand times more powerful than on a magistrate who lives in a free and respected country.[72]

Towards the end of his long plea to the jury, Aubert argued again for the 'irresistible force':

Do you understand that, in relation to the questions put to you [by the judge] all your answers should free Conradi and Polounine too? All the more so because Vorowsky's arrival in Lausanne constituted for Polounine a violent provocation. His mind was haunted by the irresistible force for justice and by a love for one's country. Do you understand? Yes, you have understood that if there are guilty persons, they are the Bolshevik leaders.[73]

The pleading by Aubert of the 'irresistible force' as an exculpation for the criminal act of Conradi and Polounine could constitute a justification for any White Russian to kill any prominent Bolshevik anywhere. But why was Vorovsky chosen to become the victim of the two former officers of the White Russian Army? The reason given by Aubert was analogous to that proffered by mountain climbers: because the mountain was there. Vorovsky was killed because he was the most prominent Soviet functionary available in Switzerland. Any other representative of similar rank would have satisfied the requirements of the killer and his accomplice.

XXI

Vorovsky had been chosen for assassination because Conradi and Polounine were pushed by an 'irresistible force' to kill a prominent Bolshevik. But once Vorovsky had been designated as the victim, features of his own personality were found to justify the choice already made. One such aspect of Vorovsky's *curriculum vitae* was constituted by proof of his significant Bolshevik past.

Early in his talk to the jury, Aubert referred to the fact revealed in the pre-trial investigation that Polounine had indicated Vorovsky to Conradi as a likely candidate for assassination: 'He [Polounine] believed that the latter [Vorovsky] had a distinguished Bolshevik past and that he would certainly be one of the more prominent Bolshevik leaders in the very near future.'[74] Several paragraphs of Aubert's speech before the Criminal Court were given over to establishing Vorovsky's importance in the Soviet hierarchy: his death was a great blow to Bolshevism, hence morally justified.[75] One example:

Vorovsky was in Stockholm to greet Lenin when he arrived there on his way to the Finland Station.[76]

Aubert showed in his oration how Polounine, and Aubert himself, were irritated by the fact that Vorovsky and other representatives of the Soviet Union were lodged in first-class hotels while travelling abroad.[77] (This was a normal way of life for diplomats and other functionaries of all the countries in the world, then and now.) Aubert underlined the fact that 'Vorowsky met his death in a luxurious restaurant'.[78] Polounine was described as being filled with 'indignation' when he learned that Vorovsky, on an official mission in Genoa, was received with great consideration, 'at these grand, over-polite dinner parties with princes and archbishops'.[79] Hence, the assassination of Vorovsky was justified.[80]

In addition to the basic plea of the 'irresistible force', Aubert discovered a further panoply of Communist 'crimes', which contributed to a justification of the murder of Vorovsky. Among these were such ill-defined conceptions as the accusation that Lenin had 'poisoned the soul of Russia':

> Gentlemen, even if, instead of misery, instead of ruin, instead of distress, instead of famine, Lenin had brought the greatest prosperity to his country, the sole fact that he poisoned the soul of Russia would be sufficient to justify Conradi pulling the trigger![81]

Among other justifications invoked by Aubert for the murder of Vorovsky were petty reasons such as the affronts to Polounine's Russian patriotism,[82] racist reasons such as the foreign (non-Russian) elements allegedly among the personnel of the Cheka,[83] or more easily understood reactionary reasons such as Soviet incitation to social unrest all over the world,[84] co-education in Soviet schools[85] and government-financed abortions in Soviet State hospitals.[86]

Aubert denounced not only the persecution of the Russian Orthodox Church, but insisted that 'the Roman Catholic and Protestant churches are persecuted quite as much'.[87] But, true to his Huguenot ancestry, he could not resist the temptation to cite a previous religious persecution, nearer to Geneva than was Russia, the persecution of the Huguenots by the French Catholics, encouraged by Catherine de Medicis, and which resulted in the Massacre of St Bartholomew and the murder of Admiral Coligny, in 1572. To justify Polounine, Aubert quoted Charlotte de Laval, wife of Coligny, as saying to her husband, 'Sir, I have on my heart so much of the blood of our people, that blood cries to God that you will be the murderer of those whose murder you did not prevent.'[88]

XXII

The Lausanne jury, by a vote of nine to zero, declared that Conradi had voluntarily killed Vorovsky by means of a firearm, at the Hotel Cecil in Lausanne on 10 May 1923. The same jury, by the same unanimity, affirmed that Polounine had been an accomplice to that murder. And the same jury, by a vote of five to four, affirmed that both of the accused were guilty. The two accused were then set free. The leading newspaper of the city, *Feuille d'Avis de Lausanne*, explained the situation as follows:

> The accused were declared guilty by five jury members out of nine and therefore benefited from a minority rule since the Vaudian criminal code requires a majority of six 'yes' and three 'no' for the accused to be declared guilty.[89]

They were guilty but free from any punishment.

The Conradi–Polounine case is a rarity in the annals of Western European justice. First, there was absolutely no doubt that Conradi had fired on Vorovsky and killed him, and that he had wounded two other Soviet citizens. Conradi self-proclaimed his culpability at the scene of the crime. Nor was there any doubt concerning Polounine's guilt as an accomplice. Despite the criminal act of Lodygensky, destroying evidence in a case of murder, as he himself years later, with a bit of boasting, confessed, the investigating prosecutor quickly found more than sufficient guilt on the part of Polounine.

In the 'Introduction' to *L'Affaire Conradi*, we can read that, when three days after the murder, Polounine was arrested, he

> did not hesitate to admit that he had helped Conradi to carry out the deed, whether this was by discussing the possibilities with him, by giving him information about Vorowsky's personality or even by giving him some money for his expenses on the trip from Zurich to Lausanne.[90]

Second, neither of the accused showed the slightest sign of regret for his act. In most cases where the accused, confronted with irrefutable proof of his guilt, can hardly plead 'not guilty', he does proclaim before the court his profound remorse. Conradi, self-righteously announced his responsibility for the murder at the scene of the crime. Nor was there any scene of contrition in the courtroom at Lausanne, when Polounine was questioned. 'To the question put by the Prosecution: Would he be prepared to do the same again? Polounine answered "yes".'[91]

Third, there was premeditation, a conspiracy. Since in one way or another, this book is entirely concerned with 'Communist Plots', it is highly relevant to underline the fact that the murder of Vorovsky was the result of an 'Anti-

Communist Plot', openly presented as such by Aubert in his discourse to the Lausanne jury.[92] I shall further here quote from the 'Introduction' to *L'Affaire Conradi*:

> The detailed examination carried out by the examining Judge of Lausanne showed that no plot existed beyond this understanding between Conradi and Polounine; the Swiss National League in Lausanne and the former Russian Red Cross organization in Geneva were notably dismissed from the case in the clearest possible fashion, both by the findings of the inquiry and by the Prosecution.[93]

(The public Prosecutor, in exonerating the 'former organization of the Russian Red Cross' from any complicity in the killing, was unaware that Lodygensky had purposely destroyed evidence of that complicity.)

It is impossible not to consider the verdict of the jury in Lausanne as a grave miscarriage of justice. There was no doubt of the physical culpability of Conradi and Polounine, who carried out the acts of which they were charged: there was premeditation, a conspiracy between the two men, and neither of the accused showed the slightest compunction for what they had done.

XXIII

I have already cited Lodygensky's description of Aubert as a 'little-known Genevan lawyer'. He apparently gave up his active practice at the bar after his defence of Polounine. His legal reputation therefore rests on the text of *L'Affaire Conradi*, which can be judged by two weights: its intrinsic value, and its efficacy. On this latter point, he scores 100; his client was freed. On the first question, he gets a grade of mediocrity. There are few courts in Western political democracies that would have admitted the 'evidence' so zealously proclaimed before the tribunal of Lausanne by Aubert. The moment that the Lausanne Court permitted Aubert to present such nebulous, ill-documented testimony, the door was wide open to allow all the components of forensic farce. It was highly significant that Conradi and Polounine were not given even short prison sentences, generally the minimum for premeditated, unprovoked murder in our Western European and American courts.

The explanation for the verdict of the Criminal Court in Lausanne lies in the highly exaggerated fear of social unrest that was sweeping the ultra-conservative country of Switzerland during the post-war years, a state of panic associated with the Russian Revolution and the Soviet Union. The reader can recall the quotation from Burckhardt, in which popular thinking in Switzerland seemingly linked the influenza epidemic with the Soviet Berzine Mission.

Aubert was not content with his success in freeing Conradi and Polounine. He wanted to establish the theses propounded before the jury in Lausanne as principles of international jurisprudence. This was the sequel to his victory in Lausanne: the political utilization of his second-rate address before the Swiss court to save a self-confessed assassin and his accomplice from a just punishment. As I have already recounted, the forensic master-piece of Aubert was published in the original French and then widely translated. It became the founding document of the EIA.

It can, of course, be argued that Aubert, lawyer for the defence, had not only the right, but the obligation, to utilize all the artifices of the Vaudian code to obtain the freedom of his client. It is quite another thing to publish this specious plea as a basic political document, as did Aubert. Scholarly research was never a strong point with Aubert and his group, despite his attribution of the following achievement to the credit of the Entente in 1933: 'The development of the information service by the method of truth and authenticity ...'.[94]

But Aubert was never seeking scholarly praise, as I have shown above. Businessmen, political figures of the extreme right, military leaders such as Mannerheim and Francisco Franco were his goals. We do not know exactly which Entente publications came into Franco's hands, but there is a very great probability that *L'Affaire Conradi* was among them, and that it contributed to his political education.

XXIV

Aubert's reputation as the outstanding anti-Communist of Switzerland was subsequent to his success in the courtroom. The murder of Vorovsky, the highly political trial and the freeing of the two culprits 'widened the breach', as Burckhardt's article had said, between the two countries. The reprisals of the Soviet Union to the verdict of extreme clemency were imme-diate and durable. Arthur Ransome wrote:

> It was felt in Russia that the lack of precautions taken by the Swiss police to protect a man who, though not a fully accredited delegate, had yet received a Swiss diplomatic visa on his diplomatic passport was a reflection of the hostile attitude of the Great Powers. In this way, the murder of Vorovsky was connected in the Russian mind with the Curzon ultimatum ...[95]

All Swiss subjects, with the exception of workmen and old residents, were expelled from Russia, trade with Switzerland was prohibited and it was announced that until satisfaction had been given, Russia would send no diplomatic or trade representative to that country. The agreement concerning the Dardanelles, which Vorovsky had been charged with negotiating before his death, was eventually signed by another Soviet representative, but this took place in Rome, not in Switzerland.[96]

XXV

I have used up a considerable amount of space in analysing the text of *L'Affaire Conradi* because one can find therein the fundamental lines of the anti-Communist argument which persisted until the Gorbachov era. These were seemingly directed against the Soviet Union, as in fact they were in part, but only in part; for, essentially, they were directed against any political movement in the world that was not to the right of the political Centre. This significant fact appeared in Aubert's discourse to the jury in Lausanne: the numerous attacks against the right of the workers to strike underlined the *reactionary* nature of the Entente, as did the disparaging remarks concerning the minority groups in the Soviet Union that participated in the Civil War, the condemnation of co-education in the Soviet educational system and of government financed abortions in Soviet State hospitals. Another obscurantist cause invoked by Aubert in his harangue was the defence of the Russian Orthodox Church, which was probably the most ultra-Rightist of the Christian churches. But his firm stand against social change was most apparent in his denunciation of the movements for social revolutions in the European colonies. Even when of indigenous inspiration, Aubert always considered them to be Communist in origin.

These themes constituted Aubert's stock in trade. For him, anti-Communism signified opposition to social change. He believed in the economic status quo as firmly as he believed in Calvinism. It was to him a revealed religion. Socialists, Anarchists and freethinkers were all implicated in the 'Communist Plot'. Aubert and his collaborators never envisaged social reform as an arm against Communism. In his incessant war against the working class everywhere in the world, it never occurred to him that he was himself engaged in the class struggle.

In countries where the Communist Party was not a politically significant factor, Aubert chose to oppose the Social Democrats, as in England in 1924, where he sought to distinguish himself and the Entente as foes of the Labour Party in the general elections. According to Aubert, *Bolshevism's Terrible Record* played an important role in the 1924 political campaign:

Since the British parliamentary elections were imminent, the Permanent Office [of the Entente Internationale contre la III Internationale] took everything it could out of this indictment of Moscow. The publication of Zinoviev's letter had just created the scandal we all know about. The election campaign was passionate and Bolshevism had a prominent role in it. *Bolshevism's Terrible Record* was published. Candidates and propagandists found everything they needed in this little book in order to contribute a terrifying image of the horrors of the Soviet regime to the debate in meetings, in the press, in brochures and pamphlets. Ten thousand copies were sold before the elections which consecrated the triumph of the anti-Bolsheviks.[97]

Aubert, very probably, perceived in the Fascist movement of Mussolini the political programme that he had been vaguely seeking ever since the October Revolution upset the security of his life in Geneva. A suggestion of this is found in his harangue to the Lausanne jury. After denouncing, in the first part of his address, the reception (too cordial, in his view) offered to Vorovsky in Italy, he came back later to the theme, with these slightly embittered words:

> Even today, if one can believe the news from Italy, in this country that Mussolini seemed to be guiding towards a noble destiny, they are preparing to negotiate with the Soviets, whom the fascists not so long ago treated as criminals ...[98]

At the same time that Aubert was fantasizing about the 'noble destinies' of Mussolini's projects, he instinctively recognized the danger in anti-Fascism. In his discourse at Lausanne, he condemned propaganda acts of the Third International in this manner. After enumerating 'strikes in Sweden, in England (miners, railwaymen), Italy (sailors), Germany (Communist insurrections)', he declaimed: 'Anti-fascism serves as a pretext to establish combat organizations.'[99]

The anti-Fascist line that appeared in Aubert's forensic declaration in 1923 was to be followed by the Entente to the end: he collaborated with the Nazis in 1933 and with Franco in 1936, with Hitler in 1940 and throughout the Nazi campaign in Russia.

XXVI

Switzerland was one of the focal points of Civic Union activity, which sought to control and stop social ferment in post-war Europe. This right-wing activity was inspired by hostility and fear of the Russian Revolution. The national Civic Union groups in each country entered into relations with the others, and an effort was made to 'create a sort of European civic federation intended as mutual aid and help in the common struggle against the subversive movements engendered by the war'. A 'secret' conference among the Civic Unions was held at Lucerne at this time, but nothing came of all these efforts.[100]

This failure served as a lesson for Aubert when in 1924 he and Lodygensky, encouraged by the former's courtroom success, decided to form a 'Preparatory Committee of the International Entente against the Third

International'. This work began on a modest scale, although Aubert had been promised financial help from three of his banker friends.

The first meeting of the 'Preparatory Committee' took place on 13 March 1924, being present the host Aubert, Colonel Odier of the Swiss army, two bankers, a doctor in chemistry, who was also secretary of the *Union Civique Romande*, and Dr Lodygensky. Aubert was named president of the 'Preparatory Committee'. The first offices were installed in rooms loaned by the *Union Civique* and the secretarial work was entrusted to a young woman who had collaborated with Lodygensky at the Red Cross.[101]

Aubert was able to procure the close collaboration of his colleagues of the *Union Civique* of Zurich. Then he obtained the support of the *Union Civiques* of France and of Belgium. The latter was headed by General Graindel. The *Union Civique* of Norway, headed by another military figure, Colonel Fugner, also joined Aubert's crusade.[102]

In June 1924, an organizational meeting to found a European Entente was held in Paris, with delegates from ten countries: France, England, Belgium, Holland, Norway, Sweden, Yugoslavia, Switzerland, Finland and the group of Russian anti-Communist refugees. Lodygensky summed up his own thoughts concerning the projected Entente in these words:

> In a good number of countries, organizations have been established in order to take up the struggle against essentially destructive, criminal communist activities. But as each organization is limited to its own country, they are dispersed, have no links with each other and are very often unaware of each other's existence.
>
> Only an international organization can fight against the Comintern, an international organization. Only together can all patriots, all men of good will in every country fight for the defence of their fatherland, family, religion and private property.[103]

These details of the first months of the Entente are in their greater part taken from the Lodygensky memoir. The two accounts of the history of the Entente, one signed by Théodore Aubert, differ in significant aspects from that of Lodygensky. Aubert, in his brochure on the first nine years of the Entente, mentions the *Union Civique* but once. He does not insist, as did Lodygensky, on the useful contacts between the CICR and the Entente's work during the early years. Nor does Aubert underline the important role in post-war Europe played by military figures in the *Unions Civiques* to repress the organizations of working men, and later in the Entente. The fundamental mission of the *Unions Civiques* was to break strikes and to put an end to any other actions considered to be 'subversive'. The French word for a strike by workers, *grève*, is treated as an obscenity in the basic texts of the Entente and also in Lodygensky's typescript, both of which were in French. Lodygensky wrote that the 'French Civic Union was led by worthy officers in retirement ...'.[104] The president of the *Union Civique* of France was a general and the secretary-general was a colonel as well as a marquis.

XXVII

Also among the first supporters of the Entente were significant members of the great Swiss banking institutions, some of whom advanced the sums necessary for the initial expenses of Aubert's project. The two brothers Gustave and René Hentsch, of the Banque Hentsch et Cie., were especially helpful to Aubert.[105] The bookkeeping of the Entente was done by an employee of the Banque Hentsch.[106] Lodygensky wrote concerning René Hentsch: 'for a time, he was the Vice-Chairman of the International Chamber of Commerce and because of this he had many contacts in the financial world of Europe and America'.[107]

Lodygensky also found his relations with the *Comité Internationale de la Croix Rouge* quite helpful for the Entente. Lucien Cramer, a member of the CICR,[108] also joined the Permanent Bureau of the Entente. 'He enjoyed a prominent position in Genevese society,' wrote Lodygensky. 'He had a considerable fortune ... He and his wife often entertained in their luxurious villa on the outskirts of Geneva.' One of Lodygensky's unwittingly revelatory anecdotes concerns a reception at Cramer's villa in honour of an international conference of the Entente. Years later, Lodygensky wrote that his wife 'said when regarding the members of our group and their guests, that it was enough to compare their heads with those of the Communist leaders to see that the former served God and the latter, the Devil'. Lodygensky continued with his own profound social commentary: 'I would add that it is not surprising since an old Russian saying states that "the Devil brands scoundrels".'[109]

In Belgium, Lodygensky profited from contacts he had made before the war through the Tsarist organization of the Russian Red Cross. It was thus that he knew distinguished persons on the Belgian scene, from Cardinal Mercier to Vandevelde, President of the Third International. However, to launch the Entente in Belgium, he depended on the Civic Union, with its president General Greindel and his assistant Major Spiltoir.[110] The latter founded an anti-Communist organization which reproduced publications originally provided by the Entente. This organization was entitled *Société d'Etudes Politiques, Sociales et Economiques* (SEPES).[111]

Another eminent member of the bourgeoisie of Geneva who joined the Bureau Permanent of the Entente was Monsieur Jacque Le Fort, who drew up the statutes for Aubert's group. Lodygensky described Le Fort as follows: 'one of the most respected members of the Geneva bar and of the International Union of Jurists; he was also very active in Swiss Protestant society, in his capacity as Chairman of the Consistory of the Genevan national Church'.[112]

Despite the support given to Aubert's enterprise by Geneva's banking community, the word *capitalism* appeared rarely, if at all, in the early statements of the EIA, nor have I found it in later bulletins. In its place was used the expression *propriété privée* (private property), words with a far wider social sweep. The four devices on the Entente's blazon could have been, in Aubert's words: fatherland, family, religion and private property. It is somewhat amusing to note that today, in the twenty-first century, in the rapidly changing society of Eastern Europe, capitalism is not always referred to by its true name, but by the euphemistic form of the expression 'market economy'.

XXVIII

The work of the Entente was strongly backed by the Swiss press, which was among the most conservative of Western Europe. The founding of the Entente was saluted by an editorial in the *Journal de Genève*, on 9 September 1924. It read in part:

> we are delighted to learn that a certain number of brave and determined men have decided to undertake a systematic struggle against the III Internationale. This movement should quite naturally take root in Switzerland, in a nation like ours which is solidly attached to freedom, the family and private property. We were not, therefore, surprised to see the Entente Internationale Anticommuniste establish its headquarters in Geneva, under the distinguished management of Mr. Th. Aubert, a lawyer who has been courageously involved in many recent incidents.

These encouraging phrases for the Entente were followed by others of high-principled counsel:

> One of the chief methods of undertaking this struggle against Bolshevism is the scrupulously precise documentation on the Bolsheviks' procedures, activities and projects. Once they are revealed to the public, these shady activities will already be half thwarted and we will only need to wait for these revelations to succeed in shaking public opinion out of its torpor and apathy. This is why we are in total sympathy with the aims of the new Entente Internationale and have decided to open our columns to its documentation, which we know to be very strictly controlled, as well as the articles and debates that its promoters will make available to us.

The editorial ended with expressions of confidence in the future work of the Entente, which was, the newspaper wrote, 'the defence of freedom and of modern civilization against the sinister propaganda of Bolshevism',

By using all our strength, we, the brave citizens who have systematically undertaken this struggle, will be accomplishing a real duty. We would add that our readers, we are sure, will find this documentation to be a source of information of the greatest interest and also new reasons for acting for the good of our country and of civilization which is threatened by an offensive return to barbarism.[113]

The true dimensions of Aubert's fight for Western civilization can only be understood when, farther on in this text, the reader realizes that the efforts of the Entente to rescue the higher values of 'civilization' were to be undertaken with the collaboration of Hitler, Mussolini, Salazar and Franco.

XXIX

In 1924, Lodygensky visited Austria, Hungary, Yugoslavia and Bulgaria in search of ideological support. In Vienna, his contact was the secretary-general of the Civic Union. He was also received by the president of the Civic Union, a former general of the Imperial Army.[114] In Budapest, Lodygensky arrived at an understanding with an anti-Communist organization which agreed to serve as liaison for the Entente with other such groups in Hungary, but which was, underlined the envoy of the Entente, unlike most such groups, not 'fiercely anti-masonic and anti-semitic'.[115] When in Yugoslavia, he had an interview with the White Russian general Wrangel, who promised Lodygensky help in gathering information concerning 'communist subversives'.[116] On the frontiers of the Soviet Union, in Sofia, Lodygensky was welcomed by the Prime Minister and by the Minister of War. He established warm relations with a leader of the Bulgarian Union of Reserve Officers, and the Union was henceforth invited to all the international conferences sponsored by the Entente.[117]

XXX

It was also late in 1924 that the Entente began to publish a series of brochures. The first was entitled *Bolchevisme et réligion*, and the second, *La lutte contre le bolchevisme*.[118] One of the brochures of the EIA that I have been able to obtain for reading was called *The Red Network: The Communist International at Work*, printed in England in 1939 but previously published in Geneva in French. It is a dry, uninteresting and unexciting work. Among the ten publications recommended in a 'Bibliography of Books [sic] for readers of *The Red Network* on Communism' are three that I have mentioned earlier in this book – Loveday's *World War in Spain*, Lunn's *Spanish Rehearsal* and the booklet *Exposure of the Secret Plan to Establish a Soviet in Spain* – all of which are worthless as journalism or history, but highly significant for the study of pro-Franco propaganda.[119]

XXXI

Switzerland, possessing neither a seacoast nor a navy, did not have any colonies in the European sense (a parent country, a body of water, a colony). However, the directors of the Entente understood quite well the importance of the colonies of the European nations to the Swiss financial institutions and in the world-wide struggle between the European empires and the Communist movements. The defence of capitalist imperialism was a constant theme in the literature of the Entente. This pro-imperialist propaganda also helped the Entente financially when, as was frequently the case, the Entente needed economic assistance. This was notably the situation in 1927, when an international economic conference was being held in Geneva. Among the participants was Professor Treub, a former Dutch Finance Minister and President of the Economic Commission of the Interparliamentary Union. Lodygensky explained the virtues of Professor Treub in these words: 'In his country, Treub presided over the large organization with overall responsibility for all Dutch companies in Indonesia. He thus became aware of progressive communist infiltration in Dutch, British and French overseas possessions.'[120]

Treub, a Protestant, on learning of the Entente's existence, requested Aubert to have prepared for him 'a detailed report on Soviet-Communist action in Asia and Africa'. Aubert and Lodygensky brought the report themselves to The Hague when it was finished. This was the beginning of a beautiful friendship. The report was published in The Hague[121] and later served as the base for studies 'concerning communist infiltration in French colonies' written by the Professor Gustave Gautherot of the Université Libre de Paris,[122] who became, in the words of Lodygensky, 'one of the most active craftsmen in our movement'.[123]

Treub and his collaborators joined with Aubert and Lodygensky in forming the International Bureau for the Defence of the Colonies against Communist Infiltration, at The Hague. Treub was elected President. The Entente took 'the undertaking to closely follow the development of Soviet-Communist action in the colonies and to regularly supply the Centre in The Hague with useful information', and 'In return, Treub promised us a contribution that would cover our costs and enable us to broaden our activities in the manner indicated.'[124] Lodygensky underlined the importance of the financial aid from Holland: 'collaborating with Treub gave us real advantages and temporarily freed our Chairman from his financial worries'.[125]

XXXII

It is from reading the anecdotal pages of Lodygensky, overly frank in revealing the class prejudices of their author, that I have tried to piece together an idea of the network of relations used by Aubert and his henchmen to promote the Entente. As I have now shown, the immediate basis was the wealthy Protestant bourgeoisie of Geneva, but there were also the *Unions Civiques* of Western and Central Europe, the upper military echelons of these countries, and influential members, economically and socially, in various European capitals, of the Conseil International de la Croix Rouge; in general, persons frightened at the thought of social change in the capitalist political democracies and, above all, of any social change in the colonies. One might admit that at the start the Entente could be classed as merely furthering the 'conservative' point of view of the time, but there were always to be found in its ranks, along with respectable bankers and lawyers, men of the extreme Right, the extreme ultra-Right, until on the eve of the Second World War, the Entente was an open and frank collaborator of Nazism and Fascism.

It is evident to me, from reading parts of the Lodygensky memoir and a goodly number of Entente publications, that in the minds of Aubert and his collaborators, the expression 'anti-Communist' never meant 'pro-Democratic', but frequently 'pro-Fascist'. The sympathies of the Entente as publicly demonstrated before 1933 were generally bestowed on autocratic regimes such as the Spain of the dictator Primo de Rivera, the Portugal of Salazar and on the Fascist government of Mussolini. It was therefore inevitable that the paths of Francisco Franco and Théodore Aubert should cross and that the greatest propaganda success of the Entente should be found in its influence on the political thinking of Franco and the old band of military leaders who prepared the revolt of the Spanish military. (I shall go into detail concerning the Entente's work in Spain before and during the Civil War a bit farther on.)

XXXIII

The year 1933, when Adolf Hitler became Chancellor of the German Reich, was a watershed year for Europe and for the world. The Anti-Comintern, a subsidiary of Dr Goebbels' Ministry of Information, was the foreign organization that worked in most intimate ideological harmony with the Entente. This collaboration between the Anti-Comintern and the Entente began shortly after the Nazis seized power. Lodygensky wrote:

> The beginnings of the Antikomintern, an important German anticommunist centre, were promising. Its leader was a level-headed and competent man, a sincere believer and not a fanatical Nazi. Although

Ehrt was anti-communist, he was still a Russophile. He shared the liberal tendencies of the EIA, inspired by Christianity and humanism.[126]

However, during one of the frequent visits Lodygensky made to Berlin to consult with the direction of the Anti-Comintern, he and another White Russian, Professor Iliin, were invited to a lecture by Alfred Rosenberg, the leading intellectual in the Nazi Party and the Nazis' expert on Russia. Rosenberg was an Estonian Balt, whose chief contribution to Nazi ideology was the 'thesis that Communism and world Judaism were identical'.[127] Rosenberg's anti-Semitism was notorious and could hardly have been unknown to the two White Russian guests, invited to the lecture by Dr Ehrt himself, then head of the Anti-Comintern. Lodygensky and Iliin were deeply shocked by the frankly pronounced racial prejudices of Rosenberg. Lodygensky later recorded the impressions of Iliin and himself, writing that Rosenberg's talk 'had disgusted us with its arrogant attitude, the idiotic glorification of the German "Herren Rasse" and contempt for the "Untermenschen" of the Slavic race'.[128] The two White Russians had not imagined that the racial prejudices of the Nazis could be other than hatred of the Jews or that Hitler really meant what he wrote in *Mein Kampf* about the German conquest of the Ukrainian wheat fields.[129]

Differences of this nature did not keep the Entente from maintaining a long and fruitful relationship with the Anti-Comintern.

After the signing of the Ribbentrop–Molotov Non-aggression Pact, in August 1939, the liaison between the EIA and the Anti-Comintern weakened considerably, according to Lodygensky, but this reaction was not evident in EIA publications. When the Nazi invasion of Russia took place, a close collaboration began anew, but then declined again with the reports of German oppression of the Russian people. Lodygensky quoted from a report by Professor Iliin to the Superior of the Russian Orthodox parishes in Switzerland: 'The Germans remain faithful to their original plan: Russia must be weakened, depopulated, occupied, driven back towards Siberia and colonized by the Germans. The ferocity of the Germans is equal to that of the Reds.'[130]

XXXIV

Whereas the Anti-Comintern, with the resources of the Third Reich behind it, could be considered the superior, ideologically and financially, of the Entente, another international ultra-Rightist organization, the *Commission Internationale 'Pro-Deo'*, was, for all practical purposes, a subsidiary of the Entente. Lodygensky explained as follows:

> From the beginning of our movement, Aubert and the members of the Office in Geneva were convinced that anti-religion was one of the essential elements of militant communism. As a result, the struggle against communism was above all fought on a religious and spiritual level.[131]

The political conclusion of this line of thought resulted in the formation of a movement, essentially religious in nature, to combat Communism. Lodygensky's chronology is disappointingly vague concerning the development of the 'Pro-Deo' movement, as the following paragraph shows:

> As the fate of believers worsened in Soviet Russia and anti-religious propaganda developed in the West, it became necessary to create a special, interdenominational organization. For this reason, on my initiative, the 'Pro-Deo' International Commission was created, under the leadership of the popular Abbé Carlier, editor of 'L'Echo Illustré' and later editor in chief of the Catholic newspaper 'Le Courrier de Genève', Jacques Fort, Chairman of the Genevan Protestant Consistory and myself. Aubert, without any direct involvement in our work, did his best to promote and encourage it.[132]

Contacts were established by the founders of 'Pro-Deo' with the Superior of the Russian Orthodox Church in Geneva, and with the high clergy of the Russian, Serbian and Bulgarian churches. Since most of the members of the Bureau of the Entente were Protestants, relations with the Reformed Churches were without difficulty.[133]

Lodygensky was responsible for the day-to-day affairs of 'Pro-Deo' and for the correspondence. The secretariat of the EIA was at the disposition of 'Pro-Deo', and at times the Entente gave financial help to the newly founded 'Commission'.[134] Aubert's friends also contributed money to 'Pro-Deo', especially Le Fort and René Hentsch.[135]

In order that 'Pro-Deo' might truly represent the Christian churches in their preparations for warfare against the Soviet Union, it was necessary that the Catholic Church become involved in the work of 'Pro-Deo'. This contact was made when a fellow member of the Geneva bar brought Aubert into rapport with the Catholic vicar-general of the Geneva diocese.[136]

XXXV

The Vatican and its national branches constituted the *fer-de-lance* of the religious attack against Communism and the Soviet Union. One might, therefore, be surprised that the Roman Catholic Church was not more closely allied with the Entente from the beginning. But, after reflection, it is not difficult to understand that an intimate collaboration between the Vatican and the Russian Orthodox Church was unlikely during the 1920s, but that, on the other hand, a close alliance was possible between certain Protestant groups and Orthodox elements. Théodore Aubert was, as I have already noted, a Protestant; his ancestors had fled France during the Huguenot persecutions. It is not inexact to say that the Entente was founded by socially reactionary Calvinists and by equally reactionary Orthodox personalities.

From the material that I have been permitted to read, any contact between the EIA and the Vatican was of a fairly low grade. According to Lodygensky's text, the EIA had excellent relations with the 'leaders of Catholic trades unionism in France, Belgium and Holland', and with a Mgr Arnoux 'who was the Vatican's and the Catholics' permanent liaison agent with the International Labour Office'.[137] Mgr Arnoux would seem to be the highest level on which the EIA maintained even semi-permanent relations with the Vatican.

XXXVI

Gustave Gautherot, a prominent French Catholic academic, as I have already written above, had collaborated with the Entente in its crusade in favour of European colonial imperialism, and had published an article which caught the attention of Lodygensky. The Russian admired 'the serious nature of his documentation' on the Communist problem. Lodygensky and Aubert went to Rome, armed with a letter of introduction to Cardinal Tisserant from Gautherot, a former comrade in arms. Tisserant was then Papal Librarian. He personally received the two visitors from the Entente and showed them some of the treasures of the Vatican Library.[138]

All of this does not add up to a very intimate association between the EIA and the Vatican. It was later, during the Spanish Civil War, that the Vatican and the Entente, through the *Commission Internationale 'Pro-Deo'*, cemented their common interests. 'Pro-Deo' played a less visible role in support of the Spanish rebels than did either the Vatican or the EIA, but its function may have been more important than is generally believed. I shall develop this theme farther on.

Concerning the collaboration between the Anti-Comintern and the Entente, Lodygensky wrote:

> Our collaboration with the Antikomintern during the Spanish Civil War was both active and fruitful, as it also was with our Italian friends. Germany and Italy supported Franco, obviously in pursuit of their own interests. It is, nevertheless, true that this support contributed to the victory of the Whites over the Reds and at the time was useful to the anti-communist world.[139]

We can affirm, therefore, that it was during the Spanish Civil War that the separate interests of the Anti-Comintern, the Vatican and the *Commission Internationale 'Pro-Deo'* coalesced most strongly with those of the Entente.

XXXVII

Since we now know that the Archives of the Entente are not irretrievably lost, although they cannot easily be consulted, the memoir of Georges Lodygensky is doubtless the best source now available for studying the relations of the EIA and Spain. Chapter 8 of Part I of these memoirs concerns, among other countries, those of the Iberian Peninsula. Portugal, one can read there, was 'the first foreign delegation accredited to Berne, that established contact with the Entente'. In this case, as in many others, Lodygensky is vague as to the exact date. However, when Salazar

> came to power and put in place a regime to maintain order, putting an end to incessant civil wars (which the enemies of the upright but severe Salazar are eager to forget), a permanent relationship between the Entente and the Portuguese authorities was assured by the representative of the Portuguese Red Cross, M. Freire d'Andrade. He was then appointed as his country's representative to the League of Nations ... He was very helpful to us; in particular, he introduced me to members of his government when I had to go to Lisbon to meet some partisans of Franco at the beginning of the Spanish Civil War.[140]

Salazar became Finance Minister and the strong man of Portugal in 1928, Prime Minister in 1932, but it was, in all probability, the first of these dates that Lodygensky wished to indicate. The year 1928 is also the date that Franco gave to Brian Crozier for his initiation into the secrets of the Entente. Lodygensky does not confirm this date with exactitude, but wrote that the establishment of the first contact of the Geneva Bureau with Spain 'relates to the time of Primo de Riviera [sic]'; that is, before 1930. Lodygensky described the first contact in these words:

> A Spanish organization had asked us for information on communism and, further to this request, we decided to send our Vice-Chairman, Colonel Odier, to Madrid. Aubert believed that the Colonel, in his military capacity, would be more easily able to achieve the desired result, that is, the appointment of a qualified officer by the leader of the government to ensure permanent contacts with the EIA and to represent his country at our international conferences.[141]

> Colonel Odier immediately won the case after having briefly given General Primo de Riviera [sic] a summary of the aims of our movement

and our 'desiderata'. The General appointed Colonel Ungría de Jiménez (future chief of Franco's military police) as responsible for maintaining contact with Geneva and for keeping him directly informed of any useful information. Colonel Ungría proved to be not only a competent collaborator but also a loyal friend with whom I had an excellent relationship whenever I went to Spain. He greatly strengthened our relationship with prominent Spanish figures.[142]

XXXVIII

In another chapter, Lodygensky wrote about the Civil War and the relations of the EIA with Franco. He began:

> When the Spanish Civil War broke, in April [sic] 1936, we believed it to be of the utmost importance to establish immediate contact with the Spanish patriots.
> When General Franco was still in Africa and he found out about our Bureau, he started subscribing to our publications in order to be kept well-informed about matters relating to communist activities. There is a photocopy of the subscription card, signed by the 'Generalísimo' in the EIA's files.[143]

Lodygensky, in all probability, was not in Geneva when he wrote 'Face au communisme', which would explain his imprecision as to dates. However, on this matter Suárez Fernández is the more acceptable guide, for Franco was in Africa in 1935 and not in 1934. Lodygensky has mixed up Franco's letter signalling his change of address to Africa, dated 18 March 1935,[144] with the membership demand he signed on 21 June 1934, when the Spanish government refused to continue paying for his subscription.[145] Nor is Lodygensky exact when he writes that Franco was in Africa when he first learned of the Entente's existence. The precise dates are here of importance for they show that for more than seven years Franco was an avid reader of the intellectually mediocre *Bulletins* of the Entente. We have four sources to show that Franco was a serious student of the *Bulletin*, and all four sources are in agreement that Franco readily believed what he read in the Entente publications.

XXXIX

Lodygensky recounts that, after the death of General Sanjurjo on 20 July 1936 and the subsequent rise of Franco to pre-eminence on the rebel side – Franco was known to Lodygensky as a reader of the EIA *Bulletin* – he decided to go to Portugal. He wrote: 'I believed it would be very easy for me to make useful contacts with [Franco's] partisans in Lisbon and to see how

the Spanish patriots could be most effectively assisted.'[146] Lodygensky and
another White Russian travelled on a Japanese ship from Marseilles to
Lisbon:

> We were unable to see Salazar who was relaxing in the countryside, but
> we were warmly welcomed by his deputy, the Minister of Finance, Mr.
> Ferre; the Minister of Propaganda and other senior officials, editors of
> pro-Spanish newspapers and several anti-communist Spaniards, one of
> whom was Mr Gil Robles. *La Voz* interviewed us and published our
> photos. *All these contacts made me realize what the Spanish patriots lacked
> more than anything: well-organized propaganda on an international scale.* On
> my return to Geneva, I immediately set to work on this propaganda.[147]

XL

Lodygensky and his colleagues did not do very much for the Franco cause
during the war. The Spanish Civil War itself was decided on a level which
did not concern the EIA, the level of actual warfare. The Entente had already
paid its contribution. This judgement is based on the Lodygensky memoir
and on an incomplete collection of EIA publications. Lodygensky wrote that
the EIA organized 'a Spanish service denouncing the crimes of the Reds'.[148]
Lodygensky himself edited an illustrated brochure entitled *Les sans-Dieu en
Espagne*, which 'was very successful'. This work bears no date, but its
contents would indicate the date of 1937. However, this brochure was not
officially published by the EIA, but by 'Editions du Bureau de la
Commission Intérnationale "Pro-Deo"'.[149] The EIA also prepared radio
programmes for Rebel Spanish radio stations, and during a session of the
League of Nations Assembly organized an 'impressive *anticommunist exhibi-
tion*', which 'received many visitors'.[150]

The Entente, in 1940, published a resumé of its activities since 1924, the
date of its founding, and therein wrote of its work on behalf of the Franco
cause:

> The EIA Office, with Spanish collaboration, created a special informa-
> tion service very soon after the beginning of the civil war. The
> Spanish-language periodical published by this service included most of
> the information on communism published by the Nationalist press and
> broadcast by radio stations in Burgos and other Spanish cities. The EIA
> and the Spanish anti-communist Agency collaborated very well
> together.
>
> The EIA Bulletins provided their readers with unpublished material
> on the Red regime in Spain ...[151]

Lodygensky gave a talk in the Orthodox church in Geneva on the subject 'Our Catholic brothers under the CROSS in Spain'. This talk was published in the French language, in Rebel Spain, during the Civil War.[152]

Such tasks hardly influenced the outcome of the Spanish Civil War. The labours of the Entente on behalf of the Franco cause were carried out before the fighting began, by influencing the ideological positioning of Spanish military figures ranging from General Miguel Primo de Rivera to General Francisco Franco, and on to the officers below them. It is highly possible that Théodore Aubert and Georges Lodygensky died unaware of the guidance their propaganda had offered to Franco and other Spanish officers; without knowledge of the only tangible results of any importance to their long years of misinformation.

However, Franco, on at least one occasion, expressed his gratitude for the work done on his behalf by the EIA. Lodygensky wrote:

> The 'Generalísimo' charged the Duke of Alba, at that time Nationalist ambassador in London, while he was on a mission in Geneva, to express his gratitude to us.
>
> During lunch one day with the Duke at the Métropole he told me that, while Russia was still under Imperial rule, he had had an excellent time hunting there and had killed a 'medved' (bear) at point blank range.[153]

XLI

I had expected to find in one of the *Bulletins* of the Entente some references to the 'Secret Documents of the Communist Plot', especially in view of the Anti-Comintern publication *Rotbuch über Spanien*, which, as I have mentioned before, appeared early in 1937 with reproductions of the three 'documents' in typescript. But even a reproduction of the 'documents' in the *Bulletin de la EIA* at that time would not have offered us the insight into Franco's phantasms that we now possess through the revelations of Crozier, Hills, Suárez Fernández, la Cierva and Lodygensky. And these were all witnesses who were testifying in favour of Franco and the military rebels and who, unwittingly, at the same time unveiled their own obsessions.

Although I have not found in any Entente publication a reference to the 'Secret Documents of the Communist Plot', the general idea of a Communist Plot, just any Communist Plot, was a recurring theme for the *Bulletin* of the EIA. In a 1936 *Bulletin*, published after the outbreak of the Civil War, one can read:

> Moscow, in fact, had a plan all ready. Once the communist leaders became aware of the success of their tactics with the Popular Front, a special meeting of the Comintern was held (27th February). A clear and

precise plan of action was drawn up which the Communist Party delegates at this meeting promised to observe. One only has to list the
points in this plan to show how close, when Franco and the other
Nationalists launched their revolution, the final hour had come to put
an end to the bloody regime of terror, still rapidly slipping towards the
left in which Spain was struggling.[154]

There followed a list of the ten points of the 'clear and precise plan of action'
established during the 'special meeting of the Comintern'. Six of these
points are more or less word for word among the nine points presented by
the Portuguese government on 20 October 1936 in a letter addressed to the
President of the Non-intervention Committee in London. Two of the
Portuguese points are combined to make one in the EIA document. Point 5
of the EIA list reads as follows: 'Withdrawal from Spanish Morocco and the
creation of an independent Soviet Morocco.' Then this commentary: 'It is
easier to understand, on reading this point, why the General hastened his
insurrection.'[155] The introduction to this issue of the *Bulletin* reported thus:

> The Entente's Bureau, faithful to its tradition of drawing on first-hand
> information and assessing the situation from the inside, sent observers
> to the Iberian Peninsula on two occasions as the situation there got
> worse. Mr Deonna, Secretary of the Antimarxist Institute, went to
> Barcelona in the spring of 1936, while Dr Lodygensky, a member of the
> Entente's Bureau and of the Bureau of the International Pro-Deo
> Commission, accompanied by Prince Kourakine, went to Lisbon in the
> month of August to make some enquiries on the ground. Their aim was
> to assess the situation without prejudice, to verify the various sources of
> the accounts of anti-religious Marxist services and of Red terrorism.[156]

It was undoubtedly in Lisbon that Dr Lodygensky discovered the details of
the Comintern meeting of 22 February 1936, and he published them in the
Bulletin one month before a slightly altered copy of it appeared in the official
'Portuguese Government's reply to the accusations made by the Soviet
Government'.[157]

XLII

As I have said above, the editors of the Entente *Bulletin*s were not fastidious
about to which 'Communist Plot' they preferred to attribute the responsibility for the Spanish Civil War. In the first *Bulletin d'Information Politique*
for 1937, we can read the following:

> The facts confirmed our previous accounts as far as the origin of the civil
> war in Spain was concerned: General Franco simply thwarted the Red

plot hatched against this country by Moscow who had drawn up a programme for it and had given precise instructions as to its execution.[158]

And in the same *Bulletin*, under the title 'The Moscow pyromaniacs', we learn of other wars being instigated by Litvinov and Dimitrov, heads respectively of Soviet diplomacy and of the Comintern. They were said to be seeking to provoke a war in Western Europe as well as a conflict between Japan and China. 'We are not exaggerating in the slightest by stating this, and this fact deserves our readers' attention all the more since it has been hardly brought to light by the international press.'[159] One of the strengths of the EIA was its presentation of exclusive news and secret reports: if the reader had not seen these 'facts' elsewhere, their importance was doubled for being 'secret' and 'confidential'.

Here is still another explanation and justification of the Spanish military revolt advanced by the political analysts of the Entente:

> Finally, one last observation which should prove useful to us is the fact that during the course of our inquiries we saw, more clearly than ever, how much of a crime it is to allow Communist propaganda to develop with impunity in a democratic regime, as a result of so-called liberalism. Inevitably, sooner or later, the country is driven into fratricidal combat, because once Bolshevist teaching has claimed people's minds it makes them unable to accept any moral criteria. Violence becomes the only set of rules, and how can we oppose it if not with violence, from the moment the nation refuses to allow itself to become definitively poisoned, to perish as a result of Bolshevist poison! And that is when blood flows, when the killing begins, one against another, by persons who only a short time previously were brothers and sons of one Motherland.[160]

XLIII

The testimony of Crozier and Hills concerning Franco and the EIA referred to the mass of the Entente's publications up to the outbreak of the Civil War, but Suárez Fernández, who has had access to Franco's archives, a quasi-exclusive access to them, has given special emphasis to two 'reports' of the Entente, 'one relating to the Comintern's meeting in 1935' and 'the Dimitrov report, stating that communism would soon take over once the Popular Front had won the elections'.

The phrasing of Suárez Fernández clearly indicates that there are two 'reports' under consideration and that both came from the 'Entente's services ... reports, secret in part, the contents received through confidential channels ...'. The first 'report', beyond any doubt, has an incontrovertible source, the Seventh International Congress of the Comintern, held in Moscow from 25 July to 25 August 1935. The second 'report', if we are to judge it rationally, was necessarily of a later date.

Let us look at the printed record of the Seventh Congress of the Comintern. The most useful text that I have discovered is the one published in Moscow in 1939.[161] I have sought in this book of more than 600 pages, references to two subjects: 'Dimitrov' and 'Spain'. Dimitrov, the Secretary-General of the Comintern, gave his report, entitled 'The Fascist Offensive and the Tasks of the Communist International in the Fight for the Unity of the Working Class against Fascism', on 2 August 1935.[162] It was in this significant lecture that he placed the Comintern stamp of approval on the Popular Front, on the policy of a wide collaboration among the parties of the Left, even Left of Centre, as the method by which Fascism could be defeated. (This was a complete about-face of the stratagem employed in Germany and which had permitted Hitler's accession to power.) It was in this speech that he used the simile of the Trojan Horse to describe the proposed undertaking of the united forces of all the anti-Fascists. He spoke as follows on this subject:[163]

> Comrades, you remember the ancient tale of the capture of Troy? Troy was inaccessible to the armies attacking her, thanks to her impregnable walls. And the attacking army, after suffering many sacrifices, was unable to achieve victory until, with the aid of the famous Trojan Horse, it managed to penetrate to the very heart of the enemy's camp. We revolutionary workers, it appears to me, should not be shy about using the same tactics with regard to our fascist foe, who is defending himself against the people with the help of a living wall of his cutthroats. *(Applause)*
>
> The mass movement for a united front, starting with the defence of the most elementary needs, and changing its forms and watchwords of the struggle as the latter extends and grows, is growing up *outside and inside* the fascist organizations in Germany, Italy and the other countries in which fascism possesses a mass basis. It will be the *battering ram* which will shatter the fortress of the fascist dictatorship that at present seems impregnable to many.[164]

The expression 'Trojan Horse' can be misleading, for the Greeks (it was a Greek horse, in reality) gave no advance warning to the Trojans, but Dimitrov publicly spelled out the intentions of the Popular Front. The Fascists – and the Social Democrats – were forewarned.

This report was the object of discussion on 3 to 5 August,[165] and again from 7 to 11 August.[166] Dimitrov replied to those observations on 13 August,[167] and he made the closing address on 20 August.[168] These interventions make up the total of Dimitrov's contributions, directly or indirectly to the Congress.[169]

I have noted few references to Spain in the sixty-nine pages of Dimitrov's report; these appeared on seven pages in all, sometimes merely the word Spain, in a cluster of other countries. At one point, Dimitrov declared, 'We greet the leader of the Spanish Socialists, Caballero, imprisoned by the counter-revolutionaries ...'.[170] This was the only mention of Spain on that page. On another page, in which the greater part is given over to the failure of the revolt in Asturias, the orator offered his audience a diatribe of twenty-eight lines against the Spanish Socialist Party in which he perceived Social Democratic tendencies.[171] This was by far the longest mention of Spain in the famous report of Dimitrov. These two statements were followed by remarks concerning Spain on five other pages, four of which dealt in passing with the Asturias revolt, and one of which dealt with Spain since the First World War.[172]

On one of these pages, where there is a reference to Spain, the following page continues the argument with these lines:

> In estimating the present development of the world situation, we see that a *political situation* is maturing in quite a number of countries. This makes a firm decision by our Congress on the question of a united front government a matter of great urgency and importance.[173]

This constitutes the clearest reference, albeit indirect, that I have found in Dimitrov's texts at the Seventh Congress of the Comintern in which he linked Spain and a United (Popular) Front. This was far from the precise formulas which were forming in Franco's mind, filled with Communist phantasms inspired by the pages of the Entente publications.

Spain did not occupy a prominent place in Dimitrov's report. In the section of his talk subtitled 'Cardinal Questions of the United Front in Individual Countries', only three countries are dealt with: the USA, Great Britain and France.[174] Spain was not considered by Dimitrov, on 2 August 1935, as a candidate for the establishment of a Popular Front.

Many of the orators at the Congress, among them Ercoli,[175] Pieck,[176] Thorez,[177] Marty[178] and Manuilsky,[179] mentioned Spain but it was always fleetingly and, usually, in connection with the Asturian revolt of 1934. These mentions were not necessarily flattering. Wilhelm Pieck, on 1 August spoke of Spain in these words:

> the Communist Party of Spain is still suffering from political weak-nesses. After the armed fighting in October 1934 our comrades in Spain, unlike the Communist Party of Austria, were not able to enlighten the masses as to the mistakes of the Social-Democratic leaders and to induce large numbers of Social-Democrats to turn towards communism. The fight in Spain is not over. The Party must now develop still greater initiative in organizing the masses and must make still greater efforts to establish a united front with the Socialist and

Anarchist workers in order to prepare itself for the impending political struggles. We are absolutely certain that the Spanish comrades, who are on the right road, will be able not only to correct the errors in their work, but also to achieve further and greater successes.[180]

The longest section of the Seventh Congress of the Comintern devoted to Spain was that of 'Ventura'. This pseudonym has been attributed to both José Díaz and Jesús Hernández. The latter identification seems to be the exact one. The secrecy and the pseudonyms in the Communist Parties are frustrating to the historian, but people lost their jobs, were imprisoned and frequently killed for belonging, or suspected of belonging to a Communist Party; and the inconvenience caused to the historian should be understood. The history of the Soviet Union began with armed warfare on the part of France, Great Britain and the United States against what was then merely the Russian Empire. This left a stain of suspicion on both sides, never completely wiped out.

In the London compilation of contributions to the Seventh Congress (1936), Díaz is named as a member of the Executive Committee of the Communist International, and 'Dolores' as a 'candidate member' of the same body. There are no other Spanish Communists on the lists under the heading 'Composition of the leading organs of the Communist International'.[181] The Communist penchant (necessity) for secrecy could explain the unrecognized presence of Jesús Hernández at Moscow in 1935, and we shall attribute to him the words of 'Ventura'.

'Ventura's' talk was printed on a bit less than four pages of text.[182] It does not appear in the London (1936) compilation. It began with the ritual tribute to Dimitrov's Report, which 'Ventura' declared, found its 'best confirmation in the October of the Asturias'.[183] His most pertinent statement for our present research was the following:

> We declare that we are ready to work out the terms of an agreement for united action with all those who want to fight against fascism in Spain; that we are ready to draw up an agreement that will include all sections of the country – from top to bottom, from the principal cities to the most remote hamlet – all the oppressed nationalities and all sectors of the labour movement; that, with the broad proletarian united front as a basis, we are ready to rally the large masses around an anti-fascist People's Front, and to work for the inclusion of all Left Republicans. The present is a particularly momentous juncture. The great experience of the victory of the anti-fascist People's Front in France with its tremendous reverberations in all sections of the working people of our country shows us the way.[184]

'Ventura' went on to say that 'The entire political activity of our Party must revolve around the task of organizing Workers' and Peasants' Alliances.' But this was hardly the manner in which the Spanish Popular Front was eventually formed.[185]

There was nothing, absolutely nothing, in any published paper emanating from the Seventh Congress of the Third International, attributed to Dimitrov or to any other participant, that would have convinced a reasonably well informed person that the Comintern 'was preparing an attack on Spain', to quote Suárez Fernández's description of Franco's way of thinking in 1962.

XLIV

However, Suárez Fernández also mentioned another 'report' involving Dimitrov and which weighed heavily in Franco's decisions late in 1935, early in 1936, and again in 1962. This 'report' 'affirmed the imminent intervention of communism in Spain once the Popular Front had won the elections'. Unlike Dimitrov's report to the Comintern in August 1935, this *informe* (report) is not dated by Suárez Fernández's text, but Suárez Fernández's reference bears within itself a reference which we can easily date: 'once the Popular Front won the elections'. The chronology of the Spanish Popular Front can be easily traced. It was only after weeks of discussion among the Leftist elements on the Spanish scene, and the presidential decree of Alcalá-Zamora calling for elections, signed on 7 January 1936, that the formation of a Popular Front of Left Republicans, Socialists and Communists, with some smaller Leftist parties, actually officially took place. The Popular Front programme was published only a month before the elections scheduled for 16 February.[186] It was therefore only in January 1936 that anybody except a certified soothsayer could have referred to the Spanish Popular Front. Nobody in Moscow or Madrid, or anywhere else, in August 1935 could have foreseen the Spanish general elections in February 1936. The historical reality does not, of course, rule out the publication of an apocryphal *Informe Dimitrov* by the EIA in February or March 1936, that is after the formation of the Spanish Popular Front and the victory of the Left. But this possibility cannot be invoked to explain Franco's actions earlier than February 1936.

Faced with the seeming impossibility of finding an EIA publication corresponding exactly to the description given by Suárez Fernández of the two 'reports' attributed to Dimitrov, one dealing with the Seventh International Congress of the Comintern in 1935, the other called 'the Dimitrov report' and 'which affirmed the imminent intervention of communism in Spain once the Popular Front won the elections', I decided that Franco did not have a photographic memory and I should, therefore, accept a publication of compromise, one that would fulfil the Franco–Suárez Fernández description, amended and coloured by Franco's phantasms.

Suárez Fernández does not really give a title to the documents being sought by Franco. He called them *informes*, a word that is generally translated into English by 'reports'. Nor have I found among the Entente material I have handled a single page marked 'secret'. Nevertheless, we have no reason to doubt Franco's own belief in the existence of the *informes* of the Entente, which convinced him that Spain would be threatened with a Communist uprising in the event of a Popular Front victory in the February elections.

Neither do we know why Franco kept silent about his relations with the Entente for so many years and then chose two non-Spanish biographers as his confidants in this matter. It seems clear that the small, exclusive group of Spanish officers who did receive Entente material maintained a certain secrecy about this affair towards the uninitiated. As for the numerous pro-Franco authorities on Communist activities in Spain before, during and after the war, such as Comín Colomer and Carlavilla, they apparently had no inkling even of the existence of the EIA.

XLV

The esoteric character of the Entente publications is responsible in part for the difficulties encountered in tracing the EIA *Informes* that weighed so heavily on Franco's thoughts and actions in the first months of 1936. This problem justifies a few pages to study some of the facts known about the Entente's publications.

The distribution system employed for the Entente publications was not that of an ordinary, commercial publishing house. The Entente was a propaganda organization, with irregular printings, according to the needs of the moment. There exists, as of this writing, no catalogue of the output of the EIA. The nearest thing to such a catalogue is to be found in the Bibliothèque Publique et Universitaire of Geneva. This institution has generously furnished me with copies of twelve pages, 23 cm by 17 cm, listing non-periodical printed matter (books, brochures, leaflets, etc.). The EIA holdings of the Geneva library are very incomplete. It is the legal deposit library of the Canton, but the very nature of the Entente publications may have exempted them from the obligation of the *dépôt légal*. The most extensive listing of Entente material in the United States is to be found in the Hoover Institution on War, Revolution and Peace at Stanford, California, but these bulletins had not been considered worthy of full cataloguing at the time of my first enquiry. This detail can be interpreted to mean that the Hoover Institution did not find the EIA material worthy of full cataloguing.

XLVI

I have come to the conclusion that the Entente was not greatly interested in placing its material in public or university libraries. The EIA preferred personal contacts with persons susceptible to its arguments, persons in powerful positions who were already convinced anti-Communists and who were capable of enlisting others in the anti-Communist crusade. In a brochure detailing, as its title – *Dix-sept ans de lutte contre le bolchevisme, 1924–1940* – indicated, the most important years of the Entente's existence, it was written: 'The EIA had assured to its cause the collaboration of thousands of persons, frequently influential or disposing of means for effective action.'[187]

We have already seen the methods used by Dr Lodygensky in his 1924 tour of Central Europe. Aubert, at a date not clearly defined, went to Belgrade and Sofia, 'where he was welcomed by leaders of the Orthodox Church, ministers and politicians'. At the same time, Aubert had the occasion to present the work of the Entente 'before a public composed of prominent people, Church leaders, civilians and the military in each capital'.[188] On the same journey, at Athens, Aubert was received by King George and the Minister of Propaganda. He did not meet with General Metaxas, who 'unfortunately, remained at home, due to illness'.[189] In 1940, an EIA publication stated that members of the Permanent Bureau of the EIA had made almost 150 trips abroad, to most of the European countries, to the United States, to Canada and even to Japan.[190]

The usefulness of such expeditions is difficult to calculate, but one journey, that of Colonel Odier to Madrid in 1927 or 1928, resulted in the cementing of relations between the EIA and General Primo de Rivera and, consequently, between the Entente and the military junta that brought about the Spanish military rebellion. The mechanism of delivering EIA publications to certain Spanish officers is illustrative of the workings of the Entente. The original agreement for the subscriptions was made between Colonel Odier, for the Entente, and General Primo de Rivera, for the Spanish military.[191]

From the information that I now have, it seems highly probable that the Entente material was received in bulk at the Ministry of War, and then forwarded to the different favourites of General Primo de Rivera. The names of the recipients were themselves probably unknown to Geneva. Suárez Fernández wrote that Franco signed his bulletin of *adhesion* to the Entente on 21 June 1934. This bulletin had been doubtless sent in reply to Franco's letter of 16 May of the same year. This chronology explains the confusion among certain persons as to the exact dates for Franco's relations with the Entente. His personal adherence to the EIA began on 21 June 1934, but he had been receiving EIA material since 1928. And the material that he had been receiving was that of a 'member', although he had not yet given his own signature, nor been himself personally accepted as a 'member'. He had been guaranteed, in principle, by Primo de Rivera. Not everybody who requested EIA publications received them. In 1933, the Academy of Leningrad requested EIA publications in exchange for a shipment of Soviet books. 'Nothing further came of this request.'[192]

XLVII

Another method, hardly new, of spreading EIA propaganda was to send free articles to newspapers and magazines in the hope that they would be reprinted, and thus read by tens of thousands. In 1940, the Entente claimed that the 'information service was already being used by publications appearing in nineteen languages'.[193] In the same brochure, it was stated that many specialists on the Soviet question 'were directly inspired by the bulletins received from Geneva'.[194]

But a more direct approach was also utilized by the Entente; this was the preparation of material destined to a specific public as shown in the following quotation: 'The EIA published the "Tables" of Soviet and communist organizations, printed in French, English and German and distributed worldwide, mainly to Ministries of the Interior and to the Police.'[195] According to Entente sources, the EIA succeeded in introducing into the Soviet Union ten thousand copies in Russian of an oration opposing the entry of the Soviet Union into the League of Nations; the speech had been delivered by Giuseppe Motta, a prominent Swiss Catholic figure, who was in charge of foreign affairs for the Helvetic Confederation.[196] In addition, memoirs and documents were addressed to governments, to members of parliaments, to the assemblies and lecture groups of the League of Nations, to international institutions, to churches, to economic and intellectual formations.[197]

There were also the periodical publications of the EIA, 'distributed worldwide by National Centres and their correspondents'.[198] A resumé of the periodicals, published in 1940, described them in this way:

> The periodical publications were published under different titles: 'Documentation', 'Information Bulletins' political, religious, social and economic, 'EIA Press Bulletins' in French and in Spanish; *Mitteilungsblätter über politische, soziale, religiöse und wirtschaftliche Fragen*; Monthly News Bulletin'.[199]

Elsewhere in the same booklet, there is mention of 'the regular delivery of documentary studies and information Bulletins ...'.[200]

XLVIII

Just as 1938 and 1939 were years of Nazi–Fascist–Falangist progression, so were they also very active years for the Entente:

> From March 1938 to March 1939, the secretariat edited seven general studies on Bolshevism, seven works on communism and religion, two on youth action, one on intellectual Bolshevism, eleven studies on the USSR, four on the foreign activities of the Comintern and of the Soviet government.[201]

France was also the scene for considerable production in Entente propaganda during the twelve months mentioned above:

> The special service for France sent that country seven special reports on Comintern activities in different countries, twenty-one specific news bulletins, more than five hundred pages of extracts from the Soviet press which particularly interested France and eighty-six articles and notes intended for different sections of the French press.[202]

It was France and not Spain that was the imagined theatre of the Communist menace. Even during the Civil War, Spain did not count for very much: 'The civil war in Spain, independently of the EIA Bulletins in Spanish, has been the subject of four notes; the anti-communist legislative measures, the subject of three reports.'[203]

As I remarked above, when I had found nothing in the EIA editions labelled *rapport* (report) or *informe*, nor anything marked 'secret' or 'confidential', I began seeking a bulletin or document with information which, although not in complete agreement with the formulas of Suárez Fernández, could, if interpreted in the light of Franco's background and known phobias, be accepted as the *informes* that Franco sought in vain in 1962.

It was then that I discovered in the EIA series entitled *Documentation* a few pages on which Franco's phantasms might well have been founded. A page headed 'Sommaire de la Documentation de 1935' indicates articles on the Seventh Congress in the July–August and September–October issues. All of the articles on the Congress in the July–August number were written before the opening of the Congress,[204] but in the following number there are more pertinent papers.

A section labelled 'General activities of the Comintern' was presented as follows:

> We dedicate this issue to a concise presentation of the works and resolutions of the Communist International ... We add a comprehensive view on the large and complicated manoeuvres of the Comintern concerning the extension and consolidation of the Popular Front.[205]

This Comintern campaign was further described in the EIA publication as a 'new general offensive of Bolshevism'. The EIA writer then characterized the acceptance of the Soviet Union as a member of the League of Nations, an act which had been hailed, he wrote, as 'the precursory sign of a new peaceful era', to have been instead an 'insidious manoeuvre which should facilitate this offensive by installing the "Trojan Horse" at the heart of Europe'.[206]

The third section of the essay entitled 'General activities of the Comintern' was called ' "The Single Front", the "Popular Front", Bolshevism's accomplices and auxiliaries'.[207] It is my considered opinion, after months studying the problem, that this essay was the document that Franco sought to recover in 1962, and which motivated his paranoiac behaviour just before the elections of 1936 and for some time thereafter.

Let us look at the contents of these four pages and two half pages. They probably came into Franco's hands in November 1935. They were in the French language, which Franco apparently read without too much difficulty. Their message conformed in general, and even in particulars, with Franco's political discourse and political behaviour from December 1935 to the outbreak of the Civil War, and even to the end of his days. The material in the Entente publication of September–October 1935 corresponds to the accounts based on Franco's papers published by Suárez Fernández and to Franco's conversations as reported by Crozier and Hills.

Franco was especially sensitive to political events in France, just across the Pyrenees. For some time, the EIA bulletins had been insisting on the growing Communist menace in France, and Franco could not have been insensitive to the following, which he certainly read in the late autumn of 1935:

> The Popular Front tactic launched and partly accomplished in France, is an innovation from 1934 and particularly from 1935. It considerably extends the Comintern's field of operations and aims to reinforce its shock troops by assuring them of the collaboration of politicians, intellectuals, those affiliated to no party, peasants and others who are unhappy with the regime and are capable of being harnessed to the chariot of the revolution. It should be pointed out that even the possibility of putting these new tactics into motion has been drawn up by auxiliary organizations of the Comintern who, in collaboration with agents of the Soviet government, have been able to penetrate their tentacles into the most diverse environments.[208]

And a bit further on:

> In practice, the 'Popular Front' has been particularly successful in France because it encompasses Communists, Socialists and a good number of radical Socialists in that country. It would appear that even at the very

heart of government and the administration, sympathisers for the Popular Front are not lacking.[209]

And, at the end of several paragraphs of denunciations of Communist inroads through organized groups of teachers, freethinkers, revolutionary Christians and writers, there was this sentence, 'It really is a centre for preparing civil war in France.'[210] In addition, there was another reference to France as the centre of Popular Front agitation: 'Thus, the "Popular Front", whose progress and aims in France and in some other countries we have outlined, was able to set foot in the international arena. It is completely futile to refuse to see this.'[211] Amongst all these details of the Red Peril just across the frontier, Franco read this: 'The situation in Spain is closest to that in France.'[212]

XLIX

In the same article where Franco had been reading of the threats posed by the Popular Front to neighbouring France, he was also learning of the menaces posed by Dimitrov's programme to the Fascist movements and assimilated groups. In the September–October number of *Documentation*, the pro-Fascist position of the Entente, usually nuanced, came out more into the open. The 'fascist danger' was declared to be a 'scarecrow'.[213] It denounced 'the recent creation of a new organization to "fight against the Ethiopian war", and the hard core of this organization is made up of Italian anti-fascists'.[214]

It was in defence of pro-Fascist movements, such as the Rightish leagues which had violently manifested in Paris on 6 February 1934, that the EAI article again turned to France.

> The Popular Front's immediate efforts are concentrated on breaking up the 'Patriotic Leagues', the 'Croix de Feu' in particular. The people in Moscow pulling the strings of all the cogs of the Popular Front, having learnt from the Italian and German experiences, obviously see a mortal danger for their organization in these leagues, and a certain threat to their plan. They know that the disintegration of the country has already made such progress that the State, alone, will soon be unable to face the Red forces. This is why the breaking up of the Leagues, the disintegration of the patriotic front in France is a matter of life or death for 'Moscow's allies'.[215]

And, on another page, the Entente writer spoke up for the development in Europe of organizations like the Croix-de-Feu:

the creation, the reinforcement, the development of parties and patriotic Leagues, similar to the Croix-de-Feu seem to be of the utmost importance. These Leagues should have as wide a social base as possible. Apart from political and civil action, they should pursue intelligent and disinterested social action.[216]

Finally, this article, which we have been assured that Franco read, came out against the Popular Front because it could become a menace to Fascist Italy and to Nazi Germany.

As far as the immediate aim of this international 'Popular Front' is concerned, it seems to be to overcome the fascist regime in Italy by taking advantage of the Italian-Ethiopian conflict. Then, all the forces brought together will turn against Germany. They state that they wish to fight fascism in the name of democracy, but they are preparing a Red dictatorship, in the manner of Moscow.[217]

L

Although it seems certain that the two *informes* concerning Dimitrov never existed in the precise formula of Franco's recollections, it is beyond argument that Franco himself believed that they did. We must take into account the effect on Franco's thinking and behaviour (he possessed little general culture) of a constant diet of Entente publications. I cannot pretend to evaluate the statistical articles dealing with the Soviet Union which appeared in the EIA bulletins, but what I can affirm is that what the Entente published about Spain and the Spanish Civil War was 90 per cent inexact, and that it was insalubrious to believe it. Moreover, Franco *acted* during the end of 1935 and during the months of 1936 preceding the outbreak of the war as if he were under the control of phantasms created by the publications of the EIA, especially of the two Dimitrov *informes*.

An example of how the name 'Dimitrov' was used in the writings of the EIA in 1940, which Franco may or may not have seen, is of interest:

The Third Republic has been ill for many years, or at least suffering from anaemia. The Franco-Soviet pact contributed to weakening it still further. And when it was decided, further to a proposal made by Dimitrov at the VII Congress of the Comintern in 1935, to surreptitiously inject it with the bacillus of communism, its death certificate began to be drawn up. The bacillus multiplied extraordinarily quickly and induced the final illness: the Popular Front. We remember riots, strikes, factory occupations, the glorification of leisure and disdain for work; the international impotence of Léon Blum's government, the veiled weakness of Daladier's government. Under this latter, it seemed that the II Republic was recovering. But it was only one of those fleeting and illusory recoveries that the dying often go through at their final hour.[218]

According to the dogma of the Entente, Dimitrov was not only responsible for the situation in Spain which forced Franco and the other military leaders to revolt, but also to blame for the fall of France before Hitler's panzer divisions in 1940.

LI

Although neither Crozier nor Hills made a specific reference to the 'Dimitrov reports', each gave to the contents of these reports, as formulated by Suárez Fernández, a contextual credibility. The constitution of the Popular Front was considered by George Hills to signify that an important step had been taken towards implementing 'the Comintern's decisions ... in Spain'.[219] Franco also told Hills:

> Developments in Spain towards the end of 1935 were disturbing. There was growing violence and disorder. What worried me however was not so much what was happening *within* Spain as outside and the relations between people in Spain and Moscow. I had had a full report of the proceedings of the VIIth Congress of the Comintern. I had however to be certain that what had been decided upon in Moscow was in fact going to be carried out in Spain.[220]

This quotation, more or less authorized by Franco, deserves study and interpretation. We can assume that Hills took notes, or wrote notes very soon after talking with Franco, and that the words used reflected Franco's thoughts. It would seem that Hills, despite his excellent knowledge of Castillian, wrote these notes in English. The translator, in an introductory note (p. vi), wrote that 'no Spanish text exists' for 'Mr George Hills' interviews with Franco and other prominent people'.

There are four sentences in the quotation. The first statement concerns law and order in Spain in the last weeks of 1935. 'Violence and disorder' may well have been 'increasing', but they were certainly less than they were to be once the Spanish Right realized that it had lost the elections. Franco was inclined to consider any civil state less than martial law as unruly conduct.

In the Spanish translation, an essential part of the meaning of the second sentence is changed. I consider this error to be the result of ignorance rather than of an intention to deceive the reader. In the translation, one can read the following: 'lo que más me preocupaba no era lo que ocurría *dentro* de España, sino lo que pasaba fuera y las relaciones entre el pueblo español y

Moscú'. But Hills wrote in English, translating Franco's Spanish, 'What worried me however was not so much what was happening *within* Spain as outside and the relations between people in Spain and Moscow'. The English word 'people' does mean *pueblo*, but in this context *pueblo* means *personas*. If Hills quoted Franco with exactitude, and we must suppose that he did, Franco meant that what he feared was relations between certain persons in Spain (Leftist political leaders, Communists, Socialists and so on) and Moscow. Otherwise, the sentence is meaningless. Still, it is curious that Hills did not correct the proofs, or that Franco himself did not look at them and at what he was supposed to have said.

The third sentence of the aforementioned declaration by Franco dealt with published accounts of the Seventh Congress of the Comintern and reveals much about Franco's powers of self-deception. There was hardly one possibility in a million that Franco 'had received a full report of the proceedings of the VIIth Congress of the Comintern' at the time mentioned, 'towards the end of 1935'. From my own research, I can express my personal doubts that there was available anywhere in the world for general distribution a *complete* report on the Seventh Congress of the Comintern at the time mentioned by Franco. What did Franco mean by a 'full report'? This phrase, in all probability, came from an impression that he had retained from reading EIA publications. It could have been a few pages or a few hundred pages. Franco had no experience with such matters. For Franco to have been able to decipher the report, it would have had to be written in Castillian or in French. To my knowledge, such a work does not exist, even today. There were available fascicules, by this speaker and by that speaker – there were fascicules on this subject and that subject – but there was not available a complete report.

But it is highly possible, even probable, that Franco had read something in the Entente publications that convinced him that he knew exactly what had been discussed and decided on at the Seventh Congress. Franco later gave the Entente as his source. This may have been in the form of a 'secret' report, but nothing permits me to believe that the Entente had any reliable 'secret' information. The complete report on the Comintern Congress, in its broad and general lines, was known to newspaper readers all over the world. The Comintern did all in its power to publicize the policy of the 'Trojan Horse'. It was because Franco had been brainwashed by his constant reading of Entente literature that he became excessively nervous over Spanish political developments late in 1935 and up to the outbreak of the Civil War.

There can be no doubt that Franco's reference to the 'Comintern meeting' meant Dimitrov's talk before the Seventh Congress of the Comintern in August 1935, which was, it would seem, as much on his mind in January and February 1936 as it was later in 1962, but this was not necessarily because of the situation in Spain; it was more probably because of the progress of the French Popular Front than that of the Spanish Popular Front.

Franco simply transferred the state of affairs in France as described by the Entente to what was happening in Spain or what he feared might happen.

LII

Hills, still more to the point, wrote that Franco late in January, on his way to London, where he had been ordered to go as Chief of Staff for the funeral services of King George V, was very concerned about developments in Spain. He had asked Major Barroso, then military attaché in Paris, to come to London with him as his aide-de-camp. On the way back, Franco invited Barroso to come up on deck, deserted because of the bad weather. Barroso told Hills:

> 'Now we can talk', he said, and he told me all about the Comintern meeting and how like him there were other officers who were worried – Mola and Goded, and so on – and Sanjurjo was being kept informed. He said that of course the Popular Front hadn't yet won the elections, but that he believed they would. Again, it all depended on what the Popular Front did *if* they won. But the Army had to be prepared. If the worst came to the worst, then it would be our duty to intervene.

Franco pointed out that a victory for the Popular Front meant that he would cease to be head of the General Staff. Barroso affirmed that Franco could count on him. Franco told him to remain in Paris and if an uprising should take place, 'your lot will be to explain to people in Paris, to people likely to be well disposed, what it is all about'.[221]

LIII

Franco did not apparently confide this incident with Barroso to Crozier who was reduced to mind-reading in his commentary on Franco's journey to London. In his account of the funeral procession, Crozier wrote: 'It is a safe guess that Franco's mind was ... on the Seventh Congress of the Third International, which – as Franco well knew – was largely devoted to Spain.'[222] Crozier was probably correct in his guess of what was on Franco's mind, as proved by what Barroso told Hills, but his analysis of the work of the Congress of the Comintern in August 1935 was, unfortunately, also guesswork.

Crozier wrote on the same page:

> It is worth noting that international communist plans to take control of the impending Spanish revolution were already far advanced by the time of the general elections of 1936. The Comintern's Seventh Congress had

begun its meeting in Moscow on 23 July 1935. It had examined the causes of the failure of the Asturian revolution. And it had launched the idea and slogan of the 'Popular Front' ... [223]

Crozier then went on to quote Dimitrov's lines on the tactics of the 'Trojan Horse', and to note that José Díaz, Secretary-General of the Spanish Communist Party, la Pasionaria and Vittorio Codovila, an Argentine– Italian Comintern agent in Spain, were all present to hear these words.[224] But the fact that Spanish Communists heard Dimitrov's presentation of the tactic of the 'Trojan Horse' does not mean that Dimitrov had foreseen the Spanish Popular Front.

Crozier then continued his mind-reading act with Franco, writing:

> Although Franco knew all this, as he walked in procession behind Marshal Tukhachevsky, he was not, at that stage unduly worried. His equanimity was not, however, entirely due to a naturally tranquil disposition. For one thing, though the party had grown considerably during the Republic, it was still small, with some 30,000 members, at the time of the 1936 elections. For another, there was still, in January, every reason to believe that Gil Robles's CEDA would sweep the board on polling day.
>
> Doubtless, this is why Franco told Dr Gregorio Marañón, the distinguished physician and supporter of the Republic, in Paris on his way back to Madrid that everything would calm down in Spain within a few weeks.[225]

The reader will note here the contradiction between what Hills reported from his conversation with Barroso concerning Franco's state of mind during the trip back from London and what Crozier wrote on the same subject. Crozier was using a footnote in Hugh Thomas's Penguin edition, for which the source seems, to me, a bit vague.[226] Anyway, Barroso's account is the more detailed and precise and the one I prefer.

Further evidence of Franco's preoccupation with the Comintern Congress can be found in his notes of the epoch, as given by Suárez Fernández. The note certainly concerns 1935 and the electoral period of 1936. It reads: '1935. Comintern meeting. Go for the three hundred. El Escorial meeting. Leader, leader, leader. Popular Front in Spain. The die is cast.'[227] This would seem to indicate that Franco believed that he had crossed the Rubicon. When? At the moment of the Popular Front victory?

LIV

There exists no more convincing evidence of Franco's trust in what he had read in the EIA publications than his own actions immediately after the

Popular Front victory on 16 February 1936. When the election results began coming in on the night of 16 February, Franco began running around like a chicken with its head cut off. During the three or four days that followed the defeat of the Spanish Right in the elections, Franco made frenzied efforts to have a state of war declared, through contacts with the Minister of War, Molero, the Prime Minister, Portela Valladares and the President of the Republic, Alcalá-Zamora. This account is well known. It first appeared in 1936, in the first official life of Franco by Joaquín Arraras. It has been reported so often as proof of Franco's superior political knowledge and understanding that readers are now apt to overlook the evident fact that Franco was merely trying to foment a coup d'état in the time-honoured tradition of the Spanish military. (In one of the latest repetitions of Franco's comportment at that time, that of Ricardo de la Cierva, it is described in these terms: 'The political activity of the Chief of the General Staff in the hectic days from 16th to 20th February is overwhelming.')[228]

May we not conclude that Franco's nervosity at that time, his fears of an immediate Communist uprising, unfounded on any Spanish reality, were based, as he declared to Crozier, on his interpretation of the situation in Spain and in the world as revealed by his gurus in Geneva? Brian Crozier, after talking with Franco, wrote, as I have already pointed out, that it was from reading the *Bulletin* of the Entente that he and his fellow officers were prepared, so that 'the events of 1936 did not come as a surprise to them, and they were ready to deal with the Communists'.[229]

LV

Unable to obtain the action which he desired by either the military or the political arms of the Portela Valladares government, and aware of the opposition of President Alcalá-Zamora to signing the decree establishing the *Estado de Guerra*, Franco finally gave up for the moment. He was quite probably assuaged for the time being by the failure of the Communists (and their allies of the Comintern?) to rise up in arms, as he seems to have expected.

Franco left the Peninsula on 9 March for his new post as military commander of the Canary Islands, but only after a tacit agreement with other high officers on the general lines of a conspiracy against the Popular Front government. Just before Franco's departure for the Canaries, a meeting was held in Madrid among the conspiring officers. The date is not exactly known, nor even the roster of those who attended. Hills, for example, writes that Goded was present, but he evidently had already left for the Balearics, where he had been sent, as Franco had been posted to the Canaries, to disarm him.[230] Hills comment on this gathering, however, is highly interesting: 'The meeting however did produce a consensus of opinion that all those present should proselytise the cause of revolt against the Popular Front since they all believed imminent a Communist takeover of Spain.'[231] It seems to me evident that their common dread of a Communist assault came not from events in Spain, but from the erosion of having been brainwashed for years by the propaganda of the Entente Internationale Anticommuniste.

Crozier, writing of the spring of 1936, when Franco was in the Canary Islands, stated:

> By now, Franco, in common with a number of Nationalist leaders, was convinced that the Soviet Union had prepared precise plans for a communist uprising, and Franco Salgado quotes him as saying that despite all the difficulties that lay ahead, a military uprising was the only way left to forestall a communist takeover.[232]

Suárez Fernández referred to these lines from Crozier's book with this commentary:

> Crozier ... obtained a handwritten note from Franco Salgado in which he stated that in those days his cousin [Francisco Franco] was convinced that the Soviet Union was preparing for an uprising in Spain. This was the information in the EIA report that Victor de la Serna had been given orders to search for in 1962 ... This conviction was fairly generally held and one had only to read the editorials in *Mundo Obrero* and Largo Caballero's speeches in order to be convinced.[233]

The profound conviction of Suárez Fernández is thus again shown to be that Franco's belief in a Soviet-inspired uprising in Spain was fundamentally established on EIA publications, which were then considered to be confirmed by the political scene of Spain in the spring of 1936. The care-taker of Franco's personal papers then wrote:

> We will not here enter into the much debated matter of whether the documents supplied in 1939 by Loveday about the communist plan for subversion for that summer are genuine or not. When there is doubt, as in this case, the historian must remain silent.[234]

This means that Suárez Fernández declines to take a position concerning the Loveday 'documents', of which he has doubts, but reaffirms his confidence in the Entente publications, especially in the two 'reports'.

LVI

Let us return again to Crozier's book. A few lines further on from the last quotation, Crozier again insisted on Franco's profound uneasiness concerning a Communist uprising. After an ambiguous discussion of the arguments concerning the 'Secret Documents of the Communist Plot', Crozier wrote about another Communist Plot:

> The point that interests us here is that Franco himself was among the leading figures on the Nationalist side who believed that precise communist plans existed for the liquidation of all Army officers and men, of whatever rank, known to be anti-communist, in the event of a 'conflagration'. A copy of communist orders to this effect, dated 6 June, is said to have fallen into the hands of the Army's intelligence service and to have reached Franco in the Canaries. He took them seriously enough to double the guard at his headquarters and order additional security measures.[235]

Again, Suárez Fernández, doubtless inspired by his incessant studies in Franco's papers, wrote concerning the atmosphere in Spain during the first fortnight of May 1936. 'All the signs pointed to an imminent communist coup d'état.'[236]

And, in another reference to the same period of time, Suárez Fernández observed:

> On examining the behaviour of the future 'Generalísimo' during these months, from March to June of 1936, one could almost sense something like tense expectation: would the Republic be able to react on its own to cut off the communist uprising which was seen as inevitable?[237]

(Here is another item referring to Franco's belief in the plans of the Comintern concerning Spain. Manuel Aznar, journalist and writer on military history, who was known to have close relations with Franco during the Civil War, indicated, as I have noted in the first part of this book, that Franco 'had detailed and exact reports on the resolutions the Comintern adopted to make the revolution in Spain possible and triumphant'. He also wrote that Franco 'knew the dates that the Marxist revolution had set to attack us'.[238] This is undoubtedly information that Aznar had from Franco himself.)

LVII

Franco and the men of the EIA were foredestined to meet. Born into the same epoch, that of Fascism and anti-Fascism, they shared the same prejudices of class, notably the unshakeable conviction that a strike by working men was both immoral and criminal. Hills writes that Franco, in breaking the miners' strike in 1917, was simply obeying orders, but I should like to point out that when he took away from the Spanish labourer during forty years the right to strike, he was obeying not orders but the deepest impulses of his own class feelings. There was not to my knowledge any branch of the *Union Civique* movement in Spain, but the effects of the war and the Russian Revolution on the working class in Spain were like those seen elsewhere in Europe, and Franco's conception of the rights of the labourer paralleled that of the *Unions Civiques*, which had engendered the Entente.

In another context, Franco and Lodygensky judged the European situation – the world situation – from the same watchtower and observed the same scenes below.

Suárez Fernández, who has probably looked more closely at Franco's personal papers than anybody else since El Caudillo's death, and always with a highly favourable interpretation, has written concerning the vital dilemma facing everybody in Europe, and many people elsewhere, during the period from 1933 to 1945, in these terms:

> the fight between the Axis and the Western allies seemed to him [Franco] to be madness on an enormous scale, only benefiting the Soviet Union. If they had all united against communism it is almost certain that the 'Generalísimo' would have decided to join in.[239]

The Entente, which had wagered heavily on Hitler to overthrow the Soviet Union, was profoundly discouraged when the war ended. Lodygensky wrote in his memoirs:

> I must admit that when I understood that, in the wake of Hitler's criminal and idiotic policy in Russia and the incurable ignorance of the Western leader Roosevelt, the Second World War would not bring freedom to the Russian people and would not rid the world of the communist nightmare and that it would, more than likely, leave things in a worse state than the First World War, I felt greatly disheartened and the effects were felt on my usual dynamism ...[240]

Franco, Aubert and Lodygensky had one guiding line of thought in common, from 1936 to 1945: they were prepared to inhabit a Europe controlled by Hitler, on condition that *der Führer* demolish for all time the Soviet Union. This same ideology can be attributed to all of the *Kollabos* of the Continent, including those who fought for Franco against the Spanish Republic.

For the people who inhabited the zones of decision in the world from 1936 to 1942 there was but one problem: Should an alliance be formed between the capitalist political democracies and the Soviet Union to overthrow Hitler? Or should an alliance be formed between the capitalist political democracies and Hitler to overthrow the Soviet Union? The presence of Hitler meant that war was inevitable. But when France did not react to the German occupation of the Rhineland, and France and Great Britain (and the United States) permitted Nazi Germany and Fascist Italy to destroy the Spanish Republic, when France and Great Britain abandoned Czechoslovakia, to which they were bound by a treaty, it was clear to everybody who wanted to see, including Josef Stalin, that the capitalist political democracies were more interested in the 'capitalist' quality of their description than in their 'democratic' attribution.

LVIII

It was hardly surprising that, in the first part of this book, I found no indications of any connection, close or otherwise, between Franco and the 'Secret Documents of the Communist Plot'. Aside from the fact that Franco was removed from such enterprises by reason of his transfer to the Canaries, there was another explanation for his lack of interest in those scraps of paper. Franco had knowledge of a more important 'Communist Plot', one that he considered to be based on irrefutable proofs, the material that he received from the Entente, *informes* telling him of what had *really* happened in Moscow in August 1935 and of what Dimitrov had *really* said. Few people in Spain had access to these reports. Small wonder that Franco possessed an unshakeable faith in the written words of the EIA.

We now know that two different versions of the 'Communist Plot' were being simultaneously exploited in Spain in the months preceding the outbreak of the Civil War. The 'Secret Documents of the Communist Plot' constituted an effort by right-wing elements, allied with the military conspirators and, probably, with Falangist groups, to brainwash, to disinform certain strata of the Spanish middle classes and of the upper bourgeoisie. At the same time that this operation was in full swing, Franco and his fellow schemers were themselves in the higher spheres of political intoxication, eagerly submitting to the campaign of misinformation carried on among the Spanish military since 1928 by the Entente Internationale Anticommuniste.

Notes

Part I: Conspiracy and the Spanish Civil War

1 I have previously dealt with this problem in *El mito de la cruzada de Franco*, Paris, Ruedo Ibérico, 1963, pp. 123, 247–258; *Le mythe de la croisade de Franco*, Paris, Ruedo Ibérico, 1964, pp. 163–176, 208–213; *La destrucción de Guernica*, Paris, Ruedo Ibérico, 1977, pp. 124–126; *Historia 16*, Madrid, no. 26, June 1978, pp. 41–57; *El mito de la cruzada de Franco*, Barcelona, Plaza y Janés, 1968, pp. 195–213, 367–370. This book attempts to include all the references to the 'secret documents' that I have discovered through years of research.

2 Gregory Zinoviev was an old Bolshevik, long-time companion of Lenin, who became in 1919 chairman of the executive committee of the recently founded Communist International (Comintern). The card catalogue of the Bibliothèque de Documentation Internationale Comtemporaine (University of Nanterre) describes the 'Zinoviev Letter' as follows:

> Document, signed Zinoviev; Chairman of the Foreign Committee Presidium of the Third International, dated 15th September 1924, addressed to the Central Committee of the C.P. in Great Britain, giving the latter orders for practical rebellion against their Government; on the eve of the vote ratifying the Treaty between G.B. and the USSR. Intercepted by the Foreign Office, it gave rise to a bitter diplomatic row between the English Government and the Soviet Government who alleged that the document was a forgery. In general, historians today believe it to be such and to have been written by Russian emigrés. In 1966, the Foreign Office made no statement on the matter.

> Another catalogue card referring to the book by Lewis Chester, Stephen Fay and Hugo Young entitled *The Zinoviev Letter* (London, Heinemann, 1967) reads as follows:

> Letter signed Zinoviev, 3rd International, 1924, actually forged by Russian emigrés in Berlin, sent to English CP to incite them to revolution and to support Anglo-Russian agreements being discussed. Intercepted by the Foreign Office, this forgery changed the course of the elections and changed political and economic relationships.

3 Whether Marinus van der Lubbe actually set the fire, whether or not his motivations were politically Communist, whatever may have been his mental

capabilities, there is no doubt that the 'Communist Plot' concerning the Reichstag fire was a Nazi invention. A recent biographer of Hitler, Joachim C. Fest, wrote in 1973:

> the communists always passionately denied any connection with the fire and in fact they had no motive whatsoever for it ... By instantly taking advantage of the fire to further their plans for dictatorship, the Nazis made the deed their own and manifested their complicity in a sense that is independent of 'whodunit' questions. In Nuremberg, Göring admitted that the wave of arrests and persecutions would have been carried out in any case, that the Reichstag fire only 'accelerated these steps'.
>
> (*Hitler*, Harmondsworth, Penguin, 1977, pp. 587–688)

Moreover in a showcase tribunal in Leipzig, where the Communist leaders were put on trial by the Nazis, Dimitrov, the Comintern head, and the others accused, were freed.

4 This policy of justifying the military uprising by references to the 'documents' continued for a long time outside Spain, but in Spain itself, this artifice was, beginning early in 1937, contradicted by the conflicting claims of the Carlists, the Alfonsine monarchists, the Falangists and the military, all of whom were, as they thought they saw victory approaching, jockeying for positions to demand their prerogatives as conspirators of the first hour. See Southworth, *Antifalange*, Paris, Ruedo Ibérico, 1967, pp. 89–91.

5 Del Moral was apparently a man of means. Douglas Jerrold, who was active in a small committee formed in England after the arrival of the Republic in 1931, and which included Luis Bolín and Sir Charles Petrie, wrote: 'The energizing factor on this committee was the Marquis del Moral, whose remarkable and overflowing hospitality kept our small group in being and in remarkable amity over a number of years.' (*Georgian Adventure*, London, Collins, 1937, pp. 361–362). Del Moral was also busily engaged behind the scenes during the Civil War. (See Southworth, *Guernica! Guernica!*, Berkeley, University of California Press, 1977, pp. 126–132.)

6 FO 371/20538. W 10767, Folio 257. Del Moral's covering note was sent from Sidmouth, on the Devonshire coast, about 240 kilometres from London. The urgency in the note suggested that he was extremely eager for the 'documents' to reach the Foreign Office. Why had he then waited three days before dispatching them to London? From whom had he received the 'documents'? See n. 159.

7 *Ibid.*, Folio 255. Mr C. J. Norton wrote: 'I should prefer not to put anything in writing to M. del Moral. I assume that he is on the side of the military party ... If he returns to the charge we could tell him orally that we don't believe them to be genuine.' As seen further on, this oral reply was evidently given to del Moral.

8 This booklet bore the imprint of Eyre and Spottiswoode, as did a great quantity of the pro-Franco propaganda published in Great Britain. The atrocity contents of the pamphlet were in reality an emanation of Queipo de Llano's propaganda services in Seville. The Burgos Committee attribution was apparently a London invention. A second volume, entitled *The Second and Third Official Reports on the Communist Atrocities Committed in Southern Spain from July to October 1936 by the Communist Forces of the Madrid Government*, was published in London by Eyre and Spottiswoode in February 1937 and bore a preface by Sir Arthur Bryant. A *Preliminary Official Report* went into three editions in October 1936 and at least two in November. The *Second* and *Third Official Reports* went into at least two editions. In spite of the eminent sponsorship given to the volumes, they are

historically of little value, except for documentation in a study of Francoist propaganda.

9 *A Preliminary Official Report* ..., p. 25.

10 *Ibid.*, pp. 26–27. Largo Caballero, called by someone in the 1930s the 'Lenin of Spain', was the bugbear of the Spanish Right during the months that preceded the Franco uprising. This notoriety, which hardly concorded with reality, explains why the authors of the 'documents' chose him to be head of the 'National Soviet'. His nomination as prime minister on 4 September 1936 could lend credibility to the 'documents', but this could not have been an acceptable argument at the moment that the 'documents' were given to the Foreign Office; for Largo Caballero was not yet prime minister and did not hold that post for long.

11 Tangye, Nigel, *Red, White and Spain*, London, Rich and Cowan, 1937, pp. 14–15. Anyone who has seen, in the flesh or in paintings or photographs, people with titles, well knows that not all of them conform with the fairy-tale images of aristocracy. In fact, there are far more actors, born commoners, who seem 'aristocrats' on the stage than there are born so-called aristocrats who conform with the popular idea of what constitutes the aristocratic appearance.

12 *Ibid.*

13 Letter to the author.

14 Letter to the author.

15 See Southworth, *Guernica! Guernica!*, pp. 124–126.

16 *Gringoire* was a typical example of the French pro-Fascist press of the years preceding the Second World War. See *Guernica! Guernica!*, p. 3. The director of the weekly was Horace Carbuccia, one of many Frenchmen who wrote propaganda for Franco during the Spanish War and who were later partisans of a Hitler-controlled Europe.

17 *Spanish Journey: Personal Experiences of the Civil War*, London, Eyre and Spottiswoode, 1936, p. 30. Tennant's military pass is dated 23 October 1936. The preface is dated 20 November 1936.

18 *Ibid.*, p. 30

19 *L'Espagne en flammes. Un drame qui touche la France de près*, Paris; Les Editions de Publicité et Propagande, 1936(?), p. 29. *Spain in Flames*, London, Burns, Oates and Washbourne, 1936(?). (I have not seen this publication, but it is advertised on the back cover of Dingle, *'Democracy' in Spain?*, London, Burns, Oates and Washbourne, 1st edition 1937). *Spain in Flames*, New York, The Paulist Press, 1936. (Cattell, David, T., *Communism and the Spanish Civil War*, Berkeley, University of California Press, 1956, p. 266.) *Spain in Flames*, New York, reprinted with permission of the author for the Fordham University Alumnae Association, 1937(?). These different appearances of Echevarría's pamphlet in three countries at almost the same time are of considerable interest for they constitute an early manifestation of the publishing network of the Catholic Church in support of the Franco cause. This interlocking system of Catholic propaganda exchanges was to prove to be the centre of Spanish Nationalist propaganda in Western Europe and North America.

20 It was Raymond Cartier, writing in *L'Echo de Paris* immediately after the outbreak of the military revolt, who mobilized French public opinion to oppose aid to the Spanish Republic. See Southworth, *Le mythe de la croisade de Franco*, p. 213.

21 *Revue de Paris*, pp. 721–760. Document I, pp. 755–757; Document IV pp. 751–752, note. Bardoux had a fixation on Communist plots, and the 'Secret Documents of the Communist Plot' was not his first venture into the field. On 15 August 1936, he had published an article in the *Revue de Paris* bearing the

title 'Le complot sovietique contre la patrie francaise'. I quote from the work by 'Pol Bruno', *La saga de los Giscard*, Paris, 1980:

On 15th August 1936, Jacques Bardoux publishes a long article entitled 'The Soviet plot against France' in the *Revue de Paris*. This sensational article received great publicity in the Catholic press, particularly in the *Documentation catholique* and in the *Dossiers de l'action populaire*. Jacques Bardoux's revelations were enough to surprise anyone.

'There is a conspiracy, which, if it succeeds, will establish a Red dictatorship and open our borders to German invasion. It is my duty to reveal it. Nearly all the facts which I will quote are known both to the judicial authorities and to the government ... Moscow knows that our people will refuse to go to the aid of Stalin. A Franco-German war is therefore, for the Soviet dictatorship, a pathological obsession. It would allow defeat to be avoided and the Revolution to be extended. A double result. A double benefit.'

Bardoux then explains that the plot was organized in three phases. First of all, the extreme left would be galvanized. The Comintern, using Boukharine as an intermediary, would provide large sums of money to Trotskyist organizations. Then, the CGT would be bolchevized. According to Bardoux, 'one of the important figures in the Soviet government, Nicolas Chvernik' would supervise this phase thanks to the European office of the Trade Union Internationale. Then, the central committee of the Communist Party would be mobilized: 'Thanks to the assistance provided by secret communist cells, one method of striking, out of many, has been chosen. The workers and the public must be familiarised with the idea that factories and plants belong to workers ... Travelling protagonists, of whom several are Poles, will be responsible for stirring up the agricultural daily workers.'

The style employed by Bardoux in denouncing the 'complot' of 15 August 1936 was similar to that later employed in 'revealing' the 'Secret Documents of the Communist Plot'. I continue to quote 'Pol Bruno':

After emphasizing the importance of the funds made available to the strikers, Jacques Bardoux denounces the role played by foreign propagandists and the passiveness of the public powers. 'This collusion and its success surprised the Communist Party. It believed itself to be master of the situation. As the trouble spread, as the population became impatient, on Sunday, 7th June, citizens Thorez, Duclos and Racamond decided to precipitate matters. The violence of Thorez's language was difficult to believe at the meeting at the Sports Palace on Sunday, 7th June. In the presence of Léon Blum, and in the middle of an indescribable enthusiasm, he stated that 'the Communist Party loyally supported the present government but had nothing in common with it and before very long it would be itself in power. I say again, comrades, before very long ...'

'There was stamping of feet, enthusiasm, an outburst of cries of hatred in this crowd of 30,000 people ... Women cried. Men yelled. The red flags fluttered. What was strange was that Léon Blum then got up and shook Thorez's hands for a long time, as the *Internationale* was sung by the whole crowd on their feet. I must point out that no newspaper reported these facts.' With the seizure of power of the CGT assured, Thorez and his colleagues envisaged taking power on Thursday, 11th June in the evening. On Wednesday, 10th June, Léon Blum was secretly approached. Distraught and nervous, he gave the impression that any resistance on his part would be a matter of pure form ...

'As all the witnesses have been able to confirm, Thursday, 11th June was really a pre-revolutionary day. The atmosphere in the streets was typical: spontaneous gatherings, threatening silhouettes. Everything was ready. The seizure of power was set for two o'clock in the morning, then, after some thought, for five o'clock, on Friday 12th, since the older communists remembered that during a war, attacks always took place in the early hours. 'The preparations did not go unnoticed. The Croix-de-Feu, once informed, mobilized partially and occupied strategic points. Ministers were alerted. Blum played the innocent.'

However, this plot failed and Jacques Bardoux explains why: 'Appeals were humbly made to the government in Moscow by that of Paris, and Nicolas Chvernik, in the belief that the army was still disciplined and that insufficient work had been carried out in this area, gives a counter-order which Thorez docilely carries out.' According to Jacques Bardoux, it was only a deferral and he states in conclusion that the Communist Party was preparing its revenge for the autumn ...

Such an article calls for some details and Georges Lefranc provides them in *Histoire du Front Populaire*. Georges Lefranc was at the Sports Palace meeting; Thorez never held the aims given to him by Bardoux. Being a scrupulous historian, Georges Lefranc questioned the witnesses of the time. Robert Blum wrote to him: 'Nothing I remember, however little, corroborates the idea or hypothesis that there was a communist conspiracy of which my father was aware or which was given up at the beginning of the June 1936 government.' (Letter of 19th September 1965).

Edouard Daladier's reply, the Minister of National Defence in Blum's government, confirms this: 'At that time, I never heard about this communist plot, neither in my interviews with Léon Blum nor in my meetings with his Minister of the Interior.' (Letter of 29th August 1965).

Finally, René Belin, a CGT leader at the time of the Popular Front and future Minister of Labour under Marshall Pétain, is even more explicit: 'No information at all about the communist plot that Jacques Bardoux talks about. It is astonishing how that text differs from the true facts. Clearly, Jacques Bardoux has chosen to play the role of the propagandist. He adopts neither fable nor bad faith. But how can one explain the fact that he is in a position to quote such little known facts as Chvernik being in contact with French trade union leaders? Who are the men, groups or clans manipulating Bardoux's pen with evident ideological intoxication? Are they patrons of the Comité des Forges? Members of Foch's general staff? Intellectuals from the Croix-de-Feu? A clear response to this cannot be given. But the fact remains: when the French working class decided to make its voice heard, the grandfather of the current President of the Republic did not shrink away from such gross lies. His political career was not however compromised.

Jacques Bardoux was, as shown in the preceding quotation, emotionally and psychologically prepared to believe in any Communist plot that was brought to his attention. On 26 September 1939, the French government dissolved the French Communist Party. 'Pol Bruno' observed:

Jacques Bardoux's militant anti-communism, from then on, found a good many occasions in which to express himself. Always careless about historical rigorousness, he explained that the war is as much a case of Russian aggression as German aggression. According to him, Stalin's ambition is to wear out Germany in a war against France and England in order to dissuade her from attacking the Ukraine. Then, to take advantage of the fact that the various adversaries are worn out, to destroy free and Christian countries in the West and to establish an atheistic, communist dictatorship.

On the back cover of Pol Bruno's book, one can read: 'A group of high-ranking civil-servants and journalists is hidden under the pseudonym of "Pol Bruno".'

22 Jacques Bardoux, *Le chaos espagnol. Éviterons-nous la contagion?*, Paris, Flammarion, 1937, Document I, pp. 32–34; Document IV, pp. 45–47, note. This pamphlet contains, under the heading 'La libération de l'Espagne', pp. 37–41, material not found in the *Revue de Paris*. An English translation of this pamphlet (*Chaos in Spain*) was published in London by Burns, Oates and Washbourne; it was undated but probably came out in 1937.

23 *Revue de Paris*, p. 763 *Le chaos espagnol*, p.30; *Chaos in Spain*, pp. 43–44. Bardoux added insult to injury by adding these lines: 'In October 1934, twenty-one months before any German or Italian pilot landed in the Peninsula, the Comintern and its Government had organized, armed and launched the Asturian revolutionary army, landed "seventy crates", supplied tanks and light armoured cars.' There is no truth whatsoever in the above quotation.

24 *Revue de Paris*, p. 761; *Le chaos espagnol*, p. 29; *Chaos in Spain*, p. 29.

25 *Spain: Impressions and Reflections*, London, Constable and Co., 1937, pp. 470–492.

26 Douglas Jerrold, 'The Issues in Spain', pp. 1–34. This and another article by Jerrold, 'Red Propaganda from Spain', which had appeared in the summer issue of *The American Review* (pp. 129–151), were reprinted as a pamphlet entitled *The Issues in Spain*, New York, The American Review, 1937. *The American Review*, which was a continuation of *The Bookman*, for many years edited by John Farrar, had been bought by the conservative, Seward Collins. The magazine's offices, 231 West 42nd Street, in New York City, also housed a bookshop and a lending library, wherein one could find all the books dealing with those schools of thought which might break the national unity of the non-Fascist countries. There were works espousing the New Humanities and *Action Française*; on anti-Semitism and on Pan-Arabism; on Southern United States regionalism and on English distributism; on Roger Casement and other heroes of the struggle for Irish independence; poetry by Hugh McDiarmid, a Communist but also a Scottish Nationalist; on Ukranian nationalism; on the Portugal of Salazar; on the Germany of Hitler; on the Italy of Mussolini; and on the Franco side of the Civil War. Many of these books, by authors such as Herbert Agar and Allen Tate, Walter Prescott Webb, Irving Babbitt, Ralph Adams Cram, Paul Elmer More, Ralph Borsodi, Hilaire Belloc, G. K. Chesterton, T. S. Eliot, Norman Foerster and others were far from being Fascist, but their texts were thought useful if provoking disunity and retreat in Great Britain, France and the United States and the Soviet Union, and unity and expansion in the Fascist countries. On the Monday morning, following the attack on Pearl Harbour, the bookshop was closed, and, I think, never reopened.

27 *The Nineteenth Century and After*, April 1937; *The Issues in Spain*, pp. 2–3. Jerrold condescendingly began his article with these words:

To wish to understand the Spanish situation is not enough. It is necessary also to know a good deal of recent Spanish history, to have made some little study of the art of war, to have a journalist's training in the assimilation of the facts; and above all, to realize the part played by propaganda in a conflict of vital interest, on the one hand to Spain, and on the other, to the revolutionary forces who have made Spain their battleground.

Alas for Douglas Jerrold, who attributed all these sterling qualities to Douglas Jerrold, they were not enough for him 'to understand the Spanish situation' or to keep him from certifying as genuine, 'documents' which were only too obviously false.

28 *Das Rotbuch über Spanien*, Berlin-Leipzig, Nibelungen-Verlag, 1937, pp. 71–73. In *Le mythe de la croisade de Franco* (n. 73, p. 203) and *El mito de la cruzada de Franco*, 1968, p. 197, I mistakenly wrote that the *Rotbuch* was printed before 26 February 1937; since there is a reference to the *Deutschland* incident on p. 210, the *Rotbuch* was printed after that date. There were it seems at least two editions of this book printed, of 50,000 copies each.

29 *Das Rotbuch über Spanien*, p. 69.

30 Josef Göbbels, *The Truth about Spain*, Berlin, M. Müller und Sohn, 1937(?), p. 8. This speech was delivered in September 1937, by which time the *Rotbuch* had certainly been printed.

31 *The Road to Madrid*, London, Hutchinson and Co., 1937, pp. 214–219. Gerahty presented these papers for posterity under the heading 'La Línea Document'. (p. 214).

32 *Ibid.*, pp. 218–219. Correspondents possessing Gerahty's small ration of political knowledge were never troubled by the evident contradiction between the 'plot' of the Anarchists and Syndicalists and the 'sovietic dictatorship'. Collaboration between the two political groups was not possible.

33 *Ibid.*, pp. 40–41.

34 Lunn defended the Franco cause in the following publications: *And Yet so New*, London, Sheed and Ward, 1958; *Memory to Memory*, London, Hollis and Carter, 1956; *Revolutionary Socialism in Theory and Practice*, London, The Right Book Club, 1939; *Spain and the Christian Front*, New York, The Paulist Press, 1937(?); *Spain: The Unpopular Front*, London, Catholic Truth Society, 1937; *Spanish Rehearsal*, London, The National Book Association, Hutchinson and Co., 1937(?).

35 *Spanish Rehearsal*, p. 174.

36 *Spain and the Christian Front*, p. 9.

37 *Spanish Rehearsal*, p. 174.

38 *Revolutionary Socialism in Theory and Practice*, p. 68.

39 *The Unpopular Front*, p. 25, which cites p. 17 of Jerrold's reprinted article.

40 Douglas Jerrold, *Georgian Adventure*, 1937, pp. 375–376.

41 *Ibid.*, pp. 374, 376. The reference to the 'elected' government of Spain was probably a Freudian slip on the part of Jerrold.

42 *Ibid.*, pp. 367–374.

43 *Revue des Deux Mondes*, Paris, 1 October 1937, pp. 640–671. Document I, pp. 646–648; Document II, pp. 648–650; Document III, pp. 655–657; Document IV, pp. 650–655.

44 Jacques Bardoux, *Staline contre l'Europe; Les preuves du complot communiste*. Paris, Flammarion, 1937. The article in the *Revue des Deux Mondes* gave the text of the 'documents' only in French; in this brochure the texts were in both French and Spanish. Document I, pp. 10–13; Document II, pp. 14–17; Document III, pp. 27–30; Document IV, pp. 18–27.

45 *Staline contre l'Europe*, pp. 9–10. A more unreliable paragraph can with difficulty be found in the vast historiography of the Spanish Civil War. (I cannot say that I have read all the works on the subject, but I have read quite extensively among

the publications favourable to the Franco cause, that is among the more doltish found on the shelves of the library on the Spanish Civil War.) This was, as I shall demonstrate, 'written evidence' of nothing at all. Bardoux seemingly believed in the mystic qualities of a 'photocopy'. It was an outright lie for him to say that he had 'verified' the 'authenticity' of Documents I, II and III. Who authorized him to publish them?

46 The Unión General de Trabajadores (UGT) existed long before the Third International.

47 *Staline contre l'Europe*, p. 10.

48 *Ibid.*, p. 27.

49 *Ibid.*, pp. 17–18.

50 *La renaissance d'Espagne*, Paris, Plon, 1938, p. 73.

51 Jacques Bardoux, *Chaos in Spain.*

52 *Spain's Ordeal*, London–New York, Longmans, Green and Co., 1938, pp. 85, 89, 91.

53 *Ibid.*, p. 85.

54 This propaganda pastoral letter is filled with counter-verities which, in a less loftily inspired script, would be characterized, correctly, as lies. The purely imaginary formation of '150,000 shock troops' is and was an insult to the intelligence of the Spanish people.

55 Bardoux, *Revue des Deux Mondes*, Paris, 1 October 1937, pp. 646–658. Sencourt, *Spain's Ordeal*, p. 89.

56 *Ibid.*, p. 91.

57 *Exposure of the Secret Plan to Establish a Soviet in Spain, London,* Friends of National Spain, 1938.

58 Douglas Jerrold, *Georgian Adventure*, pp. 361–362.

59 *The Times*, London, 3 May 1938, pp. 17–18. There was also an editorial based on the Riga dispatch, p. 17. The use of Riga as a centre for disinformation concerning the Soviet Union during the 1920s and 1930s merits detailed study. Gabriel Jackson suggests that the 'documents' were published in this article (*The Spanish Republic and the Civil War, 1931–1939*, Princeton, Princeton University Press, 1965, p. 515); in fact, the article dealt only incidentally with Spain and in no way touched the 'documents'.

60 *Exposure*, p. 3. This display of pseudo-scholarship adds nothing as an argument in favour of the authenticity of the 'documents'.

61 *Ibid.*, p. 4.

62 *Ibid.*, pp. 10, 12.

63 *Ibid.*, p. 5.

64 William Foss and Cecil Gerahty, *The Spanish Arena*, London, Robert Hale, 1938, Document I, pp. 268–269; Document IV, pp. 265–267. The preface is by His Grace, the Duke of Alba, Franco's representative in the United Kingdom. There was also a Right Book Club edition (1938). This book club boasted of having on its committee twenty-three members of parliament, including Viscount Halifax. The book was also translated and published in Germany and Italy (*Die spanische Arena*, Berlin–Stuttgart, Rowohlt, 193(?); *Arena spagnola*, Milan, Mondadori, 1938). The thesis of *The Spanish Arena* was (London, Robert Hale, p. 249):

We have shown that Spain was the victim of a vast Communist plot, inspired and controlled by continental Freemasons, largely Jewish, and international agitators, working with certain Spaniards as their tools and assistants, to establish a world domination for the Comintern ...

65 Roy Campbell, *Light on a Dark Horse*, London, Hollis and Carter, 1951, p. 351.
66 Arthur F. Loveday, *World War in Spain*, London, John Murray, 1939, pp. 176–183.
67 *Ibid.*, pp. 55–56.
68 *Ibid.*, p. 103.
69 *Ibid.*, p. 176.
70 Arnold Lunn, *Revolutionary Socialism in Theory and Practice*, p. 63. This is nonsense. There is absolutely no relationship whatsoever between the article in *The Times* and the 'documents'.
71 Merwin K. Hart, *America, Look at Spain*, New York, P. J. Kennedy and Sons, 1939, pp. 221–228.
72 *Ibid.*, p. 73. Hart did not name the source as being *Exposure*, but he did credit the 'translation' as being that 'published by the Friends of National Spain'. He also explained:

> As a matter of fact, five copies, practically identical, of the document were found in possession of Communist leaders in five different places. These places were the General Communist Headquarters in Spain, at Palma on the island of Majorca, at Lora del Río, in the province of Seville, in a town near Badajoz and at La Línea.

He did not specify the precise locality of the 'General Communist Headquarters in Spain', but he did nullify any Anarchist relationship with the 'documents'. The word 'Anarchist', useful before the First World War to scare Americans to death, had lost some of its propaganda value.

The 'Secret Documents of the Communist Plot' seems to have had a smaller public in the United States than in either England or France. However, in 1937, at least three Catholic sources in the United States made references to the contents of the 'documents'. Father Edward Lodge Curran, Ph.D., a Catholic priest in Brooklyn (a stronghold of the Christian Front), alluded to Document III: 'Plans for a Communist Revolution had already been prepared in May 1936, under the direction of Ventura, a delegate of the Third International. The people of Spain rallied behind General Franco just in time' (*Spain in Arms. With Notes on Communism*, Brooklyn, NY, International Catholic Truth Society, 1936, p. 11). The Rev. Bernard Grimley, DD, Ph.D., wrote in the same vein:

> The army also claims that just before the insurrection they had come into possession of the complete plot for a Red revolt to establish throughout Spain the dictatorship of the proletariat. Certainly such a plot, or what reads like a plot, has been published in the areas occupied by the army.
> (*Spanish Conflict*, Paterson, NY, St Anthony Guild Press, p. 23)

A Hearst newspaper, *The New York American*, in January 1937 in a series of unsigned articles, hinted at the contents of Documents I and III:

> Besides the Socialists and Communists had a revolution of their own in store, which was scheduled to take place on May 11th, then postponed for June 29th, and finally set for July 31st. Abundant evidence of the above has been gathered now from prisoners taken by the Burgos government. Plans of the revolt were carefully laid down for the capture of the most strategical points in each town, and there was also a 'blacklist' of citizens to be shot. Also, the names of the persons scheduled to form the

Central and local Soviets, and it is significant that a number of the People's Commissars now hold portfolios in the present government.

(*The Catholic Mind*, New York, 22 January 1937, p. 36)

American public opinion was also influenced by the references to material found in the 'documents' and reproduced in the *Collective Letter of the Spanish Bishops*, of 1 July 1937. This was another piece of American Catholic propaganda which received considerable publicity and which drew some inspiration from the 'documents'. It was issued by a Catholic group in 1937. It was signed by at least a dozen presidents of Catholic universities, including Notre Dame and Fordham, by Catholics who were teaching at Princeton, Stanford, University of New York, etc., by Alfred E. Smith, former governor of New York and the candidate of the Democratic Party for the presidency of the United States in 1928, as well as by Carlton J. H. Hayes, Professor of History at Columbia University and, during the Second World War, United States Ambassador to Spain. This read in part:

> as authoritative documents show, the Spanish Republican Government was preparing for a military coup for the seizure of absolute power in the late spring or early summer of 1936. The decision of the Government, strongly Communistic, was the usurpation of governmental agencies supported by lawless military agencies for the perpetuation of a radical Leftist regime.

(*Catholics Reply to 'Open Letter' on Spain*, New York. The America Press, 1937)

There was enough inexact information in this publication to disqualify any professor of history anywhere in the world.

73 Generale Francesco Belforte, *La guerra civile in Spagna*, I, *La disintegrazione dello stato*, Varese–Milano, Instituto per gli Studi di Politica Internazionale, 1938, pp. 161–176. 'Belforte' was the *nom de plume* of General Francesco Biondi Morra.

74 *Ibid.*, pp. 127–131.

75 *Ibid.*, pp. 164–170.

76 *Ibid.*, p. 170.

77 *Ibid.*, pp. 171–173.

78 *Ibid.*, pp. 173–175.

79 *Ibid.*, pp. 175–176.

80 *Ibid.*, p. 175. Readers of *Arena spagnola*, 'traduzione autorizzata' (authorized translation) of *The Spanish Arena*, will search in vain for a reference to the 'documents'. This volume lacks a great part of the original text of the English edition (pp. 112–316, for example), but at the same time includes material in the form of notes on the misdeeds of Jews and Freemasons. Some of these notes are the work of Foss, so we must conclude that the Italian text had the authorization of at least one of the original authors. Other notes are contributed by the translator Gino Garia. This book was printed on 7 December 1938 (p. 319); that is, it was undoubtedly prepared for publication during the last half of 1938, the period during which Mussolini 'decided to take the first of a series of measures designed to align his country with Germany's anti-Jewish policy' (Meir Michaelis, *Mussolini and the Jews*, Oxford, The Clarendon Press, 1978, p. 151).

81 Ernest Bredberg, *Rebellen Franco och den Lagliga regeringen*, Stockholm, Sves Rikes, 1938.

82 Robert Brasillach and Maurice Bardèche, *Histoire de la guerre d'Espagne*, Paris, Plon, 1939, p. 53. The translator and editor of the Portuguese edition of this

work. Ferreira de Costa, added details on the composition of the alleged 'Soviet' in Spain, giving as his reference the *Rotbuch* (*Historia de la guerra de Espanha*, Lisbon, Livraria Clásica Editora, 1939, Vol. 1, pp. 99–100). This Portuguese edition in 1939 and a Spanish printing somewhat censured in Valencia in 1966 are the only translations of which I know. Perhaps the chief interest of the Brasillach–Bardèche book lies in its exemplary position as a showcase of the historical ignorance concerning the Spanish Civil War held by the European Right in 1939. However, even then the truth was not difficult to uncover. Another lesson can be found in the subsequent career of Brasillach, whose French nationalism was transformed into German-Nazi nationalism and who was condemned to death and executed in France on 6 February 1945. For a recent opinion concerning Brasillach's role during the Second World War, see Gérard Loiseaux, *La Littérature de la défaite et de la collaboration*, Paris, Publications de la Sorbonne, 1984. The Brasillach book was reprinted in Paris in 1966 by Plon, the original publisher, but the authorship is given exclusively to Brasillach, and the name of Bardèche appears only in the indication of copyright owner.

83 Léon Ponçet, *Lumière sur l'Espagne: Faits, témoignages, documents*, Lyons, Presse Lyonnais du Sud-Est, 1939, p. 132. Here is another witness obnubilated by a photocopy of a false document.

84 The publication of the *Carta Colectiva* had space on the front page of the *New York Times*, doubtless the result of the activity of the correspondent of this newspaper in the Franco zone, William P. Carney, whose loyalty to the Catholic cause may at times have interfered with his professional reporting. (*Guernica! Guernica!*, p. 431, n. 101). The very day of the German-Nationalist bombing of Guernica, Carney had telegraphed to the *New York Times* that the Basques had at their disposal an air fleet of 100 aeroplanes, when in reality the government of Bilbao had less than 10 per cent of this number (*ibid.*). Carney was decorated at the end of the war in Spain by the United States fraternal Catholic Order of the Knights of Columbus. Carney never had another significant posting by the *New York Times*, and after the Second World War, entered the service of the United States government to fight the Cold War.

85 Isidro Gomá y Tomás, *Por Dios y por España*, Barcelona, Ediciones Casulleras, 1940, pp. 570–571.

86 *Ibid.*, p. 569.

87 *Ibid.*, pp. 567–568.

88 *Ibid.*, p. 568.

89 *Ibid.*, p. 568.

90 It is generally considered bad manners to question the good faith or the honesty of a churchman. This is ridiculous when one observes the nonsense that is dispersed every day under the banner of religion. It is frequently asserted that one should respect another man's religion. I would rather respect his political beliefs. The religious faith of the majority of the believers in Spain in 1936 was inherited and was not at all the fruit of reflection; on the other hand, the Leftist political ideals held by at least half the Spanish people were in great part an intellectual choice, not an inheritance.

The decision the great majority of the Catholic apparatus adopted with the advent of the military revolt – to support it with their intellectual and literary abilities – was unfortunate for their subsequent reputations, for a study of the published books and pamphlets, either written and signed by members of the clergy or printed with the *nihil obstat*, reveals a mediocrity of historical and political knowledge and an insufficiency of the reasoning processes that would have shamed a churchman of earlier centuries. Yet Cardinal Gomá, who wrote many foolish statements about the Spanish Civil War, held the highest office in the Spanish Church; he was the Primate of Spain and at the same time he was notably misguided concerning the historical and social problems of his day. Despite this ignorance, he insisted on publicizing his opinions, and we have the right to judge them. He and the other pro-clerical scribblers could have held themselves aloof, above the mêlée, but they chose the struggle. The situation was not peculiar to Spain, but was true for all Catholic countries, with the exception of France, where a hard-learned wisdom held back at least the official scribes of the Catholic Church.

I have always found it slightly amusing that the writers of Marxist persuasion or of Anarchist faith, say the Left in general, in their studies of the War in Spain were far nearer the truth than were the Catholic authors, priests and laity. The men of the Church, who claimed to be bearers of the Truth, found it extremely easy to lie for the good cause. Perhaps all were not lying, merely ill-informed. This alibi will not cover all the falsehoods countersigned by a *nihil obstat*. It is a paradox that the institution whose spokesmen showed themselves incompetent and ignorant should, through the armed victory of the Spanish Rebels, have found itself entrusted with the education of the young in Spain, after Franco's victory.

91 F. Ferrari Billoch, *¡Masones! Así es la secta. Las logias de Palma e Ibiza*, Palma, Tip.Lit. Nueva Balear, 1937. The text is dated 20 January 1937. Ferrari Billoch's previous works on Freemasonry, the Jews and other subjects dear to the Catholic obscurantists of the time had won him a certain prestige in the Spanish Catholic press (pp. 97–100). It was possible, even probable, that this 1937 work was known to Cardinal Gomá before the *Collective Letter* was published on 1 July 1937. In his book, Ferrari Billoch referred to a *Comité Nacional de Unificación Marxista*, which, he wrote, citing still another 'document', had ordered, sometime during the pre-war months, the organization of Spain's young revolutionaries in militia formations (pp. 74–75). Gomá credited this same activity to a *Comisión Nacional de Unificación Marxista* (*Carta Colectiva*, in *Por Dios y por España*, p. 575). But Gomá certainly had other sources, for Ferrari Billoch's does not use Document III, whereas the Cardinal did. Here is a sample of Ferrari Billoch's prose:

> the Symbolic Serpent of the Seven Wise Men of Zion, defeated in Italy and Germany by the leaders of the great national movements, twisted itself around our fatherland and was threatening to pulverise it with the terrible claw of its semitic grasp.

For similar views to those of Ferrari Billoch, see José María Pemán, *La poema de la bestia y el ángel*, Zaragoza, Ediciones Jerarquía, 1938.

92 *¡Masones! Así es la secta*, pp. 76–78. The code signalled in this copy of Document I was 'E.I.M. 54–22', the same as that given in the *Gringoire* copy, supposedly found in Mallorca early in the war. Ferrari Billoch did not give the source of his 'documents', but each 'document' has a Mallorcan reference.

93 *Ibid.*, p. 77.

94 *Ibid.*.

95 *Ibid.*, p. 78.

96 *España vendida a Rusia*, Burgos, Ediciones Antisectarias, 1937. This book was Vol. 3 of the collection Ediciones Antisectarias, directed by the ultra-Rightist Catholic, Juan Tusquets. Anti-Semitism in the Spain of the 1930s and later was a cherished theme of the Roman Catholic Church, a relic of the traditional obscurantism of the Defenders of the Faith. Ant-Semitism was rarely found in the writings or speeches of the Falangists or other Spanish Fascists. It had no

worthwhile role to play in Falangist imperialism. See Southworth, *El mito de la cruzada de Franco*, 1986, pp. 170–172.

97   *España vendida a Rusia*, pp. 97–99.
98   *Ibid.*, pp. 92–94.
99   *Ibid.*, p. 103.
100   *Ibid.*, p. 100.
101   G. Orizana and José Manuel Martín Liébana, *El movimiento nacional, momento, espíritu, jornadas de adhesión, el 18 de julio en toda la nueva España*, Valladolid, Imp. Francisco G. Vicente, 1937(?).
102   *Ibid.*, p. 95.
103   *Ibid.*
104   *Ibid.*, pp. 95–99. Also on p. 99:

> The Marxists, the anti-Spaniards are the only ones responsible for the Civil War. They wanted it, they prepared for it. If they made a few mistakes in their forecasts, it is their fault and they are already paying for it ... The Army, with the few resources available to it, beat them hands down.

105   Constantino Bayle, *¿Qué pasa en España? A los católicos del mundo*, Salamanca, Delegación del Estado para Prensa y Propaganda, 1937, pp. 19–20. Father Bayle was a prolific propagandist for the Franco cause during and after the Civil War. He can be considered as the archetype of the Spanish priest emotionally dedicated to the defence of the military revolt. The national branches of the Roman Catholic Church all over the world bore the principal responsibility for the propaganda of the Spanish Nationalists. The pro-Franco forces might have found a substitute elsewhere for the propaganda labours of the Church, but the reality was that the propaganda tasks in favour of Franco were in their great majority carried out by the Catholic Church, which had the newspapers, magazines and printing presses already in place and was more than ready to help out.
   ¿Qué pasa en España? was certainly known to Cardinal Gomá. It was exemplary as a model of collaboration between State and Church: it bore the *nihil obstat* of the Church and its political purity was guaranteed by the publisher, the Delegación del Estado de Prensa y Propaganda, the equivalent at that time of the Ministry of Propaganda. The head of the Delegación was none other than the notorious Falangist priest, Fermín Yzurdiaga Lorca, who was also director of the highly ideological occasional publication of the ultra-imperialists of the Phalanx, *Jerarquía* (see Southworth, *Antifalange*, pp. 168–171).
   The greatest propaganda coup carried out by the *Franquistas* was the *Carta Colectiva*. Another propaganda book dealing with the *Carta Colectiva* – *El Mundo católico y la carta colectiva del episcopado español*, Burgos, Ediciones Rayfe, Centro de Información Católica Internacional, 1938 – was apparently written or compiled by Father Bayle. It did not carry Bayle's name, but it is attributed to him in the Jesuit monthly *Razón y Fé*, September–October, 1938, and in the *Catálogo General de la Librería Española 1931–50*, entry no. 6977. *El Mundo católico* was also an example of the collaboration in propaganda between the Church and the Spanish Rebel State. The Jesuit José María de Llanos wrote, 'Constantino Bayle, named Official Director of the "Centre of International Catholic Information", established on the initiative of His Excellency Cardinal Gomá and sponsored by the Spanish State ...' (*Nuestra Ofrenda, Los jesuitas de la provincia de Toledo en la cruzada nacional*, Madrid, Apostolado de la Prensa, 1942, p. 253).

According to Luis Carreras, *El Mundo católico* ... was published in nine languages by the CICI (*Grandeur chrétienne de l'Espagne*, Paris, Sorlot, 1939, p. 124). This information is not found in the Spanish-language edition of Carreras's work *Grandeza cristiana de España*, Toulouse, Les Freres Douladoure, 1938 which lacks pp. 103–140 of the French-language copy. This detail concerning the nine translations underlines the effort made by the Church and the Franco State to extract the maximum of propaganda from the *Carta Colectiva*. Father Bayle was also the author of *El clero y los católicos vasco-separatistas y el movimiento nacional*, Madrid, Editora Nacional, 1940.

106 *Documents on German Foreign Policy, 1918–1945*, Series D (1937–1945), Vol. 3 *Germany and the Spanish Civil War, 1936–1939*, p. 8, Washington DC, US Government Printing Office, 1951.

107 *Heraldo de Aragón*, Zaragoza, 1 August 1936. During the Civil War, Zaragoza became a busy centre for pro-Franco propaganda. In November 1936, one J. Mata, in a book published in Zaragoza, asserted that a Communist revolution in Spain had been scheduled for 20 July and added such details as this: 'In Valladolid a guillotine was set up in the la Casa del Pueblo and a list of as many as 10,000 people who were to perish there.' (*¡¡España!! Apuntes histórico-críticos sobre el Alzamiento de la Patria contra la invasión masónico-bolchevique*, Zaragoza, Imp. Ed. Gambon, 1936, p. iv, n.; this note comes from Josep Fontana (ed.), *España bajo el franquismo*, Barcelona, Editorial Crítica, 1986, 'Introdución: Reflexiones sobre la naturaleza y las consecuencias del franquismo', p. 11, n. 2. According to the not always trustworthy *Catálogo General de la Librería Española 1931–50*, Vol. 3, entry no. 44.401, the author's name is Juan M. de Mata. This book bears an *imprimatur*. It will be interesting some day to catalogue the books published on the Rebel side which bore either an *imprimatur* or a *nihil obstat*. Of course, ecclesiastical authorities can emphasize that such words do not really mean that the Church guaranteed the truth of the contents of each book, but it is beyond any doubt that the majority of the readers in the Rebel Zone considered such books to contain the TRUTH. The Church could thus play with the consciences of its believers.

108 José María Iribarren, *Mola, datos para una biografía y para la historia del alzamiento nacional*, Zaragoza, Heraldo de Aragón, 1938, p. 63. Iribarren's phrases can be found word for word in Gomá's *Collective Letter*, but not in any version of Document II that I have found. This coincidence suggests, to a cynical nature like mine, that Iribarren found this information after the dates given in his diary, and added it to his book for artistic effect.

109 *Ibid.*, p. 49.

110 *Ibid.*, p. 72.

111 *Con el General Mola: Escenas y aspectos inéditos de la guerra civil*, Zaragoza, Librería General, 1937, pp. 14–15.

112 *Ibid.*, pp. 17–18.

113 *Ibid.*, p. 18.

114 Douglas Jerrold ('Jerold' on the cover), *España: Impresiones y reflejos*. Salamanca, 1937. The DEPP on the back cover referred to the Delegación del Estado para Prensa y Propaganda, which had also published the already mentioned booklet of Constantino Bayle, S.J.

115 *Ibid.*, pp. 5–7.

116 *Ibid.*, p. 6.

117 See Southworth, *Antifalange*.

118 *Dictamen de la Comisión sobre ilegitimidad de poderes actuantes en 18 de julio de 1936*, Estado Español, Ministerio de la Gobernación, [Barcelona], Editora Nacional, 1939, p. 67.

119 This part of the *Dictamen* is largely based on material found in the Portuguese document mentioned, published in Lisbon in 1937 by the Ediciones Secretariado da Propaganda Nacional. The *Dictamen* repeated the charges found in the Portuguese booklet, and occasionally repeated in Franquista propaganda, concerning a decision of the Comintern, reputed to have been taken on 27 February 1936, to provoke a revolution in Spain, based on a ten-point programme of which the final one was the provocation of a war with Portugal: 'by means of revolutionary experience'. I have not cared to mix this propaganda ploy with the present study, which deals with the use of 'documents' on a far wider scale. Sencourt's source was Léon de Poncins, *Histoire secrète de la révolution espagnole*, Paris, G. Beauchesne, 1938, pp. 174–183, which quoted extensively from the Portuguese source. One thing in common among of all of them was the affirmation of the presence of the Hungarian Communist Bela Kun in Spain during the spring of 1936. It is now well known that Bela Kun was ill in the Soviet Union at the time. The Portuguese declaration gave as its source *Le Matin* (Paris, 27 March 1936). Poncins added this note: 'Several Bolshevik leaders in Spain, such as Rosenburg, Bela Kun, Neumann, are Jews' (*Histoire secrète*, p. 179).

120 The title page bore this explanation: '(Document made available by the Friends of Nationalist Spain in England).'

121 *El por qué del movimiento nacional español*, Salamanca, Ediciones SPES, 1937, pp. 44–55.

122 Angel Viñas, *La alemania nazi y el 18 de julio*, Madrid, Alianza Editorial, 1977, pp. 149, 148, 161; Julio Rodríguez Puertolas, *Literatura Fascista Española*, Vol. 1, *Historia*, Madrid, Ediciones Akal, 1986, pp. 754–756.

123 Salvador de Madariaga, *Spain*, London, Cape, 1942.

124 *Ibid.*, p. 472.

125 This book was published by Librería Santaren in Valladolid, where many of the Rebel propaganda books appeared during the Civil War, since Madrid and Barcelona, the editorial and publishing centres of Spain, were held by the Republic. It may have even been printed before the war ended.

126 *Preparación y desarrollo del alzamiento nacional*, p. 59; The text of Document IV, pp. 59–64.

127 *Ibid.*, p. 65.

128 F. Ferrari Billoch, *Entre Masones y Marxistas*, Madrid, Ediciones Españolas, 1939, p. 8.

129 *Ibid.*, p. 351.

130 But if Ferrari Billoch's book, though written before the war, was published only after the conflict, he could not have copied Father Toni's 'documents', nor could Father Toni have copied those of Ferrari Billoch. The only explanation is that both men worked from a common source.

131 *Ibid.*, p. 8.

132 Madrid, Ediciones Españolas. The date at the end of the book is '4th of February 1936', and was probably 1936 Rightist electoral propaganda. It is significant that the two most distinguished leaders of the Alfonsine Monarchists on the eve of the Civil War, Goicoechea and Calvo Sotelo, should have lent their prestige to books of such cheap pseudo-scholarship. This level of intellectual performance was that of the Spanish Right throughout the Civil War and the Franco era. In evaluating the atmosphere in which the war was being prepared, one cannot overlook the fact that intellectually the Spanish Right, its political leaders, its military figures, its clerical dignitaries lived in a world of frightening fantasies and conspiracies, peopled by menacing Freemasons.

133 *Entre Masones y Marxistas*, p. 295. The text of Document IV is found on pp. 295–301.
134 *Ibid.*, pp. 291–295.
135 *Ibid.*, pp. 290–291.
136 The two other books of Rebel propaganda which mentioned an article in *Claridad* concerning the 'documents' were, as already indicated, that of Orizana and Liébana, probably published in 1937, and that of Father Toni, also published in 1937. If the Ferrari Billoch book had been published a few weeks before the outbreak of the war, it might have removed the word 'secret' from the 'Secret Documents of the Communist Plot', and perhaps even another word or two.
137 *Historia de la cruzada española*, Madrid, Ediciones Españolas, 1940, Vol. 2, p. 509. Documents II and I are found on pp. 509 and 510.
138 *Ibid.*, p. 510.
139 *Ibid.*, p. 481.
140 'Mauricio Karl' is the pseudonym of a Spanish police officer whose real name has been written in diverse ways. Ricardo de la Cierva gives his name as Mauricio Carlavilla de la Vega (*Bibliografía sobre la guerra de España (1936–1939) y sus antecedentes históricos*, Madrid–Barcelona, 1968, p. 140). On the other hand, the *Catálogo General de la Librería Española 1931–50*, Vol. 1, p. 438, entry 12.101, says that the real name of Mauricio Karl is Julián Carlavilla del Barrio. García Venero, however, called him Julián Mauricio Carlavilla (*Falange en la guerra de España: la unificación y Hedilla*, Paris, Ruedo Ibérico, 1967, p. 309). The pseudonym 'Mauricio Karl' seems a strange disguise for anyone called 'Mauricio Carlavilla'. For more information concerning 'Mauricio Karl', see n. 224.
141 Aznar was a well-known war correspondent on the Rebel side, after escaping from Madrid in the first weeks of the fighting (see Southworth, *Antifalange*, p. 159; Maximiano García Venero, *Falange en la guerra de España: unificación y Hedilla*, pp. 242–243; Rafael Sánchez Guerra, *Mis prisiones*, Buenos Aires, Claridad, 1946, pp. 27–28). He became a favourite of Franco and was awarded the first Premio Nacional de Periodismo 'Francisco Franco' for an article published in the *Heraldo de Aragón* on 26 April 1938. (This article was reprinted as a preface to Vol. 1 of the *Historia militar de la guerra de España (1936–1939)*, Madrid, Editora Nacional, 1958, pp. 11–15, 3rd edition). With the appearance of his *Historia militar*, Aznar became the recognized authority on the military activities of the war, from the Rebel point of view, just as Arrarás was the authority on the political side. The *Historia militar* went into three editions, the last one being published in three volumes with hundreds of photographs. The allusions to Document IV and the 'Communist Plot' were unchanged in the three editions.

Aznar was eventually named Franco's Ambassador to the United Nations. He also served the Franco regime as a journalistic hatchet-man. His greatest exploit was to shame Herbert Matthews, the *New York Times* correspondent on the Republican side, into apologizing by letter to Señora Moscardó, wife of the defender of the Alcázar de Toledo, for having doubted the truth of the dramatic story of the telephone call to the Alcázar by which a Republican leader threatened to kill Moscardó's son. This story has never been proved, and if the telephone call were made, it certainly was not the cause of the death of Moscardó's son, Luis. Matthews was in a poker game where he held all the aces and Aznar bluffed him by a tawdry appeal to his honour as a gentleman. See *Le mythe de la croisade de Franco*, pp. 52–68; Luis Bolín, *España: Los años vitales*, Madrid, Espasa-Calpe, 1967, pp. 208–209. Another who expressed his doubts about the telephone call to the Alcázar and then under pressure reneged, also by letter, was Hugh Thomas (Bolín, p. 387). Both men were the objects of moral blackmail, one of them, perhaps both, by Aznar. Matthews's letter was dated 20 September 1960 and Thomas's 25 June the same year.

142   Manuel Aznar, *Historia militar de la guerra de España*, p. 25.

143   *Ibid.*, p. 30.

144   *Ibid.*, pp. 25–30.

145   Afonso G.de la Higuera y Velázquez and Luis Molins Correa, *Historia de la revolución española. Tercera guerra de independencia*, Cádiz–Madrid, Establecimientos Cerón y Librería Cervantes, 1940, p. 29.

146   Estado Mayor Central del Ejército, Servicio Histórico Militar, *Historia de la guerra de liberación (1936–1939)*, Vol. 1, *Antecedentes de la guerra*, Madrid, Imprenta del Servicio Geográfico del Ejército, 1945. A good many years ago, finding myself in the Servicio Histórico Militar, I enquired why further volumes of this work had not appeared, and I was told that jealousies and disagreements among the commanders of the Rebel armies had prevented the completion of the projected history.

147   *Ibid.*, pp. 444–445.

148   *Ibid.*, p. 444.

149   *Ibid.* This observation recalls the handwritten remark on the typescript of Document I addressed to the Foreign Office by the Marqués del Moral.

150   *Ibid.*, pp. 438–439.

151   *Ibid.*, p. 438.

152   *Historia militar de la guerra de España*, p. 26.

153   *Ibid.*, pp. 29–30.

154   A. Ramos Oliveira, *Politics, Economics and Men of Modern Spain*, London, V. Gollancz, 1946.

155   Arthur F. Loveday, *Spain, 1923–1948. Civil War and World War*, Ashcott, nr. Bridgewater, Somerset, The Boswell Publishing Co., 1949(?), 'Foreword', pp. xv–xviii.

156   *Ibid.*, pp. 48–49. Loveday's text seems to give the impression that the 'document' was handed into the Foreign Office in June, when Loveday received it. The only mention of the 'documents' found in the files of the Foreign Office is that of the 'documents' accompanying del Moral's letter dated 30 August 1936, more than two months later.

157   *Ibid.*, p. 100. Loveday's text can be interpreted to mean that he handed the 'documents' in to the Foreign Office. There is no proof of this.

158   *Ibid.*, p. 251.

159   Since it is a valid assumption that del Moral received his 'documents' from Loveday, or from an intermediary between the two, it is of interest that Loveday never mentioned del Moral. But del Moral worked behind the scenes (Southworth, *Guernica! Guernica!*, pp. 90–95). I have not seen the other papers of either Loveday or del Moral. Del Moral, in his note to the Foreign Office addressed to H. J. Seymour, wrote that he would telephone the latter on his return to London, scheduled for 2 September. Perhaps Seymour had left London before that date, because an interior memorandum dated 8 September shows that 'Mr Seymour was unable to deal with this [the 'documents'] before he left.' (W10767 F.O. 371/20538, p. 3). Another memorandum, dated 15 and 16 September, indicates that del Moral had not yet been told that the 'documents' were considered to be a 'forgery' (*ibid.* p. 2). Del Moral was probably awaiting the return of his Foreign Office contact, H. J. Seymour. Del Moral's missive was sent from Sidmouth, on the Devon coast, and nothing in Loveday's biographical notices suggests a link with that town. See n. 6.

160   *Spain, 1923–1948*, p. 48.

161   *Ibid.*, p. 251.

162 *Ibid.*, p. 48.

163 *Ibid.*, p. 251.

164 Richard Pattee, *This is Spain*, Milwaukee, The Bruce Publishing Co., 1951, p. 507. R. Pattee and A. M. Rothbauer, *Spanien, Mythos und Wirklichkeit*, Vienna–Cologne, 1955(?), pp. 523–524. Joseph Husslein, S.J., PhD, wrote in the preface of Pattee's book (pp. vi–vii):

> if there is one person qualified reliably to inform the world about Spain today, it is this scrupulously exact and careful author, who in the writing of his present work has spared no pains and labour to give us an authentic ... account for which the entire English speaking world, still so badly misinformed [sic] upon this question, can never be too grateful ... We need but further mention his present membership in the Academies of History established respectively in Ecuador, Panama, Colombia, Nicaragua and Venezuela, while he also holds today affiliation with the Geographical Society of Lisbon. All this external evidence is backed by the absolute reliability of this book and the ease with which the author uncovers the factual errors and often, no doubt, the positive falsehoods that abound in the present-day literature on Spain. As for the thoroughly paganized products of the extreme socialist, communist and anarchist combination that has strived to submerge Spain under their own godless and destructive rule, there can be nothing but utter contempt. They are not writing history but are merely laboring to promote their own red dogmatism. Yet Spain has been cluttered with such abominations, too often taken seriously by the world at large. Every letter in the work issued by the present writer is backed by facts and evidence to the ultimate degree.

The Bruce Publishing Company was one of the most prominent Catholic editorial houses in the United States and Father Husslein was the General Editor of its 'Culture and Science Series'. I have reproduced this quotation as an example of the boundless ignorance that existed in 1951 in American Catholic intellectual circles concerning the war in Spain, and which is quite probably still in existence today.

165 S. F. A. Coles, *Franco of Spain*, London, Neville Spearman, 1955; same text issued by The Newman Press, Westminster, MD, 1956. Coles, an ardent admirer of Loveday, referred approvingly to the 'Secret Documents of the Communist Plot' three times in his book, pp. 147, 172–173, 181. He considered Loveday's mention of the refusal of the Foreign Office to accept the 'documents' to be a 'significant revelation' (pp. 172–173).

> The fact has long been proved beyond peradventure by the discovery in Spain of secret documents ... that a Red revolution was planned to follow the election in May of Azaña as President ... This mass revolution the generals decided to forestall by a narrow margin ... [Why the 'decision' by a 'narrow margin'?]
>
> (*Franco of Spain*, p. 181)

166 David T. Cattell *Communism and the Spanish Civil War*, pp. 41–43.

167 *Ibid.*, p. 42.

168 *Ibid.*, p. 42. Cattell is in error on a very minor point, when he says 'The source of the other [Document III] has never been mentioned' (p. 42). An explanation for Document III can be found in the pamphlet *Exposure*, as well as in Loveday.

The explanation is inexact, but it is an attempt at an explanation. Both the pamphlet and Loveday's first book are in Cattell's bibliography.

169 *Ibid.*, p. 42.

170 Claude Martin, *Franco, soldat et chef d'état*, Paris, Quatre fils Aymon, 1959, pp. 119–120. Claude Martin, *Franco, soldado y estadista*, Madrid, Fermín Uriarte, 1966, p. 154.

171 *Franco, soldat et chef d'état*, p. 120. Martin, *Franco, soldado y estadista*, p. 154.

172 Madariaga, *op. cit.*, p. 472; Hugh Thomas, *The Spanish Civil War*, London, Eyre and Spottiswoode, 1961, p. 108.

173 I have found no reference to the 'documents' in either the Buenos Aires fourth edition of Madariaga's book (*España. Ensayo de historia contemporánea*, Editorial Suramericana, 1944) or in *Spain: A Modern History*, New York, Praeger, 1958. This 1958 book was very probably sponsored by the Congress of Cultural Freedom. See Southworth, ' "The Grand Camouflage": Julián Gorkín, Burnett Bolloten and the Spanish Civil War', in Preston and Mackenzie, *The Republic Besieged. Civil War in Spain 1936–1939*, Edinburgh, Edinburgh University Press, pp. 261–310.

174 Hugh Thomas, *The Spanish Civil War*, 1961, pp. 107–108.

175 *Ibid.*, p. 108, n. 1.

176 *Ibid.*

177 *Ibid.*

178 *Ibid.*

179 *The Illustrated London News*, London, 1961.

180 *La destruction de Guernica*, p. 342, n. 106.

181 Thomas, *op. cit.*, 1961, pp. 419–423.

182 *Ibid.*, p. 423.

183 *La destruction de Guernica*, p. 342, n. 106.

184 *The Times Literary Supplement*, 11 April 1975, p. 40.

185 *TLS*, 13 June 1975, p. 662.

186 *TLS*, 20 June 1975, p. 698.

187 Hugh Thomas, *The Spanish Civil War*, London, Hamish Hamilton, 1977, p. 631.

188 Antonio Cordón, *Trayectoria*, Paris, Editions de la Librairie du Globe, colección ebro, p. 317.

189 *Ibid.*, p. 333.

190 See n. 187.

191 *Trayectoria*, p. 339. Andújar was the town closest to Santa María de la Cabeza and remained in Republican hands until the end of the war. It was to Andújar that the women and children of Santa María were brought after the surrender, as were the combattant prisoners. It was there that Captain Cortés was operated on in a vain endeavour to save his life.

192 London, Eyre and Spottiswoode, 1967, p. 233; Madrid, Editorial Magisterio Español, 1969, p. 338.

193 Barcelona, Instituto Gallach, 1968, p. 253.

194 *TLS*, 11 April 1975, p. 40.

195 *Le mythe de la croisade de Franco; El mito de la cruzada de Franco*.

196 See n. 194.

197 *Ibid.*.

198 Douglas Jerrold, *Georgian Adventure*, pp. 367–374.

199 Burnett Bolloten has written but one book, revised from time to time, generally by the addition of new text, or by the transfer of old material from the notes to the newer text. His first book was published with the unfortunate title *The Grand Camouflage. The Communist Conspiracy in the Spanish Civil War* (London, Hollis and Carter, 1961). This book was translated and published

with a rapidity rarely encountered under such circumstances, in Barcelona, only a few weeks after its London appearance (*El gran engaño*, Barcelona, Caralt, 1961). The author rejected this version in Spanish, not because it falsified the text, but because his scholarly feelings were bruised by the mediocre erudition of the *Franquista* authorities who, eager to rush the book into print and unable to find the numerous quotations in the original Castilian, translated Bolloten's translations from Spanish to English back into a new and usually different Spanish. Later, Bolloten found a translation team to his liking and the book was published in Mexico by an ultra-Rightist editor (*La revolución española. Las izquierdas y la lucha por el poder*, Mexico, Editorial Jus, 1962). This new translation was eventually used for another printing in Barcelona (*El gran engaño*, Barcelona, Caralt, 1967). Thus, Bolloten's original text, translated according to his own desires, was published in Spain during Franco's lifetime, eight years before the Caudillo's death. At the same time, Bolloten was working on an augmented text of his book, and a first version appeared in Paris in 1977, (*La Révolution espagnole. I. La gauche et la lutte pour le pouvoir*, Paris, Ruedo Ibérico, 1977). In 1979, a further developed copy was published in the United States (*The Spanish Revolution. The Left and the Struggle for Power during the Civil War*, Chapel Hill, NC, University of North Carolina Press, 1979). A translation of this book was published in Spain in 1980 with the note 'revised edition with new material in the Spanish language version'. Bolloten died in 1987 leaving a large and more ambitiously titled revision of his book. It was published in Spanish translation in 1989 as *La Guerra Civil española: Revolución y contrarrevolución* (Madrid, Alianza Editoria). In 1991, came the publication of its English original, *The Spanish Civil War: Revolution and Counterrevolution* (Chapel Hill, NC, University of North Carolina Press, 1991).

200 *El gran engaño*, 1967, p. 104; *The Grand Camouflage*, London, 1961, p. 97.
201 *Ibid.*, n. 6. The texts referred to in this note and the previous one are also found, in their essential words, in the French edition of the book (1977, pp. 126–127), in the American edition (1979, pp. 103–104), and in the Spanish edition (1980, pp. 165–166). The chief difference lies in the fact that the material referred to by n. 206 was in a footnote in the original version and incorporated into the texts in the later books of 1977, 1979 and 1980.
202 Hellmuth Günther Dahms, *Der spanische Burgerkrieg 1936–1939*, Tübingen, Rainder Wunderlich Verlag, 1962, pp. 63–64; *La guerra civil española de 1936*, Madrid, Rialp, 1966, pp. 110–111; *A guerra civil de Espanha*, Lisbon, Editorial Ibis, 1964, pp. 51–53.
203 *Op. cit.*, Tübingen, p. 69; Madrid, p. 117; Lisbon, p. 56.
204 'Georges-Roux' (Georges Roux), *La guerre civile d'Espagne*, Paris, Fayard, 1963, pp. 207–208; *La guerra civil de España*, Madrid, Ediciones Cid, 1964, pp. 337–338. This book is one of the most misinformed of all those written on the Spanish Civil War. It formed part of a collection called by its editor, 'Les grandes études contemporaines', and was awarded a prize by the French Academy; see Southworth, *Guernica! Guernica!*, p. 251, n. 62. 'Georges-Roux' wrote, '15,000 priests or monks or nuns, of whom 14 were bishops, had their throats cut.' ' "Fifteen thousand martyrs," exclaimed Georges Bernanos, "and not an apostasy!" ' p. 299. This figure of 15,000 priests, nuns and monks was not exclaimed by Georges Bernanos but by Paul Claudel, in his poem *Aux martyrs espagnols*, which served as a prologue to the propaganda book by Juan Estelrich, Franco's public relations agent in Paris during the war, entitled *La persecution religieuse en Espagne* (Paris, Plon, 1937). Estelrich gave the figure of 16,750 ecclesiastics killed by the 'Reds' up to his date of publication, a bit more than the poet's numbers. Among the nobler lines of Claudel's intellectual effort, one can find:

Robespierre, Lenin and the others, Calvin, have not exhausted all the treasures of rage and hatred!
Voltaire, Renan and Marx have not yet touched the bottom of human stupidity!

(Estelrich 1937, pp. ii–iii)

In a book published in Madrid in 1941, *Historia de la persecución religiosa en España 1936–1939*, written by Antonio Montero Moreno and bearing both a *nihil obstat* and an *imprimatur*, the figures for the 'clergy (lay, monks and nuns) sacrificed in the religious persecution' total 6,832 (p. 762). This figure is enormous – a problem for which I have not the time to enter at this point – but it is also but 45.5 per cent of the figures advanced by 'Georges-Roux'. Such moderating information may not have reached the eyes of a research historian in Paris in 1963, but it could have more easily become known to the person who translated 'Georges-Roux's' book into Spanish, the Falangist militant-diplomat author, Felipe Ximénez Sandoval, who nevertheless had no scruples about repeating the obviously false figures of 'George-Roux', although he did the French historian the kindness of removing the credit from Bernanos to its rightful owner, Claudel. He also did a kindness to Georges Bernanos.

205 *La guerre civile d'Espagne*, p. 55.
206 *La guerre civile d'Espagne*, p. 60.
207 Félix Maíz, *Alzamiento en España: de un diario de la conspiración*, Pamplona, Editorial Gómez, 1952, Document I, pp. 82–84; Document II, pp. 85, 174–175; Document III, pp. 143–144, 146–147, 179; Document IV, p. 66. Maíz's work is presented in great part as notations from a diary, and he was in close touch with Mola almost from the day the general arrived in Pamplona, 14 March 1936. But it is impossible to believe that the diary extracts were untouched since their first recording, and this disturbing fact places in doubt certain affirmations concerning the 'secret documents'. Maíz had a wide range of credulity. As late as 1952, he asserted that Bela Kun was in Spain in the spring of 1936 (p. 56), and he even placed Ernst Thälmann, Luis Carlos Prestes and Anna Pauker in Madrid at the same time (p. 174). For Maíz, the modern history of Spain is a tale of Masonic–Communist plots, based on the protocols of the Sages of Zion (pp. 24, 272), the anti-Semitic Argentine novelist Hugo Wast, and the books of 'Mauricio Karl' (p. 68).
208 *Ibid.*, p. 66.
209 *Ibid.*, pp. 65–66.
210 *Ibid.*, p. 83.
211 *Ibid.*, pp. 83–84.
212 *Ibid.*, pp. 84–85.
213 *Ibid.*, p. 174.
214 Enrique del Corral, *Calvo Sotelo*, Madrid, Publicaciones Españolas, 1953, p. 25 (Temas Españolas, no. 29).
215 Blasco Grandi, *Togliatti y los suyos en España*, Madrid Publicaciones Españolas, 1954, pp. 11–13. Grandi also gave great importance to the alleged presence of Bela Kun in Spain during the spring of 1936.
216 Diego Sevilla Andrés, *Historia política de la zona roja*, Madrid, Editora Nacional, 1954, p. 226.
217 Diego Sevilla Andrés, *Historia política de la zona roja*, Madrid, Rialp, 1963, pp. 259–260.
218 Eduardo Comín Colomer, *Historia secreta de la segunda república*, Madrid, Editorial 'Nos', 1954, preface Mauricio Carlavilla, p. (1) (see n. 140). Mauricio Carlavilla, 'Mauricio Karl', began writing in 1932 (*El comunismo en España*,

Madrid, Imp. Sáez Hermanos). In 1934 he published *El enemigo. Marxismo, Anarquismo, Masonería* (Madrid, Imp. Sáez Hermanos). In his first book he declared himself to be 'German and a professional tourist' (p. 5) and 'from the International Secret Service' (cover). His vision of Spanish history since 1800 took the form of a Masonic conspiracy. In 1937, he wrote of the 'foul masquerade of the Popular Front, a sinister alliance of Communism and Free-Masonry under the symbol of Israel' (*Técnica del Comintern en España*, Badajoz, Tip. 'Gráfica Corporativa', pp. 4–55). There were apparently persons who took him seriously. Maximiano García Venero wrote in *Falange en la guerra civil de España: la unificatión y Hedilla* (p. 309):

> Here is an antecedent of the unification decree. The bases were given to Nicolás Mauricio Carlavilla ... Before the Uprising began, the police officer was exiled in Lisbon, close to General Sanjurjo. He went to the Nationalist zone, making pro-Falangist statements and was an observer at the meetings in Sevilla on 30th August 1936 and in Valladolid on 2nd September of the same year when the Junta de Mando was chosen. Carlavilla reported directly to Nicolás Franco. Inspired by Nicolás Franco, Felipe Ximénez de Sandoval and Carlavilla wrote the bases that, as can be judged by later events, were used to some extent.

As is well known, both Hedilla and García Venero attempted, unsuccessfully, to prohibit the distribution of García Venero's book, as well as of my book, *Antifalange*, in France; and Hedilla filed suit against García Venero, claiming that the latter's manuscript belonged to him, since he had financed the research for the historian. Hedilla won this case in Paris and then published a slightly changed version of García Venero's book, naming himself as author (*Testimonio de Manuel Hedilla*, Barcelona, Ediciones Acervo, 1972). However, it is interesting to read on p. 4 of that book, the following: 'This work was written by Maximiano García Venero under the guidance of Manuel Hedilla.' Although *Testimonio* is in great part the book of García Venero published in Paris, there are differences between the two. There are a good many pages eliminated by Hedilla, passages rewritten and even some additions. The extract cited above concerning Carlavilla and Nicolás Franco, for example, does not appear in Hedilla's version. Already, in 1970, García Venero had published another book on the general theme of the Unification (*Historia de la unificación (Falange y Requeté en 1937*, Madrid, Agesa, 1970). The text of this book is different from the book he published in Paris three years earlier. Of the three books, two by García Venero and one by Hedilla, the Paris text by García Venero is by far the more interesting, although students should look at all three.

  In the research that I undertook to write *Antifalange*, I discovered what I deemed to be a deliberate falsification by García Venero, in parts of the speech which he attributed to Hedilla during the last meeting of the Consejo Nacional of FE de las JONS on 18 April 1937. A printed text of the speech had appeared in a book by Alcázar de Velasco, *Serrano Suñer en la Falange* (Barcelona, Madrid, Ediciones Patria, 1941, pp. 73–76). García Venero, in his version of the speech, omitted parts of the text as given by Alcázar de Velasco. The phrases omitted contradicted the thesis of Hedilla, who claimed that he had not sent his men to arrest Sancho Dávila and Garcerán on the night before, provoking a scuffle in which two men were killed. This outbreak of violence was used by the entourage of Franco to intervene and later, in part, to justify the Decree of Unification.

I was writing *Antifalange* in opposition to the Spanish Fascist movement, as can be discerned in the 61-page 'Introducción. Análisis del falangismo' which preceded the 'Notas' (pp. 63–241). I had tried to limit my comments to what I considered to be clarifications and amplification of the García Venero text. However, when I arrived at the pages where García Venero dealt with Hedilla's discourse of 18 April 1937 and wherein he made changes that differed with the only printed text available at the time of that discourse (Alcázar de Velasco), I felt obliged to adopt a frankly adversary position to García Venero. I informed José Martínez, Director of Ruedo Ibérico, of this situation and he wrote to García Venero, who replied that he had made the changes because he had written the speech of Hedilla and therefore knew what Hedilla had said, although he was not among those present.

If García Venero had written that he held the 'true copy' of Hedilla's talk, I might have reconsidered my own conclusion, to wit that Hedilla had despatched his men to detain Sancho Dávila and Garcerán and bring them before him to be judged. This conclusion was based not only on Alcázar de Velasco's text of Hedilla's talk, but also on two other elements. First, my belief formed by a long study of Falangist writings, including García Venero's book, that there existed in the Falangist tradition of hierarchy a juvenile cult of violence into which the mission entrusted by Hedilla to his subalterns entered almost mechanically. Second, the written testimony of an aristocratic Finnish mercenary, Carl Magnus Gunnar Emil von Haartman, who was directing a military school for the Phalanx in the Salamanca region in April 1937. In a book published in Helsinki in Swedish in 1939 and in Finnish in 1940, von Haartman wrote that on the night in question he was called to Salamanca by Hedilla, who charged him to 'to arrest the three main leaders of this palace revolution as soon as possible' (von Haartman, *En Nordisk Caballero I Francos armé*, Helsinfors, Söderström and Co., 1939, pp. 29–30; *Antifalange*, p. 198). Although von Haartman evidently played a leading role in the events of the night of 17–18 April, García Venero did not mention him in that connection. I had the feeling that von Haartman was fairly neutral in his sentiments about the internal quarrels of the Falange, or, anyway, that he was less partisan than were the Falangists themselves as evidenced by the complete silence in Franco Spain concerning the activities of the Finnish mercenary on the night of 17–18 April 1937.

García Venero quoted from the discourse of Hedilla, in a manner to indicate that Hedilla had sent his agents on a peaceful mission. He gave no source for his text, with the changes favourable to Hedilla's position, but wrote that 'The shorthand text of the Junta's deliberations seems to have been lost' and suggested that a copy might be in the possession of the Falangist Vicente Cadenas y Vicent. He added that if these papers should reappear some day, they might be falsified. 'Who knows if one day, some copies of the shorthand text taken by Ximénez de Sandoval will make an appearance without any guarantees of authenticity?' (*Falange en la guerra de España*, p. 383). It is worth noting that García Venero considered his memory of a lost sheet of paper to be 'authentic' copy.

The obscurity surrounding Hedilla's last speech as *jefe* of FE de las JONS was, I believe, made somewhat clearer by the publication of the text of the speech in a book edited by Vicente Cadenas Vicent, entitled, *Actas del último Consejo Nacional de Falange Española de las JONS (Salamanca 18–19 de abril 1937) y algunas noticias referentes a la Jefatura nacional de prensa y propaganda editadas por Vicente Cadenas*, Madrid, Gráficas Uguina, 1975, in which my interpretation of the events was confirmed, and by the reproduction of his 1941 text by Alcázar de Velasco in another book published in 1976 (*Los 7 días de*

Salamanca, Madrid, G. Del Toro, pp. 261–273). In a note concerning Hedilla's speech, Alcázar de Velasco wrote (pp. 278–279):

This is the text taken down by Ximénez de Sandoval in shorthand and, once it was written up, I took it and put it in my briefcase in order to take it to the Press and Propaganda Ministry's files. If I did not do as I had intended, it was because of the events [the imprisonment of Alcázar de Velasco]. Because of that, I was to be the only person who brought this document publicly to light in 1941; in my book *Serrano Suñer en la Falange*, which even Hedilla himself, and it could not be otherwise, has had to accept it had to be enough, although he did it without being honest enough to quote the source. But what is really serious is that he has omitted sentences that he does not now enjoy seeing published without warning of their omission. Such a lack of rigorousness occurs throughout his entire biography.

We may possibly never be certain as to what Hedilla said on 18 April 1937, during the last hours of FE de las JONS, but the documentary and analytical evidence is weighted in favour of the version of Alcázar de Velasco and Cadenas Vicent. This is also the opinion of Ricardo Chueca Rodríguez, author of the excellent study on Falangism, *El fascismo: en los comienzos del régimen de Franco*, Madrid, Centro de Investigaciones Sociológicas, 1983 (see pp. 160 and following).

219 *Historia secreta de la segunda república*, Vol. 2, p. 336.
220 *Ibid.*, pp. 336–337.
221 *Ibid.*, p. 337.
222 *Ibid.*, p. 467.
223 *Ibid.*, p. 466.
224 *Ibid.*, p. 467.
225 *Ibid.*, p. 468.
226 José Díaz de Villegas, *Guerra de liberación (La fuerza de la razón)*, Barcelona, AHR, 1957, pp. 42–44.
227 *Ibid.*, p. 43.
228 *Ibid.*, p. 44.
229 *Ibid.*
230 *Ibid.*, pp. 75–76.
231 *Ibid.*, p. 76.
232 *Ibid.*
233 *Ibid.*, pp. 76–77.
234 *Ibid.*, p. 78.
235 *Ibid.*
236 *Spain*, 1942, p. 472.
237 The 'documents' are not mentioned either in *España* (Buenos Aires, 1955) or in *Spain: A Modern History* (New York, Praeger, 1968). Madariaga, with his scholarly pretensions, should have at least presented his readers with the reason for abandoning the earlier warranty he had given the 'documents'.
238 *Spain*, 1942, p. 472.
239 *The Grand Camouflage*, 1961, p. 97, n. 6. Even the sub-title of Bolloten's book, *The Communist Conspiracy in the Spanish Civil War*, contradicts the extract quoted. See n. 207.
240 See *La révolution espagnole: La gauche et la lutte pour le pouvoir*, p. 127. *The Spanish Revolution: The Left and the Struggle for Power during the Civil War*, p. 104; *La revolución española*, Barcelona, Grijalbo, 1980, pp. 166–167. However, in the two latter editions, Bolloten began to hedge his bets, quoting the arguments of

Ricardo de la Cierva, 'one of the most important contemporary Spanish historians on the Civil War' (Barcelona, 1980, p. 167).

241 *Spain*, 1942, p. 472.
242 *Ibid.*
243 *Ibid.*
244 *Ibid.*
245 *Ibid.*, pp. 476–478.
246 *No fue posible la paz*, Barcelona, Ariel, 1968, p. 118; also *Españoles de mi tiempo*, Barcelona, Planeta, 1974, pp. 46–47.
247 *Spain*, 1942, pp. 474–490; *Españoles de mi tiempo*, pp. 365–372.
248 *Españoles de mi tiempo*, pp. 336–337.
249 Thomas Jones, *A Diary with Letters*, London, Oxford University Press, 1954, p. 269.
250 *Ibid.*, p. 280.
251 *Ibid.*, p. 76.
252 On Madariaga's activities during the Spanish Civil War, see Paul Preston, *¡Comrades! Portraits from the Spanish Civil War*, London, HarperCollins, 1999, pp. 153–158. For Madariaga's defence of his position, see *Spain*, 1942, pp. 486–487.
253 *Spain*, 1942, p. 379.
254 *El mito de la cruzada de Franco*, pp. 217–233; *Le mythe de la croisade de Franco*, pp. 179–189; *La destrucción de Guernica*, pp. 69–71.
255 *Spain*, 1942, p. 472.
256 *Ibid.*, p. 369. This is another example of 'history' based on gossip.
257 *Españoles de mi tiempo*, pp. 332–340; Pablo de Azcárate, *Mi embajada en Londres durante la guerra civil española*, Barcelona, Ariel, 1976, pp. 23–24. For the personal assessments of each other written by Madariaga and Azcárate, see Madariaga, *op. cit.*, pp. 324–330; *Spain*, 1942 and Azcárate, *op. cit.* p. 58.
258 Azcárate, *op. cit.*, pp. 260–261. On 23 July 1986, the date of the first centenary of Madariaga's birth, Madrid's foremost newspaper, *El País*, published an eight-page supplement highly flattering to the writer and academician, deceased eight years earlier. This portrait was achieved by overlooking his efforts to help Franco during the Civil War and stressing his opposition to Franco after the end of the Second World War. The English edition of *Spain* (1942), in which the hatred and venom he felt for the war effort of the Spanish Republic was underlined and his sympathy for the Spanish Rebels made evident, does not appear in the four-column long bibliography, which completely falsifies Madariaga's record on the Spanish Civil War. Readers of these pages on Madariaga may be amused to read the following, written by Consuelo Varela, identified as a 'contributor to the Escuela de Estudios Hispano-Americanos, of the CSIC in Seville', which appeared in the *El País* supplement (p. iii):

A passionate researcher and contraversialist, Madariaga studies each episode in its most differing aspects, deploying great erudition, together with a systematic analysis of the sources he uses, documentary sources – in print or not – which he knows perfectly ...

Certainly, none of these admirable qualities were made manifest in his judgements expressed on the Spanish Civil War.
259 *Españoles de mi tiempo*, pp. 324–330; *Spain*, 1942, p. 357.
260 *Españoles de mi tiempo*, pp. 326–328.
261 Azcárate, *Mi embajada en Londres durante la guerra civil española*, p. 58.
262 *Spain*, 1942, p. 327.

263 *General, márchese usted*, New York, Ediciones Ibérica, pp. 13–19.
264 *Ibid.*, p. 161.
265 *The Nation*, New York, 11 September 1967, 'The Cultural Cold War', pp. 198–211.
266 *Ibid.*, p. 199.
267 *Ibid.*, p. 203.
268 Southworth, ' "The Grand Camouflage" ' in Preston and Mackenzie, *The Republic Besieged*, Ch. 10, pp. 261–310.
269 *Españoles de mi tiempo*, p. 118.
270 *Ibid.*, p. 122.
271 *La crisis del humanismo* was republished in Madrid in 1945, with a preface by A. Goicoechea, but with no mention of an editor.
272 Many chapters of *Defensa de la Hispanidad* appeared in *Acción Española*, house organ of the political movement Acción Española, modelled on the French movement Action Française. Maeztu's book was published in Madrid in 1935 and carried, as did all subsequent editions, an appendix entitled 'Apologia de la Hispanidad', the text of an address delivered in Buenos Aires on the Día de la Raza, 12 October 1934, by the Spanish Primate, Cardinal Isidro Gomá y Tomás, before the International Eucharistic Congress. One can hardly imagine a contribution of Cardinal Gomá to a book of the Spanish Phalanx in 1935. But the war against the Republic brought differing thoughts together. *Defensa* was published in Valladolid in 1938 by Acción Española (Aldus, Santander), with an outspoken pro-Fascist 'Evocación' by Eugenio Vegas Latapié. In this 'Evocación', we can read (pp.xiv–xv):

> Another of don Ramiro's favourite themes was the defence of Hitler, since he believed him to be one of the greatest politicians in history for having, together with Mussolini, prevented Communism from destroying anything cultural in the world. He was enthusiastic about the Führer long before National-Socialism came to power. It is worth remembering Maeztu's interminable and violent discussions, seconded by General García de la Huerta, mainly with Eugenio Montes, at the time when this eminent thinker had still not surrendered to the evidence of the Führer's greatness.

273 *El mito de la cruzada de Franco*, 1986, pp. 306–307; *Le mythe de la croisade de Franco*, pp. 275–276; *Antifalange*, pp. 38–44.
274 *Españoles de mi tiempo*, p. 371.
275 *Casi unas memorias*, Barcelona, Planeta, 1976, pp. 393–394.
276 *Antifalange*, p. 58.
277 *Casi unas memorias*, p. 13.
278 *Españoles de mi tiempo*, p. 329.
279 *Casi unas memorias*, pp. 12–13.
280 *Ibid.*, p. 13.
281 *Ibid.*
282 *Ibid.*, p. 15.
283 *Frente de Juventudes*, November 1939, pp. 37–39.
284 *Antifalange*, p. 59.
285 Francisco Franco Salgado-Araujo, *Mis conversaciones privadas con Franco*, Barcelona, Planeta, 1976, pp. 348–349, 376, 549–550.
286 Madrid, CEDESA, 127 pp. with many illustrations. There were also editions in French and English.
287 *Spain 1923–1948. Civil War and World War*, p. 160.
288 *Memory to Memory*, p. 103.

289 *Ibid.*, p. 133.
290 *Historia pública de la zona roja*, 1954, p. 222.
291 *La literatura universal sobre la guerra de España*, Madrid, Atenéo, 1962, p. 59.
292 *Ibid.*, p. 60.
293 *Ibid.*, p. 63.
294 *Spain Resurgent*, London, Hutchinson, 1953, p. 35.
295 *Franco. A Biographical History*, London, Eyre and Spottiswoode, 1967, p. 148;
     Franco, historia y biografía, Madrid, Magisterio Español, 1969, pp. 223–224;
     Madariaga, *Spain*, 1942, pp. 434–435.
296 *Franco*, 1967, p. 530; *Franco*, 1970, not translated.
297 *The Grand Camouflage*, 1961; *El gran engaño*, 1967.
298 *The Spanish Revolution*, pp. 140, 157; *La revolución española*, p. 237, n. 100.
     Bolloten questioned the honesty of Azcárate's testimony, using as his authority
     Madariaga. As I have shown on several occasions in this book, Madariaga's
     affirmations concerning historical events are to be treated with considerable
     caution. It was the reliability of Madariaga that Bolloten should have ques-
     tioned and not that of Azcárate, but Bolloten never distrusts a witness against
     the Spanish Republic.
299 *Españoles de mi tiempo*, pp. 407–414.
300 See above. Azcárate, pp. 58–59.
301 Bolloten, *The Spanish Revolution*, p. 516, n. 23.
302 *Los documentos de la primavera trágica*, Madrid, Secretaría General Técnica del
     Ministerio de Información y Turismo, Sección de Estudios sobre la guerra de
     España, 1967, pp. 22–24, 40–42, 210–216, 386–388.
303 *Francisco Franco: Un siglo de España*, Madrid, Editora Nacional, 1972, Vol. 1,
     p. 7.
304 *Ibid.*, Vol. 1, p. 382.
305 *Ibid.*, Vol. 1, p. 423.
306 *Ibid.*, Vol. 1, p. 429.
307 *Franco*, Barcelona, Planeta, 1986.
308 *Ibid.*, p. 162.
309 *Ibid.*, p. 253.
310 See text referred to by n. 103.
311 *Claridad*, 30 May 1936, last page.
312 *Le mythe de la croisade de Franco*, 1964; *El mito de la cruzada de Franco*, 1986.
313 K. W. Watkins, *Britain Divided*, London, Nelson, 1963, p. 39.
314 *Ibid.*
315 *Ibid.*
316 *Ibid.*, p. 40.
317 *Ibid.*, p. 41.
318 *Ibid.*, p. 42.
319 *Ibid.*, p. 43.
320 *Ibid.*, pp. 43–44.
321 *Ibid.*, p. 44.
322 *Spain*, 1942, p. 470.
323 *The Spanish Republic and the Civil War.*
324 *Ibid.*, pp. 515–516.
325 *Ibid.*, p. 516.
326 *Ibid.*, p. 516.
327 *Ibid.*, pp. 516–517.
328 *Ibid.*, p. 515. Jackson is probably right in his evaluation of the work of García
     Venero. In weighing the latter's work, we must always remember his Falangist
     committments, etc., but his work should not be confused with that of
     'Mauricio Karl', Comín Colomer and others of their ilk.

329 Hugh Thomas, *The Spanish Civil War*, 1961, p. 108, n. 1.
330 *Ibid.*
331 *Ibid.*
332 *The Spanish Republic and the Civil War*, p. 516. Jackson is too kind. The authors of the 'documents' can be better described as ignorant, careless and ill-intentioned.
333 Arrarás, *Historia de la segunda república española, (texto abreviado)*, Madrid, Editora Nacional, 1965, p. 476.
334 *Ibid.*, pp. 476–477.
335 See *Le mythe de la croisade de Franco*, pp. 141–142; *El mito de la cruzada de Franco*, pp. 170–173.
336 Hugh Thomas, *The Spanish Civil War*, Harmondsworth, Penguin, 1965, p. 150.
337 *Ibid.*
338 Southworth, *La destrucción de Guernica*, Paris, Ruedo Ibérico, 1977, pp. 65–73, 83–87, 127, 165–166.
339 *Spain: The Vital Years*, London, Cassell, 1967; *España: Los años vitales*, 1967.
340 *España: Los años vitales*, pp. 361–369. Concerning the Communist menace in general, Bolín quoted from Madariaga (1942, p. 457) and from the article Dr Marañón published in *La Revue de Paris*, December 1937.
341 *Spain: The Vital Years*, pp. 339–344.
342 *Spain: The Vital Years*, p. 177; *España: Los años vitales*, p. 189.
343 *Spain: The Vital Years*, p. 339; *España: Los años vitales*, p. 361. Bolín also wrote: 'Russia sent instructions which were made public in Valencia at a meeting held on 16th May' (*España: Los años vitales*, p. 162). The English text is still more curious: 'Russia also sent instructions, made public at a meeting in Valencia on 16 May' (*Spain: The Vital Years*, p. 151). Does Bolín mean to say that the meeting held in Valencia on 16 May, reported in 'secret document' III, was a public one? Again Bolín told his readers, 'if the Nationalist Uprising had not stopped it, a Communist movement would have been launched in Spain in July or August of 1936' (*España: Los años vitales*, p. 167).
344 *Spain: The Vital Years*, pp. 339–341.
345 *España: Los años vitales*, p. 361.
346 Southworth, *The Destruction of Guernica*.
347 *Ibid.*, pp. 415–416; *The Times*, 24 August 1986.
348 Aznar, *Historia militar de la guerra de España*, pp. 29–30.
349 Francis McCullagh, *In Franco's Spain*, London, Burns, Oates and Washbourne, 1937, pp. 104–112. See *La destrucción de Guernica*, pp. 72.
350 The quotation from Madariaga had appeared in *Spain*, 1942, p. 349; *Spain: The Vital Years*, pp. 341–342; *España: Los años vitales*, pp. 361–362.
351 *Spain: The Vital Years*, p. 342; *España: Los años vitales*, p. 362.
352 *Spain: The Vital Years*, p. 343; *España: Los años vitales*, p. 363.
353 *España: Los años vitales*, p. 363.
354 *Spain: The Vital Years*, p. 343.
355 *El mito de la cruzada de Franco*, 1963, p. 256, n. 722, 1968, p. 210.
356 *España: Los años vitales*, p. 363. Bolín's story recalls Gerahty's account of the leaflet found in a flowerpot in Triana, but it concerned a different 'document' and was found some months later.
357 *Guernica! Guernica!*, parenthesis on the working conditions of the Foreign Press in the Nationalist Zone, pp. 45–59.
358 *Spain: The Vital Years*, p. 343.
359 *España: Los años vitales*, p. 363.
360 *Spain: The Vital Years*, p. 343; *España: Los años vitales*, p. 363.

361 Eduardo Comín Colomer, *Historia del Partido Comunista de España*, Segunda etapa (III), Madrid, Editora Nacional, 1965, pp. 755–756.
362 *Ibid.*, pp. 756–757. This reference to October 1934 as inspiration for the 'documents' may have come from Díaz de Villegas. See pp. 56–57
363 *Ibid.*, p. 757.
364 *Ibid.*
365 *Historia secreta de la segunda república*, p. 468.
366 *Historia del Partido Comunista en España*, pp. 757–758.
367 *Ibid.*, p. 761.
368 *Franco. A Biographical History*, p. 175.
369 *Ibid.*
370 *Ibid.*, p. 175.
371 *Ibid.*
372 *Ibid.*
373 *Ibid.*.
374 *Ibid.*, p. 174.
375 *Ibid.*, p. 175n.
376 *Ibid*, p. 92.
377 Southworth, *The Destruction of Guernica*, pp. 365ff.
378 Ricardo de la Cierva, *Los documentos de la primavera trágica*, p. 428.
379 *Ibid.*
380 *Ibid.*
381 Carta del Archivo Histórico Nacional, Salamanca, 1982.
382 Ricardo de la Cierva, *Historia de la Guerra Civil Española. Tomo primero. Perspectivas y antecedentes. 1898–1936*, Madrid, Librería Editorial San Martín, 1969, p. 709. There is striking similarity between la Cierva's dismissal of the 'documents' as being *absolutamente trivial* (1969) and Crozier's judgement of them as being *practicamente irelevantes* (1967).
383 *Ibid.*
384 *Ibid.*
385 *Ibid.* La Cierva did not mention the 'documents', either in his two-volume *Francisco Franco: Un siglo de España* (1974) or in his 1986 book *Franco*. This means that, at the same time, he was discarding the information given by Crozier concerning Franco and the publications of the Entente Internationale Anticommuniste. Yet Crozier had unwittingly showed us the true depths of Franco's intellectual obscurantism. It was understandable that la Cierva did not want to go into this matter. See Part II.
386 *Ibid.*
387 *Ibid.*
388 The only document concerning a conspiracy of the Spanish Right against the Republic was discovered by the police in Madrid early in 1937, during a search of the offices of the Monarchist-Rightist organization Renovación Española. This document was a handwritten memorandum relating an interview held in Rome on 23 March 1934 between four Spaniards (a general of the Spanish Army, two Carlists and the monarchist leader, Antonio Goicoechea) and Mussolini and Marshal Italo Balbo. According to this document, Mussolini offered to provide money and arms to Spanish elements desiring to overthrow the Republic. This agreement was at least in part carried out during the months following the agreement. At first, the Spanish Nationalist leaders denied the reports of the Mussolini–Goicoechea agreement, but later the essential details were admitted by Goicoechea. See *Manchester Guardian*, 14 December 1937, reproduced in *How Mussolini Provoked the Spanish Civil War*, London, United Editorial, 1938, pp. 9–10; also Duchess of Atholl, *Searchlight on Spain*, Harmondsworth, Penguin, 1938, pp. 40–41, 345–346. Any docu-

ments concerning the military conspiracy were never found by the Republican authorities, for such papers in real life are rarely if ever left lying around all over the country as were the spurious 'documents' of the 'Communist Plot'.

389 *No fue posible la paz*, p. 706.

390 *Ibid.*, p. 705.

391 García Escudero had actually seen few of the original sources used in *El Mito*, in his quite long article on the 'documents'; in fact, not one of those sources is cited in his notes referring to the pages in which he deals with the 'documents' (José María García Escudero, *Historia política de las dos Españas*, Madrid, Editora Nacional, 1975, Vol. 3, pp. 1333–1334, nn. 39–49). Watkins's *Britain Divided* is the only foreign language book concerning the 'documents' which had not been translated, but which was quoted. Curiously, García Escudero cited the English edition of Crozier's *Franco*, although it had been published in Spain six years before the date of Escudero's publication. Probably parts of García Escudero's four-volume work were written long before the whole was published.

392 *Historia política de las dos Españas*, Vol. 3, p. 1317.

393 *Ibid.*, pp. 1317–1318.

394 *Ibid.*, p. 1318.

395 *Ibid.*

396 *Ibid.*

397 *Ibid.*

398 *Ibid.*, p. 1319.

399 *Ibid.*

400 *Ibid.*

401 *Alzamiento en España*, p. 85.

402 *Ibid.*, p. 83. This page is part of a section bearing the indication of the date 5 May (p. 81). On p. 82, Maíz wrote of the arrival of Serrano Suñer in the Canaries, a trip which Crozier interprets as having taken place before Franco's withdrawal from the Cuenca elections which took place on 5 May. It is not worthwhile following too closely Maíz's chronology, for it seems to have been constructed to throw the enemy off the track rather than to inform historians at a later date.

403 *Ibid.*, p. 143.

404 Maíz, *Mola, aquél hombre*, Barcelona, Planeta, 1976, pp. 220–221.

405 *Ibid.*, pp. 281, 316–324.

406 *Ibid.*, p. 221.

407 *Alzamiento en España*, p. 85.

408 *Mola, aquél hombre*, p. 222.

409 *Ibid.*, pp. 316–324.

410 *Ibid.*, pp. 316, 318, 321–322.

411 *Ibid.*, pp. 322–323.

412 Angel Viñas, *La alemania nazi y el 18 de julio*, Madrid, Alianza Editorial, 1977, p. 273.

413 *Alzamiento en España*, p. 83.

414 *Ibid.*, p. 144.

415 *Mola, aquél hombre*, p. 110.

416 *Ibid.*, p. 112.

417 *Ibid.*

418 *Alzamiento en España*, p. 66; *Mola, aquel hombre*, p. 112.

419 *Ibid.*

420 *Ibid.*

421 *Alzamiento en España*, pp. 66–67. The vocabulary of Maíz here recalls the language of Hugo Wast in his novels *Oro* and *El Kahal*.

422 José María Gárate Córdoba, *La guerra de las dos Españas*, Barcelona, Caralt, 1976, pp. 38–39.
423 *Ibid.*, pp. 38–39, n. 4. It seems that Borrás died keeping his secret, if secret there was.
424 *Ibid.*, p. 9. Gárate wrote an introduction to his book, entitled: 'Panorama historiográfico sobre la guerra del 36', pp. 9–18, in which he named 'los cuatro ases' of Spanish Civil War historiography as Martínez Bande, la Cierva, Ramón Salas and García Escudero, pp. 16–17. This is instructive concerning the workings of the Franquista mentality. For an unfriendly criticism of la Cierva's *Bibliografía*, see Southworth '"Los bibliófobos". Ricardo de la Cierva y sus colaboradores', Cuadernos de Ruedo Ibérico, Paris, nos 28–29, December 1970–March 1971, pp. 19–45.
425 Luis Romero, *Cara y cruz de la República, 1931–1936*, Barcelona, Planeta, 1980, p. 306. Romero accepts the research and the conclusions drawn from that research as presented in *El mito de la cruzada de Franco*, but he carefully refrains from mentioning that book or its author.
426 *Ibid.*, pp. 306–307.
427 *Ibid.*, p. 307.
428 *Ibid.*
429 *Ibid.*, p. 306.
430 Luis Suárez Fernández, *Francisco Franco y su tiempo II*, p. 30, note 38.
431 *Who Was Who, 1961–1970*, London, 1971.
432 See n. 347.
433 I have not been able to consult a file of this publication. However, a German friend, Günther Schmigalle, who is the author of a doctoral dissertation entitled *André Malraux und der spanische Bürgerkrieg*, University of Frankfurt, and now works in the Karlsruhe Library, has studied the files of the Anti-Comintern periodicals and has found nothing on the 'documents'. Yet there must be somewhere an indication of how Documents I, II and III came into the hands of the Anti-Comintern and were published in the *Rotbuch*.
434 For recent examples of this neo-Falangist propaganda, see *El País*, 15 December 1985, pp. 26–28; on the death of Antonio Tovar Llorente; and a counteraction by the author of this book in a letter published in *El País*, 8 January 1986, p. 8. Curiously enough, in the same number of *El País*, there was a whitewash article on José María de Areilza by Professor Carlos Seco Serrano (pp. 7–8) which completely ignored the contributions of Sr de Areilza to pre-war Spanish Fascism, his role as first *alcalde* of Bilbao of the Franco era, and his co-authorship, with Fernando María Castiella, of the pro-Hitler, pro-Mussolini book *Reivindicaciones de España*, Madrid, Instituto de Estudios Políticos, 1941.
435 I wrote in a Letter to the Editor, published in *El País*, 9 January 1986, p. 8, as follows:

> 1989 is the centenary of Dr. Juan Negrín's birth. In democratic Spain, there is no street, no monument or anything in his name. He did not write sonnets to the glory of Hitler, Mussolini or Franco, he professed no admiration for the *duce*, the *führer* or the *caudillo*. He was an honourable man who fought against fascism, who did his duty for his country and who has been granted complete oblivion. Perhaps this is the price to pay for national reconciliation, but this reconciliation is far too expensive if we have to deny the historical truth. A country that does not dare to face up to its own history is condemned to historical mediocrity.

436 This statement by Pierre Vilar was cited critically by David W. Pike in his book, *Jours de gloire, jours de honte*, Paris, Sedes, 1984, p. xliii. Professor Vilar's original text had appeared in *Historia Internacional*, no.13, April 1976, p. 46, the article being entitled 'La guerra de 1936 en la historia contemporánea de España'. Professor Pike stated that 'only those who have denounced Stalin's tyranny have the right to denounce that of Hitler and Franco. To us, there seems to be no difference between the two forms of fascism, the red and the black.'

However one may judge Stalin's career in its entirety, I am obliged to regard his actions during the war in Spain as 'globally positive', to use a phrase in vogue. Stalin at least did help the Spanish Republic, whereas the leaders in Great Britain and the United States opposed help to Spain, and France aided the Republic but a little now and then. I can already hear the echoing riposte: but it was in Stalin's interests to help the Spanish Republic. And so it was. But was it not also in the interests of Baldwin and Chamberlain, of Roosevelt, of Blum and Daladier to come to the aid of the beleaguered Spanish Republicans? Is there not some credit due to the historical actors who have recognized where their true interest lay?

Pike treats the problem of the 'documents' in his book, *Les francais et la guerre d'Espagne*, pp. 259–270. Pike refers to material from Documents I, II, III and IV, basing his accounts on *Gringoire*, *L'Écho de Paris* and Bardoux's pamphlet, *Le chaos espagnol* and his subsequent article in the *Revue des Deux Mondes*. Pike mentions details from the 'documents' with a certain amount of scepticism, but does not refer to the fact that the fraudulent nature of the 'documents' had been proved in *El mito de la cruzada de Franco* twelve years before his book appeared.

Part II: The brainwashing of Francisco Franco

1 *Franco. A Biographical History*, p. 92.
2 *Ibid.*
3 *Ibid.*
4 *Ibid.*, pp. 92–93.
5 Both Crozier and Hills wrote from a point of view extremely sympathetic to Franco. Crozier claims (*Franco*, 1967, pp. xix–xx) that:

Although my conclusions are, on the whole, very favourable to Franco, I have not set out to please him ... we both hate communism ... as I wrote this book and studied the evidence, my feelings for Franco changed from antipathy to grudging admiration.

6 Hills, *Franco, the Man and his Nation*, London, Robert Hale Ltd, 1967, p. 157.
7 *Ibid.* The reference to France is not surprising, for the literature of the Entente indicated France rather than Spain as the most likely place for a Communist uprising.
8 *Ibid.*, p. 157.
9 *Ibid.*, p. 105.
10 *Ibid.*
11 *Ibid.*, p. 186.
12 *Ibid.*, p. 193, n. 18.
13 This letter is reproduced on p. 35 of the brochure published by the Bureau Permanent de l'Entente Internationale Anticommuniste, Geneva, December 1940, *Dix sept ans de lutte contre le bolchevisme, 1924–1940*. The Entente used two titles: L'Entente Internationale contre la III Internationale and L'Entente

Internationale Anticommuniste. The first title was used at the beginning; the second title somewhat later. Both titles were used in 1937. Georges Lodygensky, Secretary-General of the Bureau Permanent of the Entente, wrote years later, of the nuance between the two names:

> Since the main task of our movement was to organize the struggle against international communism, it was obvious that we had to have a clear understanding of the organization, the programme and the methods of Comintern personnel, the instruments of the Soviet Government which aims to spread its subversive activities throughout the world.
>
> (Lodygensky, *Face au Communisme. Le mouvement anticommuniste international de 1923–1950*, part 1, chap. 3, p. 38. Henceforth, Lodygensky Memoir)

The brochure mentioned at the beginning of this note was issued by the Bureau Permanent de l'Entente Internationale Anticommuniste; a related brochure, entitled *Neuf ans de lutte contre le bolchevisme*, issued by the same organization in March 1933, had been attributed to the Bureau Permanent de l'Entente Internationale contre la III Internationale. See nn. 36, 37.

14 *Franco*,1967, p. 46.

15 *Ibid.* See also Coles, *Franco of Spain*, p. 77.

16 Hills was horrified at the thought that two ministers in the first Republican government in 1931 were non-believers: 'These measures against the Church were principally the work of the agnostic, Fernando de los Ríos ... and of Marcelino Domingo, the self-confessed atheist ...' Both were ministers in the first Republican government (*Franco, the Man and his Nation*, p. 175).

17   Suárez Fernández, *Francisco Franco y su tiempo*, Vol. 1, p. 197, n. 12.

18 *Ibid.*, pp. 255–281.

19 *Ibid.*, pp. 268–269 and n. 24.

20 *Ibid.*, pp. 197–198.

21 *Ibid.*

22 *Ibid.*, pp. 9–10.

23 *Ibid.*, pp. 268–269.

24 *Dix sept ans de lutte contre le bolchevisme*, p. 8. It would be instructive to know the names of the members of the Conseil International de l'Entente, the names of the members of the Bureau Permanent and of the other dependant groups of the EIA, but this seems impossible, without access to the EIA archives. In the various publications of the Entente which have been made available to me, the names dropped here and there are generally of a conservative level, as are those found in the Lodygensky Memoir. Here is an example concerning the Conseil International de l'Entente (*ibid.*):

> Figures such as M. Georges Theunis, former President of the Belgian Council of Ministers, Prof. Treub, former Finance Minister of Holland, Lord Phillimore and Sir Waldron Smithers, members of the British Parliament, Senators Eccard and Gautherot, from Strasbourg and Paris, Donna Christina Giustiniani-Bandini, Count Giuseppe della Gherardesca, and Dr. Ehrt from the Anti-Comintern took part as members or friends of the EIA Permanent Bureau.

25   *Ibid.*, p. 13.

26 Juan Pablo Fusi, *Franco*, Madrid, Ediciones El País, 1985, p. 26.

27 *Ibid.*, p. 31.

28 La Cierva, *Franco*, p. 102. Aubert was, as Crozier wrote, a *national* councillor. La Cierva is wrong to call him a *federal* councillor, which is a far more important post. A national councillor is a legislator; a federal councillor, of whom there were but seven, was part of the executive branch of the Swiss government. One can doubt that Aubert, president of the Permanent Bureau of the EIA, had the time to be a federal councillor. In general, the ideas of Aubert were defended in the Federal Council by Giuseppe Motta, who served in that body from 1911 until his death in 1940.

29 *Ibid.* I do not know the source of la Cierva's statement concerning Mola and the EIA.

30 *Ibid.* In scholarly circles in Spain, the FNFF is said to be organized for the glory of Franco rather than for independent research. It is ironic that la Cierva should protest against this exclusionary treatment, since he himself profited from a similar monopoly during the final years of the Franco regime, not only for research but also for publishing.

31 *Franco*, 1967, p. 93, n.

32 *Francisco Franco y su tiempo*, Vol. 1, p. 197, n. 12.

33 *Ibid.*, p. 269, n. 24. M. René Engel was a member of the Bureau Permanent at the time of the liquidation of the EIA.

34 *Ibid.*

35 'Their Man in Madrid', *New Statesman*, London, 19 December 1967, pp. 907–908; 'Letters', 5 January, pp. 19, 26; 9 February, p. 968.

36 The incomplete state of the EIA material in the BPU would suggest that the library was not a regular subscriber to Entente publications. The correct title for the issuing office of the Entente publications was, according to the BPU, Bureau Permanent de la Entente contre la III Internationale. Some entry cards indicate 'Don du Bureau Permanent', others, 'Don du CICR'. Still other Entente material came from individual donors. See n. 13.

37 An entry card of the BPU of Geneva states: 'Depuis Juin 1938; Entente Int. Anticommuniste'. However, *Bulletin d'Informations Politiques EIA*, no. 4 for 1937, dated November, bears the heading *Entente Internationale Anticommuniste*. I have not seen no. 3 for 1937, but no. 2, dated 4 March 1937, carries the old title *Entente Internationale contre la III Internationale*.

38 Here is another example: 'Our Bulletin of *EIA Economic Information*, sent to more than eight hundred prominent persons in the business worlds of Europe and America, has been well received by these people' (*Neuf ans de lutte*, p. 25).

39 Dimitri Novik, *Théodore Aubert et son oeuvre. Le mouvement internationale contre le bolchevisme*, Geneva, Edition des Amis de l'Entente contre la III Internationale, 1932, p. 5.

40 *Ibid.*, p. 6.

41 *Encyclopaedia Britannica*, 1926, Vol. 31, p. 706. Carl Burchkardt was undoubtedly the Carl J. Burckhardt who in 1923 had carried out a mission during the Greek–Turkish War, on behalf of the Conseil Internationale de la Croix Rouge (CICR); ten years later he became a member of the CICR. During the Second World War, in the opinion of Jean-Claude Favez, Burckhardt played in the CICR 'a prominent role, in fact, the principal role'. This citation is found in an excellent short biography of Burckhardt, in Favez's book, *Une mission impossible?*, Lausanne, Payot, 1989, pp. 58–59, in which it is noted that Burckhardt, as High Commissioner of the League of Nations at Danzig, was the guest of honour at a Congress of the National Socialist German Workers Party in 1937. Favez points out, in the same paragraph, that, after the war, the Israeli Weizmann Institute welcomed Burckhardt as an honorary member. Burckhardt was named President of the CICR on 1 January 1945, but he never officially occupied this post, having let himself be persuaded that he would better serve

the Helvetic Federation as Minister of Switzerland in Paris, where the new
government of French *Résistance* viewed with distrust Swiss neutrality.

42 Aubert had taken the initiative in establishing a Swiss Civic Union the day after
the general strike which broke out in 1918, stirred up by the intrigues of the
Soviet delegation in Switzerland. Aubert was the secretary of the French-
speaking section of the referred Union and was thus particularly interested in
communist subversive activities.

(Lodygensky Memoir, part 1, chap. 1, p. 6)

According to Lodygensky, it was the Swiss Civic Union that, at the time of the
1918 general strike, 'put pressure on the Government which expelled the
Soviet mission from the country for having been involved in the organization
of the strike' (*ibid.*, chap. 2, p. 26).

43 *Théodore Aubert et son oeuvre*, p. 8.
44 *Théodore Aubert et son oeuvre*, p. 40.
45 *Théodore Aubert et son oeuvre*, p. 11; Lodygensky Memoir, part 1, chap. 1, p. 4.
46 *Ibid.*, p. 6.
47 Théodore Aubert, *L'Affaire Conradi*, Geneva, S.A. des Editions Sonor, p. 20.
48 Lodygensky Memoir, part 1, p. 5.
49 *L'Affaire Conradi*, p. 21.
50 *Ibid.*, p. 21.
51 *Ibid.*
52 Lodygensky Memoir, part 1, p. 5.
53 *Ibid.*, p. 4.
54 *Ibid.*, p. 5.
55 *Ibid.*, p. 6. There is nothing in Lodygensky's typescript, nor in any other Entente
material I have read, that justifies or confirms Lodygensky's panegyric
concerning his assistant.
56 *Ibid.*, p. 8.
57 *Ibid.*, p. 9.
58 As the police and judicial investigation progressed, it became clear that, despite
Lodygensky's illegal destruction of evidence, proof of Polounine's complicity
made a denial of the fact impossible to plead.
59 *Ibid.*, p. 17.
60 *Ibid.*, pp. 16, 17.
61 *Ibid.*, p. 14.
62 *Ibid.*, p. 19. Novik gave the figure of more than sixty journalists among those
present at the trial (p. 19).
63 *Théodore Aubert et son oeuvre*, pp. 13–15; *Images et Evénements Vaudois*, Geneva,
Editions Slatkine, 1989. Novik described the physical effort of Aubert as being
'A formidable task, almost superhuman' (*op. cit.*, p. 15).
64 Novik wrote that *L'Affaire Conradi* ran through three editions in Geneva and
was also published in German, Serb, Bulgarian, Spanish, Chinese and still other
tongues. A Russian printing was secretly distributed in the Soviet Union. He
also wrote that an English-language edition, in addition to the one published
in England, was printed in the United States (*Théodore Aubert et son oeuvre*, p.
19).
65 *L'Affaire Conradi: le procès du Bolchevisme. Plaidoirie prononcé pour Arcadius
Polounine devant le Tribunal Criminel de Lausanne les 14 et 15 Novembre 1923, par
Me. Théodore Aubert, Avocat au Barreau de Genève, Membre du Conseil de l'Ordre*,
Geneva, S.A. des Editions Sonor, 1924.
66 *Bolchevism's Terrible Record: An Indictment, by Maître Aubert of the Geneva Bar. Issued
under the auspices of the Entente Internationale contre le {sic} III Internationale*,
London, Williams and Northgate, 1924. Hereafter, *BTR*. In the analysis of

Aubert's plea before the Criminal Court at Lausanne, I have depended entirely on the text in the French language, *L'Affaire Conradi*. Where the French and English coincide more or less, I have indicated this fact in the corresponding footnote. The English-language text has been amputated of much of the material concerning the two accused persons, with the result that it appears to be even more the work of a pamphleteer than did the original. This political intention is more evident in details of the translation. For example, on p. 73 of the French text, one can read: 'The breakdowns were so frequent and the delays so long that we were no longer able to work.' In the English translation, the French word *pannes* ('breakdowns') became 'strikes', more pertinent to the English social and electoral scene of 1924 than the word 'breakdowns'. Another example on p. 106 of Aubert's original printing, the text reads: 'A Czech replied that he did not know why he had been arrested ...' In the London edition, the word *tchèque* is translated as 'Chekist'. A neutral word becomes a dirty word.

67 Lodygensky Memoir, part 1, chap. 1, pp. 22–23.

68 Lodygensky wrote that, at a time ill-defined, perhaps two or three weeks before the trial, three exiled Russian jurists came from Paris to study Aubert's plea to the jury. One was a political figure, Goutchkov, a former president of the Duma; the other two, described by Lodygensky as 'éminents juristes', were named Gourka and Nossovitch. This trio had been invited to Geneva to hear Aubert read the draft of his address to the jury. Lodygensky later depicted their reactions:

> Our guests confessed that they had never expected to find such sharp intelligence, such complete understanding of the case he was conducting, or such a brilliant exposition of the case in a little-known Genevese lawyer. The great undertaking Aubert had accomplished impressed them immensely. This was work for which he not only had to assimilate the enormous amount of documentation made available to him but also of which he had captured the very essence of the story, Russian literature and the Russian mentality.
>
> (Lodygensky Memoir, part 1, chap. 1, p. 18)

If the above account by Lodygensky is to be trusted, it would seem reasonable to believe that Aubert could have, from his own draft and notes, reconstructed his historic plea. The many differences, not of fundamental importance, but nevertheless differences, between the text of *L'Affaire Conradi* and its English-language authorized version, *BTR*, testify to a certain negligence on Aubert's part concerning textual authenticity.

69 *L'Affaire Conradi*, pp. 20–22. Also 'Introduction', p. 5. (Not in *BTR*.)

70 *Ibid.*, p. 25; not in *BTR*.

71 *Ibid.*, p. 27; *BTR*, p. 10.

72 *Ibid.*, p. 16; not in *BTR*.

73 *Ibid.*, p. 119; not in *BTR*.

74 *Ibid.*, p. 21; not in *BTR*.

75 *Ibid.*, pp. 34–39; not in *BTR*.

76 *Ibid.*, p. 35; not in *BTR*.

77 *Ibid.*, pp. 18, 37; not in *BTR*.

78 *Ibid.*, p. 43; *BTR*, p. 20.

79 *Ibid.*, p. 37; not in *BTR*.

80 It is perhaps pertinent to note that at that time Swiss governmental representation abroad was constituted by but one truly diplomatic post, that of the Swiss

Ambassador to France. Swiss interests were considered to be commercial and financial, and best served by officers of consular rank.

81 *Ibid.*, p. 112; *BTR*, pp. 100–101.

82 *Ibid.*, p. 23; not in *BTR*.

83 This part of his plea permitted Aubert to indulge in a bit of anti-Semitism and other forms of racism, which apparently did his cause no harm with the jury. I cite a few examples to illustrate this tactic of Maître Aubert:

> These are foreigners who delight in this power and luxury. Out of five to six hundred commissaries, there are thirty odd Russian-Slavs, the others are Jews, Hungarians, Latvians, Poles, Armenians, Germans, Bulgarians, dressed up in Russian names.
>
> (*L'Affaire Conradi*, pp. 43–44; *BTR*, p. 21)

> Chinese, Latvians, Jewish women make up the greater part of the staff in the Cheka.
>
> (*L'Affaire Conradi*, p. 44; *BTR*, p. 21)

> The troops, he writes [*The Times* correspondent] marched with their banners to the wind and their bayonets fixed. One group left general quarters with the emaciated and severe Dzerjinski in the lead dressed in furs, Unschlicht, Latsis, Peters, Aschmarine, Félix Kon, Enukidze, Eyduk, none of them Russian. It would have been quite difficult to tell which race they belonged to. Behind them came spies, policemen, investigators, secret agents. Megrim and Agrim, the two Latvian torturers, left number 11 of the great Lubyanka, the headquarters of the GPU, where executions are carried out in the basement.
>
> (*L'Affaire Conradi*, p. 44; *BTR*, pp. 21–22)

> These are the people belonging to the Cheka, Jews, Latvians, Hungarians, but the dregs of society from all these races. The Cheka is full of foreigners.
>
> (*L'Affaire Conradi*, pp. 94–95; *BTR*, p. 79)

> A few more details about the Kiev Cheka ... the Cheka leader was Latsis, of Latvian origin ... His aide was a Jew ...
>
> (*L'Affaire Conradi*, p. 104; *BTR*, p. 97)

Aside from assimilating Jewish persons with the Cheka, as indicated above, Aubert also employed the formula which consisted of following the Russian name of a prominent Bolshevik with his Jewish name, if the person was of Jewish origin. (This method became widely used during the period of the Nazi rise to power and later. It was a stock in trade of the 'Radio Priest', Father Coughlin in the United States during the 1938–1939 battle to lift the embargo on the sale of arms to the Spanish government: see *Le mythe de la croisade de Franco*, pp. 155, 156.) Here are some examples of the Aubert method: 'Kamenef alias Rosenfeld' (*L'Affaire Conradi*, p. 42; *BTR*, p. 19), 'Trotski-Bronstein' (*L'Affaire Conradi*, p. 40; *BTR*, p. 16), 'Zinovieff-Apfelbaum-Radomyseslsky' (*L'Affaire Conradi*, p. 40; *BTR* p. 16), 'Litviniof-Wallach' (*L'Affaire Conradi*, p. 40; *BTR*, p. 20). Such information is of interest in a work of history, but as used by Aubert it is demagogy of a cheap and inferior brand. Aubert was defending two veterans of the White Russian Army; Lodygensky was a devout believer of the Russian Orthodox faith. The word 'pogrom' comes from the bloody history of the Christian faith in Russia, persecutor of the Russian Jews. '*Pogrom*, i.e. organized wholesale robbery and murder of Jews' (*Encyclopaedia Britannica*, 1926, Vol. 23, p. 910).

One can find in Aubert's negative remarks against the Jews, the Chinese, the Negroes, the Hungarians and others, a positive element: pro-Slavism. It is at times the same message found several decades later in the writings of Alexander I. Solzhenitsyn, a reactionary prophet proclaimed a great writer because of his anti-Sovietism. On 18 September 1990, he published a 16,000-word article in two Moscow newspapers in which he called for the establishment of an all-Slav State, 'a Russian Union formed from the three Slavic republics of Russia, Byelorussia and the Ukraine plus a large part of Kazakhstan', separating these territories from the rest of the Soviet Union. Solzhenitsyn 'criticized the Communists for poisoning the soul of Russia with their ideology and destroying its traditions', according to a Reuters dispatch in the *International Herald Tribune*, 19 September 1990, p. 4.

This statement by Solzhenitsyn prompted an editorial in the *New York Times* comparing the tolerance of Andrei Sakharov with the intolerance of Solzhenitsyn, described as 'a prophet whose angry eloquence exceeds his political sense'. Solzhenitsyn, the editorial writer went on, 'is impatient with parliaments and elections and urges instead a paternal autocracy rooted in Orthodox religion and Russian nationalism' (*International Herald Tribune*, Paris, 1 October 1990, p. 6. This discourse resembles that of Aubert in the Lausanne courtroom, which was probably inspired by Lodygensky).

84 *L'Affaire Conradi*, p. 47; *BTR*, p. 48:

Finally, it is not only in Europe, it is in America, in the steel, electricity and railroad strikes in the United States that one finds the hand of the III International, it is in Japan, in China ... the agents of the Soviets are agents of the III International. That is why we say that Vorowsky in Rome, in Lausanne, in Stockholm, was an agent of the III International.

85 *L'Affaire Conradi*, p. 84; *BTR*, p. 85:

You know how many schools have been destroyed little by little ... You know the newly installed discipline. Now it is the children who put the professors out of the door. Moreover, sexes have been mixed in the schools and immorality has flourished.

86 *L'Affaire Conradi*, p. 89:

And this, which you can read in a newspaper, under the signature of an esteemed journalist: 'A decree permits abortion free of charge in hospitals'. The issue of abortion has come to the forefront in Central and Eastern Europe, with the changeover from a Communist economy to a 'market economy', the latter phrase being a euphemism for capitalism. With capitalism, there has come liberty for the Catholic Church which is seeking in Poland and East Germany to give the 'liberated' populations the freedom to knuckle under to the dictates of the Church.

87 *Ibid.*, p. 115; *BTR*, pp. 102–103.
88 *L'Affaire Conradi*, p. 127; *BTR*, p. 110.
89 *Feuille d'Avis de Lausanne*, 17 November 1923, p. 19; *Théodore Aubert et son oeuvre*, p. 10.
90 *L'Affaire Conradi*, p. 5.
91 *L'Affaire Conradi*, p. 10.

92 *L'Affaire Conradi*, pp. 20–21. Aubert declared to the jury: 'Together Conradi and Polounine have decided to accomplish within the measure of their limited forces, all that they could to arrive at this result (suppression of a Bolshevist leader), Polounine indicated Vorowsky' (p. 21).

93 *Ibid.*, p. 5.

94 *Neuf ans de lutte contre le bolchevisme*, p. 18.

95 *Encyclopaedia Britannica*, 1926, Vol. 7, no. 31, p. 424. Lord Curzon, the British Foreign Minister, had sent on 8 May 1923 an ultimatum to the Soviet government concerning details which today seem of little importance. The matter was finally settled by a Soviet note of 18 July.

96 *Ibid.*

97 *Neuf ans de lutte contre le bolchevisme*, p. 17.

98 *L'Affaire Conradi*, p. 121; Not in *BTR*.

99 *L'Affaire Conradi*, p. 48; *BTR*, p. 27.

100 Lodygensky Memoir, part 1, chap. 2, p. 26.

101 *Ibid.*, pp. 26–27.

102 *Ibid.*, pp. 27–28.

103 *Ibid.*, pp. 29–32.

104 *Ibid.*, chap. 6, p. 16.

105 *Ibid.*, p. 27:

> From the beginning up to the end of our work, Mr. Gustave Hentsch did not cease to render us important services. He was at the head of one of the most important private banks of Geneva. He presided over the Parish Council of the Cathedral of St. Peter and was equally occupied by evangelical and humanitarian tasks, while contributing to the development of the University of Geneva.

106 *Ibid.*, p. 41.

107 *Ibid.*, chap 4, p. 51.

108 *Ibid.*

109 *Ibid.*

110 *Ibid.*, chap. 6, p. 69.

111 *Ibid.* Lodygensky observed: 'In 1926, the SEPES organization was already well-established. We could therefore recommend it to the Conference in London' (*ibid.*, p. 70).

112 *Ibid.*, chap. 4, p. 51.

113 *Ibid.*, chap. 3, pp. 35–37.

114 *Ibid.*, chap. 6, p. 63.

115 *Ibid.*

116 *Ibid.*, p. 64.

117 *Ibid.*

118 *Ibid.*, chap. 3, p. 39.

119 *The Red Network: The Communist International at Work*, London, Duckworth, 1939. The original is given, translated from the French, as 'Organisation and Activities of the Communist International'. A note on p. 4 reads: 'It was prepared and issued by the Anticommunist Entente, of 14 Promenade St. Antoine, Geneva. A draft English edition was prepared in October 1938 and the present edition has been adapted for readers of this country.' The 'Bibliography' mentioned is found on p. 93, the last page of the book.

120 *Ibid.*, chap. 6, p. 70.

121 *Ibid.*

122 *Ibid.* The Université Libre was a euphemism for the Catholic University of Paris. Calling a Catholic school a 'free school' represents one of the great propa-

ganda successes of modern times. How can any reasonable person consider a school bound to the iron-clad rules of a revealed religion to be more free than a school subject to the laws of a government democratically elected and ever-changing?

123 *Ibid.*, p. 67.
124 *Ibid.*, p. 71.
125 *Ibid.*
126 Lodygensky Memoir, part 2, chap. 3, p. 40.
127 Fest, *Hitler*, p. 206.
128 Lodygensky Memoir, part 3, chap. 2, p. 57.
129 Adolf Hitler, *Mein Kampf*, New York, Reynal and; Hitchcock, 1937, p. 181–183.
130 Lodygensky Memoir, part 3, Chap. 2, p. 59.
131 *Ibid.*, part 1, chap. 12, p. 107.
132 *Ibid.*. Carlier was active in pro-Franco propaganda during the Spanish Civil War.
133 *Ibid.*, 'Most members of our Office were Protestants'.
134 *Ibid.*
135 *Ibid.*, part 1, chap. 4, p. 51–53.
136 *Ibid.*, part 1, chap. 12, p. 107.
137 *Ibid.*, part 2, chap. 3, p. 16.
138 *Ibid.*, part 1, chap. 6, p. 69.
139 *Ibid.*, part 2, chap. 4, p. 24.
140 *Ibid.*, part 1, chap. 8, p. 83.
141 *Ibid.*
142 *Ibid.*, pp. 83–84.
143 *Ibid.*, part 2, chap. 3, n.p.
144 Suárez Fernández, *Francisco Franco y su tiempo*, Vol. 1, p. 269, n. 23.
145 Lodygensky Memoir, part 2, chap. 3, n.p.
146 *Ibid.*
147 *Ibid.*
148 *Ibid.*
149 This twenty-two-page brochure was officially published in Geneva. The name of Lodygensky is not found therein.
150 Lodygensky Memoir, part 2, chap. 3, n.p.
151 *Dix sept ans de lutte contre le bolchevisme*, pp. 12–13.
152 Georges Lodygensky, *Nos frères catholiques sous la croix en Espagne*, Zaragoza, Tall. Graf. de *El Noticiero*, 1937, 19pp.
153 Lodygensky Memoir, part 2, chap. 3, n.p.
154 EIA, *Bulletin d'Information Politique*, EIA, no. 20, 22 September 1936, p. 4.
155 *Ibid.*, pp. 4–5.
156 *Ibid.*, p. 1.
157 *Portugal ante la guerra civil de España: Documentos y notas*, Lisbon, SPN, n.d., pp. 57–58.
158 Entente Internationale contre la III Internationale, *Bulletin d'Information Politique*, no. 1/37, 25 January 1937, p. 1.
159 *Ibid.*
160 Ibid.; *Bulletin d'Information Politique*, EIA, no. 20, 22 September 1936, p. 1.
161 *Francisco Franco y su tiempo*, Vol. 1, p. 269.
162 *VII Congress of the Communist International*, abridged stenographic report of the proceedings, Moscow, Foreign Languages Publishing House, 1939. This volume is a bit more complete than is *Report of the Seventh World Congress of the Communist International*, London, Modern Books, 1936. The latter work is a collection of pamphlets, sold separately and later bound together with an

index. In a hurried comparison of the texts, I have found no changes of any consequence between 1936 and 1939. An example: in the London (1936) edition, on p. 16 of Dimitrov's Report, one finds the words 'a peasant struggle'; on p. 135 of the same text in the Moscow (1939) edition, the same phrase reads 'a peasant war'. Such changes are of editorial opinion; they do not alter the meaning. However, there is at least one text in the Moscow (1939) edition which does not appear in the London (1936) printing; this was the most important contribution made by a Spanish Communist at the Congress, that of 'Ventura'. (See further on.)

163 *VII Congress*, pp. 124–193; *Report of the Seventh World Congress*, London, pp. 1–79, Dimitrov Report.

164 *VII Congress*, p. 160; *Report of the Seventh World Congress*, pp. 43–44. There are editorial changes in the two texts.

165 *VII Congress*, pp. 195–251; *Report of the Seventh World Congress*, 'Speeches', 4, 7, Incomplete.

166 *VII Congress*, pp. 280–355; *Report of the Seventh World Congress*, 'Speeches', 2, 6, Incomplete.

167 *VII Congress*, pp. 356–385; *Report of the Seventh World Congress*, Dimitrov, Speech in reply to the discussion, pp. 1–32.

168 *VII Congress*, pp. 551–562; *Report of the Seventh World Congress*, Dimitrov, 'The Present Rulers of the Capitalist Countries are but Temporary; the Real Master of the World is the Proletariat!', pp. 1–12.

169 *VII Congress*. Although the text is stated to be abridged, all of Dimitrov's declarations, as well as Manuilsky's two speeches are given in full. See 'Introduction'.

170 *Ibid.*, p. 132.

171 *Ibid.*, p. 135.

172 *Ibid.*, pp. 140–141. 145, 178–179, 189.

173 *Ibid.*, p. 179.

174 *Ibid.*, pp. 150–156.

175 *Ibid.*, pp. 404, 449.

176 *Ibid.*, pp. 27, 31, 42, 44, 45, 47, 49, 53, 59.

177 *Ibid.*, pp. 197, 214, 219, 227.

178 *Ibid.*, p. 467.

179 *Ibid.*, p. 275.

180 *Ibid.*, p. 117.

181 *Report of the Seventh World Congress*, 1936, pp. xv–xvi.

182 *VII Congress*, pp. 326–329.

183 *Ibid.*, p. 326.

184 *Ibid.*, p. 328.

185 Preston, *¡Comrades!*, pp. 130–150.

186 *Ibid.*, p. 142.

187 *Dix sept ans de lutte contre la bolchevisme*, p. 4.

188 *Ibid.*, pp. 13–14.

189 *Ibid.*

190 *Ibid.*, p. 9.

191 Lodygensky Memoir, part 1, chap. 8, p. 83.

192 *Dix sept ans de lutte contre la bolchevisme*, p. 6.

193 *Ibid.*, p. 4.

194 *Ibid.*, p. 5.

195 *Ibid.*

196 *Ibid.*, p. 4.

197 *Ibid.*

198 *Ibid.*

199 *Ibid.*, p. 7.
200 *Ibid.*, p. 6.
201 *Ibid.*, p. 7.
202 *Ibid.*
203 *Ibid.*
204 Entente Internationale contre la III Internationale, 'Documentation', July–August, p. C.-1–3, 'Chronique des Congrès du Comintern' (article in *Pravda*, 25 July 1935); C.-3, article from *L'Humanité*, 26 July 1935; p. C.-3–4, interview with Marcel Cachin from *L'Humanité*, 11 July 1935; p. C.-4–10, article from *Internationale Communiste*, no. 13, 1945. This material is interspersed with editorial comment which lowers its usefulness as research information.
205 'Documentation', September–October, 1935, p. C.-1.
206 *Ibid.*
207 *Ibid.*, p. C.-11.
208 *Ibid.*
209 *Ibid.*, p. C.-12.
210 *Ibid.*
211 *Ibid.*, p. C.-14.
212 *Ibid.*
213 *Ibid.*, p. C.-12.
214 *Ibid.*, p. C.-13.
215 *Ibid.*
216 *Ibid.*, p. C.-15.
217 *Ibid.*
218 *Dix sept ans de lutte contre le bolchevisme*, p. 10.
219 *Franco, the Man and his Nation*, p. 210, testimony of Barroso to Hills.
220 *Ibid.*, p. 207.
221 *Ibid.*, p. 210. Barroso followed Franco's orders faithfully when the Civil War broke out. As military attaché in Paris, he had in his hands the official message from Madrid requesting aid for the Republic. He showed these to Henri de Kerillis, editor of *L'Écho de Paris*, who orchestrated a campaign against the Spanish Republic in July and August 1936 and effectively blocked the shipment of armament to Madrid, leaving the Republic no alternative but to accept the aid that the far-away Soviet Union could, with difficulty and danger, furnish. *Le mythe de la croisade de Franco*, p. 213; *El mito de la cruzada de Franco*, 1968, p. 214.
222 *Franco*, 1967, p. 155.
223 *Ibid.*
224 *Ibid.*
225 *Ibid.*, pp. 155–156.
226 Thomas, *The Spanish Civil War*, Harmondsworth, Penguin, 1965, p. 135, n. 1. No source is given. However in the third edition, also Penguin, 1982, p. 159, n. 3, Thomas attributes this source to 'recollection of Dr. Marañón'.
227 *Francisco Franco y su tiempo*, Vol. 2, p. 11, n. 7.
228 *Franco*, p. 138.
229 *Ibid.*, p. 93.
230 *Ibid.*, p. 141.
231 *Franco, the Man and his Nation*, p. 219.
232 *Franco*, 1967, p. 174.
233 *Francisco Franco y su tiempo*, Vol. 2, p. 33.
234 *Ibid.*
235 *Franco*, 1967, Vol. 1, p. 175. June is the date given by Aznar for the distribution of Document IV.

236   *Francisco Franco y su tiempo*, Vol. 2, p. 33.
237   *Ibid.*, p. 30.
238   *Historia militar de la guerra de España*, p. 30
239   *Ibid.*, Vol. 1, p. 16.
240   Lodygensky Memoir, part 3, chap. 2, 'Guerre Germano-Soviétique', p. 64.

Bibliography

Ahora, Madrid, 1936.
The American Review, New York, 1937.
Bulletin d'Informations Politiques EIA, Geneva, Entente Internationale contre la III Internationale, 1937.
The Catholic Mind, New York, The American Press, 1937.
Catholics' Reply to 'Open Letter on Spain', New York, The American Press, 1937.
Claridad, Madrid, 1936.
L'Écho de Paris, Paris, 1937.
El Diario de Navarra, Pamplona, 1937.
El Diario Palentino, 1937.
España Roja.
Feuille D'Avis de Lausanne, 1923.
Frente de Juventudes, Madrid, 1939.
Gringoire, Paris, 1936.
Heraldo de Aragón, Zaragoza, 1936.
Historia 16, Madrid, 1978.
Humanité, Paris, 1935.
The Illustrated London News, London, 1961.
International Herald Tribune, Paris, 1960, 1990.
Jerarquía, Pamplona, 1938.
Journal de Genèe, 1924.
Manchester Guardian, Manchester, 1937.
Le Matin, Paris, 1936.
The Nation, New York, 1967.
The National Review, New York, 1973.
The New Statesman, London, 1967, 1968.
The New York American, 1937.
The New York Times, 1936, 1939, 1966.
The Nineteenth Century and After, London, 1937.
The Observer, London, 1936.
El País, Madrid, 1985, 1986.
Pueblo, Madrid, 1976.
Razón y Fé, Madrid, 1938.
Revue des Deux Mondes, Paris, 1937.
Revue de Paris, Paris, 1936.
The Sunday Times, London, 1975.

The Times, London, 1938, 1986.
The Times Literary Supplement, London, 1975.

ALCÁZAR DE VELASCO, Angel, *Serrano Suñer en la Falange*, Barcelona–Madrid, Ediciones Patria, 1941.
——, *Los 7 días de Salamanca*, Madrid, G. Del Toro, 1976.
ALEXANDER, Peter, *Roy Campbell, A Critical Biography*, Oxford, Oxford University Press, 1982.
AREILZA, José María de and CASTIELLA, Fernando María, *Reivindicaciones de España*, foreword by Alfonso García-Valdecasas, Madrid, Instituto de Estudios Políticos, 1941.
ARRARÁS, Joaquín, *Historia de la cruzada española*, Madrid, Ediciones Españolas, vols 1–8, 1939–1943.
——, *Historia de la segunda república española (texto abreviado)*, Madrid, Editora Nacional, 1965.
ATHOLL, Duchess of, *Searchlight on Spain*, Harmondsworth, Penguin, 1938.
AUBERT, Théodore, *Bolshevism's Terrible Record: An Indictment*, London, Williams and Northgate, 1924.
——, *L'Affaire Conradi: Le proces du Bolshevisme*, Geneva, S.A. des Editions Sonor, 1924.
——, *Neuf ans de lutte contre le bolchevisme*, Geneva, Bureau Permanent de l'Entente Internationale Anticommuniste, 1940.
AZCÁRATE, Pablo de, *Mi embajada en Londres durante la guerra civil española*, Barcelona, Ariel, 1976.
AZNAR, Manuel, *Historia Militar de la Guerra de España*, Madrid, Editora Nacional, Vol. 1, 3rd edn, 1958.
BARDOUX, Jacques, *Le chaos espagnol. Éviterons-nous la contagion?*, Paris, Flammarion, 1937.
——, *Staline contre l'Europe: Les preuves du complot communiste*, Paris, Flammarion, 1937.
——, *Chaos in Spain*, London, Burns, Oates and Washbourne, 1937(?).
BAYLE, Constantino, *¿Qué pasa en España? A los católicos del mundo*, Salamanca, Delegación del Estado para Prensa y Propaganda, 1937.
——, *Carta Colectiva, el mundo católico y la carta colectiva del episcopado español*, Burgos, Ediciones Rayfe, Centro de Información Católica Internacional, 1938.
——, *El clero y los católicos vasco–separatistas y el movimiento nacional*, Madrid, Editora Nacional, 1940.
BELFORTE, Generale Francesco (J. Biondi Morra), *La guerra civile in Spagna: Tomo 1: La disintegrazione dello stato*, Varese–Milano, Instituto per gli Studi di Politica Internazionale, 1938.
BERTRÁN GÜELL, Felipe, *Momentos interesantes de la historia de España en este siglo. La España de 1936. Preparación y desarrollo del alzamiento nacional*, Valladolid, Librería Santarén, 1939.
BOLÍN, Luis, *España: Los años vitales*, Madrid, Espasa-Calpe, 1967.
——, *Spain: The Vital Years*, London, Cassell, 1967.
BOLLOTEN, Burnett, *El gran engaño*, Barcelona, Caralt, 1961.
——, *The Grand Camouflage. The Communist Conspiracy in the Spanish Civil War*, London, Hollis and Carter, 1961.

——, *La Révolución española. Las izquierdas y la lucha por el poder*, trans. Carlos López, Carmen Downs de McGhee and Luis Sierra Ponce de León, Mexico, Editorial Jus, 1962.

——, *El gran engaño*, Barcelona, Caralt, 1967.

——, *The Grand Camouflage. The Spanish Civil War and Revolution, 1936–1939*, introduction by H. R. Trevor-Roper, London, Pall Mall Press, 1968.

——, *La révolution espagnole. 1. La gauche et la lutte pour le pouvoir*, Paris, Ruedo Ibérico, 1977.

——, *The Spanish Revolution. The Left and the Struggle for Power during the Civil War*, foreword by Raymond Carr, Chapel Hill, NC, University of North Carolina Press, 1979.

——, *La revolución española*, Barcelona, Grijalbo, 1980.

——, *La Guerra Civil española: Revolución y contrarevolución*, trans Belén Urrutia, Madrid, Alianza Editorial, 1989.

——, *The Spanish Civil War: Revolution and Counterrevolution*, foreword Stanley G. Payne, Chapel Hill, NC, University of North Carolina Press, 1991.

BRASILLACH, Robert, and BARDÊCHE, Maurice, *Histoire de la guerre d'Espagne*. Paris, Plon, 1939.

——, *Historia da guerra de Espanha*, 2 vols. Lisbon, Livraria Clássica Editora, 1939–1940.

BREDBERG, Ernest, *Rebellen Franco och den Lagliga regeringen*, Stockholm, Sves Rikes, 1938.

'BRUNO, Pol', *La saga de los Giscard*, Paris, Editions Ramsay, 1980.

CADENAS Y VICENT, Vicente, *Actas del último Consejo Nacional de Falange Española de las JONS (Salamanca 18–19 de abril 1937) y algunas noticias referentes a la Jefatura nacional de prensa y propaganda editadas por Vicente Cadenas*, Madrid, Gráficas Uguina, 1975.

CALVO SERER, Rafael, *La literatura universal sobre la guerra de España*, Madrid, Atenéo, 1962.

CAMPBELL, Roy, *Light on a Dark Horse*, London, Hollis and Carter, 1951.

CARLAVILLA DE LA VEGA, Julián Mauricio ('Mauricio Karl'), *El comunismo en España*, Madrid, Imp. Sáez Hermanos, 1932.

——, *El enemigo: Marxismo, Anarquismo, Masonería*, Madrid, Imp. Sáez Hermanos, 1934.

——, *Técnica del Comintern en España*, Badajoz, Tip. 'Gráfica Corporativa', 1937.

CARRERAS, Luis, *Grandeza cristiana de España. Notas sobre la persecución religiosa*, Toulouse, Les Frères Douladoure, 1938.

——, *Grandeur chrétienne de l'Espagne*, preface by Louis Bertrand, Paris, Sorlot, 1939.

Carta del Archivo Histórica Nacional, Salamanca, 1982.

Catálogo General de la Librería Española 1931–50, Vol. 3, Madrid, Instituto Nacional del Libro Español, 1963.

CATTELL, David T., *Communism and the Spanish Civil War*, Berkeley, University of California Press, 1956.

Causa General. La dominación roja en España. Avance de la información instruida por el Ministerio Público, Madrid, Ministerio de Justicia, 1944(?).

CHESTER, Lewis, Stephen Fay and Hugo Young, *The Zinoviev Letter*, London, Heinemann, 1967.

CHUECA RODRÍGUEZ, Ricardo, *El fascismo: En los comienzos del régimen de Franco*, Madrid, Centro de Investigaciones Sociológicas, 1983.

CIERVA, Ricardo de la, *Los documentos de la primavera trágica*, Madrid, Secretaría General Técnica del Ministerio de Información y Turismo, Sección de Estudios sobre la guerra de España, 1967.

——, *Bibliografía general sobre la guerra de España (1936–1939) y sus antecedentes históricos*, Madrid–Barcelona, Ediciones Ariel, 1968.

——, *Historia de la Guerra Civil Española. Tomo primero. Perspectivas y antecedentes. 1898–1936*, Madrid, Librería Editorial San Martín, 1969.

——, *Historia ilustrada de la guerra civil española*, Vol. 2, Madrid, Danae, 1970.

——, *Francisco Franco: Un siglo de España*, 2 vols, Madrid, Editora Nacional, 1973.

——, *Franco*, Barcelona, Planeta, 1986.

CLAUDEL, Paul, *Aux martyres de l'Espagne*, Brussels, Imp. Lesigne, 1937.

COLES, S. F. A., *Franco of Spain*, London, Neville Spearman, 1955.

——, *Franco of Spain*, Westminster, MD, The Newman Press, 1956.

The Collective Letter of the Spanish Bishops on the War in Spain, London, 1937.

COMÍN COLOMER, Eduardo, *Técnica del Comintern en España*, Badajoz, Tip. 'Gráfica Corporativa', 1937.

——, *Historia secreta de la segunda república*, 2 vols, Editorial 'Nos', 1954.

——, *Historia secreta de la segunda república*, foreword by Mauricio Carlavilla, Barcelona, AHR, 1959.

——, *Historia del Partido Comunista de España. Abril 1920–febrero 1936. Del nacimiento a la mayoria de edad*, Madrid, Editora Nacional, 1965.

The Compact Oxford English Dictionary, 2nd edn, Oxford, Clarendon Press, 1992.

CORDÓN, Antonio, *Trayectoría (Recuerdos de un artillero)*, Paris, Ediciones de la Librairie du Globe, Colección Ebro, 1971.

CORRAL, Enrique del, *Calvo Sotelo*, Temas Españolas 29, Madrid, Publicaciones Españolas, 1953.

CROZIER, Brian, *Franco. A Biographical History*, London, Eyre and Spottiswoode, 1967.

——, *Franco, historia y biografía*, trans. Joaquín Esteban Perruca, Colección Novelas y Cuentos, Madrid, Magisterio Español, 2nd edn, 1969.

CURRAN, Father Edward Lodge, *Spain in Arms. With Notes on Communism*, Brooklyn, NY, International Catholic Truth Society, 1936.

DAHMS, Hellmuth Günther, *Der spanische Bürgerkrieg 1936–1939*, Tübingen, Rainer Wunderlich Verlag, 1962.

——, *A guerra civil de Espanha*, Lisbon, Editorial Ibis, 1964.

——, *La guerra civil española de 1936*, Madrid, Rialp, 1966.

DIAZ DE VILLEGAS, José, *Guerra de liberación (La fuerza de la razón)*, Barcelona, AHR, 1957.

Dictamen de la Comisión sobre ilegitimidad de poderes actuantes en 18 de julio de 1936, Estado Español, Ministerio de la Gobernación, [Barcelona], Editora Nacional, 1939.

Dix sept ans de lutte contre le bolchevisme, 1924–1940, Geneva, Bureau Permanent de l'Entente Internationale Anticommuniste, 1940.

Documents on German Foreign Policy 1918–1945. From the archives of the German Foreign Ministry, Series D (1937–1945), Vol. 3, *Germany and the Spanish Civil War 1936–1939*, Washington, DC, US Government Printing Office, 1950.

ECHEVARRIA, Federico de, *L'Espagne en flammes. Un drame qui touche la France de près*, Paris, Les Editions de Publicité et Propagande, 1936(?).

——, *Spain in Flames*, New York, The Paulist Press, 1936.

——, *Spain in Flames*, London, Burns, Oates and Washbourne, 1936(?).

——, *Spain in Flames*, New York, reprinted with permission of the author for the Fordham University Alumnae Association, 1937(?).

El por qué del movimiento nacional, Salamanca, Ediciones SPES, 1937.

Encyclopaedia Britannica, The Encyclopaedia Britannica Co. Ltd, London–New York, 1926.

La epopeya de la Guardia Civil en al Santuario de la Virgen de la Cabeza. 18.VIII.1936 a 1.V.1937, Madrid, Taller-Escuela de Artes Gráficas de Huérfanos de la Guardia Civil, 1958.

ESTADO MAYOR CENTRAL DEL EJÉRCITO, Servicio Histórico Militar, *Historia de la guerra de liberación (1936–1939). Tomo 1. Antecedentes de la guerra*, Madrid, Imprenta del Servicio Geográfico del Ejército, 1945.

ESTELRICH, Juan, *La persécution religieuse en Espagne*, Paris, Plon, 1937.

Exposición del plan secreto para establecer un 'soviet' en España, Bilbao, Ed. Española, 1939.

Exposure of the Secret Plan to Establish a Soviet in Spain, London, Friends of National Spain, 1938.

FAVEZ, Jean Claude, *Une mission impossible?*, Lausanne, Payot, 1989.

FERRARI BILLOCH, F., *La masonería al desnudo. I parte: Las Logias desenmascaradas*, foreword by Antonio Goicoechea y Cosculluela, Madrid, Ediciones Españolas, 1939.

——, *La masonería al desnudo. II parte: Entre Masones y Marxistas ... (Confesiones de un Rosa-Cruz)*, Madrid, Ediciones Españolas, 1939.

——, *¡Masones! Así es la secta. Las logias de Palma e Ibiza*, Palma, Tip. Lit. Nueva Balear, 1937.

FEST, Joachim C., *Hitler*, Propyläen, 1973.

——, *Hitler*, Harmondsworth, Penguin, 1977.

FONTANA, Josep (ed.), *España bajo el franquismo*, Barcelona, Editorial Crítica, 1986.

Foreign Relations of the United States, 1937, Vol. I, Washington, DC, US Government Printing Office, 1954.

FOSS, William and GERAHTY, Cecil, *Arena spagnola*, Milan, Mondadori, 1938

——, *Die spanische Arena*, Berlin–Stuttgart, Rowohlt, 1938(?).

——, *The Spanish Arena*, foreword by His Grace the Duke of Alba and Berwick, London, Robert Hale Ltd, 1938.

——, *The Spanish Arena*, London, Right Book Club, 1938.

FRANCO SALGADO-ARAUJO, Francisco, *Mis conversaciones privadas con Franco*, Barcelona, Planeta, 1976.

FUSI, Juan Pablo, *Franco*, Madrid, Ediciones El País, 1985.

GÁRATE CÓRDOBA, José María, *La guerra de las dos Españas (Breviario histórica de la guerra del '36)*, Barcelona, Caralt, 1976.

GARCÍA ESCUDERO, José María, *Historia política de las dos Españas*, Madrid, Editora Nacional, 1975.

GARCÍA VENERO, Maximiano, *Falange en la guerra de España: La unificación y Hedilla*, Paris, Ruedo Ibérico, 1967.

——, *Historia de la unificatión (Falange y Requeté en 1937)*, Madrid, Agesa, 1970.

GERAHTY, Cecil, *The Road to Madrid*, London, Hutchinson and Co., 1937.

GIL ROBLES, José María, *No fue posible la paz*, Barcelona, Ariel, 1968.

GÖBBELS, Josef, *The Truth about Spain*, speech delivered at the National Socialist Party Congress, Nürnberg, 1937, Berlin, M. Müller and Sohn, 1937(?).

GOMÁ Y TOMÁS, Isidro, *Por Dios y por España (1936–39)*, Barcelona, Edit. Casulleras, 1940.

——, *Pastorales de la guerra de España. Estudio preliminar de Santiago Galindo Herrero*, Madrid, Ediciones Rialp, 1955.

GRANDI, Blasco, *Togliatti y los suyos en España*, Temas Españolas 118, Madrid, Publicaciones Españolas, 1954.

GRIMLEY, Bernard, *Spanish Conflict*, Paterson, NY, St Anthony Guild Press, 1937.

HAARTMAN, Carl Magnus Gunnar Emil von, *En Nordisk Caballero I Francos armé*, Helsinfors, Söderström & Co., Forlagsaktiebolag, 1939.

HART, Merwin K., *America, Look at Spain*, New York, P.J. Kennedy and Sons, 1939.

HEDILLA, Manuel, *Testimonio de Manuel Hedilla*, Barcelona, Ediciones Acervo, 1972.

HIGUERA Y VELAZQUEZ, Alfonso G. de la and MOLINS CORREA, Luis, *Historia de la Revolución Española. Tercera guerra de Independencia*, Cádiz – Madrid, Establecimientos Cerón y Librería Cervantes, 1940.

HILLS, George, *Franco, the Man and his Nation*, London, Robert Hale Ltd., 1967.

——, *Franco, el hombre y su nación*, Madrid, Librería Editorial San Martín, 1969.

Historia de la cruzada española, Madrid, Ediciones Españolas, 8 vols, 1940.

HITLER, Adolf, *Mein Kampf*. New York, Reynal and Hitchcock, 1941.

HODGSON, Robert, *Spain Resurgent*, London, Hutchinson, 1953.

How Mussolini Provoked the Spanish Civil War, London, United Editorial Ltd, 1938.

IRIBARREN, José María, *Con el General Mola. Escenas y aspectos inéditos de la guerra civil*, Zaragoza, Librería General, 1937.

——, *Mola, datos para una biografía y para la historia del alzamiento nacional*, Zaragoza, Heraldo de Aragón, 1938.

——, *El general Mola*, Madrid, Editorial Bullón, 1945.

JACKSON, Gabriel, *The Spanish Republic and the Civil War 1931–1939*, Princeton, Princeton University Press, 1965.

——, *La república española y la guerra civil 1931–1939*, Mexico, Editorial Grijalbo, 1967.

JERROLD, Douglas, *España, Impresiones y reflejos*, Salamanca, Delegación del Estado para Prensa y Propaganda, 1937.

——, *Georgian Adventure*, London, Collins, 1937.

——, *Spain: Impressions and Reflections*, London, Constable and Co., 1937.

——, *The Issues in Spain*, two articles reprinted from *The American Review*, New York, The American Review, 1937.

——, *Georgian Adventure*, London, The Right Book Club, 1938.

JONES, Thomas, *A Diary with Letters*, London, Oxford University Press, 1954.

LLANOS, José María de, *Nuestra Ofrenda, Los Jesuitas de la provincia de Toledo en la cruzada nacional*, Madrid, Aspostolado de la Prensa, 1942.

LODYGENSKY, Georges, *Les sans-Dieu en Espagne,*, n.p., Éditions du Bureau de la Commission International 'Pro-Deo', 1937.

——, *Nos frères catholiques sous la croix en Espagne*, Zaragoza, Tall. Graf. de *El Noticiero*, 1937.

——, *Face au Communisme. Le mouvement anticommuniste internationale de 1923–1950'*, Geneva, Bureau Permanent de l'Entente Internationale Anticommuniste, 1940 (Lodygensky Memoir).

LOISEAUX, Gerard, *La Littérature de la défaite et de la collaboration*, Paris, Publications de la Sorbonne, 1984.

LOVEDAY, Arthur F., *World War in Spain*, London, John Murray, 1939.

——, *Spain 1923–1948. Civil War and World War*, Ashcott nr Bridgewater, Somerset, The Boswell Publishing Co. Ltd, n.d. (1949?).

LUNN, Arnold, *Spain and the Christian Front*, New York, The Paulist Press, 1937(?).

——, *Spain: The Unpopular Front*. London, Catholic Truth Society, 1937.

——, *Spanish Rehearsal*, London, The National Book Association, Hutchinson and Co., 1937(?).

——, *Revolutionary Socialism in Theory and Practice*, London, The Right Book Club, 1939.

——, *Memory to Memory*, London, Hollis and Carter, 1956.

——, *And Yet so New*, London, Sheed and Ward, 1958.

MADARIAGA, Salvador de, *España*, Barcelona, CIAP, 1931.

——, *España. Ensayo de historia contemporánea*, Madrid, CIAP, 1931.

——, *Spain*, London, Cape, 1942.

——, *España. Ensayo de historia contemporánea*, Buenos Aires, Editorial Sudamericana, 1944

——, *La crisis del humanismo*, preface by A. Goicoechea, Madrid, 1945.

——, *Madariaga versus Madariaga, Extractos de Anarquía o Jerarquía. Ideario para la constitución de la tercera república*, Madrid, M. Aguilar, 1955.

——, *Democracy versus Liberty? The Faith of a Liberal Heretic*, London, Pall Mall Press, 1958.

——, *Spain: A Modern History*, New York, Praeger, 1958.

——, *General, márchese usted*, New York, Ediciones Ibérica, 1959.

——, *Españoles de mi tiempo*, Barcelona, Planeta, 1974.

MAEZTU, Ramiro de, *Authority, Liberty and Function in the Light of the War*, London, 1916.

——, *Defensa de la Hispanidad*, Valladolid, Acción Española (Aldus Santander), 1938.

——, *Defensa de la Hispanidad*, 4th edn, Madrid, Cultura Española, 1941.

MAÍZ, B. Félix, *Alzamiento en España: De un diario de la conspiración*, Pamplona, Editorial Gómez, 1952.

——, *Mola, aquél hombre*, Barcelona, Planeta, 1976.

MARTIN, Claude, *Franco, soldat et chef d'état*, Paris, Quatre fils Aymon, 1959.

——, *Franco, soldado y estadista*, Madrid, Fermín Uriarte, 1966.

MATA, Juan M. de, *¡¡España!! Apuntes histórico-críticos sobre el Alzamiento de la Patria contra la invasión masónico-bolchevique*, Zaragoza, Imp. Ed. Gambon, 1936.

McCULLAGH, Francis, *In Franco's Spain*, London, Burns, Oates and Washbourne, 1937.

Metodología histórica de la guerra y la revolución española, Barcelona, Editorial Fontamard, 1982.

MICHAELIS, Meir, *Mussolini and the Jews*, Oxford, The Clarendon Press, 1978.

MONTERO MORENO, Antonio, *Historia de la persecución religiosa en España 1936–1939*, Madrid, Biblioteca de Autores Cristianos, 1941.

NOVIK, Dimitri, *Théodore Aubert et son oeuvre. Le mouvement internationale contre le Bolchevisme*, Geneva, Edition des Amis de l'Entente contre la III Internationale, 1932.

——, *Neuf ans de lutte contre le bolchevisme*, Geneva, Bureau Permanent de l'Entente Internationale Anticommuniste, 1940.

ORIZANA, G. and José Manuel MARTÍN LIÉBANA, *El movimiento nacional, momento, espíritu, jornadas de adhesión, el 18 de julio en toda la nueva España*, Valladolid, Imp. Francisco G. Vicente, 1937(?).

PATTEE, Richard, *This is Spain*, Milwaukee, The Bruce Publishing Co., 1951.

PATTEE, R. and ROTHBAUER, A. M., *Spanien, Mythos und Wirklichkeit*, Vienna–Cologne, Verlag Styria, 1955(?).

PEMÁN, José María, *Poema de la bestia y el ángel*, Zaragoza, Ediciones Jerarquía, 1938.

PIKE, David W., *Les français et la guerre d'Espagne*, Paris, PUF, 1975.

——, *Jours de gloire, jours de honte*, Paris, Sedes, 1984.

PONÇET, Léon, *Lumière sur l'Espagne: Faits, témoignages, documents*, Lyon, Presse Lyonnais du Sud-Est, 1939.

PONCINS, Léon de, *Histoire secrète de la révolution espagnole*, Paris, G. Beauchesne, 1938.

Portugal ante la guerra civil de España: Documentos y notas, Lisbon, SPN, n.d.

A Preliminary Official Report on the Atrocities Committed in Southern Spain in July and August 1936, by the Communist Forces of the Madrid Government, together with a Brief Historical Note on the Course of Recent Events in Spain. Issued with the authority of the Committee of Investigation Appointed by the National Government of Burgos, London, Eyre and Spottiswoode, 1936.

PRESTON, Paul, *¡Comrades! Portraits from the Spanish Civil War*, London, Harper-Collins, 1999.

PRESTON, Paul and MACKENZIE, Ann L. (eds), *The Republic Besieged, Civil War in Spain 1936–1939*, Edinburgh, Edinburgh University Press, 1996.

¿Qué pasa en España? El problema del socialismo español, Madrid, CEDESA, 1959.

RAMOS OLIVEIRA, Antonio, *Politics, Economics and Men of Modern Spain, 1808–1946*, London, V. Gollancz, 1946.

The Red Network, the Communist International at Work, London, Duckworth, 1939.

Report of the Seventh World Congress of the Communist International, London, Modern Books, 1936.

RIDRUEJO, Dionisio, *Casi unas memorias*, Barcelona, Planeta, 1976.

RODRIGUEZ PUERTOLAS, *Literatura Fascista Española*, vol. 1, Historia, Madrid, Ediciones Alcal, 1986.

ROMERO, Luis, *Cara y cruz de la República, 1931–1936*, Barcelona, Planeta, 1980.

Das Rotbuch über Spanien, Berlin–Leipzig, Niebelungen-Verlag, 1937.

ROUX, Georges, *La guerre civile d'Espagne*. Paris, Fayard, 1963.

——, *La guerra civil de España*, Madrid, Ediciones Cid, 1964.

SAINT-AULAIRE, Comte de, *La renaissance d'Espagne*, Paris, Plon, 1938.

SÁNCHEZ GUERRA, Rafael, *Mis prisiones*, Buenos Aires, Claridad, 1946.

SCHMIGALLE, Günther, *André Malraux und der spanische Bürgerkrieg. Zur Genese, Funktion und Bedeutung von L'Espoir (1937)*, Frankfurt am Main, inaugural dissertation of the Johann-Wolfgang Goethe University, 1980.

SECO SERRANO, Carlos, *Historia de España. Epoca contemporánea*, Barcelona, Instituto Gallach, 1968.

The Second and Third Official Reports on the Communist Atrocities Committed in Southern Spain from July to October 1936, by the Communist Forces of the Madrid Government, preface by Sir Arthur Bryant, London, Eyre and Spottiswoode, 1937.

SENCOURT, Robert, *Spain's Ordeal*, London–New York, Longmans Green and Co., 1938.

VII Congress of the Communist International, abridged stenographic report of the proceedings, Moscow, Foreign Languages Publishing House, 1939.

SEVILLA ANDRÉS, Diego, *Historia política de la zona roja*, Madrid, Editora Nacional, 1954.

——, *Historia política de la zona roja*, Madrid, Rialp, 1963.

SOUTHWORTH, Herbert Rutledge, *El mito de la cruzada de Franco*, Paris, Ruedo Ibérico, 1963.

——, *Le mythe de la croisade de Franco*, Paris, Ruedo Ibérico, 1964.

——, *Antifalange*, Paris, Ruedo Ibérico, 1967.

——, *La destruction de Guernica. Journalisme, diplomatie et histoire*, Paris, Ruedo Ibérico, 1975.

——, *La destrucción de Guernica*, Paris, Ruedo Ibérico, 1977.

——, *Guernica! Guernica!*, Berkeley, University of California Press, 1977.

——, *El mito de la cruzada de Franco*, Barcelona, Plaza y Janés, 1986.

——, ' "The Grand Camouflage": Julián Gorkin, Burnett Bolloten and the Spanish Civil War', in P. Preston and A. Mackenzie, *The Republic Besieged, Civil War in Spain 1936–1939*, Edinburgh, Edinburgh University Press, 1996, pp. 261–310.

SUÁREZ FERNÁNDEZ, Luis, *Francisco Franco y su tiempo*, Madrid, Fundación Nacional Francisco Franco, vols I and II, 1984.

TANGYE, Nigel, *Red, White and Spain*, London, Rich and Cowan, 1937.

TENNANT, Eleanor, *Spanish Journey: Personal Experiences of the Civil War*, London, Eyre and Spottiswoode, 1936.

THOMAS, Hugh, *The Spanish Civil War*, London, Eyre and Spottiswoode, 1961.

——, *The Spanish Civil War*, rev. edn, Harmondsworth, Penguin Books, 1965.

——, *La guerra civil española, 1936–1939*, Paris, Ruedo Ibérico, Ediciones Grijalbo, 2 vols, 1976.

——, *The Spanish Civil War*, 3rd edn, London, Hamish Hamilton, 1977.

——, *The Spanish Civil War*, rev. and enlarged edn, Harmondsworth, Penguin, 1982.

TONI, SJ, RP Teodoro, *España vendida a Rusia*, Burgos, Ediciones Antisectarias, 1937.

VILAR, Pierre, *Metodología histórica de la guerra y la revolución española*, Barcelona, Editorial Fontamara, 1982.

VIÑAS, Angel, *La alemania nazi y el 18 de julio*, 2nd rev. edn, Madrid, Alianza Editorial, 1977.

WATKINS, K. W., *Britain Divided*, London, Nelson, 1963.

Who Was Who. 1961–1970, London, A. C. Black, 1971.

Who's Who, London, A. C. Black, 1986.

Index